Sarah Beckwith

Religious Ideology
and
Cultural Fantasy

Religious Ideology
and
Cultural Fantasy

CATHOLIC AND
ANTI-CATHOLIC DISCOURSES
IN EARLY MODERN ENGLAND

ARTHUR F. MAROTTI

UNIVERSITY OF NOTRE DAME PRESS
NOTRE DAME, INDIANA

Manufactured in the United States of America

Library of Congress Cataloging-in-Publication Data

Marotti, Arthur F., 1940–
  Religious ideology and cultural fantasy : Catholic and anti-Catholic discourses in early modern England / Arthur F. Marotti.
      p. cm.
  Includes bibliographical references and index.
  ISBN 0-268-03479-6 (cloth : alk. paper)
  ISBN 0-268-03480-X (pbk. : alk. paper)
   1. Catholic Church—England—History—16th century. 2. Anti-Catholicism—England—History—16th century. 3. England—Church history—16th century. 4. Catholic Church—England—History—17th century. 5. Anti-Catholicism—England--History—17th century. 6. England—Church history—17th century. 7. Christian literature, English—History and criticism. I. Title.
  BX1492.M34 2005
  282'.42'09031—dc22
                                                                                                2005002505

For my son, Steve,
whom I both love and respect

Contents

Figures

Acknowledgments

I AM INDEBTED TO A NUMBER OF FRIENDS AND COLLEAGUES, AS WELL AS archivists and librarians. I am grateful, first, to James Shapiro, who at just the right moment put the rhetorical question to me that served as a catalyst for this project ("Arthur, why don't you do Catholics?"). I am particularly grateful to Thomas M. McCoog, S.J., archivist at the English Jesuit Archive in London, for sharing information, for steering me towards interesting material, and for very useful conversations. I would like also to thank Rev. Ian Dickie of the Archives of the Archdiocese of Westminster, who provided crucial help. In the course of the past few years I have benefited greatly from collegial conversations or exchanged work-in-progress with a number of people who share with me an interest in early modern Catholicism and the tradition of anti-Catholicism in England: these include Cedric Brown, Ronald Corthell, Frances Dolan, Margaret Ferguson, Dennis Flynn, Lowell Gallagher, Christopher Haigh, Christopher Highley, Donna Hamilton, Phebe Jensen, Norman Jones, Jacques Lezra, Robert Miola, Anthony Milton, Michael Questier, Alison Shell, Paul Voss, and John Watkins. I have also benefited over the years from my professional and personal exchanges with a number of other scholars—particularly Richard Helgerson, Leah Marcus, Annabel Patterson, Nigel Smith, and Martin Elsky. I would like to thank (in addition to Cedric Brown) Suzanne Gossett, Jacob Lassner, Carla Mazzio, Douglas Trevor, and Richard Strier for arranging occasions for the presentation of parts of this study as lectures at their universities (the University of Reading; Loyola University, Chicago; Northwestern University; the University of Michigan; Harvard University; and the University of Chicago). I am likewise grateful to Richard Dutton for inviting me to speak at the "Lancastrian Shakespeare" conference in summer 1999, where many scholars interested in religion in early modern England gathered. I appreciate the support provided by a National Endowment for the Humanities Fellowship in the year 2000. Finally, I would like to thank Wayne State University for the generous research support I have received over the years — especially for a Charles Gershenson Distinguished Faculty Fellowship, a College of Liberal Arts Research and Inquiry Award, and a Humanities Center Fellowship.

Some of the chapters in this book constitute revised and expanded versions of the following book chapters, whose publishers I thank for permission to reprint:

"Southwell's Remains: Catholicism and Anti-Catholicism in Early Modern England," in *Texts and Cultural Change in Early Modern England,* ed. Cedric C. Brown and Arthur F. Marotti (Basingstoke: Macmillan; New York: St. Martin's Press, 1997), 37–65.

"Alienating Catholics in Early Modern England: Recusant Women, Jesuits, and Ideological Fantasies," in *Catholicism and Anti-Catholicism in Early Modern English Texts,* ed. Arthur F. Marotti (Basingstoke: Macmillan; New York: St. Martin's Press, 1999), 1–34.

"Manuscript Transmission and the Catholic Martyrdom Account in Early Modern England," in *Print, Manuscript and Performance: The Changing Relations of the Media in Early Modern England,* ed. Arthur F. Marotti and Michael Bristol (Columbus: Ohio State University Press, 2000), 172–99.

Preface

The imaginary is part of history.
— Michel de Certeau, *The Possession at Loudun*

[A] good case could be made that the last unchallenged and most
perniciously pervasive element in the Whig view of modern English
history is an unacknowledged tendency to privilege all things protestant
while sedulously marginalising all things catholic. Because England was
or became a protestant country (and arguably because "protestantism"
became a central part of English national identity until well into the
twentieth century), it is in practice widely assumed . . . that after some
indeterminate point in Elizabeth's reign, if not before, protestants and
Protestantism are central to the national story in a way that catholics
and Catholicism are not.
— Peter Lake, with Michael Questier, *The Antichrist's Lewd Hat*

THIS BOOK FOCUSES ON RELIGIOUS AND POLITICAL LANGUAGE AND MYTH-
making: in it I analyze some of the rhetorical and imaginative means by which
both a minority English Catholic community and a majority Protestant English culture defined themselves, their religious and political antagonists, and
the developing English nationhood and identity in the early modern period.
Taking the years 1580–1688 as my frame (from the first arrival of the Jesuits
in England to the "Glorious Revolution"), I consider Catholic writing of various sorts (for example, martyrdom accounts and conversion narratives), but I
am especially interested in the discourse of anti-Catholicism, a flexible instrument employed by English Protestant ideologues for both internecine Protestant struggles and polemical or political conflict with domestic and international Catholicism. Many of the texts to which I turn, some quite unfamiliar

to modern historians and literary scholars, are highly charged polemics, containing, therefore, the exaggerations, historical distortions, and, in some cases, paranoid reasoning endemic to the form.[1] I am particularly interested in the process by which real as well as fabricated historical "evidence" and events are translated into a developing set of rhetorical codes and ideological fantasies—both in religiopolitical works and in the more familiar literary texts into which they were infused. My main focus as a literary scholar, however, is not canonical literature but rather the larger world of language use in which literary texts were situated. After all, half of the books published in England before 1640 were in the fields of philosophy and religion and between the mid-sixteenth and mid-seventeenth centuries the most published author in English was John Calvin (in translation).[2] It is revealing that the first two chapters of the volume of the recent Cambridge *History of the Book in Britain* covering the years 1557–1695 are devoted to religious publishing.[3] Since in recent years so much fine literary scholarship has been done on the English Protestant tradition—especially that of John King, Deborah Shuger, Linda Gregerson, Huston Diehl, Donna Hamilton, Peter McCullough, and Kristen Poole[4]—I tend to emphasize Catholicism and Catholic writing, including texts that are less familiar to specialists in the field.

Although I did not plan the project to develop the way it did, I gave a great deal of attention to the English Jesuits—primarily because they loomed so large in the English "cultural imaginary." From the time of their arrival in England in 1580 and the high-visibility execution of Edmund Campion in 1581, they never ceased to attract the attention of the English government, of Protestant polemicists who responded to their voluminous writing, and of secular Catholic priests competing with them for ecclesiastical leadership. In addition, their international activism and influence on the politics of the various states in which they functioned gave them a prominence and reputation (for good or ill) that could not be ignored. In the vanguard of the Counter-Reformation, they made the perfect antagonists for both moderate and radical Protestants. Other scholars dealing with Catholicism and anti-Catholicism in the period have given or might wish to give less attention to the Jesuits, but I find it useful to return to them in each chapter because of their underestimated importance and because they provide some continuity in this thematically disparate study.

I confess to one further bias. In part because I have been affected by the strong, often sensationalistic language of the texts I have examined and in part because I am culturally biased towards the connection with the physical that Catholicism has traditionally maintained, I have highlighted not only Catholic material practices (such as relic collection) but also the violence associated with executions, persecutions, and war atrocities in the period. Although since the appearance of Stephen Greenblatt's *Renaissance Self-Fashioning,*[5] it has not been necessary to point out that the English Renaissance was as brutal as it was glorious, it might not be entirely beside the point to call attention to the real effects of religious prejudice, bias, and intransigence. The sufferings of lay and clerical Catholics in early modern England have not had a great deal of sympathetic attention from those writing the histories or the literary histories of the period. For too long historians ceded such tasks to confessionally apologetic Catholic scholars; and the master narrative of English literary history has had little space for Catholic writing.

With some trepidation, I consciously trespass on the territory of professional historians. I have learned much from them, especially from such scholars as Christopher Haigh, Eamon Duffy, Anthony Milton, Patrick Collinson, Peter Lake, Michael Questier, and John Bossy who have rescued English religious history from the clutches of both Catholic apologists and Marxist interpreters who betray their discomfort with religion by habitually translating religious and ecclesiastical material into economic and political realities. Although there is some overlap between my study and their projects, especially when I deal with the political uses of Catholic and anti-Catholic rhetorical codes, my focus is less on historical "facts" (who did what and to whom) than on language, fantasies, and perceptions (or misperceptions).[6] So, for example, I care little about whether or not Robert Cecil had any role in manipulating the Gunpowder Plotters before the plot's discovery or about exactly how many English Protestant settlers were actually killed by the Irish Rebels in the 1640s. I am more interested in how the Gunpowder Plot and the Irish Rebellion played out in the imagination of those writers who used these events for polemical or political purposes and produced narratives, fantasies, and coded language that became part of an official account of English national history.[7] On the Catholic side, I am interested in the persistence of certain aesthetic, devotional, and intellectual proclivities that became less and less "English" in character as English identity was consolidated as Protestant and as older paradigms of political and religious authority were culturally overthrown.

Some time ago, when I presented a paper on recusant women and Jesuits that became the second chapter of this study, a question was asked by a distinguished literary scholar who had written extensively on early modern English religion and literature that revealed strong discomfort with the fact that I did not, in discussing the Jesuits, address the issue of whether or not they had done some or all of the things of which they were accused. I indicated in my somewhat exaggerated reply that I did not care about what actually happened (the province of the professional historian) but rather that I was interested in what people thought happened, since this was at the center of the imaginings and of the polemical logic of the works I had examined. I know, of course, that I cannot avoid making some remarks and delivering some judgments about the truths that polemical texts distort (for example, the wild exaggerations of massacres and atrocities found in the anti-Irish and anti-Catholic pamphlets dealing with the Irish Rebellion of 1641), but getting the facts straight and separating fact from fiction is not my main interest—any more than it would be in discussing whether Shakespeare is fair to the historical Richard III in his early tragedy. Historical reality is the lived experience of individuals who see and interpret the world primarily through beliefs, fantasies, and ideologies, not through any supposedly objective analysis of evidence or cause-and-effect relationships. Historiography may strive (hopelessly perhaps) to be rational and free of illusions, but human experience operates by a different set of rules, so cultural history should attend closely to what people thought or believed was transpiring in their world.[8]

Brad Gregory's recent comparative study of martyrdom in early modern Europe raises a methodological issue that is inescapable: the degree to which the modern historian's interpretive (and ideological) assumptions either facilitate or impede the understanding of early modern agents. While separating himself from the confessional agendas of Catholic apologists and Whiggish-progressive Protestants, Gregory does not accept the critical and analytic procedures of what he calls "postmodern" interpretation (presumably a constellation of deconstructive, psychoanalytic, and cultural-materialist assumptions) since, he claims, they prevent a sympathetic understanding of the motives and mind-sets of the religious agents whose words and actions he wishes to accept "on their own terms." I am uncomfortable with this procedure, however, because I do not think that one can abstract oneself from the analytic insights provided by modern critical methods, for example, from a psychoanalytic understanding of human behavior. But I do take Gregory's point that modern interpreters, with atheistic or agnostic assumptions, have not taken seriously enough the zealous beliefs and religious motivations of early modern Christians.[9] I do not think, however, that it is necessary or possible to distance oneself from modern psychological and cultural analysis with the hope of some sort of unmediated access to the early modern cultural others being studied. This, of course, leaves me in the uncomfortable (but, I hope, intellectually productive) position of accepting *neither* those forms of poststructuralist interpretation that treat the words and actions of early modern English Catholics and Protestants merely as symbolic expressions of sociopolitical and socioeconomic realities *nor* the approaches of confessionally engaged historians and literary scholars who wish to cut religious discourse and realities off from other spheres of activity or contexts of interpretation. My solution is to approach the texts I examine in a way that allows the otherness of the voices from the past to disturb or disorient the modern reader, to create a sense that *our* interpretations of them are incomplete or inadequate.[10] For example, I do not introduce a perspective on those Catholic missionaries, such as Edmund Campion, who desired martyrdom that would explain their behavior in terms of psychopathology (which may have been a factor) or in terms of their being either deluded victims or self-conscious agents in a dirty game of international power politics. To do so would be to fail to take seriously their intelligence, the reality of their religious commitment and experience, and, most important, the actual cultural functioning of their words and actions. If we use the same kind of explanation of their behavior that we bring to the analysis of contemporary radical Islamic terrorist "martyrs," we smugly distort the historical realities we pretend to be observing "objectively."

I know that, especially in the case of discussing early modern English Catholics, I am writing against the grain of most historical and literary interpretation—which has operated, more or less, on the liberal, Whiggish assumption that (early modern and modern) Catholicism is an antidemocratic, antiprogressive force in world history, an attitude that, therefore, impedes a sympathetic understanding of English Catholic culture of the sixteenth and seventeen centuries. Of course, the fact that two of the three major authors of the period, Edmund Spenser and John Milton, were ideologically impassioned anti-Catholics has reinforced this point of view.[11]

The topic with which this book deals selectively is huge, some aspects of which have already been discussed in important studies by Frances Dolan, Alison Shell, Anne Dillon, and Raymond Tumbleson.[12] I am indebted to each of these works, but I deliberately steer clear of some of the subjects they address, so as to avoid unnecessary overlap. Dolan's study deals best with the issue of

gender and religion (in seventeenth-century England): she is especially perceptive with regard to the feminization of Catholicism in Protestant discourse.
Shell, who is interested in examining "the formulation of a various and dis-
tinct Catholic consciousness"[13] in the period between 1559 and 1660, skillfully
relates a number of literary texts to their religious contexts. Dillon examines
Catholic martyrdom accounts, published martyrologies, and the Catholic visual
representation of martyrdom in the context of an international public relations
struggle with Protestantism in which ecclesiastical history and martyrdom were
contested terrain. Tumbleson, who concentrates on the late seventeenth and
early eighteenth centuries, brings a real passion to his revisionist efforts, and he
makes it clear how deeply anti-Catholicism has been ingrained in English culture. I have learned much from all of these scholars and hope that my work
complements theirs.

   This study is not arranged to deliver a single or single-minded argument.
It is a collection of thematically focused essays dealing with a series of related
topics that shed light on the Catholic and anti-Catholic discourses in the period: relics and print culture (chap. 1), recusant women, Jesuits, and the cultural
"othering" of Catholics (chap. 2), martyrdom accounts, manuscript communication, and the Catholic subculture (chap. 3), Catholic and Protestant polemically charged narratives of conversion or change of religion (chap. 4), and the
uses of Catholic plots or outrages and providential Protestant deliverances in
the construction of Protestant English history and identity (chap. 5). Perhaps
only the last chapter, which deals with a pattern imposed on historical events in
order to dissociate England from its Catholic past (and contemporary Catholic
minority subculture), begins to offer an argumentatively shaped chronological
narrative, but it tells only part of the story whose elements far exceed the scope
of this study. What I am doing, finally, is urging a reevaluation of early modern
English culture to acknowledge the crucial presence of Catholic writing and
experience, which classic Whig versions (and newer Marxist versions) of English history have marginalized or ignored. To this end, I highlight some of the
varied uses of anti-Catholic fantasies, codes, and language because they are
crucial to an understanding of the religious and political crises and history
of the time. The Catholic and anti-Catholic discourses I have broadly identified are implicit in large processes of cultural change in the period: the making
of English Protestant nationalism, the conversion of a theocratic conception
of statehood into a (more visibly) secular one, and the developing relationship

of national to international institutions, forces, and perspectives. In separately published essays—one on Shakespeare and Catholicism and the other on John Donne's anti-Catholicism[14]—I deal with individual literary figures in relation to the religious and rhetorical conflict of Catholicism and Protestantism in early modern England. I decided not to focus on major writers in this study but rather to examine the broader field of language use in thematic chapters that cite only some canonical authors for illustrative purposes. Other literary scholars, I am sure, can relate the topics I examine to particular writers and works.

The recently established Society for Early Modern Catholic Studies signals the growing interest in the field in which this study is situated. Rather than being comprehensive, this book is meant to open (especially for literary scholars) less explored subjects of inquiry and to redefine some established areas of research. It is part of a scholarly conversation now under way, which, I hope, will produce fresh, intellectually nuanced accounts of early modern religious culture generally and of early modern English Catholicism in particular.

Southwell's Remains

Catholicism, Relics, and Print Culture in Early Modern England

There is tremendous talk here of Jesuits, and more fables perhaps are told about them than were told of old about monsters. For as to the origin of these men, their way of life, their institute, their morals and teaching, their plans and actions, stories of all sorts are spread abroad, not only in private conversation but also in public sermons and printed books, and these contradict one another and have a striking resemblance to dreams.

—Robert Persons to Alfonso Agazzari, August 1581[1]

But now he's gone, and my idolatrous fancy
Must sanctify his relics.

—Shakespeare, *All's Well That Ends Well,* 1.1.100–101

ENGLISH NATIONALISM RESTS ON A FOUNDATION OF ANTI-CATHOLICISM. In the sixteenth and seventeenth centuries English identity was defined as Protestant, so Roman Catholicism, especially in its post-Tridentine, Jesuit manifestations, was cast as the hated and dangerous antagonist, most fearfully embodied in a papacy that claimed the right to depose monarchs. Politically intrusive popes' vision of *international* order directly conflicted with the kind of political autonomy implicit in the ideology of the newly emerging nation-state. As the model of a polity, the Protestant nation contrasted most vividly with a transnational entity such as the Holy Roman Empire, just as, in reform theology, the spiritually enlightened, Scripture-reading "godly" believer contrasted with the "superstitious" devotee of a corporate Catholicism in which spiritual authorization always came (in mediated form) from above through a hierarchical church, an institution deformed through centuries of bureaucratic overgrowth and non–scripturally based traditions. From the time of Queen Elizabeth's accession in 1558 to that of the Glorious Revolution of 1688, Catholicism was for the majority of nationalistic English both an enemy within and an enemy without. A vocabulary of anti-Catholicism or anti-Popery was developed and deployed for a wide variety of national and international political circumstances, becoming immersed finally in the post-1688 era in a Whig narrative of English history.[2]

In the early modern era, a number of religiously coded events helped to shape English nationhood and the narrative accounts of English history: these include the Northern Rebellion of 1569,[3] the Spanish Armada of 1588, the Gunpowder Plot of 1605, the proposed Spanish Match for James I's son Charles in the early 1620s, the Irish Rebellion of 1641, the "Popish Plot" of 1678–81, and the Glorious Revolution of 1688. The failures of the Northern Rebellion, the Spanish Armada, and the Gunpowder Plot were absorbed into a providential narrative of deliverance in which God periodically saved an elect Protestant nation from the assaults of the forces of the Antichrist, the last transformed into a national holiday of thanksgiving, Gunpowder Treason Day or Guy Fawkes Day.[4]

The late-feudal rebellion of the Northern Earls in 1569 was more a provincial and conservative aristocratic backlash against the continuing Tudor centralization of power and the elevation of "new men" in the growing bureaucratic nation-state,[5] but it was portrayed as primarily a Catholic threat, retrospectively connected to Pope Pius V's 1570 Bull of Excommunication of Queen Elizabeth, which absolved her Catholic subjects of allegiance to her and thus led to the strong link between Catholicism and treason emphasized in the later proclamations and statutes directed against priests, especially missionary priests, and the recusant Catholic laity who assisted them.

There were numerous seminary priests in England in the 1570s (joining the older surviving Marian Catholic clergy), but the first Jesuits did not arrive until the 1580s—unfortunately on the heels of the Spanish-assisted Irish Rebellion of 1579. In the context of the papal bull and the danger of a Catholic uprising or assassination plot, these more militantly Catholic missionaries provoked a wave of anti-Catholic legislation and persecution. For example, Elizabeth's royal proclamation "Declaring Jesuits and Non-Returning Seminarians Traitors" states:

> [I]t hath manifestly and plainly appeared unto her highness and her council, as well by many examinations as by sundry of their own letters and confessions, besides the late manifest attempts of the like companions directed by the pope out of the number of the said seminaries and Jesuits broken out to actual rebellion in Ireland, that the very end and purpose of these Jesuits, seminary men, and such like priests sent or to be sent over into this realm and other of her majesty's dominions from the parts beyond the seas is not only to prepare sundry her majesty's subjects inclinable to disloyalty to be apt to give aid to foreign invasion and to stir up rebellion within the same, but also (that most perilous is) to deprive her majesty (under whom, and by whose provident government, with God's assistance, these realms have been so long and so happily kept and continued in great plenty, peace, and security) of her life, crown, and dignity.[6]

Although in the 1580s and 1590s only a couple dozen Jesuits came to England, one would think from the government's actions and from the rash of anti-Jesuit polemical activity that a secret army of thousands had landed on England's shores to prepare the way for foreign invasion.[7]

Edmund Campion and the Metaphorics of Catholic Martyrdom

The first Jesuit priests to arrive in England as missionaries in 1580 were Robert Persons and Edmund Campion. The former became the polemical nemesis of English Protestantism, excoriated, in the words of one impassioned antagonist, for example, as "a notorious lyer, a brasen faced Fryer, a known cozener, a sacrilegious Bastard, an incestuous villain, a cursed Fairie bratte, and bloudthirsty traytor";[8] the latter was a martyr who haunted the Elizabethan Protestant establishment. When it occurred in 1581, Campion's arrest was a high-profile one, partly because two of his prose works were perceived as arrogantly aggressive polemical assaults on English Protestantism. The first of these was

Campion's hastily composed letter to Queen Elizabeth's Privy Council defending his mission as nonpolitical, a work he did not wish to circulate until his arrest but which quickly found its way to its original addressees. It came to be known as "The Brag" because Campion announced himself able and ready to defend the truths of Roman Catholicism in debate with Protestant adversaries:

> I do ask, to the glory of God, with all humility and under your correction, three sorts of indifferent and quiet audiences: the first before your Honours, wherein I will discourse of religion, so far as it touches the commonweal and your nobilities; the second, whereof I make more account, before the Doctors and Masters and chosen men of both Universities, wherein I undertake to avow the faith of our Catholic Church by proofs innumerable, Scriptures, Councils, Fathers, History, natural and moral reasons; the third before the lawyers, spiritual and temporal, wherein I will justify the said faith by the common wisdom of the laws standing yet in force and practice.[9]

Campion's "Brag" elicited a strong reaction from the authorities, both in their subsequent treatment of him as a prisoner and in their printed propaganda. The zealous Protestant minister William Charke's *Answer to a Seditious Pamphlet by a Jesuite* (1580) responds to the manuscript circulation of "The Brag," which, for him, constituted "Libels, abusing the name and holy authority of the [Privy] Counsell" (Aiii). Charke worries about the vulnerability of Protestants to the rhetoric of clever Jesuits: he fears the peace of gospel-loving Christians might be disturbed by disputation with the religious enemy. At the same time he associates Protestantism with the life of the spirit (and the scriptural word) and Catholicism with "the feeling and wisdome of a natural man" (Ciiii^v), a religion designed to "snare the heart of a carnall man, bewitching it with so great glistering of the painted harlot" (Bviii) and other sensual baits.[10] *The Great bragge and challenge of M. Champion a Jesuite, commonly called Edmunde Campion, lately arrived in Englande, contayning nyne articles here severallye laide down, directed by him to the Lordes of the Counsail, confuted & aunswered by Meredith Hanmer* (1581) associates the Jesuit threat with that of the Family of Love and Anabaptists, suggesting as well that Jesuits were involved in homosexual practices.[11] Robert Persons's *Brief Censure uppon two books written in answer to M. Edmond Campion's offer of disputation* (1581)

was issued within days of Hanmer's pamphlet by the secret Green Street press.[12] Referring to Hanmer's book, and to his own *Brief Discours contayning certayne Reasons why Catholiques refuse to go to Church* (1580), Persons, in a bit of self-promotion, wrote to Alfonso Agazzari, rector of the English College at Rome (17 November 1580): "Nothing is spoken of here now but the Jesuits, especially after the recent publication of two books in English, which nearly everybody thinks were written by them, one in defense of the imprisoned Catholics, the other controverting the calumnies against the Society of Jesus contained in two books written by Protestants; and it is almost unbelievable what a stir has been caused by these rejoinders."[13] In another letter to Agazzari, Persons emphasized the importance of Catholics' using the press to counter the arguments of English Protestants, "to ensure that the heretics should not be able to publish anything without its being almost immediately attacked more vigorously." Persons continued, "Charke and Hanmer, Calvinist ministers[,]/ . . . wrote against Campion, abusing in wonderful fashion the whole Jesuit order and condemning expressly the life of Ignatius Loyola. But within ten days there appeared a short criticism by an unknown author, printed in type, which taxed those ministers with so many lies that both they and their followers were mightily ashamed."[14]

Campion's secretly printed defense of Catholicism, *Rationes Decem* (1581),[15] copies of which mysteriously appeared on the benches of St. Mary's Church in Oxford, provoked the bishop of London to instruct the Regius Professors of Divinity at Oxford and Cambridge, Laurence Humphrey and William Whitaker, to compose the first two (of several) Protestant refutations.[16] Both "The Brag" and *Rationes Decem* prompted Campion's captors and torturers to arrange four "conferences" in the Tower in which he was forced, with no other resources than a Bible, his associate Ralph Sherwin, and the depleted energies of his racked and fatigued body and mind, to dispute questions of religion with a team of Protestant theologians well equipped with notes and reference materials — meetings publicized quickly in biased printed accounts by his adversaries.[17] Persons wrote of these disputations: "[T]ruly it can scarcely be told how much good these disputations have done, and are doing every day. And if [Campion] dies for that cause they will certainly do still more good. For they are the common talk and subject of conversation of everybody, not only of Catholics, but of our enemies also; and always to the great honour of Fr. Campion."[18]

Thomas Alfield's narrative of Campion's execution appeared anonymously in February 1582 as *A true reporte of the death & martyrdome of M. Campion Iesuite and preiste, & M. Sherwin, & M. Bryan preistes, at Tiborne the first of December 1581 Observid and written by a Catholike preist, which was present therat.*[19] This work answered "a most infamous libel, entitled, *An Advertisement and defense for truth against her backbyters, and specially against the whispering favorers and colorers of Campions, and the rest of his confederates treasons*" (A4ᵛ).[20] Like Campion himself in his "Brag," Alfield argued that "meerely and only religion, no treason, no undutifulness to our Prince, no disobedience to her temporal lawe" (B3) lay behind the actions of the missionaries.

This work's dramatic account of Campion's execution, including his dialogue with his persecutors, who tried one final time to get him to confess treason, contains a report of a strange event connected with the execution of Campion's fellow martyr, the seminary priest Alexander Bryant: "[He] after his beheading, himself dismembred, his hart bowels and intrels burned, to the gret admiration of some, being layd upon the blocke his bellye downward, lifted up his whole body then remayning from the grounde" (D2ᵛ).[21] In his consolatory *Triumphs over Death* (1595), Robert Southwell later referred, in a collection of examples of supposed divine punishments exacted against Protestant persecutors, to "the wonderful stay and standing of the Thames the same day that Father *Campion* and his companye were martyred to the great marvayle of the Cittizens and mariners" (Bb3ᵛ).[22] Both accounts reflect the Catholic belief in miracles, associated by Protestants with the practices of magic and other forms of trickery attributed to the "old religion."[23] Such faith in the physical manifestations of the spiritual underlay the Catholic reverence for saints' relics. Referring to the martyrs of 1581 and 1582, William Allen remarks:

[F]or the Catholikes, of Italie, Spaine, Fraunce, and namely (which is lesse to be marveled at) of England, more then the weight in golde would be geven, and is offered for any peece of their reliques, either of their bodies, haire, bones or garments, yea of any thing that hath any spot or staine of their innocent and sacred bloud. Wherein surely great diligence and honorable zeale hath been shewed by divers noble gentlemen & verteous [*sic*] people, that have to their great daunger obtained some good peeces of them, to satisfie presently the godly greedy appetite of holy persons of divers nations making extreme sute for them.

Marry that is most notable and memorable, that divers devoute people of our nation that can get no part of their sacred reliques, yet come as it were on pilgrimage to the places where their quarters or heades be set up, under pretence of gasing and asking whose heades or bodies they be, and what traitors they were, whose heades are set highe above others, there, to do their devotion & praiers unto them, whose lives they knew to be so innocent, and deathes so glorious befor God and the world.[24]

Allen's comments characterize a Catholic community responding strongly to the heroism of martyrdom and incorporating veneration of their relics into their ongoing devotional practices.

Henry More's later account of the English Jesuit mission describes the way in which people who sought relics behaved at the execution of Campion, Sherwin, and Bryant:

While these martyrs were being torn asunder, the Catholics did their best to retrieve at least a few of their remains. But their enemies exercised great care to prevent this. One young gentleman, however, pushing through the people around him, let his handkerchief fall in order to get it soaked in Campion's blood, or at least that it might collect a few drops. But his attempt was instantly noticed, and he was seized and put in gaol. All the same, while he was being arrested, another took the opportunity in the general confusion to cut off Campion's finger and make off with it. That, too, was observed, but although rigorous enquiry was set on foot, it proved impossible to find the man who did it. Another young man, when he saw that nothing could be taken surreptitiously, secretly offered £20 of our money to the executioner for a single joint of Father Campion's finger, but he did not dare to give it. Their clothes were much sought after by Catholics, who tried to buy them, but so far they have not been able to get anything. It is thought that their enemies tried to burn everything so that nothing should fall into the hands of the Catholics.[25]

Supposedly one of Campion's arms was taken from the city gate where it was displayed and Robert Persons paid money for the halter with which Campion was hanged—which he kept with him and died wearing around his neck.[26] Mary, Queen of Scots, is alleged to have owned a reliquary that contained relics of Campion.[27] Catholic material practices with regard to relic collection, preservation, and use were a continuation of a pre-Reformation religious culture, a protest against persecuting authorities, and a means of binding a community under siege.

Relics, of course, were one of the strong markers of difference between Catholicism and Protestantism. In England the late Henrician assault on shrines and relics was part of a power contest between the state and the papacy.[28] In one of the first proclamations of her reign, Queen Elizabeth, repeating the language of some of Henry VIII's proclamations, ordered her clergy "to the intent that all superstition and hypocrisy crept into divers men's hearts may vanish away, they shall not set forth or extol the dignity of any images, relics, or miracles, but, declaring the abuse of the same, they shall teach that all goodness, health, and grace ought to be both asked and looked for only of God as of the very author and giver of the same, and of none other."[29] This proclamation ordered officials to "take away, utterly extinct, and destroy all shrines, covering of shrines, all tables, candlesticks, trindles, and rolls of wax, pictures, paintings, and all other monuments of feigned miracles, pilgrimages, walls, glasses, window, or elsewhere within their churches and houses."[30] To this day, the official center of the English church, Canterbury Cathedral, is marked by an absence, the space formerly occupied by the relics and shrine of Thomas à Becket.

Given the talismanic power Catholics attributed to saints' relics,[31] it is not surprising that both sophisticated and unsophisticated Catholics, at the execution scene and afterwards, acted as they did. But in this case, as in others, certain Protestants were also strongly affected by the spectacle. Supposedly Henry Walpole, then a Protestant gentleman attending Campion's execution out of curiosity, after being splashed with some of Campion's blood, had a conversion experience that led him to join the Jesuits and finally experience the same sort of martyrdom in 1595.[32]

It is clear that Campion, like so many other missionaries, came to England expecting if not desiring to be martyred. In his unfinished biography of his former colleague, Robert Persons quotes Campion's revealing remark about his decision to dress in humble rather than elegant attire: "he would say that to him that went to be hanged in England any kind of apparel was sufficient." He also notes that Campion took as his alias the name "Edmonds in remembrance of St. Edmond King and Martyr of England whom he desired to imitate."[33]

The martyred Campion's body was instantly sacralized at Tyburn—not only for Catholics but, given the powerful Protestant discourse of martyrdom that was such an essential feature of nascent English nationalism, for a larger community as well.[34] Any time there was a public execution of a Catholic priest or layman, the government created a situation in which spectators might sympathize, admire, and, in some cases, be moved to emulate the victims and react negatively to the power that condemned and killed them. Francis Bacon advised Queen Elizabeth not to hang Catholics for their religion because of the sympathy it won them: "they should never have the honour to take any pretence of martyrdom in England, where the fulness of blood and greatness of heart is such that they will even for shameful things go bravely to death, much more when they think themselves to climb [to] heaven; and this vice of obstinacy seems to the people a divine consistency; so that for my part I wish no lessening of their number but by preaching and by education of the younger sort under schoolmasters."[35] Francis Walsingham realized that executing Catholics "draweth some to affect their religion, upon conceit that such an extraordinary contempt of death cannot but proceed from above, whereby many have fallen away."[36] Robert Cotton made a pragmatic appeal for leniency: in a work belatedly published in 1641, he argued against making Catholics into martyrs because "there are too many of the blind *Commonalty,* altogether *Popish,* though not reconciled *Papists,* who, in their foolish ignorance, will say, it is pitty any should dye for their Conscience, though indeed they make honourable amends for their Treason."[37]

Torturing and executing Catholic priests, then, conferred the status of martyr on them (not only within Catholicism[38] but also in the eyes of the English public at large). The authorized spectacle of public execution, mutilation, dismemberment, and the display of the heads and quartered bodies of supposed traitors on the Tower Bridge and the gates of the city of London was designed to proclaim the morally sanctioned power of the state over the bodies of those who would destroy it, but all this could be reinterpreted in a martyrological context to yield a very different message. In a poem appended to the *True Report* of Campion's execution, the writer testifies to the politically oppositional meaning Catholics could find in such state theatricalism:

We can not feare a mortal torment, wee,
this Martirs blood hath moistned all our harts,
whose partid quartirs when we chaunce to see,
we lerne to play the constant christians part,
his head doth speake, & heavenly precepts give,
how we that looke should frame our selves to live.

$$(E_4)^{39}$$

In another poem from this pamphlet, "A Dialogue betwene a Catholike, and Consolation," the writer similarly states:

His quarters hong on every gate do showe,
his doctrine sound throgh countries far & neare,
his head set up so high doth call for moe
to fight the fight which he endured here,
the faith thus planted thus restord must be,
take up thy crosse said Christ and folow me.

$$(F_4)^{40}$$

In both these poems, the severed heads of the martyrs preach and teach the martyrs' coreligionists "precepts" and urge them to imitate the exemplary militancy of those who have died for the faith. In one sense, this is a Catholic answer to the Protestant exaltation of the preaching function of men of the cloth.

After Henry Garnet was hanged for supposed complicity in the Gunpowder Plot, his head was perceived as an instrument of miraculous pedagogy by those who observed it. One Catholic reported:

After that Father Henrie Garnett, Superior of the Societie of Jhesus in England, was executed by commandement of James now King of that realm, the third day of May . . . in the year 1606, his head appeared in that lively colour as it seemed to retaine the same hue and shew of life which yt had before itt was cutt off, soe as both heretiques and Catholiques were astonished thereat, and soe much the more, in that according to custom beinge cast into hoate water itt receaved no alteration at all; as neyther it did after yt was placed upon London Bridge, and sett upp there uppon a pole. Whereupon there was such resort of people for the

space of six weeks as that was admirable, the citizens flocking thither
by hundreds to see soe strange and wonderfull a spectacle, as the heade
of this glorious martyr did exhibit, whose face continuade without any
change retaining a gracefull and livelye countenance, and never waxed
blacke, as usuallye all heades cutt from the bodies doe. Whereuppon the
magistrates of the citye, and counsaile confounded with the miracle, and
displeased with the continuall resort of people to beholde the unexpected
event, gave order that the heade should be put soe as the face should be
turned uppwardes, and the people thereby not able to vewe the face as
they had been accustomed. There have been soe manie to see it at once
sometymes, what from the bridge, what from places near thereunto, as
from the water and houses, as divers there present have thought them to
have been to the number of 400 or 500 persons.[41]

Unauthorized gatherings of citizens obviously worried the authorities, and this
account tries to suggest that there was broad popular interest in the physical remains of the executed Garnet as well as willingness to believe that his head was
miraculously preserved from corruption as a sign of his innocence. Relics were
dangerous (like Lenin's embalmed body now in "the former Soviet Union"),
a source of power not sanctioned by state authority—in the case of executed
Catholics a focus for an alternative allegiance, not just to the foreign pope, but,
more generally, to a religious and personal devotional order outside the officially sanctioned one. Like those of Garnet or other Catholic martyrs, the physical "remains" of Edmund Campion delivered a strong political message.

In print culture, however, Campion's "remains" were present in both his
own polemical discourse and in the language of his enemies and interpreters.
In a passage excised by censorship from the second edition of Holinshed's
Chronicles (1587), the writer complains about Catholic propaganda evoked by
the deaths of Campion and the other two priests:

No sooner had justice given the blow of execution, and cut off the foresaid offendors from the earth; but certeine enimies to the state politike
and ecclesiastike, greatlie favouring them, and their cause, which they
falslie gave out to be religion, dispersed abroad their libels of most im-
pudent devise, tending to the justifieng of the malefactors innocencie, to
the heinous and unrecompensable defamation of the course of justice

and judgement against them commensed and finished: in somuch that speaking of the daie whereon they died, they blushed not to intitle them martyrs. . . . Thus slanderouslie against the administration of justice scattered these vipers brood their lieng reports, therein to the skies advancing the children of iniquitie as spotlesse; yea forging most monstrous fables, put them in print; as though God and nature had suffered violence to their unappeaseable indignation, for that men of such integritie forsooth and extraordinarilie sanctified, suffered so shamefull a death.[42]

In Holinshed what immediately follows this account of Campion's death is the discussion of another politically sensitive topic, the winding down of Queen Elizabeth's negotiations to marry a French Catholic spouse, the duke of Alençon.[43] The uncut 1587 edition has several pages that were censored after publication because this match (bitterly opposed by the more radical Protestants on the Privy Council and by many of Elizabeth's other subjects) was brought into an unsavory association with the business of executing missionary priests. In the censored version of Holinshed, the duke is introduced only at the point of his departure from England: "But leaving this tragedie now at the last act, you shall understand that about this time Monsieur duke of Anjou departing out of England, was accompanied with diverse lords, knights, and gentlemen of great traine to the sea side, and imbarked sailed with prosperous wind and weather."[44] The best Catholic was a departing one — one dying or setting sail.

In one of his more manically exaggerated letters to Agazzari, Robert Persons reported on the supposed benefits of the execution of Campion, Sherwin, and Bryant for the Catholic cause:

[T]he enemy are evidently enraged that the death of the last martyrs has inflicted such a great blow on their cause. . . . Walsingham declared lately that it would have been better for the Queen to have spent 40,000 gold pieces than to kill publicly those priests. And in truth the effect has been that we have all Protestants, who are of more moderate temper, very much on our side. For they say that they have a better opinion of our cause both on account of the uncompromising way in which we daily challenge our enemies to debate — which they see clearly that the latter shun after their experience with these martyrs — and also on account of the death of these men, which they believe to have been altogether unjust. . . . All with one voice, our enemies as well as ourselves, declare that if their lives had been prolonged to their hundreth year they could not have benefited their cause as much as has their short life, but glorious death. Many have stood firm, fearless and loyal after it, who had been timid before; some there have been who have joined the Catholic Church; countless numbers of the opposite party have begun to have doubts; and all the Catholics who are in chains and undergoing persecution bear it with such joy and exultation that they do not feel anything that they are suffering. . . . [O]ur persecutors are almost bursting with indignation and wrath. Countless is the number of books, dialogues, treatises, poems, satires, which have been composed and published, some in print, some in manuscript, in praise of these martyrs and in blame of their adversaries.[45]

Even a sympathetic reader would have perceived the high quotient of wishful thinking in this text, the writer's desperate need to find consoling and compensatory effects in the midst of the disasters befalling the English Mission.

From both Continental and secret English presses, Catholic polemicists were quick to make the case for their side.[46] In addition to Allen's *A Brief Historie,* these works include Persons's *An Epistle of the Persecution of Catholickes in England* (1582)[47] and Richard Verstegan's later *Theatrum Crudelitatum Haereticorum Nostri Temporis* (Antwerp, 1587)—the last a gruesomely illustrated series of vignettes of both Continental and English persecution from Henry VIII's time into the 1580s.[48] Verstegan's book contains a Henrician composite scene of ecclesiastical despoilation, a large cross being chopped and pulled down, a fire burning Catholic books, vandals dismantling two church structures (one an abbey), and a church being burned;[49] the executions of Sir Thomas More and Bishop John Fisher (25); the 1535 execution of the Carthusian monks, depicted as a progress from hauling the victims on a hurdle to the place of execution and hanging them to dismembering them and burning the entrails (27); the hanging of the Franciscan John Forest, accompanied by the image of St. David in the fire and abbots and religious authorities strangled, eviscerated, and dismembered (29); many scenes of Continental French and Low Countries persecutions (31–68), including one of Dutch Protestants using human heads in a game of boules; a general illustration of Elizabethan persecution in which are shown a vestment-wearing cleric, a noblewoman, and a gentleman being thrown in prison, a Catholic home raided and despoiled at night, torch-bearing pursuivants on horseback capturing their prey, and Catholic prisoners, bound together, being moved from one horrid place of imprisonment to another (71); a scene in which one man is being racked, four prisoners peer out from behind bars, armed men are moving menacingly towards a church, and the cramped prison cell called "Littlease" is depicted (73); a scene of various noble and base Catholics in prison (including the supposedly murdered Henry Percy, earl of Northumberland), one prone emaciated man naked in his cell and another compressed into a ball in a hoop device, another man in bed being awakened by torch-bearing men at night, and other Catholics in prison in leg irons (75); an illustration of the earl of Huntingdon's cruel persecution in the North, exemplified by the pressing to death of Margaret Clitherow, the suspension of a priest upside down in the stocks, a picture of a fetid dungeon in which Catholics are suffocating from the bad air, and the general crowding of English prisons with Catholics (77); scenes of abuses of justice showing a Catholic priest having his ears perforated, a Catholic being whipped behind a cart, a Catholic sewn into a bearskin and baited by dogs, and Catholics hauled before tribunals along with common felons (79); a scene of Irish persecution in which two bishops and a monk are hanged and a bishop in the stocks has his feet held to the fire (81); a scene showing Jesuits, secular priests, nobles, and other Catholics dragged to the place of execution, one man being shown a body being dismembered to terrorize him into recanting, and Catholics being hanged and dismembered, their decapitated heads and body parts then set up on display on the gates of the city of London (83) (fig. 1); and, finally, the scene of the execution of Mary, Queen of Scots (85). The last two scenes allude to the heightened political tension of the 1580s just before the Armada. Verstegan's visually enhanced propaganda constituted a Catholic recapturing of martyrological discourse from Protestant writers such as John Foxe, whose book circulated on the Continent to the disadvantage of the English government.[50]

In light of the outpouring of Catholic polemic and propaganda following Campion's execution, Laurence Humphrey of Oxford wrote to the earl of Leicester:

[T]he ghost of the dead Campion has given me more trouble than the Rationes of the living,—not only because he has left his poison behind him, like the fabled Bonasus, which in its flight burns up its pursuers

FIGURE 1. "Persecutiones adversus Catholicos à Protestantibus Calvinistis in Anglia," from Richard Verstegan, *Theatrum Crudelitatum Haereticorum Nostri Temporis* (Antwerp, 1587). Reproduced by permission of the Special Collections Library, University of Michigan.

with its droppings, but much more because his friends dig him up from his grave, defend his cause, and write his epitaph in English, French, and Latin. It used to be said, "Dead men bite not"; and yet Campion dead bites with his friends' teeth—a notable miracle, according to all experience, and to the old proverb; for as fresh heads grow on the hydra when the old are cut off, as wave succeeds wave, as a harvest of new men rose from the seed of the dragon's teeth, so one labour of ours only begets another, and still another; and in the place of the single Campion, champions upon champions have swarmed to keep us engaged.[51]

In defense of the official Elizabethan position, Lord Burghley published in 1583 his justification of the harsh treatment of Catholic missionaries in both *A declaration of the favourable dealing of her Majesties Commissioners appointed for the examination of certaine traitours* and *The Execution of Justice in England*. In the latter work, he insisted that the seminary priests and Jesuits who came to England under the cover of religion were there to get Catholics to conform to the papal bull excommunicating Elizabeth that "discharged [English Catholics] of their allegiance and obedience to their lawful prince and country . . . and . . . [made them] warranted to take arms to rebel against Her Majesty when they shall be thereunto called, and to be ready secretly to join with any foreign force that can be procured to invade the realme."[52] He claimed that the few missionary priests who were executed were those who refused to renounce their seditious purposes and that they were executed not for religion or under any new (anti-Catholic) legislation but as traitors under a treason law dating back two hundred years, to the time of Edward III. Burghley's arguments were answered (in a tract more than five times the length of Burghley's *Execution of Justice*) by William Allen's *Defence of English Catholiques* (1584), itself answered by Thomas Bilson's *True Difference betweene Christian Subjection and Unchristian Rebellion* (1585). Nicholas Sanders's posthumously published historical account of the English "schism," *De Origine ac Progressu Schismatis Anglicani,* was obviously one of the most threatening Catholic printed texts, if the English government's questioning of arrested missionaries is any indication.[53] Surprisingly, it was not until 1593 that a printed reply was published.[54] Clearly, in the years leading up to the (suspiciously engineered) Babington Plot, the consequent execution of Mary, Queen of Scots (1587), and the Spanish Armada (1588), the persecution of Catholics and the execution of Catholic missionaries and those who assisted them were deeply enmeshed in a national and international struggle for moral, political, and religious legitimacy. Campion was only one Catholic victim among many, but his case highlights the larger context. His relics and his writings and his example had a continuing cultural presence.

Robert Southwell and Literary Remains

In some ways Robert Southwell, S.J., was an even more disturbing figure than Campion for the Elizabethan (and Jacobean) government, both before and after his death. Less polemically confrontational than either his predecessor or the indefatigable Persons, Southwell circulated a number of his writings in both manuscript and print before his arrest in 1592—the printed books is-

sued by a secret press hidden in the countess of Arundel's house, the manuscript verse and prose works traveling the networks of Catholic manuscript
transmission. One of these pieces, *An Humble Supplication to Her Majestie,*
is an eloquent plea for toleration of Catholics written in reponse to the 1591
royal proclamation establishing commissions to hunt down seminary priests
and Jesuits.[55]

Southwell's execution at Tyburn was one of the most dramatic of the
Elizabethan era. The narrative of his movement from Newgate Prison to
the scaffold to the dismembering table involves several details that sacralize the
body of the priest-martyr. Southwell apparently gave his cap to the Keeper of
Newgate prison who treated it, in effect, as a relic: "which cap the Keeper, albeit
a Protestant, maketh such account of that he can be brought by no means to
forgo it."[56] When Southwell got to the place of execution after being dragged on
a hurdle through the muddy streets, he cleaned his face with a cloth that he then
threw to someone in the crowd. As he wrote one of his letters describing Southwell's experiences, Henry Garnet noted that this cloth was in his own possession (as a valued object), a kind of modern-day Veronica cloth.[57] The third holy
object was the rosary Southwell threw from the scaffold to a friend.[58] The live
martyr and his dead body were both treated by the executioner with unusual
respect. Garnet noted that the hangman did not follow the custom of cutting
down the hanging man before he was dead in order to perform the disemboweling on a live body.

> [Instead he] pulled on his legs—an act of courtesy and humanity that
> is unusual. One of the executioners several times made to cut the rope,
> but was stopped by the Lord [Mountjoy] and by the whole crowd, which
> cried out three times: "Let him be, let him be." The executioner took him
> down with great reverence and carried him in his own arms, assisted by
> his companions, to the place where he was to be quartered, whereas in all
> other cases it is the custom to drag [the bodies] brutally along the ground.
> When he was being disemboweled, his heart leaped into the hands of
> the executioner. All those who stood around spoke of him with respect,
> and there was none to cry "Traitor" according to custom.[59]

One contemporary narrative describes how some people in the crowd "dipped
handkerchiefs in the sprayed blood, and offered [the hangman] money for a

piece of bone or a lock of hair,"[60] desiring, as did some of the spectators at Campion's execution, relics of the deceased martyr.

Among Robert Southwell's remains or relics are the quarters of his dismembered body displayed on the gates of the city of London, his head mounted on a pole on the Tower Bridge, and the bloodstains obtained by devout coreligionists and sympathizers at Tyburn. Anticipating his own death, Southwell had referred to the power ascribed to a martyr's physical remains in his *Epistle of Comfort,* when he addressed Protestant persecutors of Catholics: "Our prisons preach, our punishments converte, our deade quarters and bones confound youre heresye: You have laboured to suppresse us this 29. yeeares: and yet of our ashes spring others, and our dead bones, as *Exechiell* prophesied, are come to be *exercitus grandis* a huge army."[61] Southwell's most important remains, however, were his writings,[62] some of which were rushed into print in 1595, the year of his execution: two editions of *Saint Peters complaynt. With other Poems,* and editions of *Moeoniae. or Certaine excellent Poems and spirituall Hymns: Omitted in the last Impression of Peters Complaint, The Triumphs over Death,* and *A Short Rule to the Good Life. An Humble Supplication* was published in 1600 but deliberately misdated as 1595 in order to associate it with Southwell's execution.[63] All these books and the other posthumously printed and reprinted verse and prose were the relics of the martyr the general public could most easily possess; they became part of a growing body of politically oppositionist recusant writing dealing with the faith, practices, and sufferings of the persecuted Catholic minority. Take, for example, the prose elegy Southwell wrote in 1591 to console the imprisoned Philip Howard, earl of Arundel, on the occasion of the death of his sister Lady Margaret, the wife of Robert Sackville (later earl of Dorset). This was published as *The Triumphs over Death: or, A Consolatorie Epistle for afflicted mindes, in the affects of dying friends. First written for the consolation of one: but now published for the general good of all, by R. S. the Author of* S. Peters Complaint, *and* Moeoniae *his other Hymnes* (1595 and 1596).[64] Since Howard and Southwell were both dead by the end of 1595, they could, along with Lady Margaret, take their places in the larger context of Catholic suffering and persecution evoked by such a printed work.

When he dedicated his collection of Southwell's writings to Richard, earl of Dorset, in 1620, the publisher, William Leake, used revealing language in referring to his having "first collected these dismembred parcels into one body, and published them in an entire edition,"[65] associating the dismembered body parts of the poet-martyr (a Christian Orpheus, as it were) with his scattered literary remains. Haviland's 1630 edition of *St. Peters Complaint, Mary Magdalens Funerall Teares, With Other Workes* has on the title page of some surviving copies a frontispiece portrait of Southwell identified with the following Latin inscription that reminds the reader of the martyr's dismemberment: "P. Robertus Southuell Soc. Jesu Londini pro Cath. fide suspensus et sectus. 3.mar.1595" (Father Robert Southwell of the Society of Jesus, hanged and dismembered in London for the Catholic faith, 3 March 1595).[66]

The association of an author's body with his body of work is more than a witty trope. It was historically grounded in the cultural conflicts and discourses of early modern England, related, for example, to the media shift from Catholic visual imagery and oral communication, on the one hand, to Protestant fetishizing of the word and the book (especially the vernacular Bible), on the other. After Catholic relics came under attack, starting with the depredations of the late 1530s, when the shrine of Thomas à Becket was destroyed and his bones scattered, the reverence for relics began to migrate into print culture, where the remains of a person were verbal.[67]

Although a long-term effect of print culture was the fostering of abstraction, the unbodying of the word—that is, the creation of the Cartesian mind-body split that characterizes modernity[68]—early in the print era the connection between books and the body was stressed. The corpse of the author and the corpus of his work were in closer imaginative proximity: hence even as reformist a Protestant as Milton could call "a good book . . . the precious lifeblood of a master spirit, embalmed and treasured up on purpose to a life beyond life."[69] Patrick Collinson, Arnold Hunt, and Alexandra Walsham observe: "Books were venerated as receptacles of spiritual power and revered for their totemic and thaumaturgic properties. . . . There was . . . negative symbolism, indicative of threatening power, when religious books, including missals, primers and religious pictures were ritually burned."[70] Burning books and burning heretics (or killing religiopolitical enemies) shared important symbolic features. As the historical bibliographer D. F. McKenzie has remarked: "The common use of the word 'Remaines' as a term for posthumous works ambiguously suggests both the items remaining to be published and, as the earthly relics of a departed soul, the close identity of a man's body and his printed works."[71] Addressing the countess of Pembroke, the sister of the deceased poet, Samuel Daniel referred to Sir Philip Sidney's poems as "holy Reliques"[72] (of a

Protestant kind). It is interesting to note that Southwell's famous apologetic epistle to his Protestant father was published, with a misattribution of authorship, in a book entitled *Remains of Sir Walter Raleigh* (1664).[73]

Southwell's literary remains were visibly Catholic ones, though they were subjected to a degree of Protestantizing. Gabriel Cawood's edition of *Saint Peters complaynt. With other Poems* (1595) was clearly marketed as a Catholic text. The religious ornament at the top of the title page (fig. 2) depicts a man and a woman kneeling in prayer looking upwards towards a highlighted "IHS." Between them is a table on which are the eucharistic symbols of chalice and host as well as what appear to be representations of the three nails of Christ's cross (always found along with the "IHS" in the Jesuit emblem).[74] The figures are flanked, as James McDonald has described them, by "doves with hearts for heads" over which are "crowns of thorns."[75] The book's title page, then, proclaims its connection with the martyrdom of the Jesuit poet whose work it contains. The whole volume takes its name from the title of its longest poem, "St. Peter's Complaynt"—which suggests, perhaps, a connection between the martyrdom of the first pope and that of Elizabethan Catholics.[76] Cawood printed only twenty of the fifty-two poems found in the circulating manuscripts of Southwell's verse, but some works may be missing not because of their political sensitivity but because Cawood had only the last part of the collection in its typical manuscript order and included whatever he possessed rather than omit any poems deliberately.[77]

Despite the signals of the poems' Catholic authorship and content, Cawood's and other early editions did not contain some of the more politically disturbing Catholic material found in the manuscript-circulated versions of Southwell's verse. For example, Southwell's poem on Mary, Queen of Scots, "Decease release," was not included, the fourth stanza of which reads:

> Alive a Queen, now dead I am a Sainte,
> Once Mary calld, my name nowe Martyr is,
> From earthly raigne debarred by restraint,
> In liew whereof I raigne in heavenly blisse.

Also, since Protestant apologists connected Queen Elizabeth and King John as royal victims of papal excommunications, it is not surprising that another politically sensitive poem, "I dye without desert," was also excluded, a piece found

FIGURE 2. Title page of Robert Southwell, *Saint Peters complaynt. With other Poems* (London, 1595). This item is reproduced by permission of The Huntington Library, San Marino, California.

in the Folger manuscript of Southwell's verse with the heading "Arthur Earle
of Britaine murthered by his uncle King John."[78] Finally, given Protestant/
Catholic conflicts over the meaning of the Eucharist, it makes sense that "Of the
Blessed Sacrament of the Aulter" had to wait until 1616 to appear in print in the
Continental edition of Southwell's work issued by the Jesuit press at St. Omer.

The 1599 Edinburgh edition of Southwell's poems by the "Printer to the
Kings Majestie," Robert Waldgrave, clearly Protestantized the verse:[79] for example, it drastically cut back the references to the Virgin Mary and added marginal annotations to "Saint Peter's Complaynt" that use the Protestant names
of the books of the Old Testament.[80] William Barrett's 1620 London edition,
St. Peters Complaint, Mary Magdalens Funeral Teares, With Other Workes, also
Protestantized Southwell's text somewhat, particularly in the alteration of his
translation of Thomas Aquinas's poem on the Eucharist, "An holy Hymne."[81]
Such religious revision, as Edmund Bunny's enormously popular (Protestant,
expurgated) version of Robert Persons's *The first booke of the Christian exercise,
apperyning to resolution* (1582) testifies,[82] helped Catholic texts win approval
from a large Protestant English readership. Sometimes, of course, the Protestantizing of a text necessitated radical changes: Shell points out that the Catholic William Byrd "published a musical setting of some verses on the death of
the martyr Edmund Campion with all the references to Campion excised, and
the praise of 'the Martirs of auncient times' substituted."[83]

In late Elizabethan England Catholic devotional and poetic texts could be
admired by those who did not share the authors' religious commitments. John
Harington of Stepney copied (from manuscript) the poem about Campion's
execution found in the Catholic *True Report* into his manuscript poetical anthology, as did John Lilliat into his, the former supposedly regarding it as "the
best Englishe verse . . . that ever he redd," the latter labeling the piece "A good
verse, upon a badd Matter."[84] The prison poem written by the Catholic Chidi-
ock Tichborne, "My prime of youth is but a frost of cares," was very popular in
manuscript transmission and was, surprisingly, printed in a volume entitled
Verses of Prayse and Joye writen upon her majesties preservation, a 1586 book celebrating the foiling of the Babington Plot.[85] Ben Jonson expressed to William
Drummond of Hawthornden his extraordinary admiration for one of Southwell's poems: "That Southwell was hanged yett so he had written that piece
of his the burning babe he would have been content to destroy many of his
[poems]."[86] Even Francis Bacon, whose essay "On Superstition" is a compen-

dium of anti-Catholic tropes, recommended Southwell's *An Humble Suppli-cation* to his brother Anthony soon after its publication: "I send you the sup-plication which Mr. Topcliffe lent me. It is curiously written, and worth the writing out for the art; though the argument be bad."[87] Despite confessional dif-ferences and despite the atmosphere of polemical viciousness in print culture, the literary remains of a Catholic author could be preserved *and venerated.*[88]

The 1580s and 1590s, then, were a time of religious and political crisis in which heightened fears on the part of the Elizabethan government of inter-nal subversion and foreign invasion led to harsh treatment of English Catho-lics, especially of the missionary priests entering the country to fill the gap left by the aging or deceased Marian clergy. Although their religious order con-stituted a minority among the missionary priests, men such as Campion and Southwell, both intellectually creative and resourceful adversaries of English Protestantism, had a high cultural visibility in life and in death. As part of the first cohort of Jesuits entering England (from various Continental locations) to do their pastoral and polemical work, they, along with Robert Persons, helped to shape English attitudes and fears about the Society of Jesus, that militant group of well-educated and committed men in the vanguard of the Counter-Reformation or "Catholic Reformation."[89] The anti-Jesuit mythology that de-veloped in England, related in some ways to that found on the Continent, is a special aspect of early modern anti-Catholicism that the next chapter addresses.

Alienating Catholics

Recusant Women, Jesuits, and Ideological Fantasies

Protestants, who had started Elizabeth's reign as a minority . . . [were]
able to produce an image of England as inherently Protestant because
Protestantism's opposite, popery, was inherently foreign.
— Peter Lake, "Anti-Popery: The Structure of a Prejudice"

IN THE SIXTEENTH CENTURY, ONCE THE MONARCH HAD BEEN DESIGNATED
the head of the English church, religious conformity and political loyalty were
inextricably bound. The 1559 Act of Supremacy (1 Eliz. I, c.1), "An Act restoring to the Crown the ancient jurisdiction over the state ecclesiastical and spiritual, and abolishing all foreign power repugnant to the same," sharply contrasted (royal) English with "usurped foreign power and authority."[1] It required
both temporal and ecclesiastical officers as well as "persons suing livery of
lands and doing homage, and . . . anyone taking holy orders or degrees at the
Universities"[2] to take the following oath on the Bible:

I, A. B., do utterly testify and declare in my conscience that the Queen's
Highness is the only supreme governor of this realm and of all other her
Highness' dominions and countries, as well in all spiritual or ecclesias-
tical things or causes as temporal, and that no foreign prince, person,

prelate, state or potentate hath or ought to have any jurisdiction, power, superiority, preeminence or authority ecclesiastical or spiritual within this realm, and therefore I do utterly renounce and forsake all foreign jurisdictions, powers, superiorities and authorities, and do promise that from henceforth I shall bear faith and true allegiance to the Queen's Highness, her heirs and lawful successors, and to my power shall assist and defend all jurisdictions, preeminences, privileges and authorities granted or belonging to the Queen's Highness, her heirs and successors, or united or annexed to the imperial crown of this realm: so help me God and by the contents of this Book.[3]

In addition, the Act of Supremacy stipulated penalties for those who

shall by writing, printing, teaching, preaching, express words, deed or act, advisedly, maliciously and directly affirm, hold, stand with, set forth, maintain or defend the authority, preeminence, power or jurisdiction spiritual or ecclesiastical of any foreign prince, prelate, person, state or potentate whatsoever, heretofore claimed, used or usurped within this realm or any dominion or country being within or under the power, dominion or obeisance of your Highness, or shall advisedly, maliciously and directly put in ure or execute anything for the extolling, advancement, setting forth, maintenance or defence of any such pretended or usurped jurisdiction, power, preeminence or authority, or any part thereof, that then every such person and persons so doing and offending, their abettors, aiders, procurers and counsellors, being thereof lawfully convicted and attainted according to the due order and course of the common laws of this realm, shall be subject to the following penalties: for the first offence, forfeiture of goods, or if these are not worth £20, one year's imprisonment, the benefices and promotions of eccelesiastics becoming void; for the second offence, the penalties of praemunire; the third offence is to be deemed high treason.[4]

Recusant Protestants, such as Anabaptists, and recusant Catholics were seen as political threats to the government: in refusing to conform outwardly to the state-mandated religious services, the former, with their democratic ideology, called the top-down system of political authority into question,[5] and the latter, by their allegiance to an international Catholic church answering to the authority of the bishop of Rome, either signaled a divided allegiance or, at an extreme, a traitorous commitment to foreign powers ready to invade the country. Of course, priests and laymen who were religious exiles awaiting or working for the restoration of Catholicism in England were most easily identified as a political menace, especially when they returned to the country as missionaries to strengthen the resolve of recusant Catholics, move "church papists"[6] (who observed the requirements of outward conformity to the established church while maintaining private Catholic beliefs and devotional practices) to active recusancy, and convert Protestants.

During the Elizabethan era, a series of laws, statutes, and royal proclamations were designed to punish lay Catholics for a wide range of activities—from simple nonattendance at Protestant services to hearing Mass and harboring priests to sending their sons and daughters to foreign Catholic schools, seminaries, and convents. The main laws were the 1559 Act of Uniformity (1 Eliz. I, c.2), which included a twelve-pence weekly fine for recusancy; the 1563 "act for the assurance of the Queen's Majesty's royal power over all estates and subjects within her Highness's dominions" (5 Eliz. I, c.1), which entailed loss of property for first refusal to take the oath of allegiance and death for a second refusal; the 1571 "act against the bringing in and putting in execution of bulls and other instruments from the see of Rome" (13 Eliz. I, c.2) and "Act whereby certain offences be made treasons" (13 Eliz. I, c.1), the former of which also made anyone leaving England for more than six months liable to forfeiture of lands and the latter of which covered not only those who plotted Elizabeth's death or overthrow but also those who dealt openly with the legitimacy of her rule or with the royal succession; the 1581 "act to retain the Queen's Majesty's subjects in their due obedience" (23 Eliz. I, c.1), which made treasonous those who drew subjects from their allegiance to the queen or to the Church of England and which dramatically increased the fine for recusancy to £20; the 1585 "act against Jesuits, seminary priests and such other like disobedient persons" (27 Eliz. I, c.2), confirming in law the royal proclamation of 1582;[7] and the 1593 "act against popish recusants" (35 Eliz. I, c.2), which ordered Catholics to register themselves with local authorities and to remain within five miles of their homes and which also made conforming husbands pay the recusancy fines of their wives.[8] Although there had been a small measure of toleration for the aging population of Marian priests surviving from midcentury, the laws targeted at secular and Jesuit missionaries arriving in England from the Continent after 1574[9] were especially severe: the 1585 statute identified them as "traitors" and pronounced both them and the laypeople who assisted them guilty of a capital crime.[10]

The harsh antirecusancy laws were designed not only to prevent the spread of Catholicism but also, mainly, to force external (patriotic) conformity to the ceremonies of a national Protestant church. They and the required loyalty oaths[11] were meant to terrorize Catholics into conformity: even those sentenced to death were often given the opportunity to save themselves by attending a Protestant service, hearing a Protestant sermon, or even praying with Protestants. Hard-line priests and lay Catholics faced imprisonment and, possibly, either exile or execution as well if they stood by their belief in papal supremacy (including the right to depose monarchs), declined to enter a Protestant church or engage in any religious practices with Protestant Christians, or refused to acknowledge the moral and legal authority of the state to demand oaths of allegiance from them or to judge them in matters of religion and religiopolitical activity. In part, they were caught in the middle of an international conflict not of their making, one that put their consciences or their lives in peril; in part, they found themselves in legal and judicial circumstances in which the final outcome rested on their own choices.

The laws and the social practices in late-sixteenth-century England worked both to erode the Catholicism of those who decided to become church papists and to alienate the recusant laity and the priests who ministered to them as disloyal, un-English. From a Jacobean perspective, Godfrey Goodman looked back on late Elizabethan attitudes towards Catholics and observed: "The common people did hate them above measure; for they must have ever an object to their hate. Heretofore the Welsh, the Scots, or the Spaniard, and the French upon occasion; but now in these later times only the papists."[12] In this chapter I focus on two Catholic figures of resistance alienated by their actions and by the state legal and political machinery from their status as loyal English citizens, the recusant Catholic woman and the Jesuit missionary priest. Both figures have a long history in the political mythology of English nationalism, constituting the most powerful danger when they are found in a combination that marks not only sociopolitical alienation but also essential religious differences between Protestantism and Catholicism.

Recusant Women and the Case of Margaret Clitherow

The recusant Catholic woman was an important character in the religious and cultural drama of early modern England for a number of reasons.[13] First, married either to a conforming church papist or to a Protestant spouse, she was a figure of opposition to state authority, a sign of the persistence of the "old religion" in the new Protestant nation. That the first four Stuart monarchs had Catholic queens placed this threat at the very heart of the state. The Catholic convert Anne of Denmark, the French princess Henrietta Maria, Catherine of Braganza, and Mary of Modena all were objects of anti-Catholic rhetoric and paranoia.[14] The fiercely anti-Catholic Puritan Thomas Scott, for example, writing against the possible Spanish Match of Prince Charles with the Spanish Infanta, defended his right as a subject to question the wisdom of a monarch's (or heir apparent's) having a Catholic spouse:

> [I]t is Objected, I have meddled with the mariage of the Prince, which concernes not the subject. Concernes it not the subject to pray, that the wife of his Soveraigne may be of the same Religion with her Lord? If I may pray thus, wish thus may not I endevor to have it thus? & shew the inconveniences (that I may not say mischiefs) which are likely to fall, if it be not thus? Princes are maried to the commonwealth; & the wife hath power of the husbands body, as he the husband of hers. The Commonwealth then hath power of the Prince in this point. Their Wives ought to be as Mothers to every Subject. And were not he a Foole, that would not desire a Naturall Mother, rather then a Step-Mother? Queenes ought to be nurcing Mothers to the Church: Who then would seeke a dry-Nurse, that might have another.[15]

When John Milton alludes to King Solomon's vulnerability to female temptation in *Paradise Lost,* he refers to "that uxorious king whose heart, though large, / beguiled by fair idolatresses, fell to idols foul."[16] The imagined danger such Catholic women posed to monarchs lay behind a parliamentary act of 1689 that made it illegal for an English monarch not only to be a Catholic but also to be married to a Catholic.

The recusant woman was, like Catholicism itself (the religion of the "Whore of Babylon"),[17] the target of Protestant misogyny—a masculinized,

reform Christianity, which attacked not only the cult of the Virgin but also devotion to female (as well as male) saints,[18] associated women's "carnality" with
some of the alleged corruptions of Catholicism, contrasting the devotional and
sacramental practices of the Roman church (which relied on the physical medi-
ation of the spiritual) with the supposedly more spiritual orientation of Protestant text- and language-based religion. Protestant iconoclasm and misogyny
shared a basic set of assumptions about the senses, about the place of the body
in religious practice, and about the seductive dangers of the feminine. Woman
and Catholicism were both feared as intrinsically idolatrous, superstitious, and
carnal, if not also physically disgusting. Duessa in Edmund Spenser's *The Faerie
Queene* is alternately attractive and repulsive—the Catholic church embodied
in the images of the dangerously beautiful wanton, the Whore of Babylon, and
the bestialized, filthy woman.[19] Mary, Queen of Scots, was feared and hated
by English Protestants as a "wicked Popish woman."[20] Sir Philip Sidney referred to Catherine de Medici, mother of the duke of Alençon (Queen Elizabeth's French suitor), as "the Jezebel of our age."[21] On the one hand, women
were seen as particularly vulnerable to being "seduced" into Catholicism: in
one of his literary "Characters," Samuel Butler says that the "Popish Priest" "[i]s
one that takes the same Course, that the Devil did in Paradise, he begins with
the Woman. . . . Christ made St. Peter a Fisher of Men; but he believes it better
to be a Fisher of Women, and so becomes a Woman's Apostle."[22] On the other
hand, Catholic women were seen as seductresses leading Protestant men to
their spiritual destruction—like Spenser's Duessa or Dalila of Milton's *Samson Agonistes*. At worst, Catholicism and Catholic women were associated with
witchcraft, black magic, and the diabolical arts.[23] Frances Howard, convicted
of arranging the poisoning of Sir Thomas Overbury, was an object of abuse
partly because of the Catholicism of her family.[24] When Shakespeare portrayed
St. Joan of Arc in the first part of *Henry VI,* following his sources, he cast her
as a wanton woman, "Joan La Pucelle," and as a witch, whose powers were obtained through her diabolical familiars.[25]

The recusant Catholic woman was "unruly" in her disobedience to the
state's authority and, possibly, to her husband's as well. In refusing to attend
Protestant services, she asserted her personal, individual religious autonomy—
an act that led some Protestant husbands to take rather harsh punitive measures, especially in times when men had to pay high recusancy fines for their
wives' refusal to comply with the law.[26] In the case of Catholic marriages in

which the man went through the motions of obeying the law by attending church services and his wife refused, the church papist husband put himself morally and spiritually in positions inferior to his wife, a situation that inverted the hierarchical arrangement expected in the patriarchal order.[27]

The first woman to be executed under the Elizabethan antirecusancy laws was a prosperous butcher's wife from York, Margaret Clitherow, who was pressed to death in 1586.[28] This "Proto-martyr of her Sext [*sic*] in the Kingdome of England"[29] was converted to Catholicism after her marriage to a Protestant man (who tolerated her religious practices) and for over a decade was well known as a recusant Catholic, imprisoned several times for her activities. She not only assisted jailed Catholics but also harbored priests, arranged for Catholic instruction for her children, and provided Mass for her family and friends. She was arrested during the northern campaign of persecution conducted by the earl of Huntington, in the aftermath of the passage of the 1585 Anti-Recusancy Act. Her biography was written (and circulated in manuscript in the Catholic community) by the man who was her last personal confessor and spiritual guide, the secular priest John Mush.[30] He used some of the conventions of romantically heroic hagiography[31] to portray Clitherow as the exemplary recusant Catholic woman.[32]

Mush presents a Catholic narrative of how the wife of a Protestant husband cheerfully performs her marital duties to spouse and children but, as a zealous convert to Catholicism, follows a devotional and ascetic regimen as rigorous as that of a member of a strict religious order.[33] She is reported as having said that "if that it pleased God so to dispose, and set her liberty from the world, she would with all her heart take upon her some religious habit, whereby she might ever serve God under obedience."[34] She uses the man who served as her last confessor and advisor[35] to deepen her religious commitment and to empower herself as a social agent, unwilling in matters of religion to bend to the demands of any superior earthly authority—whether that of her husband or of the state. Refusing to be terrorized into betraying her religious commitment, she heroically stands up to judicial coercion and forces the authorities to execute her so she can experience the martyrdom she wholeheartedly desires.[36]

In Mush's culturally symptomatic text, the biographer and his subject have a complicated relationship. He is at once her fatherly guide, her religious lover, and her spiritual son. Mush states that as a religiously exemplary Catholic woman, Clitherow "did utterly forsake her own judgment and will in all her actions, to submit herself to the judgment, will, and direction of her ghostly father" (378). When she asks her spiritual counselor, "[Is it right to] receive priests and serve God as I have done, notwithstanding these new laws, without my husband's consent"? (381) he tells her it is best for her husband not to know and "in this, your necessary duty to God, you are not any whit inferior to him" (382). In the spiritual matters that meant most to her, Margaret Clitherow was beyond her Protestant husband's authority. Mush portrays her emotional life as centered in the priests she sheltered and who gave her spiritual direction (389).

In a particularly emotional section of the biography, where Mush apostrophizes the city of York for its corruption and its persecution of this saintly woman, he notes how she used a deception to escape her domestic confines and have the freedom for a whole day's meeting with her confessor:

> Sometimes . . . she used to go on pilgrimage, but not in any prohibited manner; as, when she was invited with her neighbours to some marriage or banquet in the country, she would devise twenty means to serve God that day more than any other at home; for she would take horse with the rest, and after that she had ridden a mile out of the city, one should be there ready provided to go in her stead, and all that day she would remain in some place nigh hand, where she might quietly serve God, and learn of her ghostly Father some part of her Christian duty as her heart most desired, and at night return home again with the rest as though she had been feasting all the day long.
>
> This she used even from the beginning of her conversion, at which time also she procured some neighbours to feign the travail of some woman, that she might under that colour have access and abide with her ghostly Father the longer to be instructed in the necessary points of Catholic religion. (396–97)

In one sense, this wife of a Protestant husband (whose patriarchal role includes presiding over the religious affairs of his household), an independent-minded woman who changes her religion (and therefore the nature of the marital bond they share), is committing a kind of spiritual adultery in meeting her priest in a secluded place away from home. There is something of the character of a

romantic adventure to this activity and of the relationship Margaret Clitherow
has with the priests in whom she confides, thus some pretext for the slandering
of her reputation by her politically opportunistic stepfather and for the nasty accusation of one of her judges: "It is not for religion that thou harbourest priests,
but for whoredom" (414).[37] Using the testimony of a terrorized twelve-year-
old boy, the judge claims that "she had sinned with priests, and that the priests
and she would have delicate cheer, when she would set her husband with bread
and butter and red herring"—to which she answered, "'God forgive you for
these forged tales; and if the boy said so, I warrant you he will say as much more
for a pound of figs'" (427).[38] The Protestant minister, Edmund Bunny (using
a common anti-Catholic trope) accuses her of being "seduced by these Romish
Jesuits and priests" (424). Mush insists, however, that she was a model wife and
describes her husband's emotional response to her condemnation: "'Alas! will
they kill my wife? Let them take all I have and save her, for she is the best wife
in all England, and the best Catholic also'" (418). Over the years, this understanding and devoted spouse willingly paid the recusancy fines and answered
to the authorities in her defense.[39]

In defending her recusancy in the face of an intimidating judicial tribu-
nal, this proper woman refuses to capitulate to the demands of either the ma-
licious persecutors or the more merciful authorities who would like to see her
spared execution. She refuses to plead and thus forces the judges to sentence
her to death, though they obviously do not want that outcome. She is alternately
a woman with the supposed infirmities of her sex and a heroic saint whose
virtue and constancy make her superior not only to her Protestant adversaries
but also to her husband and to her spiritual guide. She answers her accusers, as
Mush puts it paradoxically, "boldly and with great modesty" (416). The cruel-
est of her judges calls her a "naughty, wilful woman" (417). Mush portrays her
as a saintly female warrior who has conquered her male persecutors on behalf
of the Catholicism they have betrayed (435).

Mush is quite conscious of the fact that he is writing about a martyr
who is also a "comely, beautiful young woman."[40] He makes much of the way
his religious-romantic heroine is clothed, or unclothed, for her execution. Although the court sentences her to die "naked" (431), she has prepared a kind
of smock to wear for her "marriage" (430) to Christ, "a linen habit like to an
alb, which she had made with her own hands three days before to suffer martyrdom in" (429). She carries this garment as she walks to her execution "bare-

foot and barelegged, her gown loose about her" (429). When reminded that she is to be unclothed for her execution, "[t]he martyr with the other women requested [the sheriff] . . . that for the honour of womanhood they would not see her naked; but that would not be granted" (431).[41] Nevertheless, when the women removed her clothes, they put the "long habit of linen . . . over her as far as it would reach, all the rest of her body being naked" (431), and she is allowed to die partly clothed with her hands bound in such a way "so that her body and her arms made a perfect cross" (432).[42]

In the imprecatory peroration at the end of the biography, Mush addresses her:

> O sacred martyr. . . . Remember me . . . whom thou hast left miserable behind thee, in times past thine unworthy Father, and now thy most unworthy servant, made ever joyful by thy virtuous life, and comfortable by lamenting thy death, lamenting thy absence, and yet rejoicing in thy glory. . . . Be not wanting, therefore, my glorious mother, in the perfection of thy charity . . . to obtain mercy and procure the plenties of such graces for me, thy miserable son, as thou knowest to be most needful to me, and acceptable in the sight of our Lord, which hath thus glorified thee; that I may honour Him by imitation of thy happy life, and by any death, which He will give me, to be partaker with thee and all holy saints of His kingdom, to whom be all glory and honour, now and for ever. Amen. (440)

At once an address to a deceased beloved (like Dante's Beatrice or Petrarch's Laura) and a prayerful petition for intercession from a saint, this final rhetorical flourish uses the language of Marian devotion to craft an utterance for the reader to internalize, so that the biography can work its religious-didactic purpose.[43] No longer father or holy lover, Mush has become son to this "glorious mother."

Many other recusant women sacrificed or suffered for their faith in early modern England, a number of them famous for harboring secular priests and Jesuits during the times of fiercest persecution. Anna Line was a convert to Catholicism who maintained a house for Jesuits in London and who died for her faith.[44] Jane Wiseman, like Clitherow, was sentenced to death in 1598 after refusing to plead, then imprisoned, but finally released at the accession of

James I.[45] Anne Vaux (with her sister) kept several houses that the Jesuits used as bases of operations, one in Baddesley Clinton in Warwickshire, another in London, and one in White Webbs at Enfield.[46] On the scaffold Henry Garnet, S.J., made a point of defending her reputation from some of the rumors about his relationship with her: "[I]t is suspected and said, that I should be married to her, or worse. But I protest the contrary; She is a vertuous Gentlewoman, and for me a perfect pure virgin."[47] The countess of Arundel (whose husband, St. Philip Howard, earl of Arundel, died in the Tower) was Southwell's protector and the "especiall frende" to whom he dedicated his *Epistle of Comfort*. Magdalen Lady Montague, who was protected against severe persecution by her nobility and old age, "maintained three Priests in her house, and gave entertaynment to all that repayred to her,"[48] making the Mass and the sacraments available to her family, servants and neighbors, so that her house was called "Litle Rome."[49] Richard Smith, who later became the bishop of Chalcedon, wrote her biography as a model story of the (noble) recusant Englishwoman, who finally died exuding the "odor of sanctity." She was (literally) a towering figure in the Catholic Montague family.[50] Mary Ward, the "female Jesuit," established her own order of uncloistered religious women that worked in England (and on the Continent) until it was suppressed in 1631.[51] Gertrude More was a descendant of Sir Thomas More who became a Benedictine nun and wrote *The Holy Practises of a Devine Lover or The Sainctly Ideots Devotions* (Paris, 1657). Elizabeth Cary, Lady Falkland, whose life and work have captured the attention of contemporary feminist scholars, is perhaps the most important female recusant writer from the period.[52] More receptive than most male Catholics to fervent baroque devotion, either as converts to or adherents of the old religion, recusant women were alienated from their native country and its dominant religious practices—especially when, in the Caroline period, they were associated with the court of a foreign Catholic queen, Henrietta Maria.[53]

The Dissemination of an Anti-Jesuit Mythology

For John Mush, Margaret Clitherow was a perfect example of Catholic martyrdom, because her motives and activities could easily be separated from charges of political subversion. Her commitment was to a life of devotion and charity rather than to political activism. The Jesuit martyrs whose deaths preceded and followed her execution, however, were entangled with larger matters of national and international import. Militantly defending the papal supremacy, including the right to depose monarchs and to sanction foreign invasion to change a state's religion, the Jesuits, whose hard-line stance led some polemicists to call them "Puritan,"[54] were at odds with more nationalistic and accommodationist lay and clerical Catholics who hoped that a less confrontational strategy might lessen the persecution and eventually lead to toleration.[55] At the turn of the century, as one of the leaders of the Appellants (those secular priests who appealed the pope's decision to appoint the Jesuit-sponsored secular priest George Blackwell as "Archpriest," or supreme religious authority for England), Mush participated in a government-supported anti-Jesuit campaign that drew a sharp line between English Catholic loyalism and the Jesuits' supposedly treasonous, Spanish-oriented subversiveness. Like the other Appellants, Mush defended his patriotism and loyalty by characterizing the Jesuits as dangerous aliens, thus hoping to redirect the government's attack on recusant Catholics towards the most militant of the missionaries who began to enter England in the latter part of Queen Elizabeth's reign.[56] Queen Elizabeth's proclamation of 5 November 1602 banishing all Jesuit and secular priests made a distinction between the Jesuits, as "men altogether alienated from their true allegiance . . . and devoted with all their might to the King of Spain,"[57] and secular priests opposing the Jesuits, but it nonetheless mandated the expulsion of all Catholic priests—leaving only the slim possibility that those priests who were willing to turn themselves in to the government and take a loyalty oath might be spared exile or other punishment. The kind of toleration hoped for by the Appellants was out of the question.

Certainly, such a distinction made sense in terms of the actual loyalism of the mass of English Catholics during the Armada crisis versus the politically treasonous stance of the pro-invasion forces represented by Cardinal Allen, Robert Persons, and most of the English Jesuits. After all, Persons, for example, whom one writer excoriates as "an Hispanized Camelion[,] . . . no true Englishman,"[58] was associated with the Guises and the militant Catholic League and in the six years leading up to the Armada and the following decade had urged the "empresa," the invasion of England by papally sanctioned foreign Catholic forces (supposedly to be aided by native English Catholics). He also later presented in print the case for the Spanish Infanta as Queen Elizabeth's rightful successor.[59] Such a political program could be disavowed by

English lay and clerical Catholics in the name of an allegedly "natural" patriotism it violated. The "Allen-Persons party" that pressed such aggressive policies were out of step with most English Catholics, but they were treated by government propagandists as though they represented what English Catholics
desired and would work for.[60] One of the most rabidly anti-Jesuit Appellants,
William Watson, accused the Jesuits of trying to "alien the mindes of most
loyall subjects, and draw them to consent to . . . unnaturall invasion, rebellion,
conspiracie, riot, or what else."[61] If loyal to any one country, it was to Spain
and to the project of establishing the "universal monarchy" of its "most Catholic King." Watson writes: "the Inventor of their order being a Spaniard and a
soldier, of what country soever any of his disciples are by their birth, in their
Sermons, and by all their indevors labored to perswade all Catholicks, that the
King of Spayne and our faith are so linked together, as it is become a point of
necessity in the Catholick faith to put all Europe into his hands, or otherwise
that the Catholick religion will be utterly extinguished and perish."[62] Treasonous Jesuits have "laboured," in the words of another writer, "nothing more
then to betray that sweete aportion, this sweete plot, our Country to Spaine, a
meere forraine and Morisco nation."[63] In his conspiracy-theory approach to
contemporary politics in the early 1620s, Thomas Scott made a connection
between the papacy, which supported the Spanish king's desire for universal
monarchy, and the Jesuits, as members of "the Spanish faction, though they be
Polonians, English, French & residing in those countries & Courts."[64] Even those
who are "the Penitents . . . and all with whom they deale and converse in their
spirituall traffique must needs be so too" (A4ᵛ). The taint of Spanishness thus
spread to everyone dealing with Jesuits, and the anti-Spanish "Black Legend"
was reinforced by anti-Jesuit propaganda.

   The growing polemical association of Jesuits with the theory and practice of political assassination made it possible for their Catholic and Protestant
antagonists to criticize them as enemies not only of national sovereignty (a consequence of their belief in papal supremacy) but also of monarchy and monarchical political theory. Juan de Mariana's justification of tyrannicide was, by
politically paranoid reasoning, made into the proof that the Jesuits were the
instigators of such political murders as that of William of Orange and Henri III
and Henri IV of France. In a work arguing against Elizabeth's naming a successor, one writer draws a parallel between the queen and William of Orange,
accusing the Jesuits of instigating his political murder: "They sawe that Prynce

sought to spell of Christe, and to abolish Romishe tyranny which mooved wicked misnamed Jesuites to enflame those papisticall devells to accomplish that horrible Acte. . . . [The two assassins were] by that damnable secte of runnagate fryers (misnamed Jesuittes) perswaded even in conscience that such their develishe Actes, should purchase Paradise."[65] Connecting Jesuits to the French assassinations, Thomas Dekker accuses them of using black magic "to conjure up a divell in the likeness of a Frier [Jacques Clement] whom these Exorcists armde to kill Henry the third."[66] The charge that Jesuits were behind the assassination of Henri IV by Ravillac (who supposedly was inspired by Mariana's theory of justified tyrannicide) was answered in France by Pierre Coton, the king's Jesuit confessor, but refuted by another writer, whose work was translated into English as *The Hellish and Horribble Councell, Practised and Used by the Jesuites . . . when they would have a Man to Murther a King. According to those Damnable Instructions, Given (by them) to that Bloody Villaine Francis Ravillacke, who Murdered Henry the Fourth* (1610) — a text that describes an elaborate ritual devised by the Jesuits supposedly to prepare the assassin for his mission.

In *A Temperate Ward-word to the Turbulent and Seditious Wach-word* [sic] *of Sir Francis Hastings knight, who indevoreth to slaunder the whole Catholique cause & all professors therof, both at home and abrode* (1609), Robert Persons ("N. D.") gives considerable space to the attack on the Jesuits (and on himself in particular), rehearsing and refuting some of the conventional charges leveled at them in the pamphlet literature. He knew that "Jesuit" had become a term of abuse: "Toplif the preest-tyrant of in famous memorie in putting them to death, is accustomed diligently to put up in his slaunders when he bringeth them to the gallowes (to do it with more solemnitie[)], *such a one traytor Jesuit,* as though the fiction only of this name Jesuit were a sufficient condemnation of the partie, and cleering of the quest that condemned him, though often tymes it falleth out that neither is he Jesuit, not ever was" (61). He is especially concerned to deny the accusation that the Jesuits had repeatedly encouraged and supported attempts on Queen Elizabeth's life (or those of other monarchs and leaders):

For as for the odde and ydle calumniation of the heretiques of our tyme, wherunto Sir Francis also as a devoted child of theirs, doth set his hand in this place, that they do practice the deathes of princes, and procure their destruction (except only he meane that practise wherin they joyne with their mayster . . . that the prince of this world may be cast forth) and that in particuler they have sought the blood of our Soveraigne of England, with such thirst as this man avoucheth, and that generally they be princequellers, king-killers, and the lyke, is an accusation no lesse found, then false and malitious, and as easie to prove, as that Sir Francis is by occupation a jugler, for what men are Jesuites to attend to such attemptes? Or what profit or emoulment can arise to them, more then to other men, by such murdering of princes, albeit you would faigne them to be so voyd of conscience, as you insinuate, or where, or when, or by whome was ever any such enterprise provided against them? (67)

Persons denies a Jesuit connection for Peter Panne, who attempted to kill Count Maurice in Holland (67–68). Finally, he says that the Jesuits, far from wanting Queen Elizabeth killed, prayed constantly for her spiritual welfare (69–70). The would-be assassins of Elizabeth, he states, had nothing to do with the Jesuits:

> Let the examinations and arraynementes of Parry, Savage, Ballard, Babington with all his fellowes, that were condemned with him, Polewheel also, Daniel, Hesket, and such others be vewed over, and see whether any of them do accuse father Persons to have byn partaker or privie to their councels, actions, or attemptes, in this behalf, let the recordes be sought out of all the preestes declarations that have byn put to death, within these twentie yeares (which are more then a hundreth) and consider whether any have confessed father Persons ever to have proposed any such matter unto them, and ye the most part of them were acquaynted with him, & many sent into England by his direction, and if he had felt such a deadly thirst of blood, and of her Majesties blood, as this accuser sayth, the readiest way for quenching therof, had byn to persuade some of these men (that come of purpose to adventure their lyves for religion, and feare not the leesing of anything in this world) to have taken the enterpryse upon them, for the common good, and for setting the use of their religion at libertie thereby.
>
> But there is no such matter, and these are but fiction and devyses of enemies, to make men odious; no preest hitherto nor Jesuite (that I

have hearde of) hath ever confessed of himself, or others of that voca-
tion, any such attempt or meaning at all. (71)

Persons dissociates John Chastel, who attempted to kill Henri IV in 1594, from
the Jesuits (with whom he had been connected polemically because he had once
been their student): "In France a yong men that sometymes had studies in the
Jesuites schools in Paris, was found afterward to offer violence to the kinges
person that now is, he was examined upon the torture, whether any Jesuit now
living, had geven him councel, courage, or instruction in that acte, or was privie
to his intention, which constantly he denyed; the lyke did his father who also
was put to torture, and so was delivered, and by publique testimonie of the
magistrate declared to be innocent" (61).

Despite such defenses, Jesuits were constantly depicted as "bloody"—
even made responsible, in some accounts, for the notorious St. Bartholomew's
Day Massacre of 1572.[67] The English government succeeded in associating the
Jesuits with the Gunpowder Plot of 1605 by convicting Henry Garnet, the Jesuit superior (on insufficient evidence), of complicity in the sordid affair. Supposedly, the Gunpowder Treason was a Jesuit plot from the start, undertaken
because the Jesuits could not get what they wanted from the new king: "this
treason may properly be called Jesuiticall, as pertaining to the Jesuites[,] . . . for
they were the chiefe plotters and devisers thereof."[68] The outlines were thus
complete of an anti-Jesuit mythology that, like the anti-Spanish Black Legend,[69]
took deep root in British culture. Some of this anti-Jesuit rhetoric was borrowed from French anti-Jesuit propaganda, which was a Gallican, "Politique,"
anti-Spanish strain in Catholic internecine disputes.[70] Jean Lacouture calls Paris
"the world capital of elegant Jesuit bashing" and Etienne Pasquier, the jurist
who unsuccessfully represented the University of Paris's case against the Jesuits
who petitioned to get their own school, "the true begetter of Jesuitophobia, the
man who raised the phenomenon to the level of a literary genre."[71] Pasquier's
most influential anti-Jesuit work was published in English in 1602 as *The Jesuites Catechisme*. His colleague Antoine Arnauld's anti-Jesuit work has been
published in English in 1594 as *The Arraignment of the Whole Society of Jesuits
in France, holden in the honourable Court of Parliament in Paris, the 12. and 13. of
July, 1594*.[72] In the wake of the Gunpowder Plot, James's chief minister, Robert
Cecil, expressed some willingness to be lenient to secular priests, but he was un-
bending in his attitude towards the Jesuits, whom he called "that generation

of vipers."[73] Joseph Hall wrote: "Some countries yeelde more venomous vipers then others; ours are the worst. . . . [A]s our English Papists are commonly more Jesuitish, so our English Jesuites are more furious, then their fellows. Even those of the hottest climates cannot match them in fiery dispositions."[74]

The Jesuits' reputation in England was the product of several interrelated international and domestic contexts. The English were aware of the record of the conflict between the Jesuits and the anti-Jesuit forces in France at two particular times: first, when the Jesuits made an attempt to establish a Jesuit college in Paris, which the Sorbonne authorities (unsuccessfully) resisted; second, when Jesuits and Jansenists battled in midcentury about the theology of grace.[75] Both disputes produced a body of anti-Jesuit writing that was translated into English for propaganda purposes. In England a series of episodes involving Jesuit protagonists were seen as threatening or as crises. These included:

1. The coming of the first Jesuits to England in 1580 (Campion, Persons, Emmison) and the political and intellectual challenge they posed;
2. The subsequent antigovernment propaganda written by Jesuits, especially by Persons, some of it connected to the threat posed by the claim to the throne of Mary, Queen of Scots, and to the "Enterprise" and the attempted invasions of England by Spanish Catholic forces in 1588 and in the 1590s[76] and some politically challenging, such as *Leicester's Commonwealth*[77] and Persons's treatise on the succession;
3. The fantasized and real Jesuit connections to the Gunpowder Plot and the trial of Henry Garnet;
4. The subsequent Oath of Allegiance controversy, in which King James's main antagonist was the great Jesuit theologian Robert Bellarmine;
5. The Jesuit connections to the Spanish Match negotiations and to the more permissive attitude towards Catholics in the late Jacobean period, as exemplified by the staging of the "Fisher the Jesuit" debates in which King James was involved as both spectator and participant;[78]
6. The founding of the English Jesuit province in 1623 as a sign of their stronger institutional presence in England;[79]
7. The supposed Jesuit connection to various Irish rebellions, from 1579 through 1641; and
8. The involvement of Jesuits in the alleged "Popish Plots" of 1640 and 1678–81.[80]

Jesuits were involved in both foreign and domestic internecine Catholic battles that shaped their reputation, especially as antagonists of the secular clergy, who generally wished for a less confrontational stance for English Catholics. Among these conflicts were the fight between the English and Welsh students at the English College in Rome and the student opposition in 1595 to the control of the college by Jesuits, which Persons had to return from Spain to settle;[81] the "Wisbech Stirs," the struggle for control of the prison community at Wisbech Castle involving the Jesuit William Weston, who wanted stricter spiritual discipline, and the seculars, who did not want to be managed by Jesuits;[82] the Archpriest Controversy (from 1598) and the Appellants' opposition to Jesuits;[83] the brief split on the issue of the Oath of Allegiance, which seculars were more inclined to approve than were the Jesuit hard-liners;[84] the controversy over the appointment of the bishop of Chalcedon as religious authority for England;[85] and the phenomenon of "Blackloism."[86]

By the time of the Stuart Restoration, the Jesuits were imagined in vivid ways as Catholic archvillains. In a pamphlet addressed to Charles II, *An Account of the Jesuites Life and Doctrine* (1661),[87] a Catholic author (identified only as "M. G." [Martin Greene]) offers a defense of the Jesuit order against the charges traditionally leveled against them.[88] This text makes it clear why the Jesuit priest was a prime target for anti-Catholic rhetoric in early modern England. Looking back to the previous two decades of civil war and political unrest, M. G. claims that Jesuits were the easiest scapegoat for England's troubles: "Many will needs conceive, or pretend they conceive, that the Papists were occasion of all our disorders, and the Jesuits the Boutefeu's [firebrands] in the ruine of both King and Country. . . . '[T]is the stile of our times to lay all to the Papists, and no Man concludes with applause, but he that Perorat's against the Jesuits" (A3). Objecting to the vicious portrayal of Jesuits in the pamphlets, libels, and sermons of the time, the author defines the Jesuit stereotype:

> Every Jesuit . . . hath a Pope in his belly, a Macchiavel in his head, Mercurie's wings on his feet, and the Mysterious feather of Lucian's cocks tail in his hand. The Pope in his belly makes him still big with malice, still giving birth to new mischief. Macchiavel in his head Orders all so dextrously as to make him out reach all the World. Mercurie's wings on his feet carry him from place to place, from Country to Country, and make him every where in a trice. The Cocks feather in his hand opens

all closets and Cofers, and Secrets, and discovers to the Jesuit, the Want and Wealth of every one, that he may know where to place his labours with thrift. (A3ᵛ–4)

Jesuits are the superpapists, the diabolical schemers, liars who justify their deceit with the doctrine of equivocation and mental reservation, the international vagrants threatening the modern nation-state, the political subversives with access to the wealthy and powerful. They also are Protean disguisers, appearing "[n]ow a Cobler, now a Preacher, now a Tinker, now a Courtier, now a Peasan [peasant or country fellow]; now a States-man, and what not," "the only contrivers of all the mischiefs in the World" (A4). They are the perfect object of paranoid imagining:

> The Jesuits are to our Fabulous heads, what the Evil-Genius's or Pestiferous Gods were to old times, when fictions made Deities. They are Presbyterians, and Episcopal Protestants, and Levellers, and Quakers, and what you will, provided it be . . . a name of disgrace. They have overthrown learning, destroyed Philosophy, undone Morals, ravaged Divinity, poysoned States, corrupted manners, betrayed Kingdomes, subverted the Church, confounded the Gospel, and as with the dregs of Pandor's box poured out more mischief on the World then all the Devils in Hell could ever have wished. (A5)

Addressing himself to "rational Protestants" (64) who are open to argument, M. G. enumerates and answers seven objections to the Jesuits' lives and four objections to their doctrine, as well as one other "objection" directed at neither. The list is revealing:

1. "[T]hey are crafty" (79).
2. "Jesuites are rich" (82).
3. "Jesuites are ambitious" (85).
4. "Jesuites are nice and lead a lazie and delicate life" (88).
5. "Jesuites are dangerous men, because they meddle in intrigues of State, and thrust themselves into Court affairs" (89).
6. "The Jesuites cannot be trusted, because they reveal all secrets, even confessions, to their superiours" (91).

7. "Jesuites make a vow to the Pope, and therefore must be supposed not to be so loyal as others, being already tyed to a forreign prince, and therefore but half Subjects" (96–97).

The last objection might be broadened to define the conflicted position of all Catholics in early modern England: their faith potentially put them in a situation of divided loyalty that in an earlier period needed to be tested judicially by "bloody questions"[89] or civilly by requiring oaths of allegiance. They were, at best, "half Subjects." The other objections more specifically constitute the Jesuit as a composite object of scorn.

The objections to Jesuit teaching allege:

1. "[T]he Jesuites teach the Doctrine of Equivocation and mental reservation, and therefore . . . can not be trusted" (100).
2. "[T]he Jesuites teach that horrid maxime, *Fides non est servanda haereticis,* Faith is not to be kept to Hereticks" (104).
3. "[T]hey maintain the Popes authority in prejudice to Sovereignty, teaching that the Pope hath power to depose Kings" (105).
4. "[T]hey teach the killing of Kings, though under the name of Tyrants" (113).

The association of Jesuits with the doctrine of "equivocation," with its sanctioning of withholding or distorting the truth by means of "mental reservation," goes back to Robert Southwell's and Henry Garnet's trials, especially the latter's since it followed that landmark Catholic outrage, the Gunpowder Plot of 1605.[90] Although the broad use of equivocation and mental reservation was later condemned by Pope Innocent XI in 1679, M. G. argues here that the Jesuits' teaching on this subject was "common Doctrine of all Schools, and Universities, none excepted" (103). The second supposed "doctrine" (not keeping faith in dealings with "heretics") is denied outright. Regarding the third, M. G. points out that two successive Jesuit generals issued prohibitions on teaching or discussing the doctrine of papal supremacy (110–12). The fourth doctrine, a theory of tyrannicide with which radical Protestants were also associated, is traced back to the teachings of Juan de Mariana, whose writings Aquaviva censured in 1606, four years before the Sorbonne condemned them, well before the assassination of Henri IV by Ravillac, who was supposed

to have been inspired by them.[91] M. G. emphatically denies the Jesuit connections of both Ravillac and the failed (Jesuit-educated) assassin Catell
with Mariana's work.[92] Long before Titus Oates's Popish Plot and the exclusion crisis centered on Charles II's Catholic brother James, this Catholic
writer takes stock of anti-Jesuit propaganda (and of "antipopery" in general)
at a moment just after the exiled Stuart court has returned from France,
where both king and queen had supposedly been exposed to dangerous Jesuit influence.

Despite their small numbers and the government's capture and execution or deportation of them through the Elizabethan era, English Jesuits and
Jesuit missionaries steadily increased between 1580 and the time of the Civil
War. As Hugh Aveling points out, "In 1593 there were forty-nine English Jesuits, of whom thirty were priests, and only nine in England. By 1610 there
were fifty-three Jesuites in England and possibly 120 in the Society. . . . By
1620 there were 211 in the Province and 106 missioners in England. By 1641
overall numbers had risen to nearly 400, and missioners to about 180."[93] While
the English Catholic community gradually grew through the seventeenth century, despite the continuing persecution, the number of Jesuits dramatically
increased and Protestant anti-Jesuit paranoia burgeoned.[94]

Jesuits (and many other Catholics, especially missionaries) were alienated
by their Continental exile, by their sympathy with Spain in the conflict in the
Low Countries between Spanish power and Dutch Protestant rebels, by their
international rather than national perspective as missionaries with a global orientation reaching both to the Far East and to the New World. The association
of Catholicism with paganism, especially the paganism of the East—which is
well illustrated in the work of both Edmund Spenser and John Milton—took
the specific form of connecting the Jesuits with both Islam and the Turks. Jesuit militancy and their direct service to the pope led to their being thought of
as the Pope's Janissaries.[95] In a Europe in which religious warfare continued
to flare up during the post-Reformation period, biblical metaphors of spiritual battle were connected with actual sectarian violence (such as the St. Bartholomew's Day Massacre), with anticolonial and other kinds of rebellion (for
example, in Ireland and the Low Countries), and with the kind of international religious conflict that led to the Thirty Years' War (1618–48). If English
Catholic laymen were regarded as potentially traitorous and secular priests
as actually traitorous, the Jesuits were, in effect, archtraitors, so thoroughly
alienated from their native country as to work tirelessly on behalf of its ene-

mies, particularly Spain. Jesuits were commonly regarded as "Hispaniolated" or "Hispanicized," and Englishmen influenced by them or under their spiritual control were called "Jesuited"—with the implication that they were un-Englished or alienated from their nationality.[96]

Jesuits and Recusant Women

One of the points that John O'Malley makes in his study, *The First Jesuits,* is that, with their emphasis on auricular confession and spiritual guidance of the laity, Jesuits were especially sought out by women. At various points they had to be concerned with the possible scandal that might arise from private home visits to female Catholics, and, O'Malley states, the interposition of a grill between confessor and penitent was developed as a partial solution to this problem.[97] In a Paul's Cross sermon of 15 February 1618, Robert Sibthorpe referred to "Romanists who creep into great houses to lead captive 'simple women laden with sinnes,'" alluding to priests', particularly Jesuit priests', power as confessors to the elite.[98] One anti-Jesuit pamphlet contains supposed instructions to members of the order on "How to procure the friendship of rich Widows" (so as to obtain money from them):

> For this purpose must be called out some of the Fathers of the liveliest fresh complexions, and of a middle age. These must frequent Their houses, and if they find a kindness towards our Society, impart to Them its great worth. If they come to our Churches, we must put a Confessour to them, that shall perswade them to continue in their Widowhood, representing to them the great pleasure, delight, and advantage that will accrue to them by remaining in that state. . . . The first thing that their Confessours are to do, is to get into their Counsels, and to let them understand how necessary it is for the good of their souls to give themselves wholly up into their hands. . . . [P]resently they must be put upon entring into some religious Order, not in a Cloister, but after the manner of Paulina. Thus when they are caught in the Vow of chastity, all danger of their Marrying again is over.[99]

The next chapter is entitled "How to keep Widows to our selves, so far as concerns the disposing of their Estates" (38).

A short popular pamphlet published in 1642 associated the Jesuit's use of confession not only with his hunger for other people's "secrets" but also with his sexual exploitation of women:

> [T]he Serpent is a Bungler to him: Confession is his engine by which he Skrews himselfe into acquaintance with all Affairs, all Dispositions; which he makes the best conducing to his ends, that is, the worst use of. But for this point of Craft, he is owing to the Serpent, to grow inward with the Woman when he dares not immediately adventure on the Man; whose Secrets whilest he indeavours to discover in Confession, if she be Obediently yielding (a matter which he earnestly presseth her unto, as a thing simply necessary for her salvation) then he proves most Indulgent unto her in Penance, which himselfe Acts upon her; and he is therefore the most Impious Lecher of the world, because he prostitutes not only her Body, but her Conscience to his Lust; the ancient manner of confessing was, the Penitents kneeled at the Confessors Side, but he humbleth the women to his Bosome, and thus he becomes a Father, by his Supernumerary Vow of Mission and getting children.[100]

The writer uses an old trope (going back at least to Boccaccio) of the conversion of the spiritual intimacy of confession into sexual intimacy in order to portray the connection of Jesuits and women as not only adulterous but also as subverting the domestic and political patriarchy. In 1612 the letter writer John Chamberlain reported on a sermon preached by one of Prince Henry's chaplains, who supposedly said "that the Prince told him not a moneth before he died that religion lay a bleeding, and no marvayle (saide he) when divers [Privy] counsaillors heare masse in the morning, and then go to a court sermon and so to the counsaile, and then tell theyre wives what passes, and they carie yt to theyre Jesuites and confessors, with other like stuffe."[101]

In the straitened circumstances of the English persecution, various English Jesuits were forced to rely on the harbor and hospitality of English recusant women, especially those of the aristocracy. Robert Southwell lived in the countess of Arundel's London residence, where he set up a press to publish Catholic books. He had a special relationship with the Bellamy family before he was betrayed by young Anne Bellamy—an episode fictionalized by Spenser in Book V of *The Faerie Queene* in the Samient-Malengin story.[102] Henry Garnet (and many Jesuits and seminary priests who moved about England) relied on the help and protection of the widowed Anne Vaux and her sister Elizabeth,[103] who was a patroness of the Jesuit John Gerard.[104] John Percy, S.J. (alias Fisher the Jesuit), converted the countess of Buckingham and lived under her protection in her household for ten years.[105] Henry More, the new Jesuit provincial in late Caroline England, relied on the help of Lady Arundel.[106]

Such relationships, however, were interpreted maliciously by those wishing to slander Jesuits and the Catholics with whom they were associated.[107] One of the anti-Jesuit Appellants wrote of Jesuits' special relationship with women:

> As all heresies began with talkative women, (these of nature being as flexible to yeeld, as credulous to beleeve) so Silly women more devout than discreet (as alwaies in extreames, either Saints or Devils,) poore soules do mightily dote and run riot after them, among these they title tatle, and lull babies a sleepe, and the ignorant multitudes of the Jesuits do use the most women gospellers, trumpetters of their praise, & with these women tatlers & women Gospellers, the Secular Priests are much troubled: but in the end, their fraud will appeare, when these hot Ladies shall lay their hands a little heavier on their hearts, with mea maxima culpa.[108]

Traditional misogynist tropes here serve the purpose of anti-Jesuit polemic. Other anti-Jesuit slanders poured from the pens of the Appellant writers at the turn of the century. Anthony Copley, for example, retails a common libel about Robert Persons as the "mis-begotten [son] of a ploughman" who "demeaned himselfe . . . in begetting two bastards male and female upon the bodie of his owne sister betweene his age of seventeene and three and twentie."[109] In the polemical give-and-take following the assassination of Henri IV of France, one French anti-Jesuit writer, whose work was translated into English, attacked the king's Jesuit confessor for his pandering and sexual license:

> he was the Messenger of the Kings love, and carryed his Love-letters unto Ladyes: a great Prince of this kingdome . . . can testifie, that . . . he wondred at this, that Father Cotton should be employed in bringing a certaine Damsell unto the King: the said Jesuit answered him, that indeed it was a sinne, but that he was rather to regard the health of the King, whose life was so necessary unto the Church, and that this evill shold be recompenced with a greatest good.

Cotton himself was supposed to have been judged guilty in his youth of "getting a Nun with childe."[110]

In *A Foot out of the Snare,* the apostate John Gee recounts a story of Jesuit adultery:

> A certaine Catholicke collapsed Ladie . . . departed from her husband (yet living) and went over to Bruxels, and was admitted into the order of Nunnerie, I meane, a Nunne at large, one of the uncloistred sisters of the order of Saint Clare, and there shee remained til there appeared in her some passion incompatible with Nunship. She came over into England a companion with a religious Jesuite, since of great note, F. D. [Francis Drury?] and remaining afterwards an inlarged Nunne in London, was (as it seemeth) more visibly taken with a disease befalling that sexe, called flatus uterinus: and thereupon, that this matter might bee carried the more cleanly, it was given out, that shee was possessed with an evill spirit, which did make her belly to swell like a woman with child. Certaine it is many were deluded by this occasion: and the practice of the Priests to hide her blemish, and gull poore people, was lewd and abominable. For a certaine Jesuite (whom I could also name, being a smug, spruce, liquorish, young fellow, a fit man to bee called Father (forsooth) at every word, & of no high stature . . .) put on the Ladies or such like womanish apparel, with a Vaile over his face: & that some found Ignaro's about the Towne might be perswaded of the Priests power for the casting out of Divels, they were suffred to come to her chamber, where were two other Jesuites (provided for the purpose, to act their parts in this Comedie); who no sooner fell to their prayers, and began to use their exorcising spells, but thereupon the supposed Ladie began to utter her mind in Italian, Latin, and Greeke: which much astonished the standers by, they little dreaming of this deceit.[111]

This account, which scorns the very existence of religious orders for women, highlights not only the Jesuits' alleged abuse of the women who trusted them but also their theatrically skilled deception of the wider public through staged "exorcisms," here a spectacle involving male cross-dressing.[112] In a subsequent work, Gee recounts several stories of women being deceived by Jesuit-contrived "apparitions": he describes a Jesuit attempt to proselytize a Protestant servant,

Mary Boucher, by means of a faked appearance of her dead godmother come from Purgatory to advise her to become a Catholic and a nun.[113] The "second Comodie of a Female Apparition" is staged by the Jesuits Fisher and Wainman to convert Mrs. Francis Peard, an orphan with £1,000; they succeed in getting control of her money (10–25). Gee exposes how by "creeping sly stealth the Master-Gamesters the Jesuites doe drive the female Partridges into their Nett by the helpe of the setting Dogge of sneaking Visions, and Phantasmes" (23). In a 1623 pamphlet, translated from French, there is a dialogue between a Jesuit and a novice in the order that includes an exchange explaining why, supposedly, Jesuits are associated with women in labor. The novice seems to look for an answer when he says: "I make no doubt, but as God hath assigned to every other Saint the cure of some one disease or other, as to St. Roch the plague, to St. Petronel the fever, to St. Main the itch, so St. Ignatius hath some certaine one unto which he is marvelously assisting." The Jesuit replies: "Thou art in the right: Father Ignatius doth assuredly and most readily assist all women that are in labor: for this vigilant pastor doth always accompanye them to be delivered, as it is written in Esay, Foetas ipse portabit, that is to say, he will looke to the Ewes, for to have their wooll and their lambes."[114]

In a 1629 pamphlet, *Speculum Jesuiticum,* published at a time of relatively lenient treatment of English Catholics, Lewis Owen engaged in a wholesale attack on the Jesuits, from the founding of the order in 1540 to the Caroline period, highlighting those international subversions with which they were associated in the current polemical literature. In the course of the narrative, Owen has a long digression to tell the story of "Father Mena," a Jesuit who is accused of abusing the sacrament of penance to court, win, and control the money of a rich and beautiful widow: "He was her ghostly Father, or Confessor, who in the end fell in love (as it is the custome among the Jesuites) with his prettie penitent or ghostly child."[115] He supposedly persuaded her to marry him, justifying the act by specious theological arguments, but, after she confessed to a "Frier" during what appeared to be a terminal illness and was told to reveal the marriage to her kinsmen (because the friar "would have the Jesuites disgraced, because he loved them not" [5]), Mena was brought before the Inquisition, only to be rescued by his order (to prevent public scandal): "The Jesuites (seeing the honor and reputation of their Order to be called in question, and mightily shaken by all the other Orders, and swarmes of Friers, their mortall enemies, and the Ladies friends . . . perswaded both the King and Inquisitors that Father Mena was frantick, and requested that they might have him into their custody to be dealt withall, and punished as they should see cause" (5–6)—after which "the matter was hushed up" (6). Owen notes that "the rest of the Jesuites knew of the mariage as well as Mena, and that they had all the money that he had from her, to the use of their College" (6). He editorializes, "I feare me that if diligent inquisition were made, and the truth knowne, there would be some English ladies and Gentlewomen found to be maried unto Jesuites, and very many that have had Bastards by them; especially such as have any good estates or portions, whereof many they convey over into Flanders, Brabant, and other Countreys to be Jesuitesses and Nunnes" (7). Another propagandist goes even further: "[T]hey have converted their confessionaries into Ecclesiastical stews: They have got the chief trading with Women from all other orders, and their vow of Chastity is their Passport, witness their familiarities with the Wives of the Genneses and Venetians, and amongst other Narratives, that of Summerman the Jesuit, who being to cast an evil spirit out of a possess'd Nun in Swisserland, made a shift to get her with Child."[116] Such propaganda, which combined charges of the sexual and economic abuse of women with the general charge of abusing religious authority, appealed to the salacious imagination of its Protestant target audience.

There is an interesting story that appears in different versions of a work translated from French into English as *A Short Treatise Touching some Very Secret and Close Studies and Practises of the Jesuits.*[117] In the course of criticizing the Jesuits for their adoption of disguises, the writer retails a story about the ways Jesuits seduce women into the subterranean vaults of their houses for bacchanalian revels. The wily porter of the Jesuit house supposedly keeps all sorts of male and female apparel not only to allow Jesuits to disguise themselves in order, for example, to "haunt Brothell houses, abandoning them-selves to all dissolution & excesse," but also to entice poor women into debauchery in the Jesuit house itself:

[F]or that which others in the secret places, and Chancells of their Temples, cannot attain by auricular confessions: this fellow easily obtaineth by flattering and sundry sorts of allurements, especially amongst the poorer sorts of widowes and women. . . . Now when this most impure Porter, hath once drawn them into his net, though before they were sluttish, in their torne and worne apparell, yet doth he daintily adorne them with other which he hath in a readinesse, and leadeth them by divers turnings and windings . . . to the Reverend Lord and Father. And these things are done, not by day light, but when it is somewhat late in the evening, & after that they spend the whole night in gormandies, & dancing. . . . [T]hey have for these purposes, certain safe or seeled, or if you will, places under the ground, as they had, which in times past at Rome were consecrated to Venus, whose beastly prostituting of themselves, to the lust and wantonesse of the flesh was so great, that the Senate fearing the wrath of the Gods for it, did utterly overthrow that Stue or brothell house. (3)

Associating Jesuit and pagan, Roman degeneracy, this passage describes a nasty form of class exploitation. Following this passage with a description of the Jesuits' underground torture chambers where they enact a diabolical theater of cruelty and engage in black magical arts of prognostication, the writer thus creates some of the outlines of the horrors later fictionalized in the Gothic novel.[118]

A Restoration pamphlet published during the Popish Plot crisis, *The Cabal Of several Notorious Priests and Jesuits, Discovered* (1679), rehearses not only the history of Jesuit political subversion, but also of scandals, especially sexual ones: the examples are French. After retailing stories of the alleged sodomitic sexual abuse of boys in Jesuit schools,[119] the writer turns to Jesuits' abuse of both lay and religious women within and outside of confession. He writes: "Somermanus an Helvetian Jesuit, feigning to cast an unclean Spirit out of a Nun, begat her with Child" (11); "John Surnius was shut up in the Vestry with a Gentlewoman, whom he loved precisely behind the Altar. Gentlewomen of Quality have complained to a discreet man of their Order, that *Peter Regginer* by his filthy and lascivious interrogatories had provoked them to evil in their Confessions, and asking them, whether they had made us of such and such wayes to take their carnal pleasures, had taught them to practice shameful Obscenities" (12).

The most space in this account is given to the exploits of one Stephen Petiot, who abused "a pretty black Maid," whom he kept as a mistress for some time: "this Wench hath told three or four several Jesuits, that *Petiot* had embraced her, felt, kissed, whip't her with his hand, &c. yea, *effundens semen in manum ejus*, oh Filthiness! had said to her, My dear heart, behold, *ex quo luto nascuntur homines*" (13). He supposedly had her disguise herself as a male so that she could come to his chamber. This same priest continued his sexual sins and crimes during his travels: he tried to force himself on a maid with the help of a bawd, with whom he had to satisfy himself in front of the maid, who reported the incident to the Jesuit superior. At Lady Mumma's house, he sexually pursued the maidservants:

> His first Act of Impurity was, as he came from saying Mass, to thrust his hands up under the Smock of a Maid as he went up Stairs, saying to her, *Fair maid, you lift your Leggs too high:* His second was more dangerous, as being more cunningly guided, for having learned of another by his Questions to her, that she was going away from her Mistresses Service, come (said he) bring me som Paper and Ink, and I will help you to a good Place with a Lady-President at Bourdeaux, which shall be a thousand times more advantagious to you than this; This poor innocent Maid, which thought already to be raising her Fortune, brought him some Paper into a remote Chamber of the house, where this Forger of Mischief writ such a favourable and recommendatory Letter, that he exceedingly rejoyced this silly Maid; then taking the Advantage of this his Letter, he said to her, Is not this to love thee most dearly at the first Sight? what art thou not bound to do for such a great Friend? who would give a Letter written not only with Ink but with his own Blood for to prefer thee well and to do thee Good, kissing her Forehead in the mean while, and her Lips, and embracing her with such a Passion, that the Maid saw the Danger she was like to be in, and withdrawing away from him *I do not intend Sir (said she) to buy our Recommendations with the Jeopardy of my Soul.* (15)

This clerical behavior, like its secular equivalent in life and (later) in fiction, is particularly outrageous as an abuse of power. Petiot's final sexual outrage was his assault on a young girl:

> This Sardanapalus, the next day, after his Return to his Colledge, went to divert himself near the house, in a Place called the Wood-Lowys, and to make his Recreation every way criminal, he inticed with some little Agnus Dei's a Farmers Daughter, who was not above nine or ten years old, under Pretence of teaching her to pray, and led her into the thick Walk of the Wood. This wicked Wretch put himself in a Posture to violate this Child, and already with his Impure Fingers *dilatabat ei vas fo-*

emineum; when her Father, hearing her cry and Complain, run in soon
enough to snatch her from this Wolf's Clutches: the Disorder wherein he
found this infamous Jesuit, and his Child's Posture, enkindled such a
Wrath in the Spirit of her afflicted Faith, that he ran, at that very Instant,
to the College to excuse him. (15–16)

Next to this sort of morally monstrous treatment of a child, the subsequent
discussion of the sexual liaisons of Jesuits and nuns seems tame. Petiot's story,
whatever its historical accuracy, stands as a kind of limit case of Jesuit sexual
abusiveness.

The supposed political threats posed by Jesuits were often associated with
their relations with women. In *Ignatius His Conclave,* an anti-Jesuit prose satire
written in the context of the protracted Oath of Allegiance controversy following the Gunpowder Plot, John Donne portrays Jesuits as Machiavellian
"innovators,"[120] threats to the modern nation-state because of their support for
papal temporal supremacy and deposing power, their practices of equivocation, mental reservation, and not keeping faith with heretics, their international spying and manipulation, their sanctioning of invasion and regicide for
changing a state's religion, and their questioning of the ideology of monarchy.
With regard to the last of these, Donne associates Jesuit antimonarchical attitudes with Protestant democratic resistance theory: he has Ignatius in Hell
favorably mention Knox, Buchanan, and Goodman (77).[121] In his speech in
Hell, Donne's Ignatius boasts that "states-men of our Order, wiser then the rest,
have found how much this Temporal jurisdiction [of Popes] over Princes, con-
duces to the growth of the Church."[122] He is proud that Jesuits have taken advantage of their familiarity with political leaders "to know times, and secrets
of state" (51). He argues that their theory of "Mentall Reservation, and Mixt
propositions" (55) gives them the flexibility to lie for political ends. Competing with the "innovator" (republican), Machiavelli, for evil preeminence, Ignatius says that the Jesuits' political theories and practices are more subversive
and antimonarchical than his: "all his bookes, and all his deedes, tend onely
to this, that thereby a way may be prepared to the ruine & destruction of that
part of this Kingdome, which is established at Rome: for what else doth hee
endeavour or go about, but to change the forme of common-wealth, and so to
deprive the people . . . of all their liberty: & having so destroyed all civility &
re-publique, to reduce all states to Monarchies; a name which in secular states,
wee doe so much abhor" (55, 57).[123] In this dystopian fiction, the Jesuits, as

internationalists and imperialists, even prove bad citizens of Hell, so they are considered for exile to the "new world, the Moone," to set up another state ruled by Ignatius, a polity that might serve as a base from which they "may beget and propagate many Hells & enlarge [their] Empire" (81). The moon is a good place for Jesuits because, says Ignatius,

> a woman governes there; of which Sex they have ever made their profite, which have attempted any Innovation in religion. . . . Why may not wee relie upon the wit of woemen, when, once, the Church delivered over her selfe to a woman-Bishop.[124] And since we are reputed so fortunate in obtaining the favour of woemen, that woemen are forbid to come into our houses; and we are forbid, to take the charge of any Nunnes[,] . . . why should we doubt of our fortune with this Queene, which is so much subject to alterations and passions? (83, 85)

Again, it is irresistible to a polemical writer to highlight a dangerous conjunction of Jesuits and women.

Thomas Middleton's *A Game at Chesse* exploits the popular beliefs about the relationship of Jesuits and women. This anti-Jesuit, anti-Spanish play was written in the wake of the popular celebration of the failure of the proposed Spanish Match for James I's son Charles, whose return from Spain with the duke of Buckingham set off unprecedented popular celebrations in London.[125] The play not only illustrates some of the conventional charges against Jesuits but also foregrounds the association of Jesuits and women as a particularly dangerous one.[126] Its induction presents a diabolical (recently canonized) Ignatius Loyola as a model Machiavellian politician whose followers are "all true labourers in the work / Of the universal monarchy"[127] sought by the king of Spain. They work their way into the houses and courts of aristocrats and monarchs to learn their secrets and manipulate them;[128] they are disguisers, equivocators, and advocates of king killing;[129] they are associated with homosexuality.[130]

Ignatius has a spiritual "secular daughter / That plays the Black Queen's Pawn" (Ind. 46–47)—that is, Mary Ward, the woman who established (on the Jesuit model) an uncloistered teaching order that functioned both on the Continent and in England. In the play's first scene, which demonstrates the attempted seduction into Catholicism of the White Queen's Pawn by a Jesuit (the

Black Bishop's Pawn), this female Jesuit assists in the evil business. In the sexualized language of anti-Jesuit propaganda, the Black King writes to the Jesuit tempter of the White Queen's Pawn "to require you by the burning affection I bear to the rape of devotion, that speedily upon the surprisal of her, by all watchful advantage you make some attempt upon the White Queen's person, whose fall or prostitution our lust most violently rages for" (2.1.20–25). In the play's allegory (since King James's Queen Anne had been dead for several years), the White Queen may signify either the English church or the English people left vulnerable to Jesuit temptation. The Black Bishop's Pawn, a gelding,[131] after being refused the kiss he requests to seal the bond of the White Queen's Pawn's "Boundless obedience" (2.1.38),[132] acts on his desire to "possess" (1.1.204) her by attempting to rape her, revealing himself as an "arch-hypocrite" (2.1.147) and the members of his order as habitual breakers of the vows of poverty, chastity, and obedience (2.1.87–88). In the sexualization of international politics figured in the dramatic allegory, the fall of the Palatinate and political exile of James's daughter and son-in-law are attributed to Jesuit subversion. The failure of the Spanish Match became another Protestant providential deliverance — even though the negotiations for a substitute French Catholic spouse began immediately. Subsequently, the French match, especially in the period of Charles's "prerogative rule" when Queen Henrietta Maria (after the death of Buckingham) had a powerful influence on the king's decisions, provoked strong objections to court Catholicism and new waves of antipopery and anti-Jesuit paranoia.[133]

Phineas Fletcher's Spenserian epic, *The Locusts, or Apollyonists,* portrays the Jesuits as the devilish masters of papal treacheries in the world.[134] In a scene of consultation in Hell, Ignatius, "in hell Apollyon, / On earth Equivocus,"[135] argues that the diabolical and Catholic forces should switch from open conflict to a subtler means of subversion. This involves getting at the Protestant male Christian through his weaker spouse. He explains that his Jesuits have worked their way into the favor of women to accomplish their purposes. They have

> . . . with practicke slight
> Crept into houses great: their sugred tongue
>   Made easy way into the lapsed brest
>   Of weaker sexe, where lust had built her nest,
> There layd they Cuckoe eggs, and hatch't their brood unblest.

There sowe theyr traytrous seed with wicked hand
'Gainst God, and man; well thinks their silly sonne
To merit heaven by breaking Gods command,
To be a Patriot by rebellion.
And when his hopes are lost, his life and land,
And he, and wife, and child are all undone,
    Then calls for heaven and Angells, in step I,
    And waft him quick to hel; thus thousands die,
Yet still their children doat: so fine their forgerie.

(Canto II, st. 34–35)

Fletcher makes the Jesuit Cardinal Bellarmine the originator of the Gunpowder Plot, the son of Loyola who leads the forces of the Whore of Babylon or the "Beast" against Protestant nations, particularly the "blessed Isle" of England (and Scotland). In his speech in a papal conclave, Bellarmine reiterates the Jesuit strategy:

. . . nothing more our Kingdome must advance,
    Or further our designes, then to comply
    With that weake sexe, and by fine forgerie
To worme in womens hearts, chiefly the rich and high.

Nor let the stronger scorne these weaker powres;
The labour's lesse with them, the harvest more:
They easier yeeld, and win; so fewer houres
Are spent: for women sooner drinke our lore,
Men sooner sippe it from their lippes, then ours:
Sweetly they learne, and sweetly teach: with store
    Of teares, smiles, kisses, and ten thousand arts
    They lay close batt'ry to mens frayler parts:
So finely steale themselves, and us into their hearts.

(Canto IV, st. 21–22)

Fletcher assumes the Jesuit will always select "the weaker sex" as his target and that men's vulnerability to what John Milton calls "Female charm" (*Paradise Lost,* 9: 999) will allow the subversion to spread to them. Fletcher illustrates the point with the examples of Samson and King Solomon, both of whom Milton also criticizes for their uxoriousness.[136]

Fletcher's short epic has been long recognized as one of the literary influences on Milton's *Paradise Lost*:[137] one can easily see how its portrayal of Hell and of devils had a strong impact on the Protestant poet-prophet. In Milton's poem, I would suggest, the seduction of Eve takes place in the context of anti-Catholic and anti-Jesuit polemic. A diabolical disguiser who is a skillful rhetorical seducer succeeds in enticing his female victim into idolatrous, superstitious practice and alienating her from both her husband and the faith in which they have grounded their marital relationship. The impassioned poet, who associated Catholicism with the pagan East, with witchcraft, idolatry, and devil worship, and who had a strong antipathy to the Jesuits, made use of the culturally ingrained codes and language of anti-Catholicism and of its recurrent anti-Jesuit subset.[138] If the Jesuit was the archhypocrite, archtraitor, and Machiavellian and diabolical antagonist of the "godly" Protestant, what better model could he have found for the character of Satan? And what better precedent for subverting the Protestant man could he have found than in the assault of the Jesuit "seducer" on the carnal female spouse?[139] Once the weaker Eve is seduced from true faith and obedience, her uxorious husband follows.[140] Although Milton was not writing a traditional epic of nationalistic celebration, he exploited English cultural codes and ideological fantasies that characterized both Catholic women and the priests who ministered to them as alien to English Protestant identity.

Milton's anti-Catholic (and anti-Jesuit) language and representations, then, are deeply immersed in the anti-Catholicism of the age, as well as in the polemical tradition of depicting Jesuits and their adherents as a continuing subversive threat to the Protestant believer and the Protestant nation. A feminized, seductive, idolatrous Catholicism promoted by priests who menaced what Milton and other Protestants saw as true Christianity was associated with diabolical agency in the world. Counter-Reformation militancy needed to be countered by militant Protestantism, not appeased, as Milton saw it, by an English (Laudian) church contaminated by popish ceremonies, practices, and beliefs. Although the English revolution of which Milton was a part, with the restoration of the monarchy, failed in some of its basic purposes, it helped to forge an anti-Catholic English national mythology, many of whose elements have had a long life in English and American culture.

3

Manuscript Transmission and the Catholic Martyrdom Account

In the morninge he rejoyced greatlye in God and gave Him thankes for all His benefites, utteringe these words, "O blessed day, O the fairest day that ever I saw in my life." He desired a minister that was there, not to trouble him, "For I will not," quoth he, "beleve thee, nor heare thee but against my will." When he was taken of the hurdell, they caused him to looke upon his companion, that was a quarteringe. When he saw the hangman pull out his bowels; "O why," sayth he, "doe I tarrye soe longe behind my sweete brother; let me make hast after him. This is a most happy day." This beinge spoken, he fell to his devotions, prainge expressly for all Catholickes and for the conversion of all heretikes, and soe ended this miserable life most glorioslye, committinge his soule to almightie God: where it enjoyeth, with the rest of the blessed sayntes, eternall blysse. Whether, by his prayers, our Lord bringe us by happy martyrdome; for Jesus sake, Who is the kinge of all martirs. Amen.
—From the account of the martyrdom of James Bell in John Hungerford
   Pollen, ed., *Unpublished Documents Relating to the English Martyrs*

IN EARLY MODERN ENGLAND, ESPECIALLY DURING THE TIMES OF HARSHEST persecution, English Catholics relied for information and ideological support not only on books and pamphlets smuggled into England from the Continent and on some works printed by secret English presses but also on manuscript documents that circulated in the Catholic community. The manuscript system facilitated the distribution of censorable or politically dangerous texts and also served to unite a scattered and embattled minority combating the English government's obvious strategy of cultural eradication. A wide variety of texts circulated in the manuscript medium, among them prose lives of Thomas More,[1] political libels such as *Leicester's Commonwealth,*[2] the formulaic Catholic last will and testament, a copy of which belonged to Shakespeare's father,[3] the politically explosive "Brag" by Edmund Campion and "Treatise of Equivocation" by Henry Garnet, the 1585 letter of Philip Howard, earl of Arundel, to Queen Elizabeth explaining his intended flight from England for religious reasons,[4] Robert Persons's "A Memorial for the Reformation of Englande,"[5] Edmund Campion's *Two Books of the Histories of Ireland,*[6] and literary works such as Southwell's poetry and prose that continued to be copied in manuscript despite repeated printings.[7] One kind of circulating manuscript text, the martyrdom account, normally in the form of freestanding ballads, poems, or prose narratives or of reports in letters that may also contain other information, spoke to a Catholic community and, propagandistically, to a larger national and international audience. I argue that these narratives speak a Catholic language, publicize Catholic beliefs, dramatize Catholic material practices, and serve as countercultural expressions for a community at odds with the religious and political order that was depicted as persecutory. These texts bind a scattered and demoralized minority and idealize strong forms of religious resistance.

The Documentary Remains

Poems and ballads about the sufferings and martyrdoms of Catholic priests and laymen circulated at various times during the persecutions. They highlight dramatic moments of imprisonment, trials, and executions, using the conventions of the prose martyrdom accounts. For example, the Jesuit Laurence Anderton's ballad about the lay martyr John Thulis (executed in 1616) recounts the usual attempts by a Protestant minister to convert the imprisoned Catholic, the authorities' unsuccessful efforts to get him to swear the Oath of Allegiance, the martyr's declaration that he is innocent of treason, his charity to the poor on the way to his execution, the sympathy of the crowd of spectators (and even the reluctance of the hangman to quarter the body), people's efforts to obtain his blood as relics, and the supernatural signs and wonders following the death (a light as bright as the sun pours from his mouth over his body, then disappears; to bury the pieces, ravens later pick the flesh from the quartered body set on the castle).[8]

In another ballad, the speaker welcomes the opportunity to suffer torture and martyrdom for the faith:

> Noe rope nor cruell tortour then
>   should cause my minde to faile;
> Nor lewde device of wicked men
>   should cause my corage quaile,
> On racke in *tower* let me be l[ai]d,
>   let Joynts at large be stretched;
> Let me abyde each cruell braid,
>   till blood frome vaines be fetched.
>
> .   .   .   .
>
> Let me be falslie condemned;
>   let Sherife on me take charge;
> With bo[w]es and billes let me be led,
>   least I escape at large;
> Let me from prison passe away
>   on hurdle hard to lye,
> To *Tyburne* drawne without delay
>   in torments there to dye.
>
> Let mee be hang'd and yet, for doubt
>   least I be dead too soone,
> Let there some devillish spirit start out
>   in hast to cut me downe;
> Let bowells be burnt, let paunch be fryde
>   in fier [e]r I be dead;
> On *London* bridg, a poule provide,
>   thereon to set my head.
>
> O *London,* let my quarters stand
>   upon thy gates to drye;
> And let them beare the world in hand
>   I did for treason dye;

Let cro[w]es and kytes my carkas eate;
 and ravens their portion hav[e],
Least afterwardes my frendes intreate
 to lay my corpses in grave.[9]

This ballad expresses a wish for the most extreme forms of suffering and humiliation as a gauge of the desire for martyrdom. What can be most feared is manically welcomed. This piece and others, such as the poems appended to the surreptitiously printed Catholic *True Report* of the martyrdom of the Jesuit Edmund Campion, were effective both within the Catholic community and in the larger social context—provoking at least one Protestant poetic refutation.[10]

Prose martyrdom accounts can be found in a number of different sorts of documents addressed to international or national readers.[11] For example, a letter narrating the martyrdoms of four priests (George Haydock, Thomas Emerford, James Fenn, and Robert Nutter) was sent to Rome to Robert Southwell. It ends with the suggestion that it should be passed on to other readers: "What I have putt downe I hard myself, and therefore I may boldly speake it. If you please, you may show it to your friends, provyded alwaies you tell not my name."[12] Missives such as this were part of the international system of Catholic news reporting used by secular priests and Jesuits on the English mission: hence, for example, the annual reports sent by the Jesuit superior Henry Garnet contain narratives of particular martyrdoms,[13] as do letters to the well-networked Robert Persons, and the Catholic news bureau managed in the Low Countries by Richard Verstegan regularly received and retransmitted such narratives.[14] English exiles and other Catholic propagandists on the Continent ran a martyrology industry that from the early 1580s kept up a steady stream of manuscript and printed martyrologies aimed both at the general European market[15] and at England. The letters that English Catholics and clerical leaders sent abroad, some of them containing eyewitness accounts of martyrdoms, were an essential source for these publications.[16]

When, in 1626, Dr. Richard Smith, bishop of Chalcedon, called for local priests to do an accounting of all the martyrs who had suffered in their areas, it was his intention to organize the information in a systematic way.[17] In effect, this involved sending back to a center information and narratives circulating in the periphery, though, of course, through reports of the martyrdoms to superiors and colleagues on the Continent there was always a centripetal force that facilitated the collection of martyrdom stories and their publication in Catholic martyrologies such as William Allen's *A Briefe Historie of the Glorious Martyr-dom of XII. Reverend Priests* (1582), John Gibbon's *Concertatio Ecclesiae Angli-canae* (1583, 1588),[18] Richard Verstegan's *Theatrum Crudelitatum Haereticorum Nostri Temporis* (1592), Thomas Worthington's *A Relation of Sixtene Martyrs: Glorified in England in Twelve Moneths* (Douay, 1601), and John Wilson's *En-glish Martyrologe* (1608).[19] Such Catholic martyrologies gathered and, in some cases, illustrated with elaborate engravings[20] the stories of those English lay-men and priests who suffered and died for their Catholic beliefs. One of the most carefully crafted of these publications, *The Life and Death of Mr Edmund Geninges, Priest* (St. Omer, 1614),[21] published twenty-three years after the mar-tyr's death, contains beautifully executed illustrations, including a depiction of the arrest of a large group of lay Catholics along with Gennings after hearing Mass at Swithen Wells's house (see fig. 3).[22]

One route of manuscript transmission of martyrdom accounts was through the Catholic family circles and networks in England. Thus the nar-rative of the martyrdom of James Duckett, a printer of Catholic texts, was penned by his son, who became a Carthusian priest (Pollen, *Acts,* 238). That of Thomas Sherwood, a middle-class hero whose father was a draper, was "A Relation written by his Brother for his Nephews."[23] The secular priest William Hart's letter to his mother also had considerable impact as a model of heroic resolve. He addressed her:

> [P]erhaps you will say: I weepe not so much for your death, as I do for that yow are hanged, drawen, and quartered. My sweet mother it is the honourablest and happiest death that ever could have chanced to me. I dy not for knavery, but for vertue. I dy not for treason, but for religioun. I dy not for any ill demeanour or offence committed, but onely for my faith, for my conscience, for my Priesthood, for my blessed Saviour Jesus Christ. . . . How glad then may he bee to see mee a martyr, a Saint, a most glorious and bright starre in heaven. . . . I wish that I were neer to comfort you, but because that can not be I beseech you even for Christ Jesus sake to comfort your self. . . . If I had lived I would have holpen yow in your age, as you have holpen mee in my youth. But now I must desire God to helpe yow and my brethren, for I can not. Good mother blesse mee. And now in your old daies serve God after the old Catholike manner. . . . [O]ne daie wee shall meet in heaven by Gods grace. (AAW 3: 237–39)[24]

Cùm veteri peragit Missæ pia Sacra sodali,
Infestat turbam turba profana piam.

FIGURE 3. Engraving of the scene of arrests of Catholics near Swithen Wells's house in
John Gennings, *The Life and Death of Mr Edmund Geninges, Priest* (St. Omer, 1614), 62. This
item is reproduced by permission of The Huntington Library, San Marino, California.

According to one martyrdom account, the mother of John Bodey "afterward hearing of her sonnes Martyrdome, made a great Feast to her neighbors, as her sonns marriage day, rejoycing of his martyrdom" (AAW 4: 118).

A 1,785-page folio manuscript now in the Bodleian Library (MSS Eng.th.b.12) contains a rich compendium of Catholic documents, apparently prepared for a patron by Thomas Jollette, a musician who was a protégé of William Byrd. Included are a description of a 1585 meeting of Catholics at the house of Lord Vaux at which a service, sermon, and exorcism were held; lists of persecuted Catholics; speeches from 1559 on by Catholic political figures; an account of a Mass and sermon held in 1606 at the Spanish ambassador's house whose participants were arrested by the authorities as they were leaving; musical material connected with William Byrd; and accounts of the interrorgations and executions of the Jesuit Roger Filcock and Anne Line,[25] both killed in 1601, and of Henry Garnet, executed in 1606.[26]

Beyond the family, however, martyrdom stories reached the Catholic community at large through the manuscript communication routes that Nancy Pollard Brown's interesting bibliographical detective work has uncovered: she has traced one route of manuscript dissemination of Catholic texts from Henry Garnet and the countess of Arundel's house in the Catholic London neighborhood of Spitalfields to the country and its dispersed Catholic population.[27] The survival in manuscript of several versions of John Mush's life of Margaret Clitherow[28] (the only full texts of the story disseminated before the nineteenth century, the printed account, presenting merely an abbreviated version)[29] testifies to the functioning of this network.

In the Archives of the Archdiocese of Westminster there is an eight-page, sewn, professionally copied booklet containing accounts of northern lay and clerical martyrs (AAW 4: 121 ff.): it deals with Edward Watterson, executed at Newcastle in 1591; four priests executed at Durham on 27 May 1590; a shoemaker-martyr killed at York on 30 November 1586; Thomas Pallicer; Edward Osbaldson, executed on 16 November 1583; James Thomson, executed in York in 1583; Peter Snow; Marmaduke Bowes, "condemned and executed, for giving a cupp of Beere at his dore to a Priest" (AAW 4: 127); Ralph Grimston; Robert Bikerdike; William Knight; and William Gibson. This collection was probably made in response to the bishop of Chalcedon's 1626 request for stories of martyrs, but it would seem that such texts were assembled both from Catholic oral folklore and from already circulating manuscript accounts.[30]

Michael Williams has suggested that manuscript accounts of martyrdom, some surviving in multiple copies, were regularly used to edify and reinforce the faith of native English Catholics but also as a means of fundraising for the Continental seminaries training priests for the English mission.[31] And, of course, since Catholic *printed* texts could only reach English Catholics from secret English presses or by being smuggled into the country from abroad, manuscript communication was a crucial medium of communication for English Catholics and for the official church that wished to retain their allegiance.

The Context of the Catholic Martyrdom Accounts

Some features of the martyrdom account reveal the religiopolitical work intended or accomplished by the form in the two related contexts with which I am concerned: (1) the Catholic community meant to be affected by such stories and (2) the public relations struggle between Protestants and Catholics, or, specifically, between the English government and the militant Catholic recusants. In terms of the first, martyrdom accounts celebrate this extreme form of religious heroism and deliberately include laymen as well as priests, women as well as men, and lower-born as well as highborn victims of the persecution. In terms of the sectarian polemical and propaganda wars, martyrdom accounts argue for the superiority of the hard-line Catholic position—in opposition both to Protestant adversaries and to less militant Catholics.[32]

Martyrdom narratives were especially meant to affect lukewarm or compromising English Catholics, particularly church papists.[33] Catholic leaders knew that such accommodation to a program designed to erode Catholicism and to reduce the functioning Catholic community (combined with the enforcement of recusancy fines and of the laws against missionary priests and those who helped them) facilitated the ultimate destruction of English Catholicism.[34] Especially after the failed invasion of 1588, when the likelihood of the military reestablishment of Catholicism in England was slight, patient suffering was idealized as the best way English Catholics could bear witness to their faith and create the best chance for its survival, while they hoped for religious toleration, less harsh treatment by the queen and government authorities, or a reestablishment of Catholicism itself with the change of monarchs. As one of the elegies published in the Catholic *True Report* of Edmund Campion's martyrdom had argued:

> God knowes it is not force nor might,
>   not warre nor warlike band,
> Not shield & spear, not dint of sword,
>   that must convert the land,
> It is the blood by martirs shed,
>   it is that noble traine,
> That fight with word & not with sword,
>   and Christ their capitaine.
> For sooner shall you want the handes
>   to shed sutch guiltles blood,
> Then wise and vertuous still to come
>   to do their country good.[35]

The poem assumes the belief in Tertullian's saying that "the blood of Christians is the seed of the Church."

Geoffrey Nuttall notes that, although the vast majority of Catholic martyrs in the long period from 1535 to 1680 were priests (219), there were also a large number of lay martyrs (93). Of these only three were peers. Others included "seven . . . schoolmasters," an Oxford don, "a barrister[,] . . . two printers, a weaver, a woolen draper, a tailor, a glover, a dyer's apprentice, a joiner, an ostler, a miller, a farmer, a husbandman, and five servants." These were also four women: Blessed Margaret Pole (Countess of Salisbury and mother of Cardinal Pole), St. Margaret Clitherow, St. Mary Ward, and St. Anne Line. However, no women were martyred between 1604 and 1680.[36]

The story of the lay martyr James Duckett, preserved in manuscript in near-complete form in the Archives of the Archdiocese of Westminster,[37] is one of conversion and heroism probably meant to inspire other lay Catholics. A younger brother from a relatively prosperous family, Duckett was apprenticed in London and raised as a Protestant (a "Puritan . . . so zealous that he would have heard 2. or 3. sermons on a day" [AAW 7: 339]). After being given a book on "the foundation of the Catholicke religion" by a Catholic friend, which he read surreptitiously while he tended the shop, he rejected Protestantism and was sent to Bridewell for nonattendance at church services but was soon freed at the request of his master. After buying out his apprentice-ship, he took formal Catholic religious instruction and was received into the church "by Mr. Weekes a venerable Priest, and a Prisener in the Gathowse" (AAW 7: 340). After two or three years, he married a Catholic widow.

> [He took up] a poore taylers trade wherin his chiefe worke was to ac-comadat priests and those who laboured for the Conversion of sowles with garmentes fitt for their necessities; to make and mend up vestmentes to prepare church stuffe and all necessities for the alter. And that he yet farther might be an instrument to helpe and sett forward the common good he resolved to deale and trade in bookes wherewith he might fur-nish Catholickes as well for their owne comfort and devotion as for the satisfaction and instruction of others and therby both benefitt him selfe and them. (AAW 7: 340)

When the authorities searched his house, they found an "impression of our Ladie psalters with the picture of the Rosarie togeather with the presse" (AAW 7: 341), and they arrested both him and his printers. After two years in jail he was freed but was arrested again after ten weeks, the stock of some devotional books having been found in his house. He was freed quickly, however, be-cause his wife was in labor but then rearrested when more Latin and English books were discovered at his house. He was sent to "Limbos[,] . . . [a] darke and dismall dungeon through which the Filth of the cittie ranne with no small stench" (AAW 7: 342). When his wife visited him there, he "came up to her smiling with a merrie and full countenance while shee with a heavie heart stood weeping thinking shee should have seene in him the picture of a dead man farr from that chearfull countanance he brought with him from this place" (AAW 7: 342). He was released after two months but was betrayed to the au-thorities by a man named Bullock, a bookbinder, hoping to escape his own pun-ishment by revealing to Judge Popham that Duckett had republished South-well's *An Humble Supplication to the Queen*.[38] When the search of the house turned up other Catholic books, Duckett was sent to Newgate, tried, found guilty (after the notoriously harsh Judge Popham sent the jury, who had de-clared him not guilty, back to reconsider their verdict), condemned to death, and executed (but not before he had cheerfully forgiven Bullock for betraying him). Not only an example of conversion, Duckett is portrayed as the steadfast assister of priests and servant of the wider English Catholic community he affected through the Catholic books he printed or distributed. Repeated arrests and incarcerations did not deter him; only execution brought to a halt his activities as a Catholic printer and priest helper. Duckett's importance derives from his status as a lay martyr, as well as from his providing a model of Catholic subordination to clerical authority, someone who served both the English mission and the whole English Catholic community.

In his manuscript account of the trial and martyrdom of Edmund Gennings and his companions, James Young recounts the heroism of a servant who refused to yield to pressure from the authorities:

> Amongst these Catholics there was arraigned one Robert Sydney [Sydney Hodgson], sometime a serving-man, taken at Mass with Mr. Geninges; he, by the entreaty of the Judge, and of the Lord Anderson, asked pardon of the Queen for his fault, which being done the Judge told him that he had showed himself a good subject, and therefore should have favour at her Majesty's hands. Presently he was unpinnioned, every man thinking he should be dismissed; for he was not condemned with the others; but only was singled out as a poor simple man whom they thought would yield easily, and so every one said unto him, "Sydney, thou must go to my Lord of London [the Bishop], and he will instruct thee in the truth." To whom he answered, "My lord, I would not have you to think that I will deny my faith, although I have asked her Majesty's forgiveness. I will die twenty times first." (Pollen, *Unpub. Doc.*, 106)

Thereafter he is condemned to death with the other prisoners. As someone from the lower social orders, Sydney is idealized as a steadfast and courageous Catholic resisting the socially superior secular and ecclesiastical authorities in order to proclaim loyalty to the Catholic church.

While lay martyrs like Duckett and Sydney exemplified patient suffering in the face of the judicial terrorism aimed at recusant Catholics, this was not always the response of strong-willed Catholic laymen. At his execution, Swithen Wells got into an argument with the Catholic-hunter Richard Topcliffe, a man whose relentless cruelty is a leitmotif of the Elizabethan martyrdom accounts. Topcliffe reproved Wells for asking for a blessing from Gennings and exclaimed, "'Dog-bold Papists! . . . you follow the Pope and his Bulls; believe me, I think some bulls begot you all." The narrator continues:

"Herewith Mr. Wells was somewhat moved, and replied, 'If we have bulls to our fathers, thou hast a cow to thy mother'" (a Catholic misogynistic swipe at Queen Elizabeth in her role as "Supreme Governor" of the English church). Wells immediately apologized for his impatient outburst and said to Topcliffe, "'God pardon you and make you of a Saul a Paul, of a bloody persecutor one of the Catholic Church's children'" (Pollen, *Acts,* 108).[39]

In their battle with the Elizabethan establishment, Catholic martyrologists tried to capture the moral high ground, appropriating from the Protestant martyrological discourse represented in John Foxe's popular (and nationalistic) *Actes and Monuments* (or *Book of Martyrs*) the role of religious victimage,[40] but, of course, the Catholic accounts differ narratologically and thematically from the Protestant ones in significant ways that reflect the changed method of execution (from burning at the stake to hanging and dismemberment) as well as the theological and devotional contrasts between Protestantism and Catholicism. Peter Lake and Michael Questier compare Protestant and Catholic emphases in the narratives: "[T]he catholic rather than the protestant accounts . . . were anxious to concentrate on the graphic details of the victim's physical sufferings. Protestants were obsessed with the internal, spiritual condition of their victims, and expressed concern with their physical actions and sufferings only when such externals could be made to yield some clue as to their inner state."[41] Protestants and Catholics had sharply different attitudes towards the meritoriousness of the martyrs' sufferings.[42] Brad Gregory points out that the Catholic perception of martyrs' meritorious participation in the sufferings of Christ (as "king of the martyrs") was alien to Protestants, who emphasized the primacy of faith, not of good works. He contrasts the Catholic desire for martyrdom with the more restrained Protestant attitude: "The Protestant imperative to martyrdom was more exclusively negative: a duty not to compromise the Gospel rather than avidly to pursue the supreme act of self-sacrifice. For Protestants, coveting martyrdom could spoil a death for Christ with a self-regarding anticipation of merit."[43]

The Conventions of Catholic Martyrdom Narratives

The Catholic martyrdom narratives contain a number of regular features: (1) the portrayal of the cruelty of the persecutors; (2) the repeated references to the sympathy for Catholic victims of Protestant jailers, hangmen, and members of the crowd at executions, sometimes resulting in actual conversions (or "rec-onciliations"); (3) the depiction of gallows humor and its power dynamics; (4) the rehearsing of the final speeches, sermons, arguments, and prayers spoken at the places of execution; (5) the sacralizing of these sites of suffering and exe-cution by means of Catholic prayer, sacramentalism, and ceremonialism; and (6) the occurrence of supernatural signs and wonders and the conversion of the bodies and body parts of the martyrs into saints' relics. While the first four might have counterparts in Protestant martyrology, the last two certainly high-light specifically Catholic practices and beliefs.

Cruelty of the Persecutors

Catholics were sometimes put in the most pestilential prisons and dungeons, sometimes in a room called "Little Ease," in which it was impossible to stand or lie down; they were tortured on the rack but then, when racking in the Tower was something of a public embarrassment for the government, the tor-turing was moved to Bridewell and even, in some cases, to Richard Topcliffe's house, which contained a well-equipped torture chamber where Southwell was tormented. Hanging on the walls for hours by the wrists and being subjected to the iron glove called the "gauntlet" and thumbscrews all were used to extort "confessions" and information. The full gruesome treatment at the executions themselves, however, receives the most narrative attention. Typically, the victims were not allowed to hang until they were dead but were cut down alive so that they would be conscious during the procedure in which they were castrated, eviscerated, and had their hearts cut out before their bodies were decapitated and quartered. A narration of martyrdoms sent to Robert Southwell at the En-glish College, Rome, describes Thomas Hemerford's treatment: "He was cutt down halfe dead; when the tormentor did cutt off his membres, he did cry 'O! Ah!' I heard my self standing under the gibbet" (Pollen, *Unpub. Doc.,* 62). The martyrs' heroic suffering during their mutilation and disemboweling is often highlighted as a mark of their sanctity.

Sympathy for Catholic Victims

Evidence of sympathy for the victims can be found in a remark of the former Catholic John Donne in one of his sermons: "We see at Executions, when men pretend to die cheerfully for the glory of God, half the company will call them Traitors, and half Martyrs."[44] Edmund Campion's keeper, who was sympathetic to him, was impressed when Ralph Sherwin kissed the bloodstained hand of the executioner who had just finished dismembering Campion (Pollen, *Acts,* 310). Ralph Miller, a husbandman from near Winchester, was allowed to come and go freely from prison by his keeper (Pollen, *Acts,* 85). At the 26 April 1642 execution of Edward Morgan, officers helped Catholics to get relics: "the officers calling for the people's handkerchiefs and gloves to wet in the blood, which they did, and delivered them again to the owners, and one got almost his whole heart out of the fire" (Pollen, *Acts,* 352). At the 12 October 1642 execution of the weak-voiced Benedictine Thomas Bullaker, a sympathetic sheriff tried to facilitate the martyr's scaffold speech despite the crowd noise and the constant interruptions of a zealous Protestant minister (Pollen, *Acts,* 356).[45] One of the witnesses of Montford Scott's and George Beesley's executions was supposed to have said: "Is this treason? I cam to see traitors and have seen saints"— whereupon he was clapped in prison (Pollen, *Acts,* 303). At Edmund Gennings's execution, "the hangman taking him yet alive and speaking, he ripped his belly and showed his heart to the people crying, 'Thus God grant it may happen to all traitors! God save the Queen!' When scarce one voice was heard amongst all the people to say Amen, at which they much wondered who were the chief executors" (Pollen, *Acts,* 109). When the hangman at the executions of Thomas Somers and John Roberts held up the heart of one of them, saying "'This is the heart of a traitor,'" expecting the crowd to answer, "'Long live the King,'" "not one person answered, but all remained silent as if struck dumb" (Pollen, *Acts,* 168). Even at the execution of the man portrayed by the government as the chief villain of the Gunpowder Plot, the Jesuit Henry Garnet, the spectators refused to respond positively to the executioner's display of the heart as that of a "traitor."[46] Thomas Reynolds, executed on 21 January 1642, was said to be "a man of singular meekness and most gentle manner, whereby he so far won the affection of the Protestants that many of them publicly declared with tears before his martydom that such a man ought not to be put to death" (Pollen, *Acts,* 340). Two criminals had last-second conversions on the scaffold when Thomas Reynolds and Bartholomew Roe were executed (Pollen, *Acts,* 342). At the execution of John Almond on 20 December 1612, "a Protestant beholding his undaunted courage and bold spirit, full of life and comfort, he concluded in himself that he only was happy for his religion. Thereupon he went from the gallows to the Gatehouse [prison], and desired to speak with a priest. They bringing him to Father Blackfan, he resolved to the best, and was reconciled within few days, for which my Lord of Canterbury clapt up close Mr. Blackfan" (Pollen, *Acts*, 193).[47] As noted earlier, Henry Walpole, a young gentleman (later a Jesuit), was converted at Campion's execution after a drop of Campion's blood fell on him.[48]

In the immediate aftermath of the Essex revolt, the execution of the priest John Pribush, according to Henry Garnet, was handled and responded to in a revealing way: "[T]hough they [the authorities] held the execution so suddenly that not many people were able to be present, a public proclamation was made that all were to depart, for fear or revolt. And in fact all the people, already discontented by Essex's ill success, lamented and said: 'See! They have put to death a poor sick priest.'"[49] Even if we make allowances for Garnet's biases, it would seem that the public relations intention of executing Catholics utterly failed as propaganda.

The English government, of course, did its best to control the public's response to the executions and tried to terrorize Catholics into religious conformity. It delivered a message to both Protestants and Catholics in local communities by sending people convicted in London back for execution to their places of residence or apprehension; more than half of those killed between 1570 and 1680 were executed outside of London.[50] The martyrdom accounts could also bring home to Catholics living outside the country's cultural and economic center the exemplary behavior of those who could be regarded as local heroes of the faith. Many were martyred in such northern strongholds of Catholicism as Yorkshire, Lancashire, and Durham, with the city of York, for example, accounting for some fifty of the executions in this period.[51] As Nuttall points out, every English county, with the exception of Cambridgeshire, produced at least one martyr, and many of these were executed locally. In 1588, a year in which there were thirty-four executions of Catholic priests and laymen, Sir John Puckering, later Lord Keeper, formulated plans to distribute indictments and executions widely so as to send a message to Catholics in all parts of the country.[52]

Even in London, places other than Tyburn were carefully chosen to deliver a message. For example, the priest Thomas Pormort was executed in 1592 before the door of a haberdasher he had converted (Pollen, *Acts*, 120). The layman Nicholas Horner, condemned for making a jerkin for a priest, was executed before his house in Smithfield (Pollen, *Acts*, 231). Swithen Wells was executed (along with the priest Edmund Gennings) in front of his house near Gray's Inn, which had been used for a Catholic Mass.[53] Henry Garnet was executed between St. Paul's Cathedral and the bishop's mansion, the location used to celebrate the victory over the Spanish Armada.[54]

Gallows Humor

Many martyrs are portrayed as cheerfully and confidently facing their deaths.[55] The night before his execution, the layman John Finch was visited in prison by his friends and relatives. They "came to comfort hyme in this last conflict and affliction; but they found hyme so merry in God and so joyfull of the next dayes banket (which he expected) that they were all mervelously comforted and edified by his rare fortitude" (Pollen, *Unpub. Doc.,* 87). On the hurdle, being dragged to the place of execution, Anthony Middleton was supposedly in such good spirits that "all the beholders, which were thousands, wondered at his gladsome countenance" (Pollen, *Unpub. Doc.,* 186). John Roberts, who was to be executed with Thomas Somers, "looking at the fire that was already burning to consume their bowels, said 'Here's a hot breakfast ready, despite the cold weather'" (Pollen, *Acts,* 166). Edward Morgan supposedly had the following exchange with the hangman and the usual antagonistic Protestant minister:

> [H]e with a merry countenance wished Gregory to do his office, and gave him a piece of money. Gregory going to dispose him in some posture, he said, "I pray thee, teach me, for I never was at the sport before."
>
> Whereupon the minister said, "Mr Morgan, this is not a time to sport, nor is it a jesting matter."
>
> "Sir," said Mr. Morgan, "I know it is not jest, but good sober earnest; but you cannot deny but that God requireth a cheerful sacrifice." (Pollen, *Acts,* 351)

Catholic victims sometimes played to the crowd. Brian Lacey, in fact, succeeded in making the hated Topcliffe laughable:

> Lacey, now having the rope about his neck, was willed by Topcliffe to confesse his treason. "For," saith he, "here are none but traitors who are of thy religion."

"Then," said Lacey, "answer me. You yourself in Queen Mary's days was a Papist, at least in show. Tell me, were you also a traitor?" At which the people laughed aloud. (Pollen, *Acts,* 110)

At his execution, the martyr Laurence Humphrey smiled at the unintended stupid rhyming of the hangman, who said: "Thou holdest with the Pope, but he has brought thee to the rope, and the hangman shall have thy coat" (Pollen, *Acts,* 237–38). The embarrassed man hit him in retaliation.

Final Words

Because those who were about to die were allowed to repent and ask the forgiveness of God and of the monarch, they had the opportunity to bear witness to and argue the truth of their faith as well as to resist the power of the government and to argue with the Protestant ministers who were usually at hand to recruit them to the official Church of England. Ironically, these occasions were the only ones offered for Catholic priests to preach or dispute openly to a congregation that often numbered in the hundreds. Henry Garnet's account of the sufferings and execution of Robert Southwell depicts the martyr both making a formal speech from the cart before hanging and disputing one last time with a Protestant minister.[56] Another account reproduced a dialogue between Oliver Plasden and Sir Walter Ralegh occasioned by the former's praying for the queen from the cart before his execution: Ralegh was so moved by the man's loyalty[57] and honesty that even after Topcliffe intervened to ask a version of the "bloody questions" used to trap Catholics into a hypothetical choice between loyalty to country and loyalty to their religion, he ordered that Plasden be allowed to hang until dead instead of being cut down for vivisection (Pollen, *Acts,* 112–14). The relentlessly cruel Topcliffe "cryed out with a loud voyce" to Edmund Gennings when the latter was about to be executed:

Geninges, Geninges, confess thy fault, thy Popish treason, and the Queene by submission (no doubt) will grant thee pardon. To which he mildly ansered; I know not M. Topliffe in what I have offended my deare annoynted Princesse, for if I had offended her, or any other in any thing, I would willingly ask her, and all the world forgivenesse. If shee bee offended with me without a cause, for professing my fayth and religion, because I am a Priest, or because I will not turne Minister agaynst my conscience, I shalbe I trust excused and innocent before God. . . . I must obey God rather then men, and must not in this cause acknowledge a fault where none is. If to returne into England Priest, or to say Masse be Popish treason, I heere confesse I am a traytour: but I think not so.[58]

In reaction to these words, the angered Topcliffe "scarce giving him leave to say a Pater noster, bad the Hangman turne the ladder, which in an instant being done, presently he caused him to be cut downe" alive, his last words on the dismembering table being, "Oh it smartes."[59]

The secular priest Edward Morgan made the best of the opportunity the sheriff gave him to speak before his death, delivering an apologia or sermon to the crowd that "the doctor or minister-assistant" felt compelled to interrupt: "'Mr. Morgan, I would wish you to dispose yourself for death, and not to go about to seduce the King's people'"—after which they disputed with one another until Morgan pleaded:

"Good sir . . . trouble me no more," and returned to his discourse with great zeal, alacrity, and to the content of all the people; until at last the minister spake to him . . . and wished him to put his trust in the merits of the Lord, and not in angels and saints. Whereunto Mr. Morgan replied, "Mistake not yourself, sir, for I put my whole trust and confidence in the infinite merits of my Lord and Saviour Jesus Christ, Who died for me."

"That is well said," said the minister, and let him alone. (Pollen, *Acts,* 350–51)

Catholic priests and laymen, in effect, had the last word at their executions.[60] Their suffering empowered them to speak with moral authority to religiously mixed audiences who were often willing to extend them deep sympathy.

Sacralizing the Sites of Execution

Judicially and propagandistically, the English government tried to identify priests and those who helped them as political subversives and to execute them for treason—a characterization countered by Catholic claims that they were victims of conscience suffering for their religious, not their political, activities.[61]

It is not surprising, then, that those about to be executed should try to create a religious and devotional aura for the occasion. Often the priest-victims used gestures and words borrowed from Catholic religious ceremony and devotional practice to convert the place and paraphernalia of execution from the secular to the sacred, from the environment of punishment for felons and traitors to the holy space of martyrdom.[62] Just as in donning the vestments for Mass the celebrant kissed the stole he put on, many of the priest-victims who were about to be hanged made a point of kissing the rope before slipping it over their necks. Some of this ceremonial sacralizing of the material conditions of martyrdom were performed by laymen as well: in a manuscript account of John Bodey's martyrdom (which was also put into print), the martyr is reported to have said when he was laid on the hurdle on which he was to be dragged to the place of execution, "Oh, sweet bed, the happiest bed that ever man lay on! Thou art welcome to me." When the hangman was about to put the halter around his neck, he said, "Oh, blessed chain, the sweetest chain and richest that ever came about any man's neck!" and he kissed it (Pollen, *Acts,* 62–63).[63] Futhermore, victims usually chose to say prayers in Latin, the language of Catholic liturgy and clerical devotion—an act that usually provoked anger on the part of the authorities. At his execution, the layman John Thomas was kicked by the hangman for insisting on praying in Latin (Pollen, *Acts,* 232–33). Even the treatment of the victims' bodies and blood after execution and dismemberment was quasi-sacramental: martyrs' relics were not just revered as ordinary saints' relics, but they took on, by association with Christ's sacrifice on the cross, a quasi-eucharistic character.[64] Clearly, each time an execution of a Catholic priest or layperson occurred, the place of execution was contested ground between Catholicism and Protestantism, between the government and the Catholic minority, and between the religious and the secular. Lake and Questier argue that "the very ideological means by which the state sought to encode its own purposes in these proceedings opened up spaces in which those purposes could be challenged and subverted," and "every time a Catholic priest was executed the issue of where legitimate royal authority ended and tyranny and persecution began was, through speech and gesture, reopened and thrust on to the public stage."[65] The Protestant authorities' concern that Catholics might succeed in defining the executions as martyrdoms is reflected in the care they took to destroy the victims' innards in the fire, to keep Catholics from access to the blood and body parts, and to place the heads and quarters on the gates of the city of London (out of access to Catholics) for the birds to pick the flesh from the bones.[66]

Signs and Wonders

An important feature of Catholic discourse in the period is the language of signs, wonders, visions, and miracles.[67] The dissemination of stories with these elements was meant to keep alive the very elements of the "old religion" that Protestantism wished to eradicate. Cressacre More's account of Sir Thomas More's execution and its aftermath contains two miraculous events:

> [T]hat which happened about Sir Thomas winding sheete, was reported as a miracle by my aunte Rooper, Mrs Clement, Dorothie Colly, Mr Harrys his wife. Thus it was: his daughter Margaret having distributed all her monie to the poore for her father's soule, when she came to burie his bodie at the tower, she had forgotten to bring a sheete; and there was not a penny of monie left amongst them all. wherefore Mris Harrys her mayde went to the next Drapers shoppe, and agreing upon the price, made as though she would looke for some monie in her purse, and then try whether they would trust her or no; & she found in her purse the same summe, for which they had agreed upon, not one penny over or under; though she knew before certainly, that she had not one Crosse about her.[68]

The second unusual sign is associated with the recovery of More's head after it had been displayed on London Bridge for a month: "the hayres of his head being almost gray before his Martyrdome, they seemed now as it were reddish or yellow."[69] Both signs are presented as proof of More's sanctity and God's favor.

An account of the experiences of the martyr Stephen Rowsam, a convert from Protestantism, notes:

> This Mr. Rowsam had divers strange visions, even being a schismatic, and many more after he was a Catholic and a priest. . . . Mr. Thompson, his fellow-prisoner . . . got them of him, and let the writer have a copy, which he dispersed into many counties of England, but yet at the writing

of this present had none with him, else he would have set them down at
all. This only he doth perfectly remember, Mr. Rowsam being in [Oriel]
college in Oxford, and running forth with many others one day to see
strange meteors that then appeared in the sky, he beheld over his own
head and very near to him a crown very bright and splendent, which he
showed to the fellows that stayed by him. God the Father and God the
Son appeared sundry times to him when a priest; so did our lady with
words as he would not utter. For the space of one night and day, or there-
about, being a prisoner, he lived in unspeakable joy, which he deemed
a taste of Heaven. As he prayed once in the Tower of London, many
singing birds came over his book and pictures which stood before him.
(Pollen, *Acts,* 333–34)

Numerous signs confirm Rowsam's status, including the "crown very bright
and splendent" that marks his sainthood and his St. Francis–like familiarity
with birds. Supposedly the very day that the priests Thomas Ford, John Shirt,
and Robert Johnson were martyred (28 May 1582) "they appeared to Mr. Rowsam in the Tower, and let him feel what pains their martyrdom had been to
them, and with what joy they were rewarded" (Pollen, *Acts,* 334). Nicholas
Horner, in prison "after his condemnation one night, as he was walking in
his . . . close room alone, saying his prayers, happening to look aside, he did see
about the head of his shadow against the wall, in proportion of a half circle, a
far brighter light than that of a candle, even as bright as the light of the sun. . . .
[A]t last he began to think with himself, that it was a sign given him from God
to signify a crown unto him. Therefore he immediately said, 'O Lord, thy will
be my will,' or to that effect, and so within a while it vanished away" (Pollen,
Acts, 230–31). The trope of the "crown of martyrdom" informs both accounts.
    The story of John Bodey's martyrdom includes a prophetic dream:

[He] saw in a dream the night before his death, two bulls attacking him
very furiously, but without at all hurting him, at which he was much
astonished. The next day two hangmen came down from London to
execute him, and as they walked on either side of him, he chanced to
ask their names, and as they one after the other answered that they were
called Bull, he at once remembering his dream, said: "Blessed be God;
you are then those two bulls who gave me such trouble last night in my

dream, and yet did me no harm." He then joyfully composed himself for death. (Pollen, *Acts,* 56)[70]

One of the purposes of this account, and of so many others, was to persuade Catholics that the pain and terror of punishment and execution were endurable. The aged Nicholas Horner, a tailor arrested first for refusing to say he would defend the queen from foreign invasion, said that in prison he chased from him a devil who appeared first as a "bush of thorns" and then "in the likeness of a blackamoor." After his gangrenous leg was amputated, he was freed, but he was rearrested. In prison he reported to a female visitor that he experienced "a great light in his Chamber, and . . . an angel did come and comfort him" (Pollen, *Acts,* 311).

Regularly, martyrdom accounts state that the hearts of the executed martyrs leaped out of the fire into which they were thrown. The account of Everard Hanse's martyrdom in the Douay Diaries claims:

> [T]he concurrent testimony of several witnesses has come to us that when his hart was thrown in the fire, it leaped up out of the flames with great violence, and being again flung in and covered with a faggot of wood, a second time it leaped up with such force as to lift the faggot out of its place and hold it for a time quivering in the smoke. "As if," adds the writer of his Acts, "God would manifest the victorious constancy of His martyr by the miraculous impetuous movement of his heart."[71]

A narrative of the execution of William Freeman, a priest executed on 13 August 1595, reports: "his hart trembled in the exequtioner's hand, & as some reported that saw yt, the same leaped thrice out of the fire: & his head chopt of, his mouth gasped twice" (Pollen, *Unpub. Doc.,* 359). The natural muscular contractions of the severed heart were thus hyperbolized and converted into a supernatural sign.

Signs and miracles demand witnesses. Hence sympathetic, neutral, and unsympathetic spectators are incorporated into martyrdom accounts to testify to such phenomena. One observer reports seeing Robert Sutton, a converted Protestant minister turned Catholic missionary, in jail "enveloped in light" while praying (Pollen, *Acts,* 325). A witness at the execution of Thomas Pilcher saw his "soul . . . carried by angels into Heaven." "The keeper of the gaol fell presently sick, and said openly unto many standing by, that the devils did strive for him, and that they would presently carry him away; but that he saw Mr. Pilchard stand with a cross betwixt him and them" (Pollen, *Acts,* 321). Rev. Thomas Fitzherbert reported that "one of the Assessors to the cheefe Judge, found his hand spotted with bloud at the tyme of Fa: Campions condemnation, and . . . he shewed yt to some with great admiration" (AAW 2: 188).[72]

Some signs and wonders are associated with relic collection and veneration.[73] The story is told of the miraculous preservation from corruption of the thumb and forefinger of Robert Sutton, a minister-turned-priest converted by a brother who later became a Jesuit:

> After the lapse of a whole year [after his execution], the Catholics, wishing to have some relics from the holy body of the Martyr, carried off one night by a pious theft a shoulder and arm. All the flesh was consumed, torn, and eaten by the birds, except the thumb and forefinger, which were found whole and uninjured and clothed with flesh; so that on these, which had been anointed with holy oil and sanctified by contact with the most holy Body of Christ, a special honour above the other fingers was conferred, even in this world, before the day of the Resurrection, when the whole body will shine like the sun in the sight of the Father.

The writer reports: "His brother, Mr. Abraham Sutton . . . showed me both these fingers thus wonderfully preserved, and gave me the forefinger. I have kept it deposited in a silver and glass reliquary with great reverence, with a paper on which the above account is briefly set down. Our Fathers in England have the reliquary with its sacred treasure, unless perchance, by the iniquity of these times, it have been made the spoil of the heretics" (Pollen, *Acts,* 325–26). The thumb of Edmund Campion, to which miracle cures were attributed, also had similar value because it was one of the fingers specially consecrated at the ordination ceremony.

Some of the accounts of relic hunting highlight the courage of recusant women. For example, a priest's narrative of the martyrdoms of the priest Roger Dickenson and the layman Ralph Milner notes that after Dickenson was killed and dismembered, "[o]ne of his quarters was taken away, shortly after they were hanged up on the gate, by a maid who was imprisoned for the Catholic faith, but yet made this adventure in the night, and returned to prison again with the quarter under her cloak; for the which afterward was made great search, but yet it could not be found" (Pollen, *Acts,* 96). Another woman yanked off a finger from one of the hands of the martyred Edmund Gennings, as his quarters were being carried back to Newgate to be boiled: "[T]aking the thumbe in her hand, by the instinct of almighty God, she gave it a little pull, onely to shew her love and desire of having it. The sequel was miraculous: for behold she not imagining any such matter would have followed, by the divine power, the thumbe was instantly loosed from his hand, and being separated she carried it away safely both flesh, skinne, and bone without sight of any, to her great joy and admiration" (see fig. 4).[74] The relic had value as a "holy and annoynted thumbe" that was "a part of his hand which so often had elevated the immaculate body of our B[lessed] Saviour Jesus Christ."[75] The woman allegedly later fled to the Continent, became an Augustinian nun, and mailed a portion of the thumb to Gennings's brother, a priest at Douay.[76]

One of the few Catholic women executed in this period, Anne Line, participated in the sacralization of her material remains: at her execution she cut lace from her petticoat and removed a stocking to give it to a friend. The Jesuit superior Henry Garnet had someone take material from her dress and dye it in the blood of two priests executed with her, then offered to send her stocking to the Jesuit General in Rome.[77]

To some extent the circulation of martyrs' relics paralleled the circulation of the texts narrating their martyrdoms, though the destinations were frequently Continental ones, which presented the safest locations for preservation. For example, some of the relics of John Roberts, a Benedictine priest, and Thomas Somers, a secular priest, were, according to Bishop Challoner, kept in England, but others were sent to the Continent—some to Douay to a Benedictine convent and one of Roberts's arms to Spain to the Abbey of St. Martin at Compostella (Pollen, *Acts,* 169).[78] Many of the relics at Douay were destroyed during the French Revolution,[79] but Douay manuscripts were preserved, ironically, by being returned to England (where many remain at the Archives of the Archdiocese of Westminster).

Martyrdom in the Larger Historical Framework

The behavior of Catholics at the religious executions, the folklore and devotional practices associated with the events and the remains of the victims, and the writing and circulation of martyrdom accounts all fostered the grassroots

Iuſsit amor pietasq̃ ſacram me tangere dextram;
Cede loco pollex; cedere iuſsit amor .

FIGURE 4. Engraving of the scene of Edmund Gennings's execution and its aftermath in
John Gennings, *The Life and Death of Mr Edmund Geninges, Priest* (St. Omer, 1614), 88. This
item is reproduced by permission of The Huntington Library, San Marino, California.

process of saint making—the older method that the Counter-Reformation church was trying to control through its institution of new, centralized, judicially elaborate procedures for canonization.[80] The Catholic church was very slow to install the English martyrs in its official calendar of saints: for example, Philip Howard, along with thirty-eight other English and Welsh martyrs, was not so recognized until 1970.[81] Although the Catholic Continental presses exploited the martyrdoms for polemical purposes in the propaganda war with English and European Protestantism, there are signs that martyrdom was being discouraged as a goal of English missionary priests and the Catholic faithful.

After the death of his colleague Edmund Campion on the first English Jesuit mission, the indefatigable Robert Persons not only used his pen to compose a steady stream of Catholic propaganda against the Elizabethan regime and its practices of persecuting Catholics but also undertook a biography of his beloved comrade.[82] Obviously much grieved by Campion's loss, Persons detailed his friend's personal and religious history, but he abandoned the project before he recorded the dramatic events of Campion's arrest, imprisonment, and torture, debate with Protestant adversaries, and execution at Tyburn. The martyr's biography left off before the martyrdom. When Campion had entered England, he did so with no reluctance, as he said to the authorities, to "enjoy your Tyburn."[83] Like other militant Jesuits, he thought of himself as a martyr in the making—a not unreasonable expectation, given the government's murderous treatment of priests, especially Jesuit priests, in the 1580s and 1590s. The problem, however, was that most Catholics were (understandably) uncomfortable with such an idealization of the path of martyrdom. And Claudio Aquaviva, the Jesuit general, was disturbed by the attitude of his missioners who seemed more eager to die for the faith than to survive and minister to Catholics or "reconcile" "schismatics" (church papists) to Catholicism. While all Catholics might have believed that "the blood of martyrs is the seed of the Church," it was also undoubtedly the case that Aquaviva preferred live missionaries to dead ones. Hence there was good reason for Persons, the survivor of the persecution who escaped England and capture (for which his Protestant adversaries accused him of cowardice), in effect to abandon the composition of the life of the martyred Campion.[84] He was more interested in overthrowing the English Protestant regime by foreign invasion or replacing it with a Catholic one by arguing succession claims of the Spanish Infanta than he was in propagating the message that the fate of English Catholics was to follow the example of those who suffered and died for their faith.

The 1604 peace treaty with Spain, King James I's irenic impulses,[85] Charles I's and Charles II's having Catholic spouses, and the negative publicity from the religious executions forced the English government to back off somewhat from persecuting Catholics fully after the Elizabethan era,[86] though, of course, especially after the failed Gunpowder Plot and at other times of crisis, such as the 1641 Irish Rebellion and Titus Oates's concocted Popish Plot, many Catholics were put to death.[87] On the other hand, opposition within the Catholic church to reckless pursuit of martyrdom caused a certain devaluation of martyrdom, and the martyrdom account was deemphasized as a literary subgenre. Although Catholics continued to be killed, the martyrdom account diminished in cultural importance and polemical usefulness. Its power, of course, could still be tapped on particular occasions — for example, to John Milton's great annoyance, by conservative Protestants who wished, in *Eikon Basilike* (1649), to depict the suffering and execution of Charles I as a martyrdom.

Sometimes texts circulated within the Catholic community were not only reproduced in Catholic books but also (recoded and) printed in new circumstances for other political purposes. Take, for example, the case of the famous speech from the scaffold of the priest John Southworth, killed during the Protectorate on 28 June 1654 in a well-attended execution.[88] He made a powerful speech from the cart before his hanging that used pointedly political rhetoric designed to embarrass a government sensitive to claims of freedom by religious dissenters. It made a sharp distinction between the religious and secular orders and made a strong claim for liberty of conscience:

> Heretofore liberty of conscience was pretended as a cause of war; and it was held a reasonable proposition that all the natives should enjoy it, who should be forced to behave themselves as obedient and true subjects. This being so, why should then conscientious acting and governing themselves, according to the faith received from their ancestors, involve them more than the rest in an universal guilt? . . . It has pleased God to take the sword out of the King's hand and put it in the Protector's. Let him remember that he is to administer justice indifferently and without exception of persons. . . . If any Catholics work against the present government, let them suffer; but why should the rest who are guiltless (un-

less conscience be their guilt) be made partakers in a promiscuous punishment with the greatest malefactors?[89]

Southworth's modern biographer points out: "[T]here were at least five contemporary versions of the martyr's speech at the foot of the gallows. Copies
were circulated among Catholics who, from the earliest days of the persecution, had treasured the final words of the martyrs. It was from one of these
copies that a printed version was published by a non-Catholic in 1679, the year
in which eighteen names were added to the Roll of Martyrs as a result of the
machinations of Titus Oates."[90] Thus the printed pamphlet, *A popish priest at
his execution at Tyburn June 28, 1654. Fully discovering the Papist's design to
obtain Toleration and liberty of Conscience; and to that end the late Rebellion
was begun and carried on. Printed from the true copy found among other papers at
the Search of a Papist's house* (London, 1679). If E. F. Reynolds is right in claim-
ing that Roger L'Estrange published the book in order to counter the forces
unleashed by Titus Oates, it is a good example of how an old text could have
new life in new political circumstances. The martyrdom account could move
from the context of communal oral communication to manuscript transmission to printed religious propaganda to nonconfessional political discourse,
its moral and sociopolitical force being used in various contexts for various
purposes.

In an era of brutal public executions, Catholic martyrs commanded audiences both at the scenes of their sufferings and afterwards—first, in the display of their body parts and in the folkloristic practices associated with their
relics, and, second, in the presentation of their experiences, words, and example in manuscript and print. Although they represented only a minority of
a minority, the English Catholic martyrs loomed large not only in the Catholic
subculture of early modern England but also in the wider national and international spheres. It may distort the narrative of English Catholic history to
concentrate on them so intently (as did some of the polemically driven Catholic histories written in the late nineteenth and early twentieth centuries), since
the less dramatic, though no less important, stories of the larger numbers of
ordinary English Catholics trying to function in their local communities have
usually been slighted, until more recent times. If we look at the means of transmission of martyrdom accounts, however, we see some of the contours of the
reporting of high-profile events to ordinary readers, from circles of families

and friends all the way to international audiences. As I have argued, the stories of the martyrs not only served polemical purposes, especially in conflicts between militant Counter-Reformation Catholicism and English (and European) Protestantism, but also held a prominent place in the cultural imagination of Catholics, instructing and binding the oppressed English Catholic community and encouraging persistence in the "old faith" and resistance to those forces that would eradicate it.

Performing Conversion

Out of these convertites
There is much matter to be heard and learned.

— *As You Like It,* 5.4.184–85

IN EARLY MODERN ENGLAND RELIGIOUS CONVERSION MEANT SHIFTING
one's social affiliation from one community to another. In the case of Protestants
joining the Roman Catholic communion, the change was simultaneously that
of affiliating with a persecuted minority in England and joining an international religious body: those former Protestants who announced or performed
their change of religion were sending a dissenting political message, opposing, as did Catholic martyrologists, the dominant Protestant English culture.[1]
On the other hand, English Catholics turning to or conforming to the official
religion were, first and foremost, joining an English church and demonstrating their English loyalty and cultural identity. Their degree of commitment to
this national Protestant religious community varied, however, from reluctant
or merely formal participation in the mandated religious services (practiced
by church papists for economic and social reasons) to, after 1606, swearing the
Oath of Allegiance to the monarch[2] to outright conversion — the last involving a deeply personal and heartfelt change.[3]

Catholics joining or rejoining the English church might take communion
as a sign that they were not just practicing outward conformity. After twelve
years as a Catholic convert, for example, Ben Jonson histrionically drained the
communion cup on his reconciliation to Anglicanism in 1610;[4] the Catholic

95

peer with whom he lived for a time, Lord Arundel, similarly signaled his conformity by taking public communion at Christmas, 1616.[5] Often when their
efforts to coerce or entice captive Catholic priests into the English church were
successful, the authorities asked the individuals to preach recantation sermons
and published the documents as part of the polemical struggle with Catholicism. The serial convert Anthony Tyrrell, for example, complied, addressing (as
did others) the key doctrinal and moral points argued in Protestant polemical texts.[6] Richard Sheldon, who published a tract in 1611 supporting the Jacobean Oath of Allegiance, preached after his subsequent apostasy a recantation
sermon that was published in 1612 and then wrote a longer work justifying
his conversion, *The Motives of Richard Sheldon Pr[iest], for His Just, Voluntary,
and Free Renouncing of Communion with the Church of Rome and Her Doctrine*
(1612), nominally addressed to the "Archpriest," George Birkhead, and to the
other Catholic clergy, a tract in which he fantasized his own martyrdom at
the hands of Catholics (A2).[7] The English government repeatedly used apostate
priests to try to persuade Catholics to conform.[8] Former Catholic priests often
received ecclesiastical preferment in the English church, becoming not only vicars but also higher-level church authorities. Christopher Perkins, thirty-four
years a Jesuit, became on his conversion an assistant to the archbishop of Canterbury and later helped him to compose the Jacobean Oath of Allegiance.[9] He
subsequently received a knighthood, married the duke of Buckingham's aunt,
and ended his life as a parish priest.[10] John Donne may have had converts such
as Perkins in mind when he remarked: "Truly I have been sorry to see some
persons converted from the Roman Church, to ours; because I have known, that
onely *temporal respects* have moved them, and they have lived after rather in a
nullity, or *indifferency* to either religion, then in a true, and established zeale."[11]
The religiously inconstant Catholic archbishop Marco Antonio de Dominis,
fictionally represented as the Fat Bishop in Thomas Middleton's *A Game at
Chesse,* first sought preferment in the English church, publishing anti-Catholic
polemics while in England, then, after a friend became Pope Gregory XV, returned to the Catholic church (only to be imprisoned by the Inquisition after
a new pope succeeded Gregory). Middleton's character based on him says that
the return is easy, involving "but the penning / Another recantation, and writing / Two or three bitter books against [the English Protestants]" (3.1.50–53):
thus de Dominis's *A Declaration of the Reasons which Moved M. A. de Dominis to
Depart from the Romish Religion* (1617) was counteracted by the later *M. A. de*

Dominis Declares the Cause of his Returne, out of England (St. Omer, 1623).[12] Thomas Gage was a former Dominican priest who, on the way to a mission in the Philippines stopped in the West Indies, grew dissolute, lost his faith, and, on returning to England in 1637, joined the English church and was rewarded with an ecclesiastical appointment as vicar of Deal.[13] The Spanish Dominican James Salgado converted, and his account was published in 1679.[14] He presents himself as having suffered under the Inquisition, attacks the claim of infallibility of the pope (who is not "an open Antichrist, but a hidden one, under the Cloak of Vicar of Christ"), and describes a conversion process by which he was led to Protestantism through the reading of Scripture. He attacks the Jesuits and, more broadly, criticizes the Roman Catholic doctrines of the sacraments, transubstantiation, and "worshipping of Saints."[15]

English Protestants who converted to Roman Catholicism performed their change of religion in many ways, including fleeing England for a Catholic country: Kent's line in *King Lear,* "Freedom lives hence, and banishment is here" (1.1.181),[16] might have been heard by the Catholics in Shakespeare's audience as a reference to their own plight. Some Catholic converts, such as Walter Montagu,[17] wrote to fathers or parents announcing their new faith, assuming that these missives might have an audience larger than a narrowly familial one. During the Caroline period, the conversion of some of the ladies surrounding the Catholic queen Henrietta Maria had a theatrical visibility (at least for zealous Protestants).[18] Archbishop Laud was furious, for example, at the conversion of Olive Porter's sister Anne, Lady Newport, who was attracted to Roman Catholicism by her sister with the assistance of the papal nuncio, George Con.[19] Some male converts, including former Protestant ministers, entered Continental seminaries and became Catholic priests, returning home to convert their former coreligionists and to "reconcile" Catholics (especially church papists) to the Church of Rome. Formerly Protestant women, such as Catherine Holland,[20] entered nunneries and let their reasons be known by autobiographical and epistolary means. Some individuals wrote conversion narratives explaining their "motives"—a polemical act, as Robert Persons knew when he encouraged Humphrey Leech, Toby Matthew, and Francis Walsingham to compose their accounts.[21] A few vigorously involved themselves in the polemical engagements between Protestantism and Catholicism on a new side. For example, James Anderton's eight-hundred-page *Protestants Apologie for the Roman Church* (secretly printed in England in 1604 and published subsequently at St. Omer under the name "John Brereley" in 1608), a text of a church papist reconciled to Catholicism before his death by his cousin Lawrence Anderton, S.J., was, in the words of Thomas Clancy, "undoubtedly the most important influential work of controversy written in the seventeenth century."[22]

An interesting feature of the phenomenon of conversion is the fact that, whether or not it explicitly attributes human change to divine agency, it religiously and politically enacts human choice.[23] Although no European country, except perhaps the United Provinces,[24] tolerated religious diversity, in effect, converts acted as though they had the freedom to choose among a recognized set of institutional options. The state, while mandating one form of religious practice, advertised the acts of converts to its official religion as a sign of consensual validation of its authority. Hence it had an interest in publicizing their change of religion. Catholic converts, however, remained a problem, especially when they were from prominent families (as in the cases of Dorothy Shirley, Elizabeth Cary, and Ann Hyde)[25] or were former Protestant clergymen or academics, for their defections could not be kept secret or disregarded as the product of ignorant superstition, so the government and the English church worked hard to recover them.

William Alabaster

William Alabaster, a Cambridge minister, is an interesting example of someone who exercised his independent judgment and will in converting to Catholicism. He was a prominent academic whom the English authorities, after his conversion, pressured strongly to reconform. He wrote a narrative of his conversion process (nominally addressed to a sympathetic friend),[26] but then, after conflict with Roman Catholic authorities over his writings, he rejoined the English church and later received ecclesiastical preferment. He started his career as a zealous anti-Catholic, composing sections of a Latin epic poem, *Elisaeis,* a work celebrating Queen Elizabeth and the English Protestant church and attacking Roman Catholicism as England's Satanic enemy.[27] In 1597 he was moved towards conversion by his encounter with the (ex-Jesuit) priest Thomas Wright,[28] a journey towards Catholicism that he detailed in his argumentatively charged narrative.[29] As Alabaster describes his conversion, it was driven by both rational, critical impulses and emotional and devotional motives—

not only by his extensive reading in theology and religious controversy but also by his inclination towards Catholic practices or devotional modes as well as his openness to extrarational forms of understanding.

Alabaster's initial reading in both theology and controversial literature became systematic when he was appointed catechist at Trinity College. His encounter with Catholic texts led him to discover, he says, the falseness of typical Protestant objections to and characterizations of Catholicism. He was led to religious doubt and then to indifference, the latter portrayed as a "most vaine and perilous" (112) stance. He says: "[I found in Catholic texts] reasons so strong and evident in diverse pointes, that I was forced to defend them, and ther opinions against Calvin and our own men in many Controversies at least in some 8 or 10, which I dyd in the hearing of all the College professing ingenuously that I could not aunswere the papistes argumentes, nor any other as I thought" (113).

The next period of his reading was generated by what he presents as a providential encounter (115) with a Catholic text he found in Thomas Wright's chamber, William Rainolds's defense of the Catholic translation of the New Testament.[30] After taking the volume away with him, he read only a quarter of an hour before "those squames [scales] that fell from St Paules bodylye eyes" (118) fell from his. He writes:

> [S]o was I lightned upon the suddene, feeling my selfe so wonderfully and sensybly chaunged both in judgment and affection as I remained astonished at my trewe state. I fownde my minde wholie and perfectly Catholic in an instante, and so to be persuaded of all and everie poynt of Catholique religion together, as I beleved them all most undoubtedly and every point and parcell thereof, though I knew not the reasons of all, nor any perticuler resolution in any other question of controversie, for I saw most evidently in my inward judgment that all were trewe, and nothing could be false which the Catholique Roman Churche dyd propose to be beleeved. And feeling this in my selfe uppon the suddene with such inward light or evidens as I cold not contradict and with such force of affection as I cold not resist, I lept up from the place where I satt, and said to myself, now I am a Catholique, and then fell down upon my knees and thanked God most hartely humbly and effecteously for so rare a benefitt. (118)

He has been prepared for his leap of faith by his previous reading, study, and contemplation, but it seems sudden and beyond the framework of rational discourse and argument.

The most familiar model of conversion by way of reading a powerful text, of course, is that of St. Augustine—a writer appropriated in the post-Reformation world by both Catholics and Protestants. Augustine's *Confessions* offers the most influential example of the transformative quality of a chance encounter with a text in the chapter in which this church father deals with his own moment of conversion. He had heard how one Pontitianus came across a book on the life of St. Anthony and "was changed inwardly . . . and his mind stripped of the world."[31] Although Augustine had been reading St. Paul's epistles already, his powerful encounter with Scripture at the moment of his conversion came by way of the accident of hearing some children chant, "Take up and read" ("Tolle, lege"), whereupon he opened Scripture and, in the manner of random textual divination, happened upon a passage in St. Paul he immediately applied to his own situation: "*Not in rioting and drunkenness, not in chambering and wantonness, not in strife and envying: but put ye on the Lord Jesus Christ, and make not provision for the flesh*" (Rom. 13.13)—a passage his friend continued to read to drive the point of conversion home, "*him that is weak in the faith, receive.*" Augustine frames this experience with a providential interpretation, drawing an analogy to the experience of St. Anthony, whose own oracular use of Scripture had to do with overhearing a passage from the Gospel read that he then took to heart: "*Go, sell all that thou hast, and give to the poor, and thou shalt have treasure in heaven, and come and follow me*" (Matt. 19.21).[32]

Having committed himself to Catholicism, Alabaster prays to God to give him at least six months of study to prepare to do battle with anticipated Protestant adversaries and authorities (121). After returning to Cambridge and breaking off his engagement (to the consternation of family and friends and against his attraction to the woman he had courted for five years), he spent some 22 or 23 pounds on Catholic books and undertook intense study.

Whereas he acted with academic scholarly rigor both before and after his conversion to deal with matters controverted between the two churches, reading deeply in the literature on both sides and arming himself for disputation and "conferences" with Protestant adversaries, when it came to explaining the crucial turn of mind and will, he portrayed his change as, essentially, extra-rational, coming from God as a sudden enlightenment. He defends this experience as genuine divine illumination and authentic experience of faith, but, later on, he denigrates comparable Protestant claims to the same kind of experience as merely a matter of "each mans fancy and particular Imagination" (147). He plays the skeptical rationalist when he looks at Protestant claims. In a book he composed during his period of hiding after his escape from confinement, he asserts, for example, "Protestants have no Divinitie at all and . . . the Divinitie they teach is no theological science, for that it lacketh the principalls, but only consisteth of conjecturall opinions" (160). That is, Protestant theology is not systematic. Nevertheless, he critiques the merely rational approach to religion when he valorizes his own devotional fervor and insights:

> My meditations whiles I was in heresie, upon the pious and devout places of the gospell and namely on the passion of Christ, were mere speculations without tendernes of compassion or desire of imitation, whereof I fownd all the contrarie as soone as I was Catholique: my often receaving of the protestantes communion wrought no effect at all in me for bettering of my life, nor my preparation thertow ever brought forth one dropp of teares, or new desyers of perfection or of punnishing my flesh, of all w[hi]ch I experienced the contrary by receaving the blessed sacrament in the Catholicque Church and by the preparation of contricion and confession to the same, whose devine force and vertue I did so evidently feele, and namely the vertewe of the keies of gods Church by my gostly fathers absolution, as when I first received the same, I seemed evidently to fele my harte and sowle disburdened of an infinite weight and so lightened and comforted as no tounge cane express the same. (130)

Treating the change of religion as both intellectual and emotional liberation, he uses language that echoes some of the terms of baroque Catholic devotion, anticipating aesthetic features that later marked the poetry of Richard Crashaw:

> [S]o soone as I was a Catholique, I felt such illustrations and illuminations of mynde, such joye, such content, such abundance of teares such tender devotions, such flames of ardent love towardes Christ and towardes all Christen people of the world for his sake; such earnest desier of suffering for him, and to be partaker of his cross, such hatred of synne

such resolution to avoyde it, such a greef and contrition for that was past, such thirst of fastinge, prayer, punnishing of my body doing pennance and satisfaction, such aversion from vaine pleasures, such contempt of the world and all that is in it, as before I had never tasted of in protestantes religion, but rather the contrary, and therfore if these effects be fruites of the spirite of god, that spirite must needes be in the Catholique Doctrine, and the contrarie in the protestantes. (130–31)

Alabaster's conversion resulted in the composition of religious sonnets in the midst of a period in which amorous sonnet sequences were the vogue. Like Robert Southwell,[33] he knew he was swimming against the literary current in penning his religious verse in the 1590s—as did Thomas Lodge, when, after his conversion, he composed his prose devotional work, *Prosopopeia, Containing the Teares of the holy, blessed, and sanctified Marie, the Mother of God* (1596), in which he bade farewell to his earlier amorous writing, "the leprosie of my lewd lines."[34] Conversion, then, in Alabaster's and Lodge's, and Henry Constable's[35] cases, meant a shift in literary priorities. Alabaster's poems have a Catholic devotional as well as polemical character. For example, the fifth sonnet distinguishes the "deaths of heretics"[36] celebrated by John Foxe in his *Book of Martyrs* from what Alabaster regards as true Christian martyrdom. Sonnet 7 celebrates the sufferings of persecuted English Catholics, and Sonnet 8 condemns those who accommodated themselves to the state religion. Sonnet 9 criticizes "damned Luther, swollen with hellish pride" (9.5). In a run of sonnets dealing specifically with his conversion (Sonnets 46–52), Alabaster dramatizes his sacrifice of "dearness, affection / Friends, fortune, pleasure, fame, hope, life" (47.6–7) and the dangers he faced, "Want, prison, torment, death, shame" (47.8). He celebrates a kind of religious masochism as he calls for powerful divine action:

> O strike my heart with lightning from above,
> That from one wound both fire and blood may spring,
> Fire to transelement my soul to love,
> And blood as oil to keep the fire burning,
> That fire may draw forth blood, blood extend fire,
> Desire possession, possession desire.
>
> (48.9–14)

In an astounding poem to his former fiancée, he tries to persuade her to convert to Catholicism, portraying the act as a return to a true mother:

> Let us upon our mother's bosom rest,
> Our Mother Church, from whose undried breast
> The fairies after baptism did us steal,
> And starved us with their enchanted bread.
> Our mother of Christ's treasure hath the seal,
> And with sweet junkets doth her table spread.
>
> (49.9–14)

Clearly the poems connect directly with the devotional and polemical themes of the conversion narrative.[37]

Alabaster describes the process by which his private devotions were socialized. He explains that he gave the verse to others to stir them to devotion, as he tried to proselytize his family, relatives, and friends: "thes verses and sonnetes, I made not only for my owne solace, and conforte, but to stir up others also that sold reed them to soew estimation of that which I felt in my self, for which cause my desier was so extreme ardent to imparte this my happiness with others that I felt in me the trew force of that St Dionysius Ariopagita saith, *bonum est sui diffusivum,* the nature of goodness is to spredd itself to many" (123). He apparently effected the conversion to Catholicism of several members of his family at this time.[38]

Without priestly guidance or communal Catholic support, Alabaster improvised a regimen of asceticism and devotional practices that included performing his new spiritual identity before a university audience, which he left puzzled and worried about his welfare. His devotional behavior took a decidedly baroque Catholic turn: "[D]evotions . . . came upon me with such force and abundance of teares as I could not tell oftentymes what to do, for it seemed that my hart was like to breake for joye, and having no spirituall man to guyde me, nor tried Catholique nere me to instruct me in thes begynninges I was utterly at the ende of my witts, how to behave my self in this newe world, and in the visitation of thes unacquainted guestes" (121–22).[39] When he added physical mortifications to his devotions, such as fasting and sleeping on the floor, he writes: "All the College wondred at me, and afterwards some begane to discurse that I was distracted and tended to madnes" (122).

One of the experiences or circumstances that moved Alabaster towards Catholicism was his cultural encounter with Mediterranean Catholicism during his service to the earl of Essex on the Cadiz expedition. He says that, impressed by the austere Christian way of life of the religious he saw in Cadiz, he concluded: "The protestantes [religion] seemed swete, by [the f]acility of salvation by only faith and belefe; and the Catholic hard and intollerable by the burden of good woorkes and keeping the Commandements" (105). After his escape from prison to the Continent, his arrival in Catholic countries is portrayed as both a cultural liberation and an experiential proof of Catholicism's universality and of Protestantism's factionalism and parochialism:

> I came over the sea and tooke by Journy by fraunce, flaunders Germany and Italy towardes Rome, and wonderfull was the change which I seemed to have made by cominge owt of Ingland, to witt from a little Iland and corner of the world into the maine contenent of Europe, wher the largnes of Cownrtries, the variety of people, the diversity of tonges, the aboundance of Citties, townes and Provinces, and a thowsand thinges more did greatly enlarge the borders of my harte from that straightnes which at home [I had] felt in myself, yet nothing more or so much as the uniformity and universalityre of Catholique Religion, which endured with us from Callis to Rome about a thowsand miles except some odd Cittie or tow uppon the way, wher notwithstanding the profession of protestancy is farr different from that of England. But the Catholique profession I fownd all one; both in language, forme of service, number of Sacramentes Ecclesiasticall government, and pointes of beleefe in all which the Protestantes of different Cowntries do differ and jangle infinitely amonge themselfs no one agreeing either the other in all pointes, and herby I came to see and consider indeed what was trewly *Catholicum*, to witt, universall generall, uniform agreeing and lyke to it self everywher, and what was *hereticum*, that is choosing and appropriating to them selves which every towne and Cittie fancieth most. (163)

He views England as parochial and provincial and Catholicism's transnational reach as a sign of the "universalitye" of the true church. At this point in his life internationalism trumps nationalism.

On the Continent, Alabaster responded to the material plenitude of Catholic ceremony and religious practices:

> The piety also of Catholique people every wher and ther liffe and actions the frequenting of Churches and sermons ther often communion uppon all holy daies in great abowndance ther adorning ther churches, ther precessions ther pil[grimag]es, ther doing of penance ther large [almes] ther many sodalities for setting forward and advauncing all manner of pious workes. . . was a matter of wonderfull consolation, and edification, and made exceeding contemptable unto me the barren bare profession of owr Englishe poore Protestanticall religion at home. (163–64)

He admired the "holy bodies and reliques" and the "monuments of owr Christian Religion" (165) he saw in Rome. Leaning already in a Catholic direction before his conversion, Alabaster was moved "frequently to prayer . . . especially in reverence and love towards the saints" and inclined to repent his sins by means of "bodily penance" (106). His natural "inclination to give alms" (106) was inhibited only by the Protestant doctrinal denigration of good works and his desire for fasting frustrated both by his stomach and by the Protestant aversion to such a practice. Before he left Cambridge he had delivered a Good Friday sermon, as he says,

> with much more fervour and feeling of Devotion, and with a greater tendernes of harte towardes Christes Crosse and Passion, then it seemed to the hearers that the protestantes were wont to feele or utter; or ther spirit abyde; yet can I not tell nor distinguish now, wherof this motion preceeded in me at that tyme; except it were some secrett disposition of our sweet Saviour, without my knowledge and will towardes that which soone after his heavenly majestie was to woorke in me which I am the sooner induced to beleve, for that at this very tyme, I begane to have certayne sweet visions or apprehensions in my sleepe as though I had seene owr Saviour casting down fruite from a tree, which never before had hapned to me. (114)

He was in the process of religious and cultural alienation from Protestant Englishness.

Despite his emphasis on the emotional and devotional aspects of his conversion, Alabaster's account subordinates its autobiographical material to its polemical content, highlighting the series of encounters and conferences he had with Protestant adversaries who tried to reclaim him for the English church, mostly while he was in the custody of the bishop of London or in prison.[40] It thus reproduces the form of the "true report," used to convey a biased account of Protestant-Catholic debate — for example, the Protestant and Catholic presentations of Edmund Campion's famous Tower "conferences."[41] The model is that of the intellectual and spiritual combat for truth, the kind of confessional conflict Spenser allegorized repeatedly in *The Faerie Queene* in terms of chivalric combat. Alabaster's champion is Campion, and he seems to be imitating his example not only in his "brag" that he could face any Protestant adversary in debate and his offer of "sixty or eightie reasons" (150) for Catholicism he wished his antagonists to attempt to disprove (a number considerably exceeding Campion's *Rationes Decem* [1581]) but also in his thirst for suffering and martyrdom. Responding to Campion's example and that of other celebrated Catholic martyrs, Alabaster fantasized what would happen after his revelation of his Catholicism to the authorities:

> [I wish] to speake with the protestantes and dispute for the Catholique faith; which I was resolved to defend, even unto death itself[,] . . . to be called before the commission or the Councell, or the Queene herself, or to be arrayned for denying of the supremacy[,] . . . to holde upp my hand at the barre, and to be tried for my life or to be thrust into some darke dungeon with as many chaines as I could beare. . . . I devised what sonnetts and love devices I would make to Christ, about my chaines and irons and what woordes I would speake when I should be carying to the racke, and how I would carye my countenance upon the racke, and what I would speake all the way that I should be dragged upon the hurdell: but amonge all one thing which I thought of oftenest and found exceeding joye thinking theron, was that I purposed with myself when I should stand uppon the ladder with the halter abowt my neck and see the fyer burninge to receave my bowels, and the hangman redye to open my breast and to pull forth my heart, that then I would make an earnest suite to Toplife the preest . . . to grante me one suite before my death. Which should be this, That because I had suffered so little for Christes sake, whoe suffered so much for myne, and was now to dye and make an end of all sufferinges, that he wold shew me so much favor as not to lett me hange any tyme at all, which some tymes they use to do, but to cutt me downe as soone as might bee that I might have suffitient vigour

of cense both to feele first the paine of the rope and much more after-
warde the smarte of the knyfe that should unlace me. (120)

This agitated religious fantasizing, no doubt stimulated by the conventions of
Catholic martyrdom accounts, stands in sharp contrast to the relentlessly rational argumentation of most of the rest of Alabaster's text.

At the end of his long study of religious controversy, Alabaster finally
determines to write a manuscript tract of his "Seven Motives" to the earl of
Essex to persuade his patron also to become a Catholic: "I sent some of my
said reasons to London to be seene by a freende, who impartinge them to
another withowt my knowledge or consent they passed from hand to hand
until they came to the Cowncells knowledge, and therupon came downe
order to Cambridge for my apprehension" (124).[42] Just before Alabaster was
arrested, he was readying himself to preach a sermon at Trinity defending
his new beliefs. Dr. Nevel, the master of his college, reacted strongly to Alabaster's declaration of conversion, beating himself on the breast and weeping (132), then putting Alabaster in confinement in the beadle's house, where,
Alabaster says, "[I felt] unspeakable comfort" because God was "diligent and
mercyfull . . . in visiting me continually with inward joyes and illustrations
of minde" (132–33). His desire for disputation with other scholars at the university was frustrated, and he was moved to London to the custody of Richard Bancroft, bishop of London, so as to undergo a complex process of conferences with bishops, learned Protestant ministers, and renegade Catholic
priests such as Christopher Perkins and Ralph Ithell that was intended to win
him back to the English church.[43]

Aware of Alabaster's relationship with Essex, the authorities treated
him relatively gently. Repeatedly Alabaster's attempts to dispute points of religion were thwarted. He wrote a letter to Essex explaining that the bishops
were afraid of debate, about which he wrote:

[M]y Lord . . . imparted the matter to others at the Court, wherof there
grewe very much talke among the Courteours and much musing at such
an offer, and condemning of the dastardy of the Bishops so that it came
unto the Queenes eares who took it very yvell also, that ther Bishopes
should shewe themselves so fearefull and weake and spake with angry
wordes as seemed to disgrace the whole rank of them present at the

Parlement, wher upon woord was brought to the Bishopes, what wordes the Queene had used against them, threatening them that shee would turne them all forth of ther Bishoprickes if they did not aunwer me, with which mesure they being nettled, sent me paper & inke but bookes could I not obtaine. . . . I wrote downe towarde the number of seaven or eight score of reasons. (150–51)

He then circulated the document among Catholics "over all Ingland" (152), along with his transcription of his meeting with a large group of secular and ecclesiastical authorities before whom he defended his religious change. After further attempts through conferences to persuade him to change his mind, Alabaster suggests they deliberately allowed him to escape confinement: "[I]t seemed to me that themselvese desired to be ridd of me" (158). After some months in hiding (with the Jesuit John Gerard),[44] he fled to the Continent.

Alabaster's account rests on a basic contradiction: on the one hand, he portrays the conversion itself as a suprarational or intuitive leap of understanding that occurred while he was reading Rainolds's book; on the other hand, as a scholar and as one who surveyed the body of Catholic and Protestant controversial literature, he presents himself as a rationalist able to trap his adversaries in logical inconsistencies and absurdities.[45] Although Alabaster criticizes Protestant claims of receiving faith by divine inspiration, in his conference-dispute with Lancelot Andrewes, this is exactly what he portrays in his own conversion experience. He commends Catholic devotion, during which he repeatedly experiences strong feeling leading to the profuse shedding of tears but at the same time dramatizes his cool rationality in debates in which his adversaries sometimes lose emotional control. During Alabaster's fifth conference with various authorities, his argument with the bishop of London became heated: "[M]y Lord of London was so moved that he not only prayed to God to confound or convert all Papistes, but said farther that a little thing would make hym to strike me, I aunswered out of St Paul that a B[ishop] must be no striker he said that though he did not him selfe he might commaunde it to be donn (this was a Protestanticall exposition of scripture)" (149).[46]

One of the odd things about Alabaster's story is how little the recusant community figures in it. There are occasional references to sympathetic Catholic friends and visitors, and, of course, Alabaster would not have wished to endanger specific individuals by naming names, but one still gets the sense that he found pleasure in going it alone, in immersing himself in the role of the solitary fighter for truth, not only willing to suffer and die for his new faith but also taking comfort and pleasure in any pain he might suffer. He is an example of the romantic religious masochist, someone at the extreme, presenting himself as more courageous than most of his coreligionists.

Like Ben Jonson, however, Alabaster eventually rejoined the English church. Having come into conflict with Robert Persons and having had his study of the Book of Revelation declared heretical (it was put on the Index by the Inquisition in 1610),[47] he returned finally to England with the intention of conforming. He did not, however, make his religious change official until 1614, when he renounced Catholicism before the synod at Westminster. He was restored to his functions as an Anglican minister, given a doctor of divinity degree at Cambridge, and granted ecclesiastical preferment, functioning, by 1618, as a royal chaplain.[48] Too eccentric theologically for both Catholic and Protestant authorities, he was, Michael O'Connell notes, "suspected of Catholic opinions, and no less than Oliver Cromwell, in his first parliamentary speech, mentioned what he called the 'flat popery' of a sermon preached by Alabaster in 1617."[49] He continued to vacillate religiously and to write somewhat eccentric religious works.[50] He died in 1640 on the eve of the English Civil Wars.

Francis Walsingham

Francis Walsingham, namesake and kinsman of Queen Elizabeth's Catholic-hating secretary of state,[51] performed his conversion in stages. First he tried to approach King James directly at Greenwich on Good Friday, 1604, to pass on to him his annotated copy of a Catholic book by which he was strongly moved, Robert Persons's *A Defence of the Censure, gyven upon two bookes of William Charke and Meredith Hamner Mynysters, whiche they Wrote against M. Edmond Campian* (1582), to which he added his own comments, or "Memoriall" (31). This act signaled his desire to see full, open religious debate between Catholics and Protestants, but it provoked a strongly negative response from the king— "he spake aloud & with a great Oath (as was reported) smiting with his hand, said: this is some Papist" (31)—who commanded that Walsingham be brought to him directly, after which the young man was handed over to ecclesiastical authorities to have his doubts settled by them. Next Walsingham performed his conversion, as Alabaster had, by standing his ground in many conferences with the archbishop of Canterbury and other Protestant persuaders. Finally, after being received into the Catholic church and becoming a Jesuit, he formally announced his change of religion to King James and to all his countrymen by publishing a 512-page tract (dedicated to the king), *A Search Made into Matters of Religion* (1609), a work that foregrounds the polemical engagement of English Catholics and Protestants from the time of Elizabeth's accession to the early Jacobean period. Like Alabaster, Walsingham highlights his religious conferences with the archbishop of Canterbury and other Anglican apologists and leaders, but he uses these inconclusive interviews as a lead-in to a period of extended study of books of religious controversy written on both sides of the polemical divide. He presents himself as troubled and in doubt, so that his "search" for truth by means of reading and study somewhat resembles that of John Donne as well, who, in declaring his change of religion in *Pseudo-Martyr* (1610) by writing on King James's side in the post–Gunpowder Plot Oath of Allegiance controversy, informed his readers that he did not switch churches until he had "survayed and digested the whole body of Divinity, controverted betweene ours and the Romane Church."[52] The Jesuit Walsingham not only performed a similar survey, but he provided for his Catholic and Protestant readers a mass of data and argument intended to demonstrate the intellectual inadequacies and falsifications of Protestant polemicists and the justness of Catholic defenses against them. The personal, emotional, and devotional aspects of his journey from Protestantism to Catholicism are lost in the argumentative and expository prose.[53]

In the course of his many conferences with Protestant apologists, Walsingham experienced doubts and uncertainty, in which state he resolved, as he says, "neither to turne to the right hand, nor to the left, by myne owne will, which peradventure might be drawne to the one, or to the other by feare of trouble, affection of frends, or hope of preferments, with other temporal inducements" (74). Instead:

> [I] put on as indifferent a mynd, as possibly I could towards both Catholicke & Protestant Religion, to the end, that weighting, and considering with most diligent and serious ponderation, and advisement the force and strength of such arguments and indicements, as should eyther move me to follow the one, or neglect the other, I might resolutely imbrace that

fayth and constantly professe that religion, which Almighty God should propose to me, for the only true way to eternall lyfe. (74)

In this intellectually open attitude, he prays for divine action to effect the crucial (Augustinian) turning of his will:

> O Lord Jesus Christ . . . refresh my wearied soule, inlighten me with the knowledge of thy truth. . . . Turne thou me, O Lord, unto thee, and then shall I be truly converted: my hart is ready, O Lord, unto thee, and then what simplicity and singlenes of mynd thou best knowest, I know it not: Create in me, O my God, a cleane hart, and renew a right spirit within me: give me the comfort of thy saving health, and confirme and strengthen me in the same by thy holy spirit: then shall I teach sinners thy wayes, & the ungodly shalbe converted unto thee. (75)

In his own rhetorically skillful, polemical conversion account, Walsingham thus dramatizes the final preconversion moment as one in which there is a smooth process from doubt to intellectual impartiality to divine enlightenment and movement of the will to proselytizing others.

Walsingham moves from a narrative of his own reading in theological and polemical literature to a historical survey of religious controversy. After the many chapters dealing with the latter, he dramatizes his meeting with an old Catholic man who advises him concerning his continuing doubts and perplexities. Since Walsingham expresses his intention to continue his reading in polemical literature, the old man gives him some advice about how to proceed: (1) Read "sincerely, and in conscience, making God himselfe the Judge, and proposing for that end the only knowledge and finding out of this truth for your direction and instruction, and his glory and service. . . . [B]e humble, devout, indifferent, pray much, and be earnest with God to inlighten you in this behalfe" (475); (2) "[A]pprehend well & briefly the true state of the Question, not believing one side only, but searching out, what each side sayth and holdeth therin; for that in this point above others, you shall find fraud oftentimes to be used by your Protestant writers of divers sortes and sectes, every one proposing the state of the Question advantageously, as himselfe would have the Reader to understand it, and not as his adversary doth hold it indeed" (476);[54] (3) "[W]hen you have the true state of the Question, you must be very careful to hold the same continually in your mind, making often reflection & re-course therunto, about the discourses which you shall read in your Author, con-sidering well & attentively whether they be to the purpose in hand, and do lev-ell right at the marke proposed, or no, or runne aside to impertinent matters, as often you shall find they do, and fill up leaves with things that are farre from the principall substance of the Question" (477); (4) "[P]onder well the weight of all such arguments, as are alledged" (477–78).[55]

In effect, Walsingham is offering his reader a set of prescriptions for criti-cal reading of religious polemic. But as this chapter develops, it becomes clear that potentially endless reading in controversy is not the way to settle doubts but to add to them. The old man advises Walsingham, instead, to prefer the authority of a church that preserves the wisdom of all the great theologians and the apostolic succession to the authority of his own inadequate intelligence. In fact, this is the hub of the Catholic/Protestant disagreement in his expla-nation: Protestants prefer their individual judgment; Catholics, the authority of the church. In light of this and of Walsingham's ceasing to read contem-porary religious controversy, the work he is writing takes the form of a kind of self-consuming artifact: the hundreds of pages of polemical engagement are ultimately an experience of frustration, the record of a failed attempt to settle doubts and resolve perplexities, useful only, perhaps, as the exposure of Protes-tant misrepresentation and faulty argumentation. The old man rejects the read-ing of proliferating religious controversy as the way to truth or salvation—especially since most people are ill equipped to do so:

> [S]ome cannot understand, some cannot buy books, some have no lea-sure, some cannot judge of what they read, and must less resolve doubts that may arise theron; and yet must all have meanes to be saved. But by the other way of following the visible Church, and knowne Pastours therof, all men may be directed both learned and unlearned, rich and poore, yong and old, idle and occupied. Wherin is seene Allmighty God his holy providence and provision for all, leaving no man or woman with-out sufficient meanes of direction for their salvation, if they will accept thereof, and use the same. (485)

Because wandering in the fields of controversy will do little good at this point ("it will be impossible for you," the old man observes, "to quiet & settle your judgment without some more certaine rule, then reading at randome" [481]),

Walsingham is advised to concentrate on reading St. Augustine, the church father central to both Protestant and Catholic thinking. The old man particularly points him to passages of St. Augustine's *Confessions* (489).

In the *Confessions* Augustine deals with his own journey from Manichaeanism to Christianity, offering a model of conversion that underlies many of the narratives from the early modern period: he portrays conversion as a turning towards God and a turning away from the world and its pleasures (a rejection of *cupiditas* for *caritas*), but he also emphasizes the distinction between the search for intellectual certainty (which is doomed to fail) and the turning of the will towards God and the openness to the extrarational understanding that accompanies faith.[56] As Questier notes, Catholics and evangelical Protestants both chose the will, rather than the intellect, as the locus of conversion— though the different understandings of the theology of grace and of human agency were crucial:

> Even if the will may be said to cooperate with grace after the initial conversion this is not of its own volition. Grace remains in control though in different forms (preventing, working and co-working grace).
>
> But an equally powerful patristic and subsequent tradition stressed a relative freedom of the will assisted by grace and this dictated a different perception of conversion. For Catholics (and some Protestants who did not sympathise with a severe Reformed view of grace and sin), the elements of conversion which Reformed Protestants regarded as efficacious in the first moment of grace extended into the process which is frequently described as sanctifiction (when the will actively cooperates with grace after their initial encounter).[57]

It is significant that immediately preceding the account of his actual conversion experience in Book 8 of the *Confessions,* Augustine has a long meditation on the nature of the will. John Calvin discusses the relation of the will to conversion in the third chapter of the second book of his *Institutes of the Christian Religion.*[58] In Catholic accounts, the transformation of the will is often connected to the experience of the strong feelings associated with Catholic devotion.

Walsingham uses Augustine (along with Tertullian) to criticize the heresies of his own times and to settle all interdenominational arguments and prove the validity of those Catholic beliefs disputed by Protestants, such as papal supremacy and justification by both faith and works:

And I passe over heere many other poynts of controversie which I read very largely disputed by *S. Augustine,* as about the Sacraments of the new law, their nature and number, the custome of the Church in baptizing infants, of the ancient Ceremonies of Baptisme, the signe of the Crosse, Exorcisme, Exsufflations, thrice dipping in the water. And the like of the Sacrament of Confirmation & Chrisme: of the Eucharist and Reall Presence very largely: of the externall Sacrifice of the Masse, how it was held for propitiatory for the quicke and dead in *S. Augustins* time, and offered also specially for the dead, and in the memory and honour of Saints, though not unto Saints, but only to God, that it was held for an Apostolicall tradition in *S. Augustins* time, to offer wine in the Sacrifice mingled with water: that the said Sacrifice was to be offred upon Altars, and only by them that were fasting, and other like points. (493–94)

He thus quite self-consciously reappropriates for Catholicism the favorite church father of Protestant reformers.

Walsingham, however, loses his desire to read controversial literature, finding the need to appeal to an authority larger than that of his own "wit," "the sense of the Church" (491). He says he told the old man in whom he confided:

I was ready to follow his advise, & resolve my selfe upon the direction of the Church according to S. Aug. counsell. . . . [H]e did assure me notwithstanding, that I should not leese the freedome of my own judgement in subjecting it to the Church, but rather perfect the same. For that Catholicke men (said he) do allow as great a latitude unto their reason and discourse as Protestants can do, though for the conclusion they have farre greater helps then the other to make it well, which is the direction of the said Church: which direction besides the multitude of almost infinite learned men, that are of that Church, being priviledged by the most certaine assistance of Gods holy spirit . . . is a happy restraint, if it be a restraint. (495)

He reaches a kind of paradoxical conclusion: obedience to the church is intellectual freedom. At this point he concludes that he is a Catholic and is directed to the sacrament of penance and to a spiritual retreat. The whole conversion account culminates with the experience of performing the Jesuit spiritual exercises.[59]

In assessing his whole conversion experience, Walsingham concludes "that both reason and Religion, prudence, and all true piety doth require, that the everlasting salvation of our soules should be preferred before all other respects humane whatsoever: which is the true and sincere cause of this my resolution" (512). Having worried earlier in the account about temporal considerations, he here addresses a potentially wavering Catholic audience in a way designed to strengthen their faith and determination, hence their recusancy.

One of the reasons Walsingham foregrounded religious controversy in his *Search* is that he hoped, as he did when he approached James in his period of religious wavering, to persuade the king to sanction religious debate between Protestants and Catholics—a tempting prospect for a king who was fond of intellectual disputation. Although this was a practical impossibility at the start of the Jacobean era, when the Hampton Court Conference (1604) was designed to reconcile differences among Protestants so that the reign could begin with some religious stability in the established church, in the later years of James's rule such religious debate could be sanctioned in a semipublic venue. When the duke of Buckingham's mother was inclining to Catholicism, James agreed to a series of three disputations between the Jesuits John Percy ("Fisher the Jesuit") and John Sweet and their Protestant adversaries, Francis White, William Laud, and, in the second (least publicized) meeting, the king himself. These events were broadcast in print for polemical purposes by each side, the duchess of Buckingham meanwhile converting to Roman Catholicism.[60] Campion, Walsingham, Percy, and other Jesuits consistently called for such confrontations, confident of their intellectual, rhetorical, and doctrinal superiority. Walsingham's conversion account–cum–polemical performance made of the English government's usual avoidance of public debate on matters of religion both a sign of Protestantism's doctrinal unsoundness and an indication that those who conformed to England's state religion were not entirely comfortable with their religious commitment.

Sir Toby Matthew

One of the most noticeable conversions of the period was that of Sir Toby Matthew, son of the bishop of Durham, who embarrassed his father not only by becoming a Catholic but also by entering the Jesuit order.[61] Matthew functioned socially and politically within the Jacobean and Caroline establishments with a

remarkable degree of freedom and had powerful and prominent friends, such
as John Donne,[62] Francis Bacon, and the earls of Salisbury, Carlisle, Buckingham, Portland, and Strafford, as well as Queen Henrietta Maria. He was especially close to Bacon, for whom he served as an intellectual sounding board.
Matthew translated the *Essays* and *De Sapientia Veterum* into Italian (the former,
however, was subsequently placed on the Index by the Inquisition). He was offered the hospitality of Bacon's house at crucial times. The two men disagreed
on the subject of religion (which they avoided) but bonded intellectually and
homosocially, if not also homoerotically.

Matthew's is an extraordinary case. Like Richard Crashaw,[63] he embraced
Catholicism in part to define himself against a Protestant father who disap-
proved of his early profligacy and later Catholicism; both of the younger Matthew's parents are portrayed in his writing as unwilling to offer their son love
and support. In the intervals between his political exiles, Matthew was allowed
to function as a courtier and political power player. For example, he worked
to relieve the conditions of English Catholics as he tried to facilitate the Spanish Match for Prince Charles, the latter service for which he was knighted by
King James. Called "littel prittie Tobie Matthew" by Prince Charles,[64] he used
his role as a kind of court fop and affable busybody as a mask to conceal serious religious and political goals.[65]

Matthew converted to Catholicism in Italy in 1606 after conferring in
Rome with Robert Persons. He was ordained by Cardinal Bellarmine in 1614
and became a Jesuit in 1619.[66] He initially composed an account of his conversion in 1611, at the request of Mary Gage (to whom it is addressed), a nun who
was a sister of his longtime companion George Gage,[67] but he made sure a
copy was transcribed and in circulation for self-protective purposes after he
was arrested in the late Caroline period on Archbishop Laud's orders in connection with a fictitious "popish plot."[68] In 1640,[69] when he had this conversion
account retranscribed, he had it signed and authenticated by nine witnesses
and appended another work that set forth twenty-five reasons for his fidelity
to Catholicism, *Posthumus, or The Survivor with Certain Considerations which
Follow.* In it, he anticipates the publication of his conversion account, or at least
its dissemination in manuscript to a wide audience: "[T]he story of my whole
conversion is drawn particularly and exactly by myself; and as, if it ever come
to public view, it will perhaps be the less unpleasing to any reader in regard that
it opens a fair way to many passages of several kinds, so I can and do affirm,

upon my conscience, as in the sight of Almighty God himself, that all the parts of it are most perfectly and precisely true" (146). In effect, Matthew also re-defines the earlier document as both his last will and testament and an apologia for his life as a Catholic convert. The appended work that follows is meant to persuade "A Protestant Soul which is piously affected, and procures to be saved" (156).

The intellectual preparation for Matthew's conversion included his reading of the church fathers, especially St. Augustine, much of this study done in the library of St. Mark's in Florence. After absorbing the defenses of Catholicism found in controversial literature, he felt no need to reread Protestant texts, because, he says, he knew their objections already, but he hesitated before committing to Catholicism, the final step portrayed as taking place only with divine help, coming through "the intercession of the immaculate and ever-blessed Virgin" (50). Having resolved to convert, he stated: "I was delivered from all reluctation of mind" (51). Like Alabaster, Matthew found rational argument insufficient to move the will and effect conversion, but once he converted he was ready for theological disputation with Protestant authorities, facing Richard Bancroft, archbishop of Canterbury, and all the other Protestant persuaders he was forced to confront in the many conferences to which he was subjected after his return to England. He defended his refusal to take the Jacobean Oath of Allegiance not only against the arguments of his Protestant adversaries but also contrary to the imprisoned Catholic archpriest's (ill-considered) approval of the Oath. He also held his own against the mild-mannered Bishop Launcelot Andrewes. After his exile, when he was back in England to try to assist with the negotiations for the Spanish Match, Matthew stood his argumentative ground in his father's house against a formidable group of "eminent clergymen, Archdeacons, Doctors, and Chaplains" (124), whom he challenged to "show . . . some such Church of their religion, as had continued ever since Christ our Lord, and had been derived down to this age" (125). He said he would turn Protestant under the following condition: "if they could show me any such men as believed but even the self same canon of Holy Scripture, and the same number and nature of sacraments, which were received by them at this day" (125). Their response signaled his victory: "they wrung their hands, and . . . their whites of eyes were turned up, and their devout sighs were sent abroad to testify both their wonder and grief that I would utter myself after that manner" (126). After pressing

them further with his challenge, they refused to engage him and avoided
him thereafter.

Before and after his conversion Matthew was a connoisseur, serving at
various times as a broker or buyer of art for the earl of Arundel and others.[70]
His attraction to Catholicism, especially Italian Catholicism, was aesthetic and
cultural, as well as religious. For example, he responded deeply to the litany
to the Virgin sung by boy singers in Neapolitan street processions: "I know
not by what chance, or rather Providence of Almighty God, the tune of that
sweet verse, *Sancta Maria, Ora pro nobis,* came so often in at mine ears, and con-
tented me so much that at length my tongue took it up. . . . [W]hen I found
myself alone, my usual entertainment would be to sing *Sancta Maria, Ora pro
nobis,* in the tune of those babes and sucklings, who showed forth her praise"
(13–14).[71] His viewing of Roman religious antiquities, particularly the catacombs, left a strong positive impression on him: "the sight of those most ancient
crosses, altars, sepulchres, and other marks of the Catholic religion, having been
planted there in the persecution of the primitive Church . . . did strike me with
a kind of reverent awe, and made me absolutely resolve to repress my insolent
discourse against Catholic religion ever after" (22). He responded positively to
the kind, fatherly treatment of him by Cardinal Pinelli, chief of the Congregation of the Inquisition: he emphasizes the cardinal's "civility" and hospitality
(22–24). His sight of a tearfully devout man praying in a side chapel in a church
in Florence moved him deeply, and he registered the difference between an English and Italian sensibility: "it would not be a matter of much ease in England
to find such a person, in such an action as that for substance and circumstance;
whereof, though I saw then but one, yet I daily saw multitudes afterward" (8).
His whole encounter with Italian culture drew him towards Catholicism. He
says, for example, that he was filled with "admiration" (39) for the devotions
and charitable works of virtuous Italian Catholics.

During his banishments and exile from England, Matthew wrote and
translated a number of works, including *The Confessions of the Incomparable
Doctour S. Augustine* (St. Omer, 1620);[72] *The Flaming Heart,* the autobiography
of St. Teresa of Avila; *The Life of Lady Lucy Knatchbull,* founder of the English Benedictine monastery at Ghent;[73] *Charity Mistaken* (n.p., 1630);[74] Francisco Arias's *Treatise of Patience* (1650); and *A Missive of Consolation sent from
Flanders to the Catholics of England* (1647).[75] He also wrote some mediocre religious poetry.[76] Having spent the last part of his career in England at the court

of Henrietta Maria, where his kind of Catholic baroque devotion was culturally naturalized, he fled to the Continent before the religious and political ten-
sions of the early Stuart period erupted into civil war. His conversion and way
of life enacted a cultural alienation from Protestant Englishness and a turning
to a cosmopolitan European Catholic sensibility.

James Wadsworth Sr. and James Wadsworth Jr.

Theological disputation was not necessarily the mode adopted by those who
moved from the Church of England to the Church of Rome or in the opposite direction. The cases of James Wadsworth Sr. and James Wadsworth Jr. are
illustrative.

James Wadsworth Sr. was a staunch anti-Catholic who traveled as chap-
lain to the English ambassador to Spain and converted to Roman Catholicism
while abroad.[77] Ten years after his conversion he published at the Jesuit press at
St. Omer a book announcing his conversion, a primarily devotional work that
avoided both detailed personal narrative and intense polemical engagement:
*The Contrition of a Protestant Preacher, Converted to be a Catholique Scholler.
Conteyning Certayne Meditations upon the Fourth Penitential Psalme, Miserere.
Composed by James Waddesworth, Bachelour of Divinity in the University of Cambridge, & late Parson of Cotton, and of Great Thorneham in the County of Suffolke.
Who went into Spaine with the Kinges Majesties first Embassadour-Legier, as his
Chaplayne: Where by the great Goodnes of Almighty God, he was fully converted
to the Catholique Faith* (1615).[78] In his preface "to his favorable reader: and to
all his loving friendes in Norfolke, Suffolke, London, Norwich, Cambridge, or
elsewhere" (B1), Wadsworth insists, "I have chosen first to exercise my pen in
some poyntes of devotion, before I should be challenged with any disputes of
controversy" (B1r–v), declaring an aversion to polemic (which he nevertheless
cannot finally resist).

Not properly an account of the dynamics of conversion, the *Contrition*
uses a discourse of Catholic devotion to argue, in an indirectly polemical fashion,
for the truth of Catholic doctrine and practice: confessional self-abasement carries a (usually indirect) polemical argument about the falseness of English Protestantism and the truth of the Catholic church.[79] Wadsworth portrays his Protestant past as a life of sin and error from which he has been rescued by God and

a welcoming Catholic church. Only occasionally in the course of his "meditations" does he directly raise issues of contention between Protestantism and Catholicism, though they are major ones: the relationship of faith and good works (73–75), the status of the sacrament of penance (94 ff.), and transubstantiation and the Mass as a valid sacrifice (102–12). He also incorporates features of a Catholic devotional mode repellent to Protestants, for example, the importance of Mary and the saints as mediators and the practice of praying for the dead in Purgatory.[80]

To counter the Protestant argument that Catholics deny God's part in the work of conversion and personal salvation, he states: "[W]e are not able by our selves alone to get out of the Divells slavery, to forsake sinne, nor to alter and amend entirely the course of our lives. . . . [W]e have need of Gods helpe and grace to deliver us; first preventing and stirring us up to have a good will, and afterward allso working with our will to bring our conversion and repentance unto a full worke" (B3v). Within the framework of persuading Christian readers "to practice the examination of your consciences, and the exercise of devout prayer, directing us all unto Contrition, Confession, and Satisfaction" (C2v), he offers a defense of orthodox Catholic devotional and sacramental practices and beliefs. For example, against Protestant criticisms of Catholicism's idealization of virginity and celibacy and supposed denigration of marriage, he states that "no Catholiques ever termed lawfull mariage duely used, to be uncleanes, pollution, & carnall filthynes (as Calvin & others doo sclander us herein, as they use to doo allse almost in all other pointes)" (30).

The personal confession of his own faults portrays his previous life as a Protestant minister as inherently sinful. He prays to God:

> I have dishonored thee, & scandalized men, for I was a publique preacher of the protestantes false Doctrine, wherin peradventure by my meanes some have bene seduced, many hardened, & others offended: I have profaned thy sacred churches sometime dedicated to thy catholique services; and for mine owne body & soule, which should have bene thy spirituall temples, o how have they bene polluted? By errors which I supposed to be truthes, by presumption of knowledge when I was in ignorance, by some vices which I reputed vertues, & by many faults which I neglected. . . . I was a Swynehearde, a protestante minister, feeding my selfe & others with the huskes of heresy . . . in which I coulde never taste of true comforte,

nor obteyne peace unto my conscience. . . . [H]ere I renounce any plea of passed integrity: I disclayme my wonted profession: I lament & detest my errors & my sinnes. (5)

He thus characterizes preaching, which Protestants valued above ecclesiastical ceremonies and rituals, as a pernicious practice, spreading erroneous doctrine. In a passage in which he comes as close as he ever does to describing the process of his conversion to Catholicism, he uses biblical language to portray his rescue from Protestantism as a kind of exorcism: "In the gospell it is said, though wouldest not suffer divells to enter into swyne but with me thou haste cast divells out of a swyne. Doo I debase my selfe to say so? *Beholde* o lorde, *thou lovest truthe.* I knowe no swyne so filthy and so degenerate from his kinde, as I was, being a Protestante, from thy *truthe:* If S. Mary Magdalene had seaven divells of vices; how many had I of heresyes" (48).

Wadsworth occasionally attacks Lutheran and Calvinist beliefs and behavior. For example, he relates two anti-Protestant anecdotes:

[A] dronken Calviniste minister with a foule red nose, bragging against a Catholique, that our Saviour had given him the keyes of heaven, as much as to S. poeter, or to the Pope: surely I doubte it, said the Catholique; rather by your nose, I doo suppose, you have in your custody, the keyes to the buttry. Thus often times arrogant men are confounded in their owne wordes. And so like wise some malitious persecutors of Catholiques have bene intangled in their owne spitefull diligence: as he who being tolde that in such a chamber was a Priest: called the constables & officers to breake open the doores & to enter with haste, where they found his owne daughter in bed with a brother of the Puritanes. (4)

But such satirical swipes at polemical adversaries are infrequent. Though Wadsworth sometimes takes direct issue with particular Protestant doctrines, far more frequently, in the course of his devotional meditations, he lets his idealization of Catholic beliefs and practices serve his argumentative purpose. The work, then, is supposed to attract Protestants to Catholic modes of devotion and to a church for whose sacraments, ceremonies, and beliefs the author expresses great affection.

James Wadsworth Jr. moved in the opposite direction. Born in England but educated in a continental Catholic context, he decided as an adult to return to the land of his birth and facilitated his reincorporation into the English Protestant community by publishing the picaresque, autobiographical *English Spanish Pilgrim* (1629), demonstrating his conversion to English Protestantism as the necessary outcome of his coming-of-age — an act that reversed the religious defection of his father.

Wadsworth's story is generically a captivity narrative,[81] the kind of tale that in the context of anti-Catholic discourse involves the metaphor of Protestant "deliverance"[82] from a Catholic "Babylon." It highlights its author's escape from the institutional clutches of the Jesuits, by whom he was educated. Given the reputation of the Jesuits as the most militant of Catholics and given the notoriety of those converts who left the English church and joined the order (e.g., Edmund Campion, Robert Southwell, and Francis Walsingham), Wadsworth certainly knew that his rejection of Jesuit-inflected Counter-Reformation Catholic culture would send the strongest possible signal of his desire to join the community of conforming English Protestants. As noted earlier, the Jesuits were demonized in English (and French) polemical works, including John Gee's *Foot out of the Snare* (1623), another self-justifying escape narrative,[83] so it is not surprising that Wadsworth should stage his change of religion with reference to what was regarded as this "Hispaniolated" religious order.[84]

Wadsworth's account of his father's conversion plays on the usual Protestant associations of Catholicism (and the Jesuits) with trickery. He portrays his father as religiously assaulted by the Jesuits: "at his first arrivall, the Jesuites held with him a subtle dispute about the Antiquity and the Universality of the Church of Rome, which they make their preface to all seducements, his great opposers being Joseph Creswell & Henry Walpole, two of the most expert polititians of our Nation, that then maintained the state of the triple crowne" (2). After resisting,

the Jesuites perceiving how littel they prevailed used other illusions, stronger than their Arguments, even strange apparitions and miracles, amongst others, the miracle which they pretend to bee true to happen to the eldest sonne of the Lord Wotton at his death, in the City Valladolid where a Crucifix framed him this articulate sound: Now forsake your heresie, or else you are damn'd, whereupon the young Lord and my

Father became Proselites to their jugling Religion. . . . And so my Father leaving the Embassadors house privatly, was conducted forthwith by means of Father Creswell to the university of Salamanca . . . where he was admitted with no little joy to their Church, where he prostrating himselfe on the ground, and the inquisitor putting (as their custome is) his right foote on his head, said with a loud voyce, here I crush the head of heresie. (2–3)

This account treats the "conversion" purely as a result of being duped by Jesuit illusion making, and it also characterizes conversion as not only a breaking of allegiance to a national community (in favor of one presided over by the wearer of the "triple crown") but also an abandonment of family. Wadsworth Sr., however, eventually succeeded in persuading his wife to join him in Spain and in his new religious affiliation, bringing with her their four children, including James Jr., who was only five years old at the time: "[H]aving withstood for five yeeres space all his letters and inticements, with those also of the Jesuites and Prests (But where the husband goes first, the wife commonly followes after, it being the weakenesse of that sexe) [she] was at length seduced by one Kelly a jesuite, who coming for that end with a letter from her husband misled her away, having brought her to sell all she had, carried her forthwith in to Flanders with her four children [before taking her to Spain]" (4).

The young Wadsworth was first educated in Spain, then sent to the new Jesuit school at St. Omer in Flanders in 1618, where he remained for four years. He offers details of life at that school (which was the main preuniversity continental educational institution to which English Catholics sent their sons), including the indoctrination at meals in dissident English Catholic culture: "[O]ne of our side reades the Latin Martyrologe, and other after him the English, which containes the Legend of our English Martyrs, and Traitours together, sometimes two in one day. . . . The students heare out the relation with admiring and Cap in hand to the memory of Champion, Garnet, Thomas Becket, and Moore" (17). He retails the story of a student who resisted this indoctrination and was subjected to theatrically spectacular sadistic retribution:

[A] Gentleman of Yorkeshire by name of Mr Henry Fairefax, sonne to Sr. Thomas Fairefax, who not yeelding to their inchanting allurements, one night being a sleepe in his bed, two Jesuites clad in gorgeous white as they had been Angels, approaching his bed side with two good disciplines [whips] in their hands, the ends of some stucke with wyery prickes, having uncovered him, they did after so savage a manner raze his skinne, that he became for a while sencelesse, speaking unto him in Latine that they were Angels sent from the Virgin to chastise him for some offences by him committed, viz. for resisting the power, and reviling the proceedings of his superiours, exhorting him to that Order by vertue of the testimony given by the Virgin of the holy Order of the Jesuites, which said, they departed, and left the rest so farre astonished that they knew not whether they had been Angels or divells. (20)

When, at seventeen, Fairfax was admitted to the Jesuits, they confessed the trickery but justified it as being "onely done for his good" (21).

Another example of the Jesuits' attempts to seduce someone to their order is the case of William Abinton, whom the Jesuit Francis Wallis tried to convince was destined to be a Jesuit because Wallis had a "divine revelation from St. Ignatius Loiola, that the first Student hee saw going by his doore, he should declare unto him he had chosen him to be one of his apostles, and that without delay he must be for his orders" (21). Abinton, who said he was convinced of the truth of the vision, asked to be allowed a month "to take farewell of his friends in England," but "he no sooner had arrived in his owne Country shores, but he utterly disclaimed their [the Jesuits'] superstitious reveales" (22)—a rejection of Jesuitical Catholicism that Wadsworth himself later makes.

The third case is that of the Oxford-educated Herbert Crafts, who, visiting his father in the town of St. Omer, was steered towards Catholicism by way of doing the Ignatian spiritual exercises and recruited to the Jesuits, against his father's wishes, having been told "that St Ignatius received by divine revelation, that none of his Order should ever bee damned for 200 yeeres terme" (24). Wadsworth boasts that although he also did the spiritual exercises, he was not tricked, and he offers other examples of Jesuit coercion practiced on students who wanted to escape their tyranny—for example, Estenelaus Browne, son and heir of Anthony Browne, brother of Viscount Montague, who after two years at the college of St. Omer forged a letter from his father requesting his return to England but was caught and punished.

Wadsworth then launches a general attack on the Jesuits as "meer Machiavillins, who doe nothing but imploy themselves in matters of State, and insinuate themselves into the secrets of great ones, and giving true intelligence to none, save to the Pope and his Catholic Majesty [the King of Spain], whose sworne vassals they are" (28). "As for their religion," Wadsworth asserts,

> they make it a cloake for their wickednes, being most of them Atheists or very bad Christians; these are they that observe these ten Commandements which follow.
>   1. To seeke riches and wealth.
>   2. To governe the world.
>   3. To reforme the Clergy.
>   4. To be still jocund and merry.
>   5. To drinke white and red wine.
>   6. To correct Texts of Scripture.
>   7. To receive all Tithes.
>   8. To make a slave of their ghostly child.
>   9. To keepe their owne and live on another mans purse.
>   10. To governe their neighbours wife. (28)

Wadsworth ridicules the Jesuits' pedagogical practices, which include, he says, "reading for the most part to their white boyes loose and lascivious Poems" (29). He admits there are holy and honest Jesuits, but they are only used "to colour the courses and the Actions of the more cunning and politicke ones" (30). He mocks Mary Ward's "Jesuitices or wandring Nuns" (30) who have schools on the Continent but whose aim is "to convert their Country" (31). Having been thoroughly disillusioned by the Jesuits, Wadsworth says, "[I] laboured with all possible meanes to get out of their clutche, and, though I promised them to turne Jesuite, yet had I leave to goe to Sivill with their Mission and from thence to Madrid to take leave of my Parents, and so to returne again to them" (31–32).

On the way from St. Omer to Spain with other boys, their ship was captured by pirates, and they were put on another vessel, after the goods were taken. Bound with the other youths for four days, he was then forced to row the galley and exposed to sexual predation: "At midnight, two Moores come downe unto us, & secretly selecting two of the youngest and fairest amongst us, abused their bodies with insatiable lust" (38). After an uprising the captives were put in chains. Once ashore, they were carried to a castle, fattened up like capons, and given to different masters ("Moriscoes" [40]) to be sold as slaves. Wadsworth himself was taken by the captain of the ship (who had been expelled from Spain by Philip III), put to menial tasks, beaten, but then ransomed by a French captain along with other boys before they made a narrow escape to Spain. Wadsworth draws a parallel between the capture and abuse by pirates and the treatment of young students by Jesuits at St. Omer or of English Protestants by the Inquisition. The irony is that the Jesuits supposedly used the story of the boys' journey and rescue as a fund-raising device. After Wadsworth told his father of the Jesuits' doings, however, the elder Wadsworth "grew into dislike with the Jesuites" (46).

The younger Wadsworth was in Madrid in 1623 when Prince Charles and the duke of Buckingham arrived to arrange the Spanish Match, his father having served as the Infanta's English tutor and Wadsworth himself befriending several Englishmen: Francis Browne (Viscount Montague's son and heir), Henry Barty (Lord Linsey's brother), and Anthony Inglefield (Browne's cousin). Once the Jesuits learned their pupil had no intention of returning to them, they "sought by all meanes they could to disgrace [him] to [his] parents and friends." "But," he writes, "I before foreacquainted with their dealings, kept me out of their clutches" (48). Wadsworth reveals that Benedictine monks tried to recruit Inglefield and control Browne and then cites the case of Henry Challoner ("sonne to Sir Thomas Challoner, late Tutor to Prince Henry" [51]): they kept him by force in the English Jesuit College, but he escaped by trickery, only to be vulnerable to "a certain Austin Fryer . . . then travelling to Madrid, [who] . . . well observing the comelynesse and ingenious lookes grew forthwith inamoured with him, insomuch that he desired to be his bed fellow, and in condition thereof he promised him a nights lodging with his sister, who for her beauty was then parallel'd but by very few in all Spaine, but this young Gentleman not giving way to his requests, as exceeding the bounds of reason and modesty, left the Fryer much perplexed in his unnaturall desire" (51–52). Wadsworth thus makes priest and pirate similar in their homosexual predation. Challoner, however, escaped danger and returned to England.

Wadsworth reports that his father, now opposed by the Jesuits, died disillusioned. Thereafter the younger Wadsworth procured his father's Spanish pension and lived with his mother in Madrid for another seven or eight months. During that time, his friend Inglefield escaped the custody of the monks and was sheltered by him, subsequently traveling with him to Flanders, by way of Valladolid, where the Jesuits tried to entice Inglefield into their order (55). On the resumed journey an ex-pirate Jesuit attempted to persuade Inglefield to go to St. Omer and tried to sow dissention between him and Wadsworth.

Wadsworth digresses into a discussion of the English fugitives under the Spanish king's protection, including the notorious Sir Anthony Sherley, "a great plotter and projector in matters of State . . . [who] undertakes by sea-stratagems to invade and ruinate his native Countrey" (62); Sir Edward Bainham, "a grand complotter of the Gunpowder treason" (63); and many other men and women. He thus dramatizes his alienation from the English Catholic community abroad as a prelude to his discussion of his reasons for converting to Protestantism and coming to England.

Wadsworth says that at the age of eighteen he began to read Scripture closely and to discern the differences between Protestantism and Catholicism— the latter involving such issues as "the Popes supremacy, the reall presence of Christ in the holy Eucharist, the Indulgences, pardons, and profits of Purgatory, with the Popes authority to depose and set up Kings" (78). He says, "I found more resemblance and probability of the truth in the Protestants religion then in our owne" (78), rejecting Catholic "pretended miracles" as "Impostures" (79). He objects to the pope's beatification of Edmund Campion and Henry Garnet "under the pretext of religion" (80), and he particularly criticizes the Jesuits for stating "that it is lawfull and meritorious to lye and write such things to that end the common people might with greater zeale serve God and his Saints, and that otherwise there wold be no meanes to governe them, and especially to draw the women to good order, being by nature more facile and credulous, and for the most part addicted to novelties and miraculous events" (80). He attacks the Spanish as "little better then Atheists, onely making use of the Pope for their owne particular ambition and end, to confirme and establish him in unlawful Monarchies, and under colour of Religion to make Subjects become Slaves" (81). The intellectual reasons for his conversion, however, seem less compelling than his experiential ones.

After his resolution to convert, he served as a spy for a time, then was imprisoned in Calais for ten months, freed only when at his trial no one appeared as witness against him. When he finally arrived at Dover, he was free, as he says, to enter God's "holy Church" (94). His progress from Catholic superstition and various forms of metaphoric and real captivity to English Protestant religion and freedom are celebrated in the narrative.

The *Dictionary of National Biography* article on Wadsworth fills in biographical details that the narrative elides. Having failed, after the collapse of the Spanish marriage negotiations, to obtain employment with the Infanta, Wadsworth got a commission in the Spanish army in Flanders from

King Philip and thereafter called himself "Captain Wadsworth." He headed instead for England in 1625 and announced his conversion from Catholicism to the English authorities at the same time that he volunteered his services to native English Catholics (on whom he then spied for the government). He went to Brussels and, in 1626, to Paris but was imprisoned for six months for debt and released only by his mother's help. He then went to Calais, where he was identified as a spy by his old schoolmate George Gage (Toby Matthew's friend) and imprisoned for ten months. After this he went to England in 1628 and requested the earl of Pembroke's permission (as vice chancellor of Oxford) for a license to collect money at the university to cover the costs of printing *The English Spanish Pilgrim,* which appeared in print in 1629, then, in a second edition (along with *Further Observations of the English Spanish Pilgrim*) in 1630.[85] He finally found employment as a pursuivant.[86] Henry Foley quotes, for example, the account of the trial of the martyred Jesuit Thomas Holland that includes Wadsworth's testimony.[87] His opportunistic change of religion entailed both a change in national allegiance and an estrangement from the Catholic community in England and abroad.

Motives and Metaphors for Conversion

Because they involve a justification of separation from a great and powerful international Catholic church affiliated with the imperial power of Spain and the Holy Roman Empire, Protestant conversion accounts such as Wadsworth's sometimes find the escape-from-captivity narrative useful to employ. The adventurous escape from a persecutory Catholicism was sometimes figured as a movement from Satan's clutches to God's bosom or from what John Donne called the "Italian Babylon"[88] to the Christian community of the saved. Ferdinand Texeda also used the metaphor of the escape from Babylon as a conversion trope.[89] The related metaphor, that of the Protestant "escape from Rome," is used in such works as Anthony Munday, *The English Romayne Lyfe* (1582), and Antony Wotton, *Runne from Rome, Or, a Treatise Shewing the Necessitie of Separating from the Church of Rome* (1624).[90] Sometimes an escape is coded as "miraculous"—for example, in Christopher Musgrave's *Musgrave's Motives, and Reasons, for his Secession from the Church of Rome* (1621).[91] Anthony Tyrrell celebrated the fact that he "miraculously escaped and [was] delivered"[92] from the Roman church. In his recantation sermon the renegade priest William Tedder used the metaphor of the return of the prodigal son, another possible model, to figure his conversion to Protestantism.[93] John Gee also uses the figure of the returned prodigal to characterize his reconforming to the English church: "Like a Prodigall, I now return home with a Peccavi in my heart and pen, to God and our blessed mother the Church of England."[94] The conversion story of Henry Yaxlee portrays his joining the English Protestant church as a cure for the disease of Catholicism: *Morbus et Antidotus: The Disease with the Antidote. Or A Declaration of Henry Yaxlee of Bonthorpes in the Countie of Norfolke Esquire. Wherein he Sheweth how he was a Papist, and how by Gods Grace he is now lately Converted* (1630). The Jesuit-turned-Protestant Thomas Abernethie's conversion is presented as the testimony of a repentant sinner: *The Abjuration of Poperie by Thomas Abernethie: Sometime Jesuite, but now Penitent Sinner, and an Unworthy Member of the True Reformed Church of God in Scotland* (Edinburgh, 1638).

By contrast, Catholic conversion narratives often characterize joining or returning to the Roman Catholic church as a vivifying entry into a large community of the living and the dead, a church rich in practice, tradition, and belief: such a model bears some resemblance to the typical romance story of lost children found and divided families made whole. Alabaster and Matthew both find father substitutes in their movement towards Catholicism. Humphrey Leech, in discussing one of his "motives" for conversion, portrays his conversion to Catholicism as the discovery of a loving mother: "it was my desire . . . to find out the true Church, that so I might referre my selfe unto her decision, and rest within her bosome."[95] Benjamin Carier conceives of his new commitment to Catholicism both as a return to a "Mother Church" and as an entry into the communion of saints from which Protestants had cut themselves off by their "schism" and their rejection of the invocation of saints.[96] The prodigal son and lost sheep metaphors are also used by some writers to figure their return to Catholicism: for example, Thomas Vane's *A Lost Sheep Returned Home* (1648), Laurence Claxton's *A Lost Sheep Found, or, The Prodigal Returned to his Fathers House* (1660), and E. L[ydeott], *The Prodigal Return'd Home, or, the Motives of the Conversion to the Catholick Faith of E. L., Master of Arts in the University of Cambridge* (1684).

Conversion performances enacted the polemical and political competition between churches. This certainly is clear in one of the summary statements made by Sir Toby Matthew after his own conversion account. Looking generally at the phenomenon of change of religion, he claims that the Catholic converts are more edifying:

> Consider and compare such persons as having been Catholics are become Protestants; and such Protestants, on the other side, as have grown to be Catholics; and most particularly consider such Catholic priests as have turned Protestants, and much more if they have proved ministers, and, on the other side, such Protestant laymen as have either proved Catholic priests or Religious men. And to weigh with an equal hand whether the Catholics who became Protestants did not live notoriously worse than they had done before; and the Protestants who became Catholics much better. (164)[97]

Furthermore, he argues that deathbed conversions are almost inevitably to, rather than from, Catholicism: "Consider whether you have heard of any Catholics who, at the point of death, have, merely through the desire of saving their souls, renounced Catholic religion to become Protestants; and, on the other side, whether you have not heard that many who have lived Protestants all their life did yet, when they came to die, renounce that religion to become Catholics, through the only fear which they had left, lest otherwise their souls would be lost" (164–65). Matthew himself effected the 1635 deathbed conversion of one of his patrons, Richard Weston, earl of Portland.[98]

   In midcareer individuals could change their religion for any number of good or bad reasons—worldly ambition, rebellion against parental or other authority, aesthetic-devotional inclinations, intellectual reasons, moral revulsion against the religion in which they were raised, personal psychological or emotional motives, and so on—but end-of-life conversions were another matter, especially powerful as examples since no one could argue that the influence of coercive secular or ecclesiastical authority was the cause (though psychological and rhetorical pressure was no doubt applied). The rumors that various prominent figures had deathbed conversions to Catholicism (including monarchs from Elizabeth I on forward) were especially troubling to English Protestants, for they cast doubt on the authenticity of many people's religious commitment to the established Church of England and testified to the power of the "old religion" to reclaim the "heretics" or "schismatics" it had lost.[99]

5

Plots, Atrocities, and Deliverances

The Anti-Catholic Construction of Protestant English History

[T]hey [Catholics] were our enemies in 88. when they provoked by their *Excommunications,* dangerous invasions, and in that capacity as they were our enemies in 1605. when they bent their malice even against that place, where the Laws for the maintenance of our religion were enacted, so they are our enemies still, if we be still of the same religion. He that by Gods mercy to us, leads us, is as sure that the *Pope* is *Antichrist,* now, as he was *then;* and we that are blessedly led by him, are as sure, that their doctrine is the doctrine of *Devils,* now, as we were then.

—John Donne, *The Sermon of John Donne*

[T]he Great Fear of Popery . . . had been fostered by the long struggle against Spain and the Counter-Reformation. . . . [A]nd it would remain formidable for three centuries, a national neurosis which could be awakened again and again: in the myth of the great Irish massacre of 1641 . . . , in the great scare of the Popish Plot of 1678, in the fable of the Warming Pan in 1688; even, though with dwindling force, in the Gordon Riots of 1780 and the "Papal Aggression" of 1851.

—Hugh Trevor-Roper, *Catholics, Anglicans, and Puritans*

THE HISTORIOGRAPHICAL PROJECT OF ENGLISH PROTESTANTISM UNFOLDED from the late sixteenth century to the time of the Glorious Revolution and the solidification of the "Whig" view of English history. It was structured by what was perceived as recurrent Catholic dangers, plots, and outrages—moments that were recapitulated and reinterpreted in cumulative fashion over the years, especially in religious polemic, commemorative sermons, broadside prints, popular celebrations, and other forms of historical retrospection. If English Catholic history developed from the story of (economic and other) persecution of a sizable and persistent body of believers holding on to the "old religion" to that of a seigneurially centered, fragmented, and small minority church, the larger English history became a Protestant one, celebrating both the providentially shaped triumph of the reformed religion and the formation of an English national identity that could be contrasted with both the internationalist assumptions of Catholicism[1] and the religious and political absolutism of some European Catholic states.[2]

I concentrate here on three moments of crisis in the seventeenth century: the Gunpowder Plot, the Irish Rebellion, and Titus Oates's fabricated Popish Plot. Each generated anti-Catholic texts that were part of a developing narrative of English history structured by the model of domestic Catholic outrage or threat followed by Protestant deliverance. The attempted invasion of England by the Spanish Armada in 1588, of course, provided a model of *international* Catholic threat followed by providential deliverance, incorporated into a national mythology.[3] I focus, however, on the domestic events that, while perceived in their own time as connected to a foreign menace, were at the heart of English Protestant-Catholic relations. Although I refer to a large number of texts, I pay special attention to the official published account of the trial of Henry Garnet, S.J., and others after the Gunpowder Plot, three Fast Sermons delivered to the Long Parliament and the propaganda associated with the Irish Rebellion of 1641, and Andrew Marvell's *An Account of the Growth of Popery, and Arbitrary Government in England* (1678), Titus Oates's published narrative of the Popish Plot and other texts from that era (1678–81) and its immediate aftermath. Together, these writings give a sense of the ways the rhetoric of anti-Catholicism was used to create a narrative of contemporary English history in which English identity could be fixed as Protestant and English nationhood could be distinguished from that of continental Catholic states.[4]

The Propagandistic Figuration of Catholic Atrocities and Massacre

The official and nonofficial propaganda following the discovery of the 1605 Gunpowder Plot and the 1641 outbreak of the Irish Rebellion was largely responsible for creating the image of Catholics as treasonous, ruthless, and murderous. The Gunpowder Treason plotters, a fanatical fringe of the Catholic community, were characterized in a way to suggest that committed Catholics were deluded political subversives willing to massacre Protestants, overthrow state authority, and bring in foreign invaders. It was not possible to accuse the English Catholic population of any extensive collaboration with the Spanish in 1588 (though some Catholics, encouraged by Cardinal Allen and Robert Persons, might have supported the invaders had they landed on English soil in any substantial number), but the Gunpowder Plotters were Catholics who could be recognized as attempting a direct assault on the political center of the state—not only on the monarch and royal family but also on the Parliament—in effect, the nation's political and social elite. They were, therefore, the confirmation of the worst politically paranoid imaginings. To make this model of religiopolitical subversion and threat complete, however, the government had to portray the plot as originating with those figures of extreme religious militancy, the Jesuits. Thus it was essential for the authorities to capture and bring to trial the head of the English Jesuit mission, Henry Garnet, and to portray the Gunpowder Plot as, ultimately, his (and the pope's) responsibility.[5]

The published account of the Gunpowder Treason trials of the surviving plotters and Garnet, *A True and Perfect Relation of the proceedings at the several Arraignments of the Late Most barbarous Traitors* (1606),[6] is a masterpiece of official propaganda, especially the rhetorical performances of Sir Edward Coke and the earl of Northampton, which played not only during the trials to the judges, the jury, and the monarch overhearing the proceedings[7] but also in print to the political nation as a whole. This voluminous work, largely produced under the direction of the earl of Northampton and edited by his client Sir Robert Cotton,[8] contains an account of the separate arraignments and trials of the main surviving lay plotters (Robert Winter, Thomas Winter, Guy Fawkes, John Grant, Ambrose Rookwood, Robert Keyes, and Thomas Bates), along with the separate indictment of Sir Everard Digby, the arraignment and trial of Garnet, and supplementary material. In all the proceedings the government spokespersons, primarily Sir Edward Coke, the earl of Northampton, and the earl of Salisbury, kept up a steady attack on the Jesuits as the alleged masterminds of the plot, which, for maximum rhetorical effect, Coke called "The Jesuit treason" (P1ᵛ).

In addition to proving the guilt of those tried for their involvement in the plot, *A True and Perfect Relation* was designed to drive home two points: first, that the Gunpowder Plot was only one of a series of continuing Catholic assaults on English monarchs, the true religion (Protestantism), and the nation itself, and second, that Jesuits were England's worse enemies, a diabolically crafty order of political subversives defending the papal deposing power and sanctioning regicide, the killing of heretics, the practices of lying and equivocation, and the invasion of the country by foreign powers. What is quite surprising about *A True and Perfect Relation* is the limited attention it gives to the agency of the lay plotters. From the start it is focused on the Jesuits and on the larger history of Catholic subversion, plotting, and (attempted or actual) political assassination.

The formal indictment names the Jesuits caught in the prosecutorial net before mentioning the laymen and repeatedly returns to the clergy (highlighted below in italics) to hammer home the point about their control of the conspiracy against the English nation:

> [W]hereas our Sovereign Lord the King had by the advice and assent of his Councell, for divers weightie and urgent occasions concerning his Majestie, the State, & defence of the Church and Kingdome of England, appointed a Parliament to bee holden at his Citie of Westminster, *That Henry Garnet superior of the Jesuites within the Realme of England, (called also by the severall names of Wally, Darcy, Roberts, Farmer, and Henry Philips,), Oswald Tesmond Jesuite, otherwise called Oswald Greenwell, John Gerard Jesuite, (called also by the severall names of Lee and Brooke)*, Robert Winter, Thomas Winter Gentlemen, Guy Fawkes Gentleman, otherwise called Guy Johnson, Robert Keyes Gentleman, and Thomas Bates yeoman, late servant to Robert Catesby Esquier, together with the said Robert Catesby and Thomas Percy Esquiers, John Wright and Christopher Wright Gentlemen, in open Rebellion and Insurrection against his Majesty lately slaine, and Francis Tresham Esquier lately dead, as false Traitors against our said Sovereigne Lord the King, did traiterously meet and assemble themselves together; and being so met, the said *Henry Garnet, Oswald Tesmond, John Gerrard and the other Jesuites* did maliciously, falsly, and traiterously moove, and perswade aswell the sayd Thomas Winter, Guy Fawkes, Robert Keyes, and Thomas Bates, as the said Robert Catesby, Thomas Percy, John Wright, Christopher Wright, and Francis Tresham, That our said Sovereign Lord the King, the Nobilitie, Cleargie, and whole Commonaltie of the Realme of England (Papists excepted)

were heretiques, and that all heretiques wer accursed and Excommunicate, and that none heretique could be a King, but that it was lawfull and
meritorious to kill our said Sovereign Lord the King, & all other Heretiques within this Realme of England, for the advancing and enlarge-
ment of the pretended and usurped Authoritie and Jurisdiction of the
Bishop of Rome, and for the restoring of the superstitious Romish Religion within this Realme of England; To which traiterous perswasions,
the said Thomas Winter, Guy Fawkes, Robert Keyes, Thomas Bates,
Robert Catesby, Tho. Percy, John Wright, Christopher Wright, and Francis Tresham traiterously did yeeld their assents, And that thereupon the
said *Henry Garnet, Oswald Tesmond, John Gerrard, and divers other Jesuits,*
Tho. Winter, Guy Fawkes, Robert Keyes, and Thomas Bates, as also the
said Robert Catesby, Thomas Percy, John Wright, Christopher Wright,
and Francis Tresham, traiterously amongst themselves did conclude and
agree, with Gunpowder, as it were with one blast, suddenly, traiterously
and barbarously to blow up and teare in pieces our said Soveraigne Lord
the King, the Excellent, vertuous, and gracious Queene Anne his deer-
est wife, the most Noble Prince HENRY their eldest sonne, the future
Hope and Joy of ENGLAND, and the Lords Spirituall and Temporall,
the Reverend Judges of the Realme, the Knights, Citizens and Bur-
gesses of Parliament, and divers other faithfull Subjects and Servants
of the King in the said Parliament for the causes aforesayd, to bee assembled in the House of Parliament, and all them without any respect
of Majestie, Dignitie, Degree, Sexe, Age or Place, most barbarously, &
more then beastly, traiterously and suddenly to destroy and swallow up:
And further did most traiterously conspire and conclude among themselves, That not onely the whole Royall issue male of our sayd Sovereigne Lord the King should be destroyed, and rooted out, but that the
persons aforesaid, together with divers other false Traitors traiterously
with them to be assembled should surprise the persons of the noble Ladies ELIZABETH & MARY, daughters of our sayde Sovereigne Lord
the King, and falsly and traiterously should proclaime the sayd Lady
ELIZABETH to be Queene of this Realme of England: And thereupon
should publish a certain traiterous Proclamation in the name of the sayde
Lady ELIZABETH, wherein as it was especially agreed by and betweene
the sayde Conspirators, That no mention should be made at the first of

the alteration of Religion established within the Realme of England, Neither would the said false Traitors therein acknowledge themselves to bee
Authors or Actors or Devisers of the foresaid most wicked and horrible
Treasons, untill they had got sufficient power and strength for the assured
execution and accomplishment of their said Conspiracie and Treason,
and that then they would avow and justifie the sayd most wicked and
horrible Treasons, as Actions that were in the number of those, *Quae non
laudantur nisi peracta,* which bee not to be commended before they bee
done. (A4–B2)

This document emphasizes the Jesuit use of aliases and disguises, their rhetorical skills in persuading Catholics to commit treasonous acts, the barbarity
of Catholics in the terrorist plan to blow up the Parliament building and kill
large numbers of people, and the willingness of Catholic zealots to die for political and religious ends. The indictment states further that the conspirators
were given the sacrament by the Jesuits to seal their bond of conspiracy—a
ritual associated in the polemical propaganda of the time with other assassination attempts. The account notes simply that the prisoners pled guilty and
names Garnet, Tesimond, and Gerard as "Jesuits not then taken" (C3), thus
pointing ahead to the account of Garnet's trial as the centerpiece of the book.

   After Edward Philips has expatiated on the indictment and provided
a chronology of the plot, Sir Edward Coke delivers a long speech narrating
at great length the course of the conspiracy (D2–L4ᵛ). He internationalizes
the plot and emphasizes "the principall offendors[,] . . . [that is,] the seducing Jesuits, men that use the reverence of Religion, yea even the most Sacred
and blessed name of Jesus as a mantle to cover their impietie, blasphemie,
treason, and Rebellion, and all manner of wickedness" (F1). In associating
the Jesuits with two D's (deposing of kings and disposing of kingdoms), he
harks back to the old charge that they were responsible for the assassination of King Henri III by James Clement (G1). He returns also to the mid-
Elizabethan period and the 1570 bull of Pius V excommunicating Elizabeth,
making this the foundation of Catholic subversion and treason. He identifies
recusancy with "an acknowledgement of the Popes power" (H2), that is, the
papal temporal power by which, he suggests, the deposing or assassination of
the queen was authorized. Comparing the number of Catholic executions
during Elizabeth's reign ("in al not 30. Priests, or above five receivers and har-

bourers of them" [H3]) with the three hundred Protestants slain during the reign of Queen Mary, Coke seems to argue that the Elizabethan regime practiced a greater degree of religious toleration or a lesser degree of cruelty than did the previous, Marian one.

Coke cites the oath the conspirators allegedly swore for their plot in connection with receiving the Eucharist, but he is more interested in the function of Jesuit-sanctioned lying in the conspiracy and its judicial aftermath. He thus launches an attack on the conspirators' "perfidious and perjurious Equivocating, abetted, allowed, and justified by the Jesuites, not onely simply to conceale or denie an open trueth, but Religiously to averre, to protest upon salvation, to sweare that which themselves know to be most false, and all this by reserving a secret and private sense inwardly to themselves, whereby they are by their Ghostly fathers perswaded, that they may safely and lawfully delude any question whatsoever" (H4ᵛ–I1). Coke refers to the "Treatise of Equivocation . . . seene and allowed by Garnet, the superiour of the Jesuits, and Blackwel the Archpriest of England" (I1). The Jesuitical practice of equivocation and mental reservation — perceived as a direct assault on the state's policing powers and judicial system (in an era in which rights to avoid self-incrimination were not protected) — became one of the lasting legacies of the Gunpowder Treason trials, casting suspicion on any testimony by Catholics, a context available for prejudicial exploitation by Protestant prosecutors and judges. In a society that still had faith in one's word as one's bond (a legacy from an earlier oral culture), equivocation could be seen as striking at the heart of social relations.[9]

After the main lay conspirators are found guilty and there is a discussion of the arraignment, trial, and sentencing of Sir Everard Digby, *A True and Perfect Relation* presents a long speech made at Digby's arraignment by the earl of Northampton, a politically opportunistic crypto-Catholic looking to solidify his power as Jacobean privy councillor (M1–N3ᵛ). Only then does the text move to Garnet's arraignment and trial, in which Coke took the prosecutorial lead, delivering a long, elaborate speech (O2ᵛ–V4). In his rhetorical tour de force, Coke sets the Gunpowder Treason in the context of Garnet's alleged career of subversion from 1586 onward, repeatedly associating him and other Jesuits with a long series of assassination attempts, invasion plans, and conspiracies. The pattern Coke emphasizes is clear: the Catholic plots of the late Elizabethan and early Jacobean eras were masterminded, encouraged, or sanctioned by Jesuits, many individually associated with Jesuit-authored polemical texts.[10] For example, Coke states that "[Patrick] Cullens Treason was accompanied with a book called *Philopater*, written for the abetting and warranting such a devilish act in generall by Creswell the legier Jesuit in Spaine, under the name of Philopater" (Q1ᵛ–Q2). The plan of Williams and York in 1594 "[t]o kill the Queene," he says, was undertaken "by father Holt the Jesuite, and other his accomplices." "And that Treason likewise was accompanied with a Booke written by the legier Jesuite and Rector at Rome, Parsons, under the name of Doleman, concerning Titles, or rather tittles: a lewde and lying booke, ful of falshood, forgery, and malediction" (Q2). The planned invasion of England at the end of Elizabeth's reign "was accompanied with the Popes owne writing[,] . . . two Briefs or Buls, one to the Clergie, and an other to the Laitie" (Q3), which demanded that they not accept a non-Catholic successor. Coke claims that these two papal breves were seen by the Gunpowder Plotters as justification for removing a Protestant monarch, as well as for preventing a Protestant successor (R4ᵛ). Basically, Coke traces a short history of Catholic subversion from the time of the Northern Rebellion to the Gunpowder Plot, asserting that just as no four-year period passed after Elizabeth's excommunication without a significant Catholic plot, so too in James's time no four-month period passed without Catholic treasonable activity. This is the larger context in which he places the Gunpowder Treason and the pattern he has it follow.

When he details the beginnings, growth, and culmination of the plot, he insists that the evidence shows total Jesuit involvement. Supposedly the Jesuits knew about it from the start, provided the ideological and moral justification for it, facilitated the international and domestic planning, and ritualistically and sacramentally sanctioned it. Coke quotes the supposed oath of secrecy sworn by the plotters: "You shall sweare by the blessed Trinitie, and by the Sacrament you now purpose to receive never to disclose, directly or indirectly, by word or circumstance, the matter that shalbe proposed to you to keepe secret, nor desist from the execution thereof, untill the rest shall give you leave" (R4). Connecting this oath to Catholic sacramentalism, Coke says, "They all were confessed, had absolution, and received thereupon the Sacrament, by the hands of Gerrard the Jesuite then present" (R4). He portrays the conference between Oswald Tesimond and Henry Garnet, in which the former told the latter of the plot and which Garnet says was a confession covered by the seal of secrecy governing that sacrament, as "a disguised confession" (S1ᵛ) or mere conversation.[11] But whether or not the information came by means of confession, the government held that Garnet should have warned the authorities. In fact, to some extent, Garnet felt guilty about this concealing or (felonious) misprision of treason.

Coke's anti-Jesuit rhetoric is relentless. He says that Garnet and the other Jesuits recognized that the discovery of the plot "prophesied the overthrow of the whole order of the Jesuites" (S3ᵛ), the "more violent and firie" Tesimond acting to "incite such as he could to rise up in open Rebellion . . . under the . . . pretext and colour, That it was concluded that the throats of all the Catholiques in England should be cut" (S4). Garnet is characterized as follows:

> a man of many names, Garnet, Wallye, Darcy, Roberts, Farmer, Phillips[,] . . . by Countrey an Englishman, by birth a Gentleman, by education a Scholer, afterwards a Corrector of the Common Law Print, with M. Tottle the Printer, and now is to be corrected by the Law. He hath many gifts and endowments of nature, by Art learned, a good Linguist, and by profession a Jesuite, and a Superior, as in deed hee is Superior to all his predecessors in devilish Treason, a Doctor of Jesuites, that is, a Doctor of five Dd. As Dissimulation, Deposing of Princes, Disposing of Kingdomes, Daunting and deterring of subjects, and Destruction. (T1ᵛ–2)

As Coke runs through his five D's, he attacks the papal deposing power and the practice of excommunicating princes as the ideological foundation of Catholic sedition and assassinations. He likens "the Spanish treason" to "this Powder treason" (V1ᵛ) as threats to the state from within and without, and he celebrates both the general divine deliverance of England from danger and "the wonderfull providence of God in the admirable discovery of this Superiour Jesuite to be partie to this treason" (V2ᵛ).

In the speech of self-defense that follows, Garnet rebuts the charges as best he can (often interrupted by Coke, Northampton, and Salisbury).[12] The narrator summarizes what Garnet says rather than reproduce the full rhetorical performance.[13] Garnet defends the doctrine of equivocation, the papal deposing power, the general innocence of English recusants, and the specific innocence of Jesuits, who, he claims, had no part in the conspiracy (V4–X2). He says the letters of commendation he wrote for individuals later involved in the conspiracy were pro forma rather than endorsements of seditious plans.[14] Referring to a conference he had with Catesby, in which the latter asked him if it were lawful to destroy "Innocents with Nocents" (X2ᵛ), he says he treated the question as a hypothetical matter, not as an opportunity to endorse bloody sedition, and he wrote to the pope to secure his help in preventing any rash action on the part of the more belligerent Catholics. His "Prayer for the good success of the great Action, in the beginning of the Parliament" (X3ᵛ), was not for the success of the plot but for better treatment of Catholics through parliamentary action. Finally, he says that "father Greenwel [Tesimond] told him the whole Plot, and all the particulars thereof, with which he protested, that hee was very much distempered and could never sleepe quietly afterwards, but sometimes prayed to God that it should not take effect" (X4).

The narrative of the trial gives ample space to the interruptions and questions put to Garnet during his defense by Salisbury and Northampton. Northampton refutes Garnet's claim about the secrecy of confession by pointing out that Garnet was now breaking that very seal in his testimony (X4ᵛ). Salisbury, eager to emphasize that the government did not mistreat its Catholic prisoners, gets Garnet to admit he was well handled and that it was "Digitus Dei" (Y2ᵛ), not torture, by which the government obtained information about the jailhouse conferences of Garnet and another priest (Edward Oldcorne, alias "Hall"). He points to Garnet's reply to Catesby's general question about killing the innocent with the guilty as the moral authorization on which the conspirators acted, and then presses the attack on the theory of equivocation. When Garnet says that King James was "not yet Excommunicated" (Y3ᵛ) by the pope, this leads Salisbury to pose a new sort of "bloody question": "Whether in case the Pope *per sententiam Orthodoxam,* should Excommunicate the Kings Majestie of great Britaine, his Subjects were bound to continue their obedience?" (Y3ᵛ–4). The narrator then says, "To this [Garnet] denied to answere, by which the hearers might see his mind" (Y4). The last record of Garnet's defense, following Salisbury's mention of the two papal breves requiring a Catholic successor to Elizabeth, is noted simply: "Then Garnet beganne to use some speeches that hee was not consenting to the Powder treason" (Y4ᵛ), after which Coke, as attorney general, rebutted the defense point by point and reminded Garnet and the court that to know of treason without reporting it to the authorities (whatever one thinks about the seal of confession) was "by the Common Law . . . *crimen laesae Majestatis*" (Z2), a felony for which the court could clearly convict the Jesuit. This narrower ground of guilt is constantly expanded by the prosecution to a wholesale indictment of Jesuits and the recusant Catholics influenced by them.

Coke's summation is followed in turn by a long speech by the earl of Northampton (Dd1–Eee4), augmented for the publication of the trial proceedings for the purposes of self-advertisement and propagandizing. Northampton's performance, no doubt originally aimed primarily at the king, is followed by the Lord Chief Justice's sentence. The earl has, in fact, two speeches, one before and one after the rendering of the guilty verdict, addressed to Garnet and the court and, in the expanded printed version, the monarch and the nation. They are a polemically overblown assault on the papal deposing power, on equivocation, and on recusant Catholic political oppositionism. Unlike the more economical speeches of Coke and Salisbury, Northampton's turgid and pedantic Ciceronian performance repeatedly waxes metaphoric,[15] using, for example, conceits having to do with the diabolical associations of the Gunpowder Treason that were picked up in later commemorative and polemical texts. Setting the Gunpowder Treason in a history of the devil's mischiefs on earth, Northampton says that the old curse of the serpent, that he should crawl on his belly and eat the "dust of powder," is altered for him "to snuffe gunpowder" (Bb2). He says the devil "now . . . sets upon the great Lieutenant of Gods authority and dignitie with an *auferam tibi omnia,* both life and crown, *ex penetralibus ubi Christ non est,* as wee are taught by his Evangelist. The dragons ambition extended to no further then the sweeping away with his taile of the third part of the starres in the firmament: But now the plot of him & his disciples, was to sweepe away the Sunne, the Moone, and the Starres, both out of Starre-Chamber and Parliament, that no light be given in this kingdome to the best labourers" (Aa4ᵛ). The main thrust of Northampton's argument is that the papacy's historical claim of temporal authority and the right to depose kings represents a delegitimizing corruption of that institution, which turned its back on piety and set its sights on power and wealth. With the historical research and documentation provided by his client, Sir Robert Cotton (especially the materials drawn from English history),[16] Northampton indulges in rhetorical overkill.

Like Coke, Northampton delineates the history of Garnet's activities in England from the year 1586 because he wants to connect the Jesuit superior to foreign invasion, particularly by the Armada, as well as to other conspiracies and assassination plots of the late Elizabethan and early Jacobean periods. He thus draws on the popular association of the Jesuits with a Catholic activism that repeatedly threatened the state from within and without. But the larger history that interests Northampton is the one that includes the evolution and implementation of the theory of papal temporal authority and the deposing power. Thus he notes several moments from English history during which the English Crown and the papacy clashed, alluding, for example, to the times of King Henry II and King John.

In effect, Northampton's mammoth speech in the *True and Perfect Relation* makes that publication primarily a critique of papal temporal authority and a defense of the full prerogatives of the absolute monarch whom no one, Catholic or otherwise, should resist. The prime audience for this performance, in the courtroom and in its expanded form in print, was King James, who, according to the Venetian ambassador, was so pleased by it that he ordered the book translated into French, Latin, and Italian.[17] It was, in effect, a work that led directly to the international controversy over the subsequent Oath of Allegiance in which some of the same issues were at stake.

Northampton's speech is followed by a justification of its length. The editor says that the version of the speech he got was an "unperfect" or "maimed copy" (Eee4) and that after he gave it to the earl for correction, the Earl sent him "two Copies[,] . . . the one *secundum literam,* as neere as his Lordship could call to minde, the other amplified and enriched upon the same grounds, but with greater variety of Arguments, (in respect that Canon *Nos Sanctorum,* had bene the chiefest base and false foundation of this and many other precedent conspiracies)" (Eee4^{r–v}). Given the choice, the editor assumes the reader would prefer the speech "in folio, then in decimo sexto, in the fruit then in the blossom, and the larger the better" (Eee4^v). The crypto-Catholic privy councillor's scholarly refutation of the ideological grounds of the Gunpowder Plot and of any other form of Catholic resistance thus appears in a form that would have been inappropriate to the trial itself. In fact, its unsuitability for the trial is underscored by the hasty, anticlimactic handling in half a page of the delivery of the verdict on Garnet and of Garnet's brief response to Salisbury's question whether he wished to make some final comments: "Garnet answered, no my Lord, But I humbly desire your Lordships all, to commend my life to the Kings Majestie, saying, That at his pleasure hee was ready either to die or live, and doe him service" (Eee4^v). The implication in the way these words are presented, after the sentence of death, is that he is admitting he is guilty not only of misprision of treason (in his refusal to disclose what he heard from Tesimond about the conspiracy) but also of the broader charge of promoting the plot from the start as yet one more Jesuit effort to subvert the English Protestant state and its lawful monarchs.

What follows this section of the *True and Perfect Relation* are (1) the description of Garnet's execution; (2) a narrative that dramatizes the plot's discovery through the warning letter to Lord Mounteagle (which the king is portrayed as wisely decoding) and the search of the basement of the Parliament house that resulted in the arrest of Guy Fawkes; (3) the confession of Guy Fawkes in the Tower; and (4) the alleged confession of Thomas Winter. In the account of the execution of Garnet, there is some clear editorializing—for example, when the narrator describes Garnet's appearance on the scaffold, with "feare, and guiltinesse appearing in his face" (Fff1). Supposedly, when Garnet prepared for death, "[i]t appeared he could not constantly or devoutly pray; feare of death, or hope of Pardon even then so distracted him: For oft in those prayers he would breake off, turne and looke about him, and answere to what he over-heard, while he seemed to be praying" (Fff2ᵛ–3). The gruesome details of the execution are only briefly alluded to in the last words of the narrative: "then [he] was turned off, and hung till he was dead" (Fff3ᵛ). Determined not to make the account into the story of a martyrdom, the narrator gives more attention to the public relations debate with the authorities that continued in this new venue, as some of the points of the trial are rehearsed and Garnet reiterates his position, admitting only to the misprision of treason involved in concealing what he knew through confession. In the much longer narrative that follows, the suspenseful story of the discovery of the plot is told, emphasizing the king's wisdom in interpreting the famous letter of the conspirators to Lord Mounteagle that warns him not to attend the opening of Parliament at which the Catholics' enemies "shall receive a terrible Blow" (F3v).

The Aftermath of the Gunpowder Plot

The Gunpowder Plot had powerful short-term and long-term effects on the English cultural imagination.[18] It was commemorated in anniversary sermons, alluded to in both radical and moderate Protestant polemical literature, depicted in political and satirical prints, and transformed into the subject matter and symbolic language of major and minor literary works, from Shakespeare's *Macbeth*, Thomas Campion's *De Pulveria Conjuratione*, Barnabe Barnes's *The Devil's Charter*, Thomas Dekker's *The Double PP. A Papist in Armes*, John Donne's *Ignatius His Conclave*, and Ben Jonson's *Catiline* to John Milton's "In

Quintem Novembris."[19] Milton wrote his Gunpowder Plot poem at Cambridge in 1625 or 1626 in his seventeenth year, using the diabolical context associated with earlier Gunpowder Treason literature and other literary precedents for dramatizing the hellish origin of earthly political crises. In this work Satan is an international troublemaker envious of England's peace and prosperity, bothered by its not accepting his yoke (i.e., Roman Catholicism). The devil goes to Rome and sees the pope carried on men's shoulders and kings bowing to him, and then in the pope's bedchamber he argues that the pope should destroy their enemies by blowing them up and invading with either French or Spanish troops to enable the return of the Marian age. The pope makes a speech encouraging the plot, but finally Fame and God expose it as the bold cruelty of the papists and the poem ends in celebration of the divine deliverance.

The Gunpowder Plot produced England's first national holiday (Gunpowder Treason Day, later Guy Fawkes Day), and it established a firm association of Catholicism with terrorist ruthlessness, heightening the fears of Catholic murderousness and subversion that lasted not decades but centuries.[20] David Cressy has remarked, "Of all historical providences engrained in the memory of English Protestants, the discovery of the Gunpowder Plot on the eve of 5 November, was the most enduring."[21] He defines the officially mandated commemorations of the day as "one of the earliest examples of legislated memory," becoming part of a "cycle of Protestant deliverances."[22] In the aftermath of James I's failure to arrange the Spanish Match for Prince Charles, Bishop George Carleton published *A Thankfull Remembrance Of Gods Mercy. In an Historical Collation of the great and mercifull Deliverances of the Church and State of England, since the Gospel beganne here to flourish, from the beginning of Queen Elizabeth* (1624).[23] In its revised edition, his 291-page history chronicles a series of domestic (but externally supported) Catholic conspiracies through the reign of Elizabeth and into the Jacobean era, highlighting the Armada and culminating in the Gunpowder Plot; it emphasizes the constant machinations of Spain and the papacy aimed at overthrowing the English Protestant state. The pattern of threat and deliverance is asserted in each one of its eighteen chapters to assure the English Protestant readership of God's continuing protection of England and her state church. In the period of revived anti-Spanish feeling following the collapse of negotiations for a Spanish Catholic bride for the heir apparent, this assertion of the Protestant providential scheme was timely and the choice of the Gunpowder Plot story as the end point of the narration appropriate.[24] But, of course, once the Gunpowder Plot entered the English national mythology it could be inserted in other historical narratives of succeeding events and crises.

Thus in later times of political and religious crisis the Gunpowder Plot could be invoked to define or sharpen partisan differences. For example, on the eve of the Civil Wars, John Vicars republished, in expanded and supplemented form, his 1617 translation of Francis Herring's 1606 Latin poem on the Gunpowder Plot (*Pietas Pontificia*) as *November the 5. 1605. The Quintessence of Cruelty, or, Master-peice of Treachery, The Popish Pouder-Plot, Invented by Hellish-Malice, Prevented by Heavenly-mercy. Truly related, and from the Latine of the Learned, Religious, and Reverend Dr. Herring, translated and very much dilated* (1641).[25] This work warns against the influence of contemporary court Catholics and suggests the dangerousness of a supposed Catholic menace that perpetuates the political threat exemplified by the Gunpowder Treason. Vicars, a radical Protestant, emphasizes what he claims was a Catholic plan at the time of the plot to blame it (had it succeeded) on Puritans so as to provoke persecution against them. The book contains commendatory poems by such figures as William Prynne and Joshua Sylvester (who interpolated in his translation of DuBartas, as Susan Snyder points out, "a long passionate outburst . . . against the promoters of the Gunpowder Plot").[26] Vicars's work was aimed mainly at a London middle-class audience and is illustrated with a series of woodcuts reproducing the familiar Protestant imagery associated with the plot, its discovery, and its aftermath. The dedication is to "all loyall-hearted English Protestants which sincerely relish the power and purity of Christs Gospell" (A2), and the last poem in the book is dedicated to a series of London authorities, including the lord mayor and aldermen. The frontispiece reproduces the illustration of Fawkes and the devil, the Parliament house with barrels of gunpowder underneath, and the eye of heaven sending a beam down to disclose the treachery. Several other woodcuts precede the main text and the sections of the main poem.

The main poem narrates the course of the Gunpowder Plot along familiar ideological and fictional lines: the Jesuits, diabolical schemers, are at the center of the evil, encouraging the plotters and confirming them in their mission by means of an oath, the sacrament, and absolution. The treason is generated in Hell as the firstborn son of Pluto and "Rome's strumpet" (1), who then enters the breast of Guy Fawkes (though the marginal note identifies

Robert Catesby as the author of the conspiracy). The Jesuits Garnet and Gerard are invited to join the plot and "these holy Fathers of that Sect, / Confirm the plot, advise, instruct, direct" (15). The poet dramatizes the moment Catesby asked Garnet (in general terms), "Whither our friends may dye with enimies / Whither: with nocents, innocents may die" (16). Garnet, who gives the signal to proceed, is cast as a ruthless advocate of violence, for the Jesuits "hold it lawfull to kill friend or foe" (20). The poem even imagines graphically some of the scenes that would have resulted from a successful plot:

> . . . bodies batterd, shatterd, torne and rent,
> Arms, heads and legs, flying i'th firmament,
> Dismembred bodies all besmeard with gore;
> A sight, which very Scythians might deplore,
> Yea roare to see, and seeing, curse the hearts
> Of all such barbarous Actors of such parts. . . .
> . . . .
> Women with blubbering tears bedrensh their faces,
> Wringing their hands and running up and down,
> Fearfully frighted with foes rage and frown;
> Children in Parents arms trembling and quaking,
> Mothers into their lapps their infants taking
> With gushing tears, kissing their tender cheeks,
> Chambers even ring with Damsels wofull screeks:
> Aged-men murthered, Young-men butchered,
> Wives widows made, chaste Virgins ravished.
>
> (26–27, 30)

What is also imagined to follow the explosion is a massacre of Puritans, who would be blamed by the Catholics for the disaster.

Like John Milton, Vicars had no qualms about giving God a speaking part in a poem: the deity directs an angel to England to Lord Mounteagle to start the exposure of the plot to government authorities, the king himself finally, with providential help, interpreting the letter of warning that Mounteagle's Catholic friends gave him to avoid the planned destruction of the Parliament building (reproduced verbatim in the text). James immediately understands the letter as part of a Jesuit stratagem to commit regicide by blowing up Parliament at its opening session. The anti-Jesuit theme continues with the association of the captured Fawkes with Jesuitical equivocation (45) and with the mention of the example of the (supposedly Jesuit-inspired) French regicide, Ravillac (47). The anti-Jesuit editorializing is made relevant to the political crisis of 1641 with the call to "cast out these accursed Canaanites, / These subtill foxes, bloody Jesuites" (53). The Jesuits are dramatized as central to the postplot events, especially their connection to possible Catholic uprisings in various counties of England and Wales.

Vicars's narrative concludes with references to the display of the severed heads of the lay plotters and with the Devil's speech of disappointment. But, once again, the contemporary situation is invoked in a marginal comment on Satan's prediction of a "richer prize" to come in the future: "This hath bin most fully confirmed by Satan and his Agents, our Church & State projectors, in this lately discovered plot, by our blessed Parliament, 1641, which would have far transcended this of the Pouder-plot had it taken effect. O the desperate inventions of mans more than divelish heart!" (80). The "Habernfeld Plot"[27] and the wider hysteria about possible popish plots in the last years before the Civil Wars are here connected with the most horrific of the Catholic conspiracies as true Protestants (as distinguished from court Catholics and popishly inclined Laudians) are warned to be ready to fight a new Catholic menace. The book concludes with "An Epigram to Jesuites, the Principall Disturbers of Peace and Unity, the Authours and Firebrands of Sedition and Treachery throughout the Christian-world. Or, The Romish White-Devil" (98–101), "An oenigmaticall-Riddle to Romes Jesuiticall black-Crows, who pretend themselves to be religions white-Swans" (102–3), and "A Paraphrasticall Psalm of thanksgiving for Englands most happy-deliverance from the most horrible intended Gun-pouder Treason, practised by the Synagogue of Satan, the Romish Babylonians; and fitted toone of the familiar Tunes of Davids Psalms, to be sung November the 5th" (104–5).

Popish Plotting, Irish Massacres, and the Anti-Catholic Mythology of Political Revolution

Anti-Catholic rhetoric was intensified in 1641–42 to interpret the Irish Rebellion, to portray Stuart absolutism and conservative Anglican ecclesiology as "popish," and to mobilize radical Protestant and parliamentary opposition to the Crown. In fact, Catholics were ultimately blamed for the outbreak of the

Civil Wars, or the War of the Three Kingdoms.[28] Caroline Hibbard, Frances Dolan, and others have examined the anti-Catholic language evoked by the Catholic queen, Henrietta Maria, and her court, by the long years of Charles I's prerogative rule, and by the ecclesiastical conservatism of William Laud.[29] Hugh Trevor-Roper states:

> The charge that Laudianism led directly to Roman Catholicism was a charge of guilt by association, and the use of the Great Fear of a Popish Plot by its enemies was in essence the cynical exploitation of public credulity in order to destroy a political system which they believed—rightly—was hardening into political absolutism. For it was the real absolutism which it undoubtedly served, not the speculative popery to which it was alleged to lead, that was the determining cause of the attack on it.[30]

He quotes John Selden's remark: "We charge the prelatical clergy with popery . . . to make them odious, though we know they are guilty of no such thing."[31] The political tumult surrounding the Habernfeld Plot of the late 1630s, which was as much a fiction as the later Popish Plot of Titus Oates, was a symptom of religious and political opposition to Stuart absolutism, as well as an indirect response to Protestant anxieties about the progress of the Thirty Years' War and the fate of Protestant areas of Europe in the wake of Catholic military victories.

When the Irish Rebellion broke out in fall 1641—a rising provoked not only by the native (Catholic) Irish response to their oppression but also by English misgovernment, heavy taxation, and the failure of the English authorities to extend the "Graces" that gave some property security to the Catholic "Old English"[32]—Protestant planter lobbying of Parliament as well as parliamentary and radical Protestant political propaganda made use of virulently anti-Catholic rhetoric to associate the king, on the one hand, with a supposedly serious Catholic threat to English liberties and religion, and Parliament (particularly the House of Commons), on the other, with the defense of English Protestantism and the constitutional rights of English citizens.[33] The "popery and tyranny" conjunction that resurfaced later in the Restoration Popish Plot and Exclusion Crisis was thus highlighted in this pre–Civil War moment as a way to express opposition to Stuart royal absolutism. And, in this rhetorical context, parliamentarians were not the rebels against royal authority; the Irish were.

The published accounts of the course of the Irish Rebellion, culminating in Sir John Temple's copiously documented *The History of the General Rebellion in Ireland . . . Together with the Barbarous Cruelties and Bloody Massacres which ensued thereupon* (1646),[34] expressed, in the form of supposedly objective reporting and documentary evidence, a set of fantasies about both Irish barbarity and Catholic cruelty that drew on traditional English anti-Irish prejudices and the long history of anti-Catholic polemic.[35] These works, intended both to provoke parliamentary action and to inform both popular and elite public opinion, had a powerful impact not only on the immediate political situation but also on later political struggles, shaping, as they did, the developing narrative of English Protestant nationhood by means of a set of anti-Catholic assumptions and prejudices. For example, the foiling of the plot to take Dublin Castle early in the campaign was cast in the traditional form of Catholic treachery/Protestant deliverance. One pamphlet inserts it in a history of frustrated Catholic schemes— from the attempts on Queen Elizabeth's life to the Gunpowder Plot to the danger of the Spanish Match to the threats to the queen of Bohemia's life to the aborted Spanish attack on Holland in 1639.[36]

One of the traditional charges leveled against Catholicism was that it was ruthless in its attempts to suppress or destroy Protestantism ("true religion"). The cruelties of the Spanish and Italian Inquisitions, the St. Bartholomew's Day Massacre, and the various military aggressions of Catholic powers, from the history of Spanish fighting in the Low Countries through the various battles of the Thirty Years' War, were cited as evidence of intrinsic Catholic brutality and evil. Thus the reports of the alleged atrocities committed by the Irish Rebels on English Protestants in Ireland are part of a tradition of anti-Catholic propaganda—though, of course, the language and imagery used are available to political propaganda in almost every age.

The pamphlets and books on the Irish Rebellion continually portrayed the Irish as "cruel" and "bloody." In fact, the old image of the Irish "cutthroat" (imagined to appear suddenly on English shores and in English towns, or to emerge from hiding places all over England ready to attack English Protestants) was one that could be evoked as a bogeyman for decades and centuries to come. The product of colonialist propaganda (one has only to think of Book V of Spenser's *The Faerie Queene* and of *A View of the Present State of*

Ireland, first published in 1633), this image was associated with an intransigent Irish Catholicism and with a history of repeated foreign Catholic incursions into the British Isles by way of Ireland.

Temple's *History,* which was frequently reprinted for more than a century after its composition, synthesizes material from a number of the sensational reports and pamphlets occasioned by the 1641 rising. This enormously influential anti-Catholic and anti-Irish text reinforced the association of Catholicism with bloody violence and brutality, and of priests and Jesuits with sedition and murder. Reflecting mainly the property interests of the "New English" Protestant planters and highlighting the religious dimension of the conflict, Temple's work portrays the rebellion as arising out of native Irish barbarity and Catholic murderous hostility to Protestants.

A long section of Temple's book is devoted to "Some of the most notorious Cruelties, and barbarous Murthers committed by the Irish Rebels, attested upon Oath as they appear in severall Examinations annexed in the Margin" (90–111)—a list of atrocities and outrages documented with court testimonies, letters, and other questionable evidence.

> Some [Protestant victims] were deadly wounded and so hanged upon Tentorhooks. Some had ropes put about their necks, and so drawn thorow the water; some had withes, and so drawn up and down thorow Woods and Bogs; others were hanged up and taken down, and hanged up again several times, and all to make them confess their mony, which as soon as they had told, they then dispatched them out of the way. Others were hanged up by the Arms, and with as many slashes and cuts they made experiment with their Swords how many blows an Englishman would endure before he died. Some had their Bellies ript up, and so left with their guts running about their heels. But this horrid kind of cruelty was principally reserved by these inhumane Monsters for Women, whose sex they neither pitied nor spared, hanging up several Women, many of them great with child, whose bellies they ripped up as they hung, and so let the little infants fall out; a course they ordinarily took with such as they found in that sad condition. And sometimes they gave their Children to Swine; some the Dogs eat; and some taken alive out of their Mothers bellies, they cast into ditches. And for sucking children, and others of riper age, some had their brains knockt out; others were trampled under-foot

to death. Some they cut in gobbets and pieces, other they ript up alive; some were found in the fields, sucking the breasts of their murdred Mothers; others lay stifled in Vaults and Cellars; others starved in Caves, crying out to their Mothers rather to send them out to be killed by the Rebels, then to suffer them to starve there. (95–97, 102–3)[37]

The violence against women and children, especially against pregnant women, marks the anti-English or un-English rebels as barbarous. According to Temple: "[they] taught their children to kill English children, and the Irish women did naturally express as much cruelty as the chiefest Rebels among them" (100–101).

Temple states that 105,000 "British and protestants" (both English and Scottish) were killed "from the time of the beginning of the rebellion, Octob. 23, 1641. unto the month of April following" (106). During and after the rebellion, various English propagandists estimated the total Protestant casualties as high as 200,000 (John Milton's wild exaggeration).[38] The rebellion gave English anti-Catholic (and antiroyalist) writers free rein to propagate their most gruesome fantasies about Catholics and to confirm their bigotry. A popular piece of propaganda issued in 1647, *Ireland. Or a Booke: Together with An Exact Mappe of the most principall townes, great and small in the said Kingdome,* contains a cartoon version of the Irish Rebellion in a section of twenty-two crude woodcuts, including a scene at a Mr. Atkins's house where the rebels ("Papists") broke in, beat out the brains of the husband, raped the pregnant wife, ripped open her belly to remove the child, and burned it in the fire (a man is shown with a knife over the mutilated body of the woman while another man in the background is throwing the baby in the fire);[39] a scene of armed men driving before them Protestants they have stripped naked to suffer the winter cold; a man bound on a table as two men attack him, one cutting off his legs, the other putting a hot iron in his mouth; an image of four men, two in the foreground pulling women by the hair and two in the background smashing the heads of naked children against a wall; a scene of a "Mr Blandry Minister hanged after they pulled his flesh from his bones in his wifes sight," showing a cavalier-like soldier pulling flesh from the near-naked man while his wife and two other women scream in agony; an image of "Mr Davenant and his Wife bound in their Chaires stripped of the 2 eldest children of 7 years old rosted them upon spittes before their parents faces. Cutt their throat and after murdered him," in which the husband and wife face the fire where a man is turning and roasting two naked children; a Philomel-like violation of a fourteen-year-old girl who is deflowered, the hair pulled from her head, and her tongue cut out; a scene of a man kneeling before a priest, illustrating how "[t]he Preestes & Jesuites anoint the Rebells with there Sacrament of unction before they goe to murther & robe assuring them that for there meritorious Service if they be killed he shall escape Purgatory & go to heaven immediately"; an image of a soldier pushing an emotionally distraught mother as another swings a naked child by the legs to dash its brains out against a wall; and the castration of a Protestant minister. The writer makes a summary judgment: "The Irish nation is a people both proud and envious. The Commaltie ignorant and illiterate, poor, and lazie: and will rather beg or starve, then work; and therefore fit subjects for the Priest and Jesuits to spur on upon such bloudy actions and murtherous designes."[40] In later times other atrocities were added to the list of those committed by Irish Catholics, including the story that Catholics made candles from the fat of slaughtered enemies ("Hereticks Sewet") to be used for Marian devotion.[41]

In its first year or two the Irish Rebellion was incorporated into English as well as Irish political struggles.[42] When it broke out the Long Parliament was already in session and a contentious political context already existed into which the new crisis could be inserted. In 1640 Cornelius Burges had preached the first of the Fast Sermons to the House of Commons on Queen Elizabeth's Accession Day (November 17), which had become a nationalistic Protestant holiday.[43] Combining traditional reformist Protestant language with parliamentary antiabsolutistic rhetoric at a moment of political crisis, Burges played the role of a biblical prophet calling on his listeners to make a new covenant with God to forward the processes of reformation so as to avoid the danger of a return to a Romish "Babylon" implicit in court Catholicism, Laudian Anglicanism, and a rumored new popish plot gestating "in the womb of the Jesuitical faction" (60). Using religious ideology to authorize political and legal reforms, he alludes to the larger context of English Protestant history, especially to the "miraculous deliverances" (40) from the earlier Catholic threats such as the Spanish Armada and the Gunpowder Plot.[44] But in a passage detailing the course of the English Reformation from the time of Henry VIII, he stops with Queen Elizabeth, passing over the reigns of both Stuart kings in silence as he implies that reformation either halted or was reversed (52–54).

Although he attacks "Anabaptism" and "Familisme" (77) along with "Armini-anisme, Socinianisme and Popish Idolatry" (49), he takes a clearly reformist but not politically or religiously radical stance.

Almost a year later, on Gunpowder Treason Day, 5 November 1641, Burges preached another Fast Sermon to the House, this time with greater urgency, since the news of the Irish Rebellion had recently reached London and greatly exacerbated the political crisis. Here he traces a history of Catholic plotting against Crown and country, inserting the Gunpowder Plot and the perceived contemporary political threats into the (by now) conventional account of Catholic outrages and Protestant deliverances. Obviously with the Irish Rebellion in mind, especially "the unspeakable persecutions, and butcheries of the poore Protestant Party" (17), Burges emphasizes the barbarity and cruelty of Catholic would-be assassins or rebels—"not men, but Tigers; not Beasts, but Devills. The Hunnes, the Heruli, the Turcilingi (all branded for inhumane Caiteifs in the height) were mild and temperate creatures, in comparison of these" (14).[45] As in the earlier sermon, he retails a post-Reformation anti-Catholic history of England, starting with the 1570 papal bull excommunicating Elizabeth and its supposed provoking of the French and Spanish kings to covet the crown of England. Reversing chronology, he identifies the Northern Rebellion of 1569 as "the first poysoned fruit of the Popes Bull" (22), which set the stage for the many treasonous plots by Catholics in England and Ireland during the late Elizabethan period. To relate this history to the contemporary Irish Rebellion, Burges emphasizes the "continuall Treasons and Rebellions in Ireland" (23). He sees the Irish Rebellion as an indicator of what Catholics would do if they were powerful enough "to be able to master the Protestants in England" (31). Looking at the court, he prepares the way for what the Grand Remonstrance has to say about the Catholic or papist "malignants" around Charles I.[46] He particularly opposes any toleration of Catholics, whom he regards as inherently dangerous and perfidious.[47] In fact, to promote the cultural eradication of English Catholicism, he recommends the seizure of Catholic children for forced Protestant education (35). Returning to the old theme of Protestant providential deliverance from popish threats and assaults, he depicts the House of Commons as the protector of English Protestant identity and national security—it, not the monarchy, serving as the divinely authorized center of power in the polity. The more radical Stephen Marshall, who had also preached a Fast Sermon on 17 November 1640, emphasized parliamentary governance in calling the Commons "the Representative Body of the whole Communality of the Kingdome" (99).[48]

Marshall preached his more religiously and politically militant sermon, "Meroz Cursed," as a Fast Sermon to the House of Commons on 23 February 1641/2,[49] encouraging "godly" Protestants to declare a holy war. Trevor-Roper says of this remarkable text:

> The bloodthirsty sermon in which, six months before the outbreak of hostilities, he denounced the "neuters" and called for total war would become the most famous of all his works. It was also the sermon which he himself most admired. According to his own account, he afterwards preached it up and down the country, sixty times, and it was several times printed. It caused him to be known as "the great incendiary of this unhappy war."[50]

Although most of the sermon is taken up with the need for sincere, humble, and heartfelt prayer as a precondition to religious militancy, there are signs that Marshall was particularly alarmed by the (real and alleged) sufferings of the English Protestants in Ireland and that he wanted the Parliament to appropriate funds for the campaign against the Irish rebels. He says that his advice is "seasonable" since "the occasion of this dayes meeting . . . is purposely for the helpe of the Lord and his cause, and people now distressed in Ireland" (4). He employs apocalyptic rhetoric, urging the "Saints," "the Lambes followers and servants," to fight the "Kings, and Captaines, Merchants, and Wisemen [who are] drunke with the Wine of the Whores fornications" and who "make warre with the Lambe, and . . . give all their strength unto the Beast" (8). He clearly draws the lines between the kind of zealous Protestants he represents and the corrupt members of the Laudian church who ignore Protestant suffering on the Continent and in Ireland.

In exploring the nature of the divine curse of those who will not fight for the cause of the Lord, he issues a call to religious violence that sounds like holy revenge for the reported atrocities of the Irish rebels:

> *Cursed is every one that withholds his hand from shedding of bloud:* the strengest reason of a curse that ever was read of, if ever a man might have pleaded (with Peter when the voice said unto him. *Arise Peter kill and*

eate) not so Lord. I have not been accustomed to this, here were roome for such a plea, when his worke was to go and *embrew* his hands in the *bloud of men,* to spill and *powre* out the *bloud* of *women* and *children, like water* in every street. But he is a *cursed man that withholds his hand from this,* or that shall do it *fraudulently,* that is, if he do it as *Saul* did against the *Amalekites,* kill some and save some, if he go not through with the worke. . . . Another place you shall find in *Psal.* 137.v.8,9. The daughter of *Babylon* was there to be destroyed, observe now the epithete which God gives to the *executioners* of his *wrath* against *Babylon. Blessed is the man that makes Babylon drinke the same cup, which Babylon had made Gods people to drinke.* Now he that reades the booke of the Lamentations, may finde how *Babylon* had used the Church of God, they had *broken* their *bones* as a *Lion* breaks the bones of a Lamb, brought their *necks* under *persecution,* made their *skin blacke like an oven, hang'd up their Princes by the hand,* and which is most of all cruell, had *dashed their children against the stones.* Now saith the Spirit of God, *Blessed is the man, that thus rewards Babylon, yea, blessed is the man that takes their little ones and dashes them against the stones.* What *Souldiers heart* would not start at this, not only when he is in *hot bloud* to cut downe armed enemies in the *field,* but afterward *deliberately* to come into a subdued *City,* and take the *little ones* upon the *speares point,* to take them by the heeles and beat out their *braines against the walles,* what inhumanity and barbarousness would this be thought? Yet if this worke be to revenge God Church against *Babylon,* he is a *blessed man that takes and dashes the little ones against the stones.* (10–12)

For Babylon, of course, read the Catholic church—specifically, the behavior of the Irish Catholic rebels as reported in the Protestant propaganda produced during the Irish Rebellion. Marshall is not only calling for a holy war; he is calling for holy revenge that spares neither the militant enemies nor their families.[51]

Although Marshall suggests that the privileged classes are largely corrupt and the ambitious courtiers are anti-Christian, he is somewhat restrained in his attack on the king. He speaks generally about those "who instead of *helping the Lord against the mighty,* do help *the mighty against the Lord[,]* . . . who instead of joyning all their strength, and giving all their assistance to the Church in her distresse, doe give all the assistance they can to the enemies of the *Church,* that they may do mischief against the *Church*" (20). He even criticizes those MPs who are "endeavouring to hinder the building of *Sion,* and to further the repairing of the walls of *Babylon*" (21), presumably High Church Laudians with an anti-Puritan agenda. He also attacks religious (and political) "neuters" (22) who act either out of crafty "policy" (23) or "sluggishnesse" (24). In the call for fervent Protestant unity, he says, *"he that is not with me, is against me"* (23). He urges all his listeners to abandon self-interest and to pray and struggle for the common (religious) good, reminding them of the ways "God miraculously discovered wicked enterprises against you, and almost miraculously preserved you by his own naked arme, ever since the beginning of your meeting" (44), using language associated with the defeat of the Armada and the Gunpowder Plot discovery to describe the Long Parliament's proceedings.

Though the fiction of unity of king and Parliament is maintained, the call for militancy seems more a matter of defending Parliament against the Crown's forces than of protection against external enemies: "God hath put it into the heart of *Kings Majesty and your selves,* to put the whole kingdome into a *posture of prayer;* we hope your care in putting the Kingdome into a *posture of defence,* will be serviceable" (45). Marshall seems most concerned to use "godly Ministers and godly people" (45) as the best preparation of defense for church and state, but when he decries the unresponsiveness to "Germanies afflictions" (46) during the Thirty Years' War and the failure to "help either England, Scotland, Ireland, King, or Parliament" (46), he seems to look beyond prayer and general concern to military activism. Most immediately, he argues, "many *great things* are yet to bee done; much rubbish to be removed; many obstructions to be cleared, many enemies to be overthrown. *Ireland* is to be relieved, Religion to bee established; *Prayer* may doe all this; we may overmatch all our enemies by *prayer,* discover all their plots by *prayer.* . . . [Y]et prayer is not all the means" (46–47). Only selfishness, he argues, holds "false-hearted Christians" (51) back from making the financial sacrifice needed to support religious warfare: "[T]hey love the Church, they pitty the miseries of the Church, they are sorry for Germany, when they think on it, an that is but seldome: They grieve for Ireland; but require either their hands to underwrite, their legs to walk, their purses to contribute, their authority to command or countenance, &c., they can spare none of all these" (50). He urges the members of the House of Commons to be self-sacrificing, selfless, even zealous in their support of the holy war to which he calls them: "[T]he Church at this present time requires from you many other things [than prayer]. It may be some of you may be called, as souldiers, to spend your blood in the Churches cause. . . . It may be others of you may . . . be called from your own ease and honour to some wearisome task, embrace it readily. It is like your collections and contributions wil be more frequent than ordinary, and very shortly in an extraordinary occasion, for the reliefe of our distressed brethren in Ireland. . . . What you give in this case is interpreted by Christ as given to his own person" (53–54). It finally takes a parliamentary subsidy to fund the forces Marshall wants sent to crush the Irish rebels.

The ongoing Irish Rebellion and the king's relationship with royalist forces in Ireland and with the Irish rebels helped to make the English Civil War into the War of the Three Kingdoms, for such it was perceived in its own time as both Scottish and Irish events were inseparable from English political and military struggles. Of course, once again strong anti-Catholic fantasies came into play — especially those concerning the quite unlikely Irish Catholic invasion of England or those having to do with imminent dangers on English soil from Irish cutthroats and arsonists as well as from English Catholics. Keith Lindley observes, for example: "One incredible story of an allegedly popish plot in early 1642, depicted English catholics as preparing to blow up, and burn, the chief English cities and create havoc, as soon as the rebels had conquered Ireland and landed an army in England."[52]

Because the parliamentary victory in the English Civil Wars had to be consolidated before the Irish Rebellion could finally be crushed by Oliver Cromwell, one set of events overlapped with the other and made an especially strong impact on the English cultural imagination, incorporated finally into the dominant Protestant, then Whig, version of English history. When Cromwell invaded Ireland with his troops in 1649, he said: "We are come to ask an account of the innocent blood that hath been shed; and to endeavour to bring them to an account . . . who, by appearing in arms, seek to justify the same. We come to break the power of a company of lawless rebels, who having cast off the authority of England, live as enemies to human society; whose principles (the world hath experience of) are, to destroy and subjugate all men not complying with them."[53] Cromwell's methods, strainedly justified by John Milton in his *Observations upon the Articles of Peace,* included killing 2,600 at Drogheda and 2,000 at Wexford in an exemplary show-no-mercy method of conquest.[54] But such brutality was seen as divinely sanctioned and just punishment for

Irish barbarity—a prelude to King William's crushing of Irish Jacobite forces in 1690. Milton's and Cromwell's response to the massacre of the Waldenses in Piedmont in 1655, the poet calling for holy revenge in his famous sonnet on the topic ("Avenge O Lord thy slaughter'd Saints"), was stimulated by the sort of atrocity stories associated with the Irish Rebellion, confirming, again, the cruelty of the Catholic forces serving the "triple Tyrant," the pope.[55]

The Popish Plot: A Political Romance

One thing the 1641–42 and 1678–81 political crises have in common is the use of anti-Catholic language and the threat of alleged popish plots to mask a more direct struggle between Parliament and the Crown. In his political poem, "Naboth's Vineyard," John Caryll characterizes the Restoration-era Popish Plot as a "romance."[56] It was a political fiction attuned to popular fantasy and the indirections of politically oppositionist discourse, what Harold Love has called "a fearsome cocktail of disinformation."[57] Royal policy, of course, was more favorable to Catholics and to France than either public opinion or the majority of members of the House of Commons would tolerate. The foreign policy and domestic political stance of Charles II's government that so alarmed the opposition, especially the more politically radical Protestant nonconformists, could be perceived to have the kind of controlling intelligence and larger design implied by the word *plot,* but it was less "popish" than it was royal absolutist. The elaborate fiction constructed by Titus Oates and others was exploited by the Crown's political opposition as a convenient imaginative form for the expression of a specific antimonarchical and anti-Catholic political agenda. Unfortunately, real people caught up in this "romance" were persecuted and killed.

The populace, of course, could accept Oates's allegations as an embodiment of their political anxieties about their country's foreign and domestic political struggles. Jonathan Scott argues that Oates's conspiracy story was "true" in the sense that it accurately reflected real public fears about the dangers posed by Charles II's government and policies:

[T]he crisis of 1678–81 was not imaginary but real. It had its root not in ignorance, or hysteria, but in well-informed public belief. It was not "about" Oates's story; that was an expression, not the cause, of this fear. It was not "about" the Duke of York who was, again, a symptom, not the cause, of the problem. This crisis was "about" the policies of Charles II, in their European context, which left the nation feeling dangerously vulnerable. Once again England faced its European nightmare: a government on the wrong side of the Reformation/Counter-Reformation divide.[58]

The fear, in short, was of an imminent invasion, led by France and involving Ireland, resulting in the "extirpation" of Protestantism "root and branch," by "fire and sword" in the manner understood to have occurred in Germany, France, Ireland, and Piedmont.

Oates's fiction, then, metaphorically refracted the truth as many people perceived it. As Dryden put it in "Absolom and Achitophel": "Some truth there was, but dash'd and brew'd with lies, / To please the fools, and puzzle all the wise."[59] On a popular level, the Popish Plot expressed a set of traditional fantasies and prejudices that could be manipulated by more astute political game players in times of crisis. The repertoire of anti-Catholic codes and language could be used in yet another political context, but by comparison, for example, with the late 1630s and early 1640s the religious language here had a more secular meaning, particularly since struggle for religious reform against the religious authority and changes of the Laudian church was so intense in the earlier period. For at least the preachers and the more zealously religious MPs, anti-Catholic language at that time had both religious and political valence, while during the Restoration-era Popish Plot and Exclusion Crisis, the religious feelings were less strong than the political ones.[60]

The anti-Catholic furor of the Popish Plot was, then, a cover for anti-Stuart feeling—in the sense that the Stuart conception of a strong monarchy conflicted with the nascent Whig (and older republican) desire for parliamentary governance.[61] It is interesting that once the Glorious Revolution took place the persecution of Catholics diminished greatly,[62] just as it did during the period of Cromwellian rule. The twenty-four (mostly clerical) Catholics who were executed during the Popish Plot crisis were scapegoats for the forces of "popish tyranny"—that is, royal absolutism.[63] Thus Charles was forced to allow the trials and executions to run their course. Exclusion of James II from the crown may have been the goal of the parliamentarians who supported the prosecution of the "plotters," but James was not only a Catholic threat to English religion and national security (like his brother, he was connected to Louis XIV's France) but also someone who would extend his brother's drive to royal absolutism.

Conspiracy Theory and the Threat of "Plots"

The immediate political context into which Oates's conspiracy story was inserted was delineated by Andrew Marvell in *An Account of the Growth of Popery, and Arbitrary Government in England, More Particularly from the Long Prorogation, of November, 1675, Ending the 15th of February, 1676, till the Last Meeting of Parliament, the 16th of July 1677* (1677).[64] In this work by Marvell and other members of the "country party" in Parliament, the phrase "popery and tyranny" signified not a simple anti-Catholic stance but a vilifying of Stuart absolutism by means of the religious-polemical code.[65] It begins with a powerful, blunt statement: "There has now for divers years a design been carried on to change the lawful Government of England into an absolute Tyranny, and to convert the established Protestant Religion into downright Popery: than both which, nothing can be more destructive or contrary to the interest and happiness, to the constitution and being of the king and kingdom" (248). Scott rightly emphasizes the way European religiopolitical conflicts, especially the Thirty Years' War, entered the consciousness and political struggles of the English from the late sixteenth through the late seventeenth century. He argues that the Catholic powers' gains in the Thirty Years' War and the consolidation of strong monarchical states on the Continent were seen by English wishing to preserve Protestant reform, constitutional liberties, and the institution of Parliament as an ongoing threat to the nation—even when the danger of military invasion was not imminent. Certainly there was a continuity of concerns about "popery" and "arbitrary government" running from the Jacobean period through to the time of the Glorious Revolution—concerns that made anti-Catholic discourse a fixture of political rhetoric in the period.[66]

In the context of royal foreign policy from the end of the second Dutch War (1665–67) to the request for a military subsidy to ready the army and navy for possible combat with a foreign aggressor (France), Marvell narrates the struggles between the House of Commons and the Crown over the international religious and commercial allegiances of England—the king leaning towards France and relying on periodic subsidies from Louis XIV and the Parliament trying to force the king to forge an alliance with the Dutch and, possibly, with Spain and other anti-French confederated states — both for national security and for the preservation of English Protestantism from the threat of a French-supported restoration of Catholicism.[67]

Marvell's treatise, published with a false foreign imprint because of the government's refusal to license any accounts of the 1677 proceedings in Parliament, identifies a "conspiracy" for the subversion of constitutional government and the promotion of "popery," refusing, however, to name the "conspirators," though the courtly servants of Charles II who are targeted (primarily the earl of Danby) were known to all. Conal Condren says that "Marvell's was a conspiracy theory, and with all such theories simplicity of causation must be maintained [and] events must be tailored to fit." He does call it, however, a "remarkably prescient conspiracy theory."

> Charles was effectively in the pocket of Louis XIV. He . . . was committed to the promotion of more than the simple toleration of Catholicism in England. How far Charles would really have gone is a moot point, but suffering an invasion by his own and French troops was not beyond the bounds of possibility. As England and Holland were effectively just about all that was left of the Protestant Reformation, it was well within the bounds of fear. Further, the reforms of the Long Parliament and the Interregnum had all but been undone after the Second Settlement of 1662. Whatever the latitude of the notion of a mixed monarchy . . . Charles gave it but grudging lip-service and would have preferred to rule as his father had tried to and as Louis managed to, as an absolute monarch. He also believed that Catholicism was the religion best suited to such a form of rule. There is, in short, enough truth in the drift of Marvell's argument and the yoking of Catholicism to arbitrary rule for Marvell to have scored a palpable hit and to have encouraged deeply-felt prejudices.[68]

Without directly blaming the king for the attempt to overextend royal prerogative and assert royal absolutism, Marvell uses the politically transparent device of accusing opportunistic and ambitious evil counselors of the king of attacking English liberties and the Protestant religion. He also criticizes the court party in the House of Commons and all those who neglected their duty as faithful representatives of the people as they catered to the wishes of the

Crown and promoted their own selfish interests. Despite this, he portrays the House of Commons, in contrast to the sycophantic Lords,[69] as the best protector of English liberties, property, constitutional government, and the established Protestant religion.

Marvell's tract focuses on the post–third Dutch War (1672–74) period, particularly the early 1676 French invasion of Flanders, "our natural out-work" (319). He gives an account of the parliamentary debates, petitions, and bills, as well as the official royal responses to the 1677 Parliament—in the form of carefully ambiguous messages, a final blunt rebuke, and forced adjournments or prorogations—to suggest that the king and his evil ministers were dealing with the Parliament in bad faith, asking for a subsidy whose uses the suspicious Commons could not control, and resisting (finally with great vehemence) the Commons' attempt to force the Crown to make an anti-French alliance. The conflict of parliamentary power with royal prerogative (particularly with reference to the king's right to make treaties and wage war) reprises some of the pre–Civil War clashes between early Stuarts and their parliaments, overlaid here with the religious dimension implicit in earlier struggles, as the Parliament pressed for a Protestant militancy and an anti-Catholic foreign and domestic policy.

Although foreign relations and the House's use of its taxation power to control government policy are at the center of Marvell's discourse, religious issues are also addressed, especially (1) in his exposure of two antipapist bills forwarded by the House of Lords as a Catholic ruse; (2) in his contempt for the 1672 Declaration of Indulgence as a device to use toleration or religious liberty to promote Catholicism;[70] (3) in his allusion to the 1673 marriage of James, duke of York, to the Catholic Mary of Modena (and, by implication, James's own conversion to Catholicism, which was well known by 1677);[71] and (4) in Charles's treatment of the bill formulated to guarantee Protestant education to the next minor who would be in the line of succession. Marvell portrays Charles's cozy relationship with the French as part of a conspiracy to promote the growth of popery in England—especially during the elaborately ceremonial visit of the French ambassador and his large entourage during one of the periods of Parliament's adjournment when, Marvell suggests, the king allowed this French group to usurp the role of parliamentary counsel.[72]

An international context to which Marvell attends is that of strengthening monarchies in Catholic countries such as France and Spain at the expense of representative bodies:

[T]he kings of England rule not upon the same terms with those of our neighbour nations, who, having by force or by address usurped that due share which their people had in the government, and are now for some ages in the possession of arbitrary power . . . and exercise it over their persons and estates in a most tyrannical manner. But here the subjects retain their proportion in the Legislature; the very meanest commoner of England is represented in Parliament, and is a party to those lawes by which the Prince is sworn to govern himself and his people. No money is to be levied but by the common consent. No man is for life, limb, goods, or liberty, at the Sovereign's discretion: but we have the same right (modestly understood) in our propriety that the prince has in his regality. . . . (248–49)

This passage makes it clear that when Stuart kings moved towards a royal absolutism—for example, during Charles I's "prerogative rule" or in Charles II's abusive prorogation of Parliaments—they approached the tyranny most English perceived in the rule of Louis XIV of France, "the Master of Absolute Dominion, the presumptive Monarch of Christendom, the declared Champion of Popery, and the hereditary, natural, inveterate enemy of our King and Nation" (263).

Marvell also sets the English Protestant state against Roman Catholicism, celebrating the English freedom "from that Roman yoak, which so great a part of Christendom do yet draw and labour under" (250). He refuses even to consider Roman Catholicism "a Religion; nor is it to be mentioned with that civility which is otherwise decent to be used, in speaking of the differences in humane opinion about Divine matters" (250–51).[73] He attacks the papacy and its abuses, underscoring the political dangers posed by Catholicism and obedience to a pope who claims temporal authority and the right to depose princes: "[T]hey [Catholics], being all bound by strict oaths and vows to obedience to the Pope, should evacuate fealty due to the Sovereign. Nay, that not only the clergy, but their whole people, if of the Romist perswasion, should be obliged to rebel at any time upon the Pope's pleasure" (257). This is the old charge that all Catholics are potentially disloyal and seditious.

To provide the larger historical context, Marvell rehearses the (anti-Catholic) history of England from the time of Queen Mary:

The whole reign of Queen Mary, in which the Papists made fewel of the Protestants: The excommunicating and deprivation of Queen Elizabeth

by the Pope, pursued with so many treasons and attempts upon her person by her own subjects, and the invasion in 'eighty-eight by the Spanish;
the two Breves of the Pope, in order to exclude King James from the succession to the crown, seconded by the Gunpowder Treason: in the time of
his late Majesty, King Charles the First, (besides what they contributed to
the Civil War in England) the Rebellion and horrid Massacre in Ireland,
and, which was even worse than that, their pretending that it was done by
the King's Commission, and vouching the Broad Seal for their authority:
the Pope's Nuncio assuming nevertheless and exercising there the temporal as well as spiritual power, granting out commissions under his own
hand, breaking the treaties of peace between the King, and, as they then
styled themselves, the confederate Catholics: heading two armies against
the Marquess of Ormond, then Lord Lieutenant, and forcing him at
last to quit the kingdom: all which ended in the ruine of his Majestie's
government, and person; which, but upon occasion of that Rebellion,
could never have happened. So that we may reckon the reigns of our
late princes, by a succession of the popish treasons against them. And, if
under his present Majesty we have as yet seen no more visible effects of
the same spirit than the firing of London (acted by Hubert, hired by Pied-
delou, two Frenchmen) which remains a controversie, it is not to be attributed to the good nature or better principles of that sect, but to the wisdom of his holyness; who observes that we are not of late so dangerous
Protestants as to deserve any special mark of his indignation. (258–59)

Marvell especially emphasizes the Irish Rebellion in this account. He goes on
to stir up Protestant fears that a Catholic restoration would mean the clerical
appropriation of the old monastic lands seized by Henry VIII (260). This is
the context of the "conspiracy" "to introduce a French slavery, and instead of
so pure a religion, to establish the Roman idolatry" (261). And such a conspiracy is worse than a plot to assassinate a lawful monarch: "For, as to matter of government, if to murther the King be, as certainly it is, a fact so horrid,
how much more hainous is it to assassinate the Kingdom? And as none will
deny, that to alter our Monarchy into a Commonwealth were treason, so by
the same fundamental rule, the crime is no less to make that Monarchy absolute" (261). Thus "popery" and monarchical "tyranny" are inseparable.

In this historical context Marvell announces he is writing a "naked narrative of some of the most considerable passages in the meeting of Parliament

the 15th of February 1676[–77]" (263). First, however, he returns to the first
of the Restoration Dutch Wars and its aftermath and to the Parliament of
1670, which the court wished "after the old wont [to] be gulled to the giving
of money" (266). He analyzes some of the discussion of the Triple Alliance
supported by Parliament but opposed by "the conspirators" who have "fidelity
to the French King" (273). After the prorogation and before Parliament reassembled in 1672, he says there was "competent scope for so great a work as
was designed, and the architects of our ruine might be so long free from their
busie and odious inspection till it were finished" (273), the Triple Alliance being
abandoned in the meantime and a war with Holland begun on a flimsy pretext
as England then allied with France. The "hellish conspiracy" (279) to serve the
interests of France was, according to Marvell, coupled with a religious ruse in
the 1672 Declaration of Indulgence, by which "all the penal laws against the
Papists . . . and against Nonconformists . . . were at one instance suspended, in
order to defraud the nation of all that religion which they had so dearly pur-
chased" (280). He calls the issuing of the declaration "the master-piece . . . of
boldness and contrivance" of "these conspirators" (282), one that undermined
the security of the state. He criticizes the toleration of Catholicism by alluding
to the French king's stated purposes in invading Flanders—"for extirpating of
heresie" in a "war of religion, and in order to the propagation of the Catholick
Faith," referring to a demand the king made on the Dutch for "not only an in-
tire liberty, but a publick exercise of the Catholick Apostolick Roman Religion
throughout al the United Provinces" (285). Toleration of Catholicism, then, was
inherently a threat to Protestantism.

When Charles's war with the Dutch depleted royal finances, he was
forced to call Parliament to vote a new subsidy. But, as part of the deal, the
Parliament passed the Test Act, "by which the Papists were obliged to pass
thorow a new state-Purgatory, to be capable of any publick imployment" (291).
Without saying directly that the duke of York had to quit his navy post because of the Test Act, Marvell turns to the matter of the heir apparent's pro-
jected marriage to Mary of Modena, which immediately became a subject of
discussion in 1673 in the reassembled Parliament. The MPs warned:

> for his Royal Highness to marry the Princess of Modena, or any other of
> that religion, ha[s] very dangerous consequences: that the minds of his
> Majesty's Protestant subjects will be much disquieted, and thereby filled
> with infinite discontents and jealousies: that his Majesty would thereby

be linked into such a foreign Alliance, which will be of great disadvantage and possibility to the ruin of the Protestant religion: that they have found by sad experience how such marriages have always increased Popery, and incouraged priests and jesuits to pervert his Majesty's subjects: that the Popish party already lift up their heads in hopes of this marriage: that they fear it may diminish the affection of the people related to the crown: that it is now more than one age, that the subjects have lived in continual apprehensions of the increase of Popery, and the decay of the Protestant religion: finally that she having many kindred and relations in the court of Rome, by this means their enterprises here might be facilitated, they might pierce into the most secret counsels of his Majesty, and discover the state of the realm. (296–97)

Assuming that a monarch's or an heir apparent's marriage to a foreign Catholic would open Protestant England to innumerable dangers, Marvell expects his readers to think back to the Catholic spouses of James I and Charles I (especially to Henrietta Maria), as well as to keep in mind Charles II's Catholic queen, Catherine of Braganza.

After Parliament successfully pressed the Crown to conclude a peace treaty with the Dutch, it dealt with such other matters as "questioning ministers of State" (303), "quashing the indulgence" (303), and proposing "further bills against Popery, and for the education, and Protestant marriage henceforward of those of the royal family" (301). It expressed the fear that the English regiments recruited for the service of the French might be used against the English.[74] The court party in Parliament raised the fear that the kind of conflict that led to the Civil Wars was being renewed: "That the nation was running again into 'forty-one" (303). This suspicion was confirmed when a bill was offered in the House of Lords, resembling one brought to the House of Commons at Charles I's Oxford Parliament, to require members to swear an oath not "upon any pretence whatsoever to take up arms against the King" or to "indeavour the alteration of the Government either in Church or State" (305). In conditions of press censorship, meanwhile, "many books [were] then printed by license, writ, some by men of the black, one of the green cloth, wherein the absoluteness of the English monarchy is against all law asserted" (308).

After the next session of Parliament, which considered appropriations and bills "for *Habeas Corpus* . . . against Papists sitting in either House[,] . . . for speedier convicting of Papists [and] for recalling his Majesty's subjects out of the French service" (312), Parliament was prorogued again between 22 November 1675 and 15 February 1676/7, during which time certain suspicious judicial appointments were made (including that of Sir William Scroggs, who was prominent during the Popish Plot trials). Ammunition and ordnance were shipped from England to France, and the very day the Parliament was to reassemble, 15 February 1676/7, "the French king appointed his march for Flanders" (319). In the House of Lords the duke of Buckingham was called to the bar for speaking against the prorogation of Parliament and, consequently, he, the earl of Salisbury, the earl of Shaftesbury, and Lord Wharton were "committed to the Tower, under the notion of contempt, during his Majestie's and the Houses' pleasure" (322). Marvell observes that "nothing but Parliament can destroy Parliament," by denying the "liberty of speech which the King verbally, and of course, allows them" (322). He notes that one-third of House members "have beneficial offices under his Majesty" (323) and thus constituted a court party voting the interests of the Crown rather than serving as "the representatives of the people of England . . . impowered by them to transact concerning the religion, lives, liberties and the propriety of the nation" (324). He classifies another third of the House as office seekers who have "cheated the countries into electing them" (327) by posing as anti-French and anticourt. Supposedly, only the minority third of the House was honest: "a handful of salt, a sparkle of soul, that hath hitherto preserved this gross body from putrefaction, some gentlemen that are constant, invariable, indeed Englishmen: such as are above hopes, or fears, or dissimulation; that can neither flatter, nor betray their king or country: but being conscious of their own loyalty and integrity, proceed throw good and bad report, to acquit themselves in their duty to God, their prince, and their nation" (329). One of the purposes of Marvell's tract, like others of the era produced by the "country" party, was to argue that new parliamentary elections should be held.[75]

The House, in considering grievances, formulated an address to the king to protect the country against the French threat: "'strengthen yourself with such stricter alliances, as may secure your Majestie's kingdoms, and secure and preserve the . . . Spanish Netherlands'" (354). The king curtly replied that "'the preservation of Flanders was of great consequence and . . . he would use all means in his power for the safety of his kingdoms'" (354). The House then sent a fuller address to the king emphasizing the importance of anti-French alliances in preparation for an impending war with France, for which they would provide ready money. Marvell reproduces some of the arguments for and against this parliamentary pressure in the field of foreign policy (which was traditionally reserved for the monarch), supporting what he thought was the stronger (parliamentary) argument in favor of protecting the nation against a danger he thought the king was courting.

The address was sent to the king on 30 March; the House had to wait until 11 April for his reply. The king's response was to ask for resources to prepare for war, saying nothing about anti-French alliances. This led, after a parliamentary adjournment, to a constitutional pitched battle between the House and the Crown—the former unwilling to appropriate any money until the king formed a Protestant, anti-French alliance, the latter standing firm on his prerogative to conduct foreign policy, make war, and make treaties. While French military victories continued, the Parliament-Crown dispute, Marvell sarcastically suggests, served the French interest (374). With Parliament recessed again, a great French embassy visited England. Marvell expressed outrage that "the English Parliament was kept aloof from the business of war, peace, and alliance, as improper for their intermeddling and presumptuous; yet with these three estates of France all these things were negotiated and transacted in the greatest confidence" (374–75).

Marvell notes the deathbed regret of Philip II of Spain that he had tried to obtain "the universal monarchy" (386), a desire the English had countered by an alliance with the Dutch. He argues that the English should renew the Dutch alliance to oppose the new aspirant to "universal monarchy," Louis XIV.[76] The Parliament's foreign policy address to the king, formulated by a special committee, pressed for this course of action. After some debate about the wisdom of sending it—the pro-court members arguing that it was "an invasion upon his Majesty's prerogative of making peace, war and leagues" (395)—the House rejected an amendment to omit mentioning the league with the Dutch, then passed the motion to transmit the document.

The king called the House to Whitehall for his answer, but when they appeared before him he took a surprisingly hard line in defense of the royal prerogative and rebuked them for meddling in foreign affairs. He argued: "Should I suffer this fundamental power of making peace and war to be so far invaded . . . as to have the manner and circumstances of leagues prescribed to me by Parliament, it's plain that no prince or State would any longer believe that the sovereignty of England rests in the crown" (404). Assuring the MPs that he was doing all he could to protect the country, he forced a two-month adjournment on them, leaving them "greatly appalled" (405). When House members offered to speak, they were silenced by the House Speaker, who, Marvell claims, abused his authority on this and subsequent occasions to cut off discussion and adjourn the House on his own authority. To add insult to injury, the proceedings of the Parliament were forbidden to be printed "but even all written copies with the same care as libels to be suppressed" (406), while the king's speech was printed in a royalist newspaper. Marvell is contemptuous of the House of Lords for serving as "meer property to the conspirators" (407) and their design of promoting popery and arbitrary government. When the adjournment ended, the king signified he wished another right away: "these frequent adjournments [were] calculated to give the French more scope for perfecting their conquests, or to keep the Lords closer, till the conspirators' designs were accomplished" (408). The Parliament was kept out of session until 4 April 1678, while the French king continued his conquest of Flanders. The adjournment was then extended to 15 January 1678.

Marvell concludes that he has exposed "the conspiracy against our Religion and Government" (411). He notes the increase in conversions to papacy at court, the "considerable defection of considerable persons both male and female to the Popish religion, as if they entered by couples clean and unclean into the ark of that church, not more in order to their salvation, than for their temporal safety" (412). He bemoans the state of Ireland, the pro-Roman inclination of royal policy, the readiness of an English cardinal (Howard) to manage the restoration of Catholicism "like Cardinal Pool" (412). He justifies not naming the conspirators, the conspirators he opposes being, in his eyes, "the living libels against the government" (413). He asserts his loyalty and respect for the king and ends with a cry: "'From all privy conspiracy, &c. Good Lord deliver us'" (414). This perception was widespread and although many anti-Catholic Englishmen might have been inclined early or late to disbelieve Titus Oates's evidence, they had a strong belief in a conspiracy to promote what Marvell called "popery and arbitrary government." Hence the furor over the Popish Plot.[77]

Oates's Narrative and Its Consequences

Oates's belatedly published deposition itemizing the elements of the plot story, *A True Narrative of the Horrid Plot and Conspiracy of the Popish Party Against the*

Life of His Sacred Majesty, The Government, and the Protestant Religion (1679) (see fig. 5), pretends to be concerned primarily with the well-being of King Charles II, to whom Oates dedicates the pamphlet — though it contains, by way of other people's libelous speech about the king, a number of critical remarks about Charles's behavior. Oates alludes to the history of Catholic and Jesuit subversion and murder — mentioning the Gunpowder Plot, the supposed poisoning of King James by the Jesuits, and the assassination of Henri IV of France as precedents for the alleged plan to assassinate Charles. Professing loyalty to the monarchy, Oates stupidly connects the republican John Milton with Catholic plotting because Milton allegedly "was a known frequenter of a Popish Club."[78] Associating the Jesuits with belief in absolute monarchy, tempting kings to rule "by Will" rather than "by Law" (169), Oates positions Charles as a monarch constitutionally in harmony with Parliament rather than one seeking to reinstall prerogative rule.

Oates's narrative begins with the Jesuits and a reference to one of the many letters he says he was asked to deliver on their behalf:

> Richard Strange, Provincial, John Keins, Basil Langworth, John Fenwick, and Mr. Harcourt, Jesuits, did write a Treasonable Letter to one Father Suiman, an Irish Jesuit at Madrid . . . in which was contained the Plotting and Contriving a Rebellion in Scotland, of the Presbyterians against the Episcopal Government: In order to which they had employed one Matthew Wright, and William Morgan, and one Mr. Ireland to go and Preach, under the notion of Presbyterians, and give the disaffected Scots, a true understanding of their sad condition, in which they were, by reason of the Episcopal Tyranny, exercised over them: and withall to tell them, they had now a fair opportunity to vindicate their Liberty and Religion; and that it could be done by no other way but by the Sword, and that now the King was so addicted to his pleasure, that he would, and could take but little care in that concern. And in the said Letter it was expressed, that they had gotten an interest in His Royal Highness, but they would deal with him as they thought fit; and that they were resolved to use all means to weaken the King of England's Interest, by informing his friends of his own intent to betray them into the hands of a Forein Power, to wit, to send them to fall by the Sword in the French King's Wars, against the Confederate Princes. (173–74)

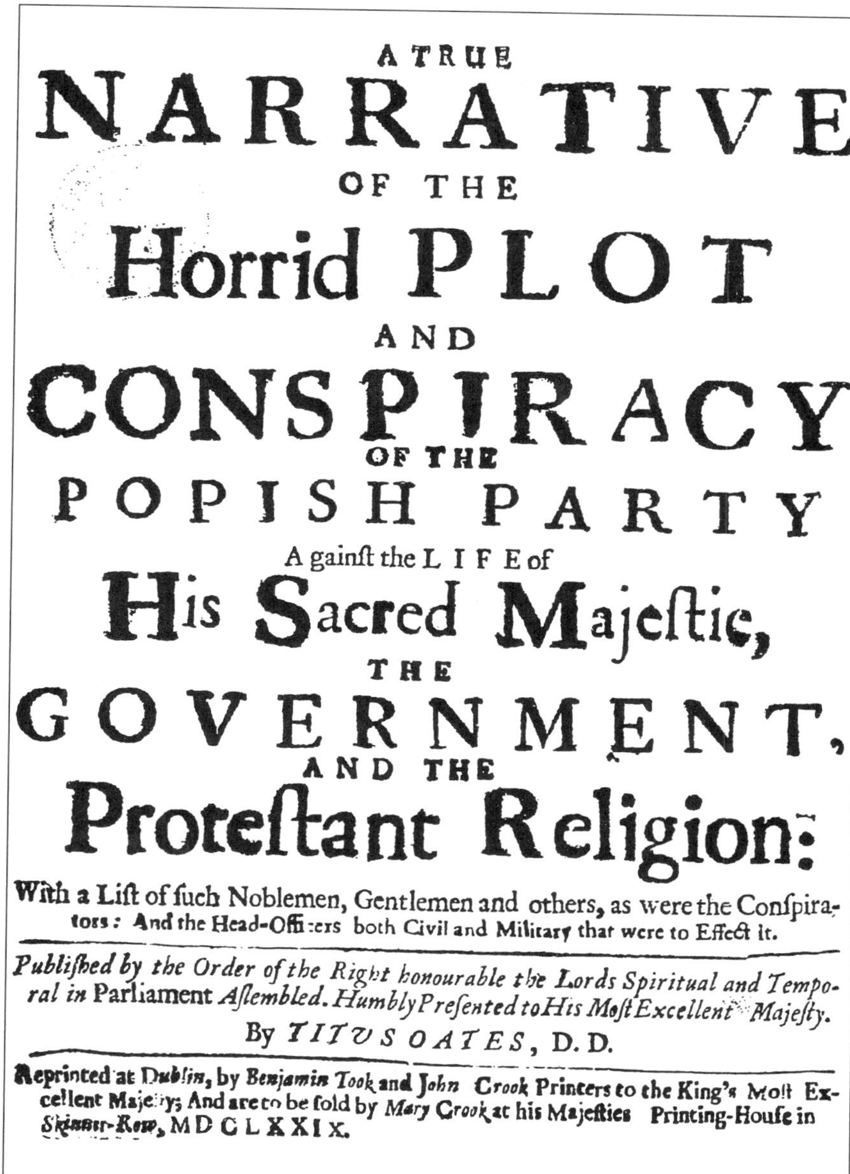

A TRUE
NARRATIVE
OF THE
Horrid PLOT
AND
CONSPIRACY
OF THE
POPISH PARTY
Agaínſt the L I F E of
His Sacred Majeſtie,
THE
GOVERNMENT,
AND THE
Proteſtant Religion:

With a Liſt of ſuch Noblemen, Gentlemen and others, as were the Conſpira-
tors : And the Head-Officers both Civil and Military that were to Effect it.

Publiſhed by the Order of the Right honourable the Lords Spiritual and Temporal in Parliament Aſſembled. Humbly Preſented to His Moſt Excellent Majeſty.

By TITUS OATES, D.D.

Reprinted at Dublin, by Benjamin Took and John Crook Printers to the King's Moſt Excellent Majeſty; And are to be ſold by Mary Crook at his Majeſties Printing-Houſe in
Skinner-Row, M D C L X X I X.

FIGURE 5. Title page of Titus Oates, *A True Narrative of the Horrid Plot and Conspiracy of the Popish Party Against the Life of His Sacred Majesty, The Government, and the Protestant Religion* (1679). Reproduced by permission of the Special Collections Library, University of Michigan.

Oates revives the old association of Catholic and Calvinist resistance theory, connects the Jesuits with Scottish and Presbyterian opposition to the English king and church, and portrays them as ready to embarrass Charles by revealing the very conspiracy between the king and France that they fostered.

Continuing his assault on the Jesuits, Oates alleges that they sent twelve of their students to Spain, requiring them "to renounce their Allegiance to His Majesty of Great Britain" (174–75), taught by their master at Valladolid "that the said Oath of Allegiance is Heretical, Antichristian and Devilish; and that Charles Stuart the King of England is no lawful King, but comes of a spurious Race, and that his father was a Black Scotch-man, and not King Charles the first" (175). He claims the English Jesuits, who "had procured one Father Beddingfield to be Confessor to His Royal Highness" (175), were ready to murder both him and his brother within the year if he did not "answer their expectations" (175) for restoring Catholicism in England. Oates says assassins were recruited and that the Jesuits "had an intent to procure one to stab him [the king] at his Court of Whitehall; and if that could not be conveniently done, they would employ one of his Physicians to poison him" (178). In a larger international conspiracy, the Scots would be stirred to rebellion and "a way . . . made for the French King's landing an Army in Ireland: And further, that the Irish Catholicks were ready to rise" (179).

In his account Oates mixes trivial and serious matters. On the one hand, he alleges that one of the Jesuits said that "the late King [Charles I] was no Martyr but an Heretick, and withal added, that he was none of King James Son, but a Bastard begotten upon the body of Anne of Denmark by her Taylor" (185). On the other hand, he claims there were plans for a general uprising in Ireland: "That the Irish were ready to rise at ten days warning, with 20000 foot and 5000 horse, and would let the French King into that Kingdom[,] . . . that there are persons that have secretly taken Commissions from the General of the Society of Jesus, by vertue of a Breve from the Pope, dated Octob. 1.1673. and that they resolve to cut the Throats of the Protestants again, when once they arise" (189). He reports that the Jesuits planned to murder a polemical adversary, "the Author of the Jesuits Morals" (Israel Tonge, his coconspirator) and that the Jesuit provincial, Thomas Whitebread (who had expelled Oates from St. Omer as morally unfit), said "That he and the Society in London would procure Dr. Stillingfleet to be knockt on the head, and also Poole, the Author of Synopsis Criticorum, for writing some things against them" (191). He alludes several times to a plan to have the queen's physician, Sir George Wakeman, poison the king, and he claims there were also plans to assassinate the bishop of Hereford as "an Apostate from the Roman faith" (193). He has the Jesuits confessing to starting the Great Fire of London of 1666, for which they used "700 Fire-Balls" (196), a blaze in which they supposedly intended the king to be killed.

Oates accuses Jesuits of trying to subvert the position of the prince of Orange "and his Party" (199) in the Netherlands, to "make a Commotion there" (208).[79] In Ireland, he claims, "[f]our Irish Jesuits had undertaken the death of the Duke of Ormond; and that after his death the Irish were ready to rise" (214). Catholics in London are said to be ready to "Rise and Cut the Throats of a hundred thousand Protestants" (207). "Jesuits and their agents" (220), with the help of some Benedictines, were supposedly planning in 1676 to set fires around London but hesitated because they were uncertain of help from the French king. The narrative keeps returning to the main plan, that of assassinating King Charles II, a project that involved elaborate fund-raising. Oates reproduces a list of bishops and other ecclesiastical authorities for England he says he saw in a papal bull—the assumption being that the pope was preparing for the Catholic overthrow of English Protestantism. After England's return to Catholicism, the Jesuits would be empowered to teach "Philosophy and Divinity" throughout the country in their colleges.

Oates's deposition, in the form of eighty-one chronologically arranged items, is a tissue of fabrications and lies dressed up as a legal document. It is presented as a record of unlikely conversations and overheard conversations and of snooping into the contents of letters Oates was supposedly entrusted to deliver both in England and abroad. It ends with his dramatization of the Jesuits' turning against him—the provincial first beating him and then sending someone to murder him. It constructs a national as well as a personal paranoid scenario of Jesuit perfidy, internal British instability, and foreign menace. It concludes with several lists. The first contains "The Names of the Conspirators"—including, in England, nine Benedictines, three Carmelites, two Franciscans, ten Dominicans, twenty-five Jesuits (plus twenty-two on the Continent, three in Scotland, and twelve more "whose names [he] know[s] not" [230]), fourteen secular priests, eight laymen (including "Four Irish Ruffians" [231]), and some others. There is a separate "List of such Noble-men and Gentry, as are present in this Conspiracy" (233). Finally, the work closes with an outline of "The General Design of the Pope, Society of Jesus, and their Confederates in this Plot[,] . . . the Reformation, that is, (in their sense) the Reduction of Great Britain and Ireland, and all His Majesties Dominions by the Sword[,] . . . to the Romish Religion and Obedience" (235). This plan involves the pope's assertion that he is "Entitled . . . to the Kingdomes of England and Ireland," his appointment of "Cardinal Howard his Legat for England to the same purpose" (235), his use of Jesuits to commission military officers to assassinate King Charles, and his order to kill Charles's brother James if he did not consent to "the assassination of the King his Brother, [the] Massacre of His Protestant Subjects, firing of his Towns, etc." (236). Oates also alleges "another French Plot or Correspondence carried on by Sir Ellis Layton, Mr Coleman and others" (236) to eradicate the Stuart line, including the king, the duke of York, and the prince of Orange, "because that Family hath not answered their expectations" (236).

As Love has observed, Titus Oates used the authority of the print medium to great advantage:

> Oates's fabrications . . . withdraw credibility from voice and script in order to confer it on their own preferred medium of print. The world of Jesuit intrigue, as Oates, William Bedloe and the tribe of informers present it is a world of whispers, covert meetings, overheard conversations and secretly transmitted letters and commissions, all directed toward the horrific overthrow of the social order. With voice and script branded as the media of concealment and dissimulation, the witnesses can be credited with the heroic, Promethean act of having transferred this concealed information into print where it was available to all and could be properly assessed. . . . [T]hey were able to appeal directly to the power of the printed page to confer objectivity and impersonality upon the texts it presented.[80]

The printed exposé had all the more power in an era of suddenly lapsed print censorship. It also highlighted the conflict between, on the one hand, the openness to political discussion found in parliamentary debate and the emerging public sphere and, on the other, the politics of royal prerogative and conspiratorial scheming.

One of the many other conspiracy mongers was a Catholic goldsmith, Miles Prance, who published his main contribution to the Popish Plot propaganda, *A True Narrative and Discovery Of several very Remarkable Passages Relating to the Horrid Popish Plot* (1679). This pamphlet targets Jesuits and other priests, four Catholic lords (Arundel of Wardour, Bellasis, Peter, and Powis)[81] and their servants, and various other militant Catholics (some of whom are connected to the Queen's Chapel), concentrating first on the alleged Protestant martyr of the Popish Plot era, Sir Edmund Berry Godfrey, the judge to whom Oates first told his story of the plot and whose mysterious death is blamed on Prance's Catholic associates. It then delineates a supposed plot to murder the political hero of the Popish Plot, the earl of Shaftesbury. The work assumes a large-scale Catholic conspiracy, not only to kill the king, but also to undertake a civil war to restore Catholicism: "one Mr. Paston . . . said [to him] . . . It was true the King was a great Heretick, but the Lord Bellasis, the Lord Arundel, the Lord Powis, and Lord Peters . . . would have a gallant Army for the Deposing, or Disposing . . . of the King, and utter subversion of all the Protestants; and then the Catholick Religion should be establisht and flourish in this Nation" (4). Prance portrays his own guilt as an accomplice, for example, in the supposed murder of Godfrey, but then, through his testimony (once recanted, then reasserted), his heroism as a patriot and newly converted Protestant. After his testimony before the king and council, he says,

> Reverend Dr. Lloid Dean of Bangor, [who] was charitably pleased to give him a Visit, & betow'd much pains with him at several times, instructing him in the grounds & reasons of the Protestant Religion; from whose pious Amonitions & labours, by the Divine blessing, he reaped much benefit for the comfort and setling of his perplexed Soul, and thinks it his duty, for the same publikly to return him his hearty Thanks, Being wholly taken off from the Apostatiz'd bloody Roman Church, which he utterly renounces, and doth freely, cordially, and intirely embrace the Protestant Religion, and therein particularly submits himself to the Church of England, resolving (by Gods Grace) therein to live and die. (24)

From the vantage point of a newly converted Protestant, in the last part of the pamphlet, he attacks "The Immoral Behaviour, Cruel Expressions, and Vile Practises of serveral other Popish Priests with whom [he] hath been acquainted" (30). This section of the work contains examples of clerical sexual corruption, financial trickery, and religious deception of the sort found in the long tradition of anti-Catholic writing.

The Trial and Execution of the Five Jesuits: Public Relations, Propaganda, and the Press

Political crises—whether spontaneous or fabricated—need focuses. Large dangers and threats need specific embodiments in order for political propaganda to work and for the political nation to grasp the situation imaginatively. After the Gunpowder Plot it was convenient to portray the subversive, radical Catholic underground's desperate attempt to attack the whole Jacobean political establishment as an internationally motivated "Jesuit Treason" engineered on the local level by such priests as Henry Garnet, Oswald Tesimond, and John Gerard. During the Popish Plot era, it was politically convenient to bring charges against the English Jesuit provincial, Thomas Whitebread, and four other Jesuits (William Harcourt, Anthony Turner, John Fenwick, and John Gaven) as the masterminds or at least the chief agents in the alleged assassination plot against Charles II.[82] The Jesuit reputation for being in the militant vanguard of the Catholic Counter-Reformation, of course, made them the perfect antagonists.[83] The judicial murder of these five men was mandated by the logic of the political situation: it was part of Shaftesbury's and the Whigs' attack on the "popishly affected" court (and, indirectly, at first, on the Catholic heir apparent, James, duke of York), a process the king felt powerless to stop, since he and his brother actually needed the Jesuits as scapegoats to prevent the more direct assault on the monarchy, the Catholic queen, and the royal brother (the last two eventually targeted as the conspiracy charges expanded).[84]

At the height of the plot hysteria, the Jesuits did not stand a chance of escaping with their lives. They were tried in the Old Bailey, where the Whig London sheriffs rigged the juries with rabid anti-Catholics and the courtroom was packed with a London audience ready to vocalize their prejudices during the proceedings.[85] The presiding judge, Sir William Scroggs, played to the galleries with his sarcastic anti-Catholic comments and delivered prejudicial instructions to the jury, inviting them to return a swift guilty verdict. This was, in Scott's words, "political theatre."[86] As was the case with earlier show trials

and executions of Catholic priests and laypersons, different accounts of what
happened in the courtroom and on the scaffold were publicized to manipulate both national and international public opinion. These texts demonstrate
in sharp contrast the differing Catholic and anti-Catholic mind-sets, codes,
fantasies, and sensibilities, but, since the central political struggle was between
Whigs and Tories, Parliament and the Crown, much of the debate was an internecine Protestant one within the Restoration political establishment: this became clearer as the Popish Plot and Exclusion Crisis developed and the publicity war was more obviously being waged by Tories such as Roger L'Estrange
and opponents patronized by the earl of Shaftesbury and other Whigs.

The trial of the five Jesuits took place on 13 June 1679, early in the
course of prosecutions of the alleged Popish Plot conspirators. William Ireland, Thomas Pickering, and John Grove had already been tried and sentenced
to death as traitors, but the Jesuits were the real catch, since Oates's perjury
centered on his characterization of the regular triennial assembly of English
Jesuits (for their regular business)[87] as the central planning session for the large
conspiracy against the king, Parliament, and English Protestantism. This meeting had taken place on 24–26 April 1678 in St. James Palace in the quarters of
the duke of York (who had to be dissociated from it).[88] Given the popular and
propagandistic image of Jesuits as political schemers and planners or sanc-
tioners of regicide, it was important for Oates and the court to put these five
men and the internationally networked order they represented at the heart of
the perceived political danger.

As Scott points out, at the trials of Catholic clergymen during the Popish Plot crisis (particularly in 1678–80), a regular feature of the proceedings
was the association of the priests with a long-standing "counter-reformation
design" to defeat Protestantism and subvert the English state:

> Thus all trials began with a lengthy recitation of its history.
> This reminded the jury [that] "ever since the reformation there
> hath been a design carried on by priests and Jesuits, that came from be-
> yond the seas . . . to subvert the government, and destroy the protestant
> religion established here in England."[89] This involved the expected char-
> acters: the pope, the French king and at least "four Irish persons";[90] the
> expected equipment: poison, fire, daggers and the sword; and the ex-
> pected *dénouement:* an invasion followed by the customary slaughter.[91]

As Edward Coke, Robert Cecil, and the earl of Northampton had done at the trial of Henry Garnet, William Scroggs[92] used the occasion of the trial of the Jesuits to rehearse propagandistic anti-Catholic history as the context of the current alleged treasonable acts.[93] During a later trial, at a point at which he was suspicious of the testimony of Oates, Bedloe, and the other plot "witnesses," Scroggs nonetheless, in an outburst at three Benedictine defendants, also revealed his ingrained anti-Catholic prejudices, evoking the Protestant historiographical schemes that portrayed Catholicism as a persistent menace to the English nation:

> I do believe it is hardly possible for an atheist to be a papist, but it is hardly possible for a knowing Christian to be a Christian and a papist. . . . Your doctrine is a doctrine of blood and cruelty; Christ's doctrine is a law of mercy, simplicity, gentleness, meekness and obedience. . . . Therefore never brag of your religion, for it is a foul one, and so contrary to Christ, that it is easier to believe anything, than to believe that an understanding man may be a papist. . . . If we look into the bottom of you, we know what you were ever since Queen Mary's days; and if we look into the Gunpowder Treason we know how honest you are in your oaths, and what truth there is in your words, and that to blow up King, Lords and Commons is with you a merciful act, and a sign of a candid religion. But that is all a story with you, for it is easier for you to believe that a saint, after her head is cut off, did go three miles with her head in her hand, to a place where she would be buried, than that there was a Gunpowder Treason.[94]

At the end of this passage he responds to those Catholic historical revisionists who claimed that the Gunpowder Plot was concocted by Sir Robert Cecil to entrap Catholics so as to justify intensified persecution.

After the trial of the five Jesuits and before his own arrest, the Jesuit Nicholas Blundell composed a narrative of the proceedings, which he intended to send in a letter by way of Madam Katherine Hall to "his Friends the Jesuits at Cambray." This document was printed as a broadsheet, *Blundel the Jesuit's Letter of Intelligence . . . taken about him when he was Apprehended at Lambeth, on Munday the 23th of June 1679* (1679). It was countered soon after by another broadsheet, *An Answer to Blundell the Jesuits Letter* (1679).[95] The context for the publication of both pieces and for all publications between 1679 and 1685 was the greater press freedom made possible by the lapsing of the Licensing Act,[96] which provided for prepublication censorship.[97] In his account Blundell portrays the five Jesuits as patient, composed, and saintly in their demeanor, and the judge, prosecution witnesses, and courtroom spectators as intemperate, bigoted, and inhuman.[98] Blundell gives few details about the testimony of Oates, Bedloe, Prance, and Stephen Dugdale but concentrates on the failed efforts of the Jesuits to have their witnesses heard in order to prove that Oates was actually at St. Omer at the time he claimed to have been in London: "Judge *Scroggs* askt each witness as he did appear, of what Religion he was, and upon answer that he was a Roman Catholick, the whole Court gave a shout of laughter, then the Judge would say to them, well, what have you been taught to say, and by many scoffing questions (which moved the Court to frequent laughter) he did endeavour to take off the credibility of the witnesses." The old post–Gunpowder Plot association of Jesuits and lying is here extended to all Catholics: since Catholics are liars, their testimony in court under oath cannot be trusted. The Catholic-liar association is connected to the general suspicion that those Catholics who took the Oath of Allegiance did so without full assent.

Assuming that the many Catholic witnesses against Oates demonstrated that he perjured himself in this trial, Blundell suggests that the other defense witnesses who testified that Oates had lied at the priest William Ireland's trial (when he claimed that he was in London when he was really in Shropshire) pointed to a pattern of perjury on Oates's part. As a contrast to Oates, Blundell presents John Gaven (see fig. 6) as a convincing spokesperson for the falsely accused Jesuits: "then did *Gaven* . . . with a great deal of clearness and eloquence and with a cheerful countenance draw up their Justification, shewing the face of their Evidence, and how fully their witnesses had proved Mr *Oates* perjured. Then he did lay open the improbability of such a Plott, and how unlikely Mr *Oates* should be intrusted in delivering Commissions to persons of Honour, and Estates, whom he never (as he acknowledge) had seen before or since." Blundell sets Gaven's rationality and equanimity against Judge Scroggs's injudiciousness and intemperateness: "this was delivered by Mr *Gawen* with a countenance wholly unconcerned, and in a voice very audible, and largely and pertinently exprest: the *Judge* was incensed at this speech which he often interrupted him, but *Gawen* still urg'd my Lord, I plead now for my Life, and

FIGURE 6.   Portrait of John Gaven, S.J., from *Brevis Relatio Felicis agonis, quem pro Religione Catholica gloriose subierunt Aliquot e Societate Jesu Sacerdotes in ultima Angliae persecutione, Sub Annum 1678. A Protestantibus excitata, Violenta morte sublati* (Prague, 1683), 57. Shelfmark 860.i.13. By permission of The British Library.

for that which is dearer to me then life, the honour of my Religion, therefore I beseech you have a little patience with me." Scroggs's instructions to the jury are presented as clearly prejudicial: "the Judge made his Arrayne to the Jury telling them that what the Prisoners had brought was only the bare assertions of boyes, who were taught it as a point of their Religion, to lye for the honour of that Religion, whereas Mr *Oats* Mr *Bedlow* and others were upon their Oathes, and if Oathes were not to be taken no Courts could subsist." Blundell is contemptuous of the four additional witnesses Oates then sprang upon the court, "an old Parson in his Canonical Gown, an old Dominican Priest . . . and two women that swore they saw Mr Oates in the beginnning of May 1678." The response of the spectators and the rest of the judicial proceedings are then presented as a shameful spectacle: "at this the whole Court gave a shout of laughter and hallow, that for almost a quarter the Cryers could not still them; never was a Bear-baiting more rude and boysterous than this Tryal: Upon this the Judge dismist the Jury to consider and bring in their Verdicts, who after half an hours absence brought in the five Prisoners at the Barr all Guilty of High Treason; thereupon the whole Court clapt their hands and gave a great hallow." Unlike the judge and the spectators, the Jesuits "comported themselves most Apostolically at the Barr, not the least passion or alteration appeared in them, at the invectives of the Judge, or at the clamours of the people, but made a clear and candid defence, with a cheerful and unconcerned countenance (as a stander by said) if they had been a Jury of Turks they had been quitted."

Blundell reports that the next defendants were brought in: Richard Langhorne, the Jesuits' lawyer, Sir George Wakeman, the queen's physician, and Mr. Corker, Mr. Marsh, and Mr. Rumbly—the last three Benedictine priests.[99] He notes that the first was tried and condemned to death. Then he recounts how "on Thursday the day before the five Jesuits were Executed, my *Lord Shaftesbury* was with *Turner* and *Gaven*, promising the Kings Pardon if they would acknowledge the Conspiracy, [but] Mr *Gaven* answered he would not murder his Soul to save his Body, for he must acknowledge what he knew not, and what he did believe was not." Thus Blundell suggests that the Jesuits were not, ultimately, the real target of the Popish Plot prosecutions. The aim was higher: the king and the heir apparent.

The last part of Blundell's account concerns the punishment of the five Jesuits, from their journey to Tyburn on sledges to their executions and dissections. The narrative is interrupted only to note that Shaftesbury put pressure on the condemned and imprisoned Langhorne to reveal the Jesuits' real estate holdings.[100] Blundell's description of the Jesuits' demeanor is consistent with his portrayal of their behavior in court. We are told that they each made a speech, "all averring their ignorance of any Plott against His Majesty, secondly pardoning their Accusers, thirdly, hartily praying for them." Unlike the hostile courtroom spectators, the crowd at Tyburn was supposedly sympathetic to the condemned men: Blundell says that when, after an eloquent speech by Gaven and "an Act of Contrition, which was much liked by all," "they all betook themselves to Meditation, for more then a good quarter . . . there was a profound silence, and their most Religious comportment wonderfully allayed the fury of the People." Earlier Catholic martyrdom accounts, of course, described similar responses of a religiously mixed audience to the final words and acts of Catholic martyrs. The rejection of the last-minute offer of pardons in exchange for a false acknowledgment of the existence of this "conspiracy" is also a conventional feature of some martyrdom narratives. Blundell does not describe at length the hanging and quartering of the victims (no need to do so since such descriptions were well known in martyrological literature). He does note, however, that "their Quarters were given to their friends" for burial instead of being reserved by the state for official display.

Since the broadside stands as a strong indictment of the operation of the justice system during the Popish Plot era, it elicited what appears a Whiggish and radical Protestant response "to confute [Blundell's] errors, and for Vindication of the wholesome Laws, and Impartial Judicature of this our English Nation." Rather than renarrate the trial and execution, the author contests the polemical force of Blundell's account by appealing to a familiar set of anti-Catholic assumptions and an anti-Jesuit mythology, setting the punishment of the five Jesuits in the larger framework of the long history of English Protestant and Jesuit Catholic struggles. The writer begins with the same assumption Scroggs articulated in court, that Jesuits, who "can Dissemble . . . with their own Friends, and send them Fallacies to keep them Ignorant for their Diabolick and most unheard of Villanies," are liars who "can Equivocate with us for their own Interest, whom they mark out as mortal Foes." He then broadly indicts Jesuits for responsibility, in the larger international context, for

Rapes and Massacres, and Murdered Kings, Poysoning and Devastations, Tortures, and all the Cruel rage that the Infernal Legions arm'd with fatal Counsels e're could prompt them to; for they the barbarous Executioners of Tyrant Rome, disperse themselves abroad throughout the Earth, and gather in the Slain to fill her Babilonish Cup with reaking Blood from Tender Hearts of Innocent distill'd. . . . They rove like thirsty Tygers in their uncontrouled paths, but if restrain'd from their pernitious Deeds by interposing Justice arm, they never look back to view what they have done to others, but cry themselves are opprest.

Any claim of innocence by the five Jesuits, given the habitual villainy of the whole order, rings hollow. Thus Blundell's account is "an Erronious Letter or Lybill."[101]

The pamphlet does not present the process of the trial sequentially but takes issue with some of Blundell's claims and reinterprets the behavior of the courtroom spectators. First, it maintains the accused were well treated in prison, given "all the favours and priviledges imaginable," and afforded the opportunity both to speak for themselves and to bring witnesses. The writer maintains, however, that the Jesuits' witnesses "were suborned and sent by their Tutors in St Omers, and other places"—that is, they were all liars. The courtroom laughter they provoked, he says, was caused "by their confounding themselves in their Averrations, for they not being well versed in Roman Lyes, or that their premeditated Doctrine being not well digested, they baffled one another more erroniously in their Discourses . . . so that their Attestations proved not only Ineffectual, but also prejudicial to the Prisoners." He claims that the main point of their testimony, concerning Oates's presence in St. Omer in April 1678, was undercut by the fact that "many of them never saw him, nor in Court had not known which was he unless they had been shewed." The three college employees testifying (supposedly to protect their jobs)—a tailor, a butler, and a gardener—were "by publick Confession absolved for what they should say or Swear, [and] came merrily over, but went as shamefully home after they had Disgorg'd their Popish Element, vowing never to bring any more Lyes into England, seeing they were no better accepted, and no more regard taken of them; they being Mint of the Popes own stamp." In discussing the butler, he says the man was "made to Swear he would never Lye with any Nun in France, nor Fast a whole Lent together, till he had performed the Rectors Will, who put him in remembrance of the brave Atchievements of those Hero's, who were sent over in King Jameses Time, supposing to excite Father

Garnet, and the rest of the jesuits, in the daring Powder-Plot." The writer thus connects the most outrageous Catholic attempted act of terrorism with the present circumstances (and invokes the supposed sexual immorality of nuns and priests). Oates's witnesses, by contrast, are seen as reliable: "one of them being a Dominican Fryer, a Chicken of the Popes own Hatching; and Three more honest Protestant Attestators."

To counter Blundell's portrayal of the courtroom proceedings and the behavior of the crowd as resembling a bear-baiting, the author blames "their foolish Witnesses" for "any disturbance or incivility from unruly spectators," then conjures up another episode in English anti-Catholic history: "give me leave to ask the Monsieur Jesuit what Bear-baitings were in Ireland committed in 41. By the barbarous and bloodly Papists, when 300,000 innocent Protestants unjustly fell, not being suffered so much as to speak for themselves, but were inhumanely sacrific'd by their devilish rage." Protestant judicial murder supposedly pales by comparison with Catholic massacres. The author notes that the penal laws made the Jesuits' very presence in England a capital crime (one not usually prosecuted by Protestants, who are naturally "merciful"). Then he expresses strong doubt whether Shaftesbury ever visited the Jesuits in prison with a deal to spare their lives, "knowing them to be Priests, and therefore irreclamable."

Blundell's depiction of the demeanor of the martyrs on their way to execution is dismissed by conjuring up the image of Jacques Clement, the supposedly Jesuit-inspired assassin of Henri III: "'tis objected, that they went joyfully to the place of Execution, so did the Monk that Stab'd King Henry of France, the Dagger being Consecrated, dipped in the Euchrist, and wrapt in the reliques of a Saint, to make it more forcible for Execution." The writer alludes to the familiar charge that Jesuits both theoretically justify and practically promote king killing, referring further to the familiar fantasy that there was a special elaborate Catholic ceremony for preparing the assassin to do his dirty work.

The pamphlet denies the last-minute offer of reprieve to the Jesuits at the gibbet, emphasizing again the main point that to provide an example to those wishing to imitate their "Diabolick practices," they "dye with lyes in their mouths, which lying and equivocating may be seen at the late Apprehending of this Blundell, about whom (as it is credibly reported) this Letter was found; who both to the Justice Dr Oates, and the Constable, forswore himself, his Name, and Function." The main theme of this pamphlet, Jesuit lying, thus extends from the condemned and executed priests to the Jesuit author of their story.

The greatest public relations impact of the trial and execution of the five Jesuits came through the printing of their last speeches. Kenyon suggests the initial publication was a government decision that backfired:

> The government itself may have authorized this step, on the assumption that it would discredit the authors . . . but the opposite was the case. The appetite of the public for works of piety was insatiable, and Catholic piety did as well as any other. It soon became *de rigueur* for every prospective martyr to compose a long farewell speech protesting his innocence and justifying his Catholic faith. . . . Richard Langhorne even composed lengthly meditations in verse. The government made no effort to interfere. . . . But the concern of the Church of England is shown by the haste with which many clergymen, led by the Bishop of Lincoln, rushed into print to rebut them.[102]

Thus the first of the pamphlets dealing with the last speeches of the five Jesuits is presented as "Published by Authority": *The True Speeches of Thomas White-bread, Provincial of the Jesuits in England, William Harcourt, Pretended Rector of London, John Fenwick, Procurator for the Jesuits in England, John Gavan, and Anthony Turner, All Jesuits and Priests, Before their Execution at Tyburn, June the 20th DCCLXXIX. With Animadversions Thereupon: Plainly discovering the Fallacy of their Asseverations of their Innocency* (1679).[103] The pamphlet inserts into the text of the Jesuits' speeches aggressive interruptions by the sheriff. He tried to stop Turner's protestation of innocence, directing him to pray instead (4), and while the priests were "at their private [silent] Devotions for about an hour" he instructed them to "Pray aloud . . . that we may joyn with you," adding, in addressing Gavan, the accusation that he "did preach at the Quakers meeting" (8). The "Animadversions" that follow, as a separate document with separate pagination, attempt to counter the force of the Jesuits' protestations with a long discussion of Jesuit equivocation, plotting, and sanctioning of king killing, alluding to Henry Garnet as a bogeyman whose behavior was a model for these Jesuit malefactors. The writer concludes: "I have great reason to be confident that these Speeches were contrived for the promoting of their Grand Plot, upon which their hearts were so much set . . . that the thoughts of Death could not divert them. Their Design in that was to destroy Us and Our Religion, and in order thereto, by these specious words they would deceive us." But evidently the "specious words," like other scaffold speeches from the martyrological tradition, convinced both live and print audiences otherwise.

A subsequent attempt to neutralize the effects of the five speeches similarly tried to connect them to the long history of Jesuit deception: *The Last Speeches of the Five Notorious Traitors and Jesuits: viz. Thomas White, alias Whitebread, Provicial of the Jesuits in England, William Harcourt alias Harrison, pretended Rector of London, John Gaven alias Gawen, Anthony Turner And John Fenwick, Procurator for the Jesuits in England. Who were justly Executed at Tyburn, June 20, 1679, for Conspiring the Death of His Sacred Majesty, and the Subversion of the Government and Protestant Religion* (n.d.). Emphasizing the Jesuit practice of using disguises and aliases, this work begins with comments on the exploitation of the dying speech for propaganda purposes: "Those men know that the last words of dying Men bear a great sway amongst the Living, and that the swanlike sentences of those that sing at their departure, being cunningly insinuated and politickly made use of, penetrate more deeply than can be imagin'd into the hearts of the credulous and unstable" (1). The author acknowledges that the speeches were disseminated in manuscript in increasingly corrupt versions, in "Transcripts conveyed from Person to Person, and consequently subject to those alterations, additions, and diminutions, as may be most advantageous to the interpreter" (1). He claims that he reprints accurate texts of the speeches before he comments on them. Quite possibly, the whole scheme is an excuse to practice the trick that Catholic or pro-Catholic writers had used to disseminate Catholic texts under the guise of attacking or refuting them. In any event, the short interpretive section of the pamphlet rather perfunctorily rehearses the usual charges that Jesuits are liars or equivocators as well as believers in the doctrine of king killing. To illustrate the latter, the author narrates the supposed elaborate ritual Jesuits use "at the Consecration of the Person and the Dagger, which they design for a Royal Massacre. . . . An invention of Men worse than Devils, enough to maze Heaven it self: which shews that the words of dying men are not always Oracles, when they go about to palliate embodyed Villany" (7). He then retails a list of supposed Jesuit mischiefs perpetrated throughout Europe. Catholics could buy this pamphlet to have copies of the speeches; radical Protestants could buy it for the critical framework in which the speeches are embedded. It was a case of clever marketing.

Another pamphlet, which refers to two previous works criticizing the last speeches of the Jesuits,[104] republishes an earlier anti-Jesuit tract to connect the executed Jesuits with general Jesuit perfidy: *Autokatakritoi, or, the Jesuites*

*condemned by their own Witness, Being an Account of the Jesuits Principles, In the
matter of Equivocation, The Popes Power To Depose Princes, The King-Killing
Doctrine. Out of a Book Entituled An Account of the Jesuits Life and Doctrine. By
M. G. [a Jesuit] Printed in the Year 1661. And found in possession of one of the five
Jesuits Executed on the 20th of June last past. Together, with Some Animadversions
on those passages, shewing, that by the Account there given of their Doctrine in the
three points above-mentioned, those Jesuits lately Executed, were, in probability,
guilty of the Treasons for which they suffered, and died Equivocating (1679).*[105]
The author claims that Gaven's speech was partly borrowed from the pro-
Jesuit tract (A1ᵛ). His main purpose, however, is to prove, through a discussion
of their support of papal deposing power, of king killing, and of equivocation[106] and mental reservation, that the Jesuits are congenital liars and thus
their claims of innocence are not to be believed: "[T]hey are all a pack of
Juglers. Those of them who have little or no conscience will Equivocate without scruple, and therefore we may justly despair of ever learning the Truth
from them" (18).

The 13 October 1682 issue of Henry Care's *A Weekly Pacquet of Advice
from Rome* contains a satiric poem that mistranslates a Latin poem celebrating
the Jesuit martyrs:

> All hail! you Pseudo-Martyrs blest,
> With Hell, or Purgat'ry at best,
>   For love of Pope your Lord:
> All hail dear Lads! That bravely dy'd
> Like Father Garnet Hangefi'd,
>   By Parliaments abhorr'd.
>
> Five Bonny Fathers o'th'Society,
> Each of the Order of Impiety,
>   Prodigal of their stinking Breath;
> Right Jesuits, living and dying,
> Traytors In Fact, but Truth denying,
>   At Tyburn-Cross did yeild to death.
>
> Grant Heav'n! their Quarter'd Limbs, Burnt Guts,
> May Caveats prove to Rogues and Sluts,
>   And stop Romes Catter-wauling:

> May Tory Shams leave Holy Church
> (As she, poor Coleman) in the Lurch,
>   And cease L'Estrange's Bawling!

This poem drags the spectacle of the execution of the five Jesuits down to the level of sick-joke popular satire.

The Jesuits' lawyer, Richard Langhorne, prepared a speech for his own execution, the written text of which was taken from him so that he had to recite it from memory. It was subsequently published, along with other material, in *Mr. Langhorne Memoires with some Meditations and Devotions of his, During his Imprisonment: As also his Petition to His Majesty, and his Speech at his Execution* (1679). This work is an effective self-defense against the false charges of Oates and Bedloe, reasonable and tactful in tone. It carries an anti-Whig message and recounts how Shaftesbury and others approached the condemned Langhorne with a deal to save his life by admitting the existence of the Popish Plot (the same offer extended to others at the time).

The petition Langhorne submitted to the king denies any involvement in the Popish Plot and is worded to refute the usual claim that Jesuits and their disciples practiced calculated lying:

> I doe make this Declaration, and every Part thereof in the Plain and Or-
> dinary Sense of the Words . . . as they are commonly understood by En-
> glish Protestants, and the Courts of Justice of England, without any Eva-
> sion, or Equivocation, or Delusion, or Mental Reservation whatsoever.
> And without any dispensation, or Pardon, or Absolution already granted
> to me, for this, or any other purpose, by the Pope, or any other Authority
> or person whatsoever, or without any hope of any such Dispensation.
> And without thinking or believing that I am, or can be acquitted be-
> fore God or Man, or absolved of this Declaration, or any part thereof,
> although the Pope, or any other Person or Persons, or Power whatsoever,
> should Dispense with, or Annul the same, or Declare that it was, or is
> Null or Void from the beginning. (10)

Although this declaration has an especially lawyerly style, it reproduces a formula often used by Catholics at their trials, one necessary because of both prosecutorial assumptions and popular belief in Catholic mendacity.

The scaffold speech itself is an eloquent apologia in which Langhorne says: "[M]y Religion to be the sole Cause of my being the Object of the Malice of my Enemies, who are the causers of my death" (11). He states that for the English to disbelieve his protestation of innocence because of his religion is to cast aspersions on all Catholics, past and present, and to invite a retaliatory mistrust of English Protestants—"To lay a Foundation for the total destroying of all Trade, as well as Conversation, with all those Princes, States, and People" (11). He does not accept the restriction of mistrust to Jesuits "and those who make use of them": "For there is scarce any Prince of this Religion now living, who doth not make use of a Jesuit for his Ghostly Father, which will likewise be a clear Evidence, that those Princes (known to all the world not to be Fools or Mad-men) have not an Opinion, That the Doctrines and Principles of the Jesuits, are any wayes Pernicious and Dangerous to Government, as the Pulpits of England repute them to be" (11). Langhorne argues that Jesuits can more easily be cleared of responsibility for the acts of assassins such as Clement and Ravillac than can English Protestants for the killing of Mary, Queen of Scots, and King Charles I — the Catholic assassins being "private Villains" (11). He claims, in fact, that there are "more Authors, reputed Protestants, who justifie the People to have a Power to Depose, and take away the Lives of Kings, than there are found Authors, reputed to be Catholiks, who assert the Pope to have Power to Depose Princes" (11). He finally denies any wrongdoing on his part and prays for forgiveness for "Mr. Oates and Mr. Bedloe, and all Others, who are any ways guilty of my Death, or of my not obtaining my Pardon, or of rejoycing at the shedding of my Innocent Blood" (12).

The editor of the pamphlet writes that Langhorne was not allowed to speak from notes, so that what he said at his hanging was imperfectly remembered. Even so, Sheriff How is reported to have interrogated him after his denials of guilt and to have attempted to cut short his speech: "Shorten your business, you have, Mr *Langhorne,* and your Party, so many wayes to Equivocate, and after Absolution you may say any thing" (21). The full text of the speech, which the sheriff has in his hands, he declares "not fit to be Printed" (21). The editor then gives a short version of the end of Langhorne's speech and an account of his charitable exchange with the executioner: "The Writer [says] The Lord have Mercy on your Soul," and Langhorne answers, "The Lord in Heaven reward your Charity" (22), before crossing himself, praying, and signaling the executioner that he was ready to die. The whole work is a power-ful piece of anti-Whig propaganda.

It elicited a response in *The Confession and Execution of Mr. Richard Lang-horn, Late Counsellor in the TEMPLE, Who was Executed for his Treasonable Practices against the Life of His Most Sacred Majesty, And the True Protestant Government . . . With an Account of his Deportment in Newgate, and at the Place of EXECUTION. With several other Remarkable Circumstances* (n.d.). This pam-phlet begins by associating Langhorne with Jesuitical equivocation and with "ambitious Tyrants far remote" (2). In contrast to the reasonable, charitable, and tactful tone of the pamphlet it answers, this work is nasty, vituperative, and bigoted, rehearsing the charges of conspiracy with foreign agents and priests that were leveled against Langhorne, but when it moves to a description of Langhorne's journey to Tyburn and actual execution it sometimes seems posi-tively sympathetic to him, suggesting that the title and initial tone of the piece are only a disguise for an anti-Whig (if not also pro-Catholic) document. For example, Langhorne is described, on the sledge, as "seemingly very Peni-tent," denying "that he knew any intreague of Design on foot by Catholicks around this nation, of any of his Majesties Countries or Dominions" (3) and protesting his loyalty to the king. Although the writer seems to take an anti-Catholic tack in expressing a suspicion of "[t]hese and many other Protesta-tions so common to those kind of desperate People, who trust in Romes In-dulgences and Pardons, and pin their Consciences thereon, not weighing the displeasure of an angry God" (4), he acknowledges the positive responses of spectators to Langhorne's behavior: it "moved the Hearts of many to pitty him, by reason of his Age and Gravity: being a tall man, of a Sanguin Complexion, of a moderate Grace and Gesture and of brave and Eloquent and authentick parts, having been a Counsellor for this many years" (4). The next sentence skips the details of the execution but notes the disposition of Langhorne's re-mains: "After he was Cut down and Quartered, his Quarters were by his Maj-esties Order delivered to his Friends, in Order to his Burial, &c" (4). There are mixed signals in Langhorne's treatment, both by the king, who allows for a re-spectful burial rather than the state's propagandistic display of a traitor's body parts, and by the pamphlet's writer. The concluding paragraph sounds like anti-Catholic propaganda, but there are doubts cast on its message by the pre-vious treatment of Langhorne: "Now one would suppose that this and many other the untimely Ends of such like Miscreants, who have of late for their ab-horr'd Crimes been justly made the Trophies of pursuing Justice, should stand as marks to warn their Brethren least they should headlong press upon those dangerous shoals of an untimely Fate: but 'tis vain, pernicious men that bend on black Designes, Rush forwards not caring where they go, so they accomplish their destructive ends" (4). Langhorne's portrayal in the pamphlet does not comport with the rash miscreant depicted in this peroration.

As Scott points out, persecution and execution of Catholics during the Popish Plot era have been difficult to assimilate to the classic Whig account of English history: "[W]ithin a Protestant historiographical tradition founded, in part, on the myth that it invented liberty of conscience, the hanging, drawing and quartering of at least twenty-four catholics between 1678 and 1681, purely on account of their religion, in the face of unflinching protestations of their innocence, has proved an insuperable obstacle to a satisfactory account."[107] Certainly the Jesuits (and someone, such as Langhorne, connected closely to them) bore a disproportionately large share of the persecution of Catholics during that time, and the judicial murders connected with this sordid episode in English history are part of the dark underside of the progressive Whig narrative.

When the Tory propagandists had gotten the upper hand in the war of political propaganda, there appeared in 1683 a Catholic apologetic work that included the scaffold speeches, private devotions, letters, and other material of executed Catholics, as well as Catholic material designed not only to defend the English Catholic population but also to win converts to the faith: *A Remonstrance of Piety and Innocence: Containing The last Devotions and Protestations of Several Roman Catholicks, Condemned and Executed on Account of the Plot. Faithfully taken from their own mouths as they spoke them, or from the Originals Writen and left under their own hands. To which are annexed certain Lessons, Psalms and Prayers, selected out of Holy Scripture, Church-Office, and Roman Missal, proper for the present exigence of the times. Hereunto is also added a Summary of Roman Catholick Principals, in Reference to God and the King, explained in a short Treatise formerly Writ, and Published upon that Subject.* The words of Edward Coleman, Thomas Whitebread and the other Jesuits, Richard Langhorne, Oliver Plunket,[108] and others are offered as protestations of innocence and of Catholic piety.

Republication and the Narrative of English Protestant History

In part because of the lapsing of the Licensing Act between 1679 and 1685 and in part because of the Whig campaign against Catholicism and royal absolutism during the Popish Plot and Exclusion Crisis, the late 1670s and early 1680s (like the time of the Glorious Revolution and its immediate aftermath) were marked by the republication of a number of anti-Catholic works and the appearance of new works that surveyed the history of real and alleged Catholic outrages in England (and Ireland) from the time of Queen Elizabeth to that historical moment.[109] In 1678 William Prynne's *Romes Master-Peece,* his 1643 account of the earlier fictitious Habernfeld Plot, was reprinted (minus much of the topical material concerning Archbishop Laud) as *The grand designs of the papists, in the reign of our late sovereign, Charles the I: and now carried on against His Present Majesty, his government, and the Protestant religion.*[110] In 1679 the old account of the treason trial of the earl of Essex, which highlighted his conspiring with the "popish" earl of Tyrone, was republished.[111] In the same year the official government account of Henry Garnet's trial for involvement in the Gunpowder Treason was republished for the first time since 1606 to draw direct connections to the contemporary Popish Plot.[112] The new preface, written by Thomas Barlow, bishop of Lincoln, blames the Gunpowder Plot on "the impious Subtilty of the Jesuits (and their Associates)" (4) and refutes the Catholic allegation that Robert Cecil arranged it as a way to trap Catholics.[113] Barlow argues for a continuous chain of Catholic conspiracies from the late Elizabethan through the Restoration eras:

> [I]t is notoriously known to this, and other Nations; that during the times of Queen Elizabeth, King James, Charles the Martyr, and our Gracious Soveraign now happily restored, they have impiously designed and indeavored, by open War, by Poison and Pistol, Gunpowder Plots, and horrid Conspiracies, to destroy our Princes and our Religion; So we have little reason to doubt but while there are such Persons, possess'd with a belief of such principles, they will continue to Design, and (when they have abili[t]y and opportunity) execute such damnable, and (to Protestant Princes and People) destructive Conspiracies. (41)

Barlow focuses on the Jesuits as English Protestants' archenemies: "Father Campian (who though hang'd at Tyburn for High Treason, yet at Rome is reputed a famous Martyr) tells us . . . That ALL THE JESUITS in the world have long since entred into Covenant, ANY WAY TO DESTROY all heretical KINGS; nor do they despair of doing it effectually, so long as any one Jesuit remains in the world" (42). The bishop cites a Jesuit source to prove Catholics are instructed and encouraged "to kill Hereticks" (42) without any moral qualms, and he alleges further that Jesuits claimed "they cannot commit any mortal sin: For Ignatius their Founder, by his Prayers obtain'd that priviledge for them, that for an 100 years (beginning from the confirmation of his Order) that none of his Society should commit any mortal sin; and their great Saint Xavierius procured the continuance of that priviledge for 200 years longer" (43). Despite the continuing Catholic and Jesuit danger, Barlow assumes that God's Providence will continue to protect England. The various messages of the Gunpowder Treason account itself—that all Jesuits were potential king killers or sanctioned regicide and were not only equivocators or liars but also promoted equivocation and lying within the Catholic population at large, that Catholics were actually or potentially ruthless and bloody, that papism posed an international threat to English nationhood—all were seen as relevant during the Popish Plot crisis.[114]

In 1679 a new edition appeared of a pamphlet formerly banned and burned by the authorities, a work blaming Catholics for starting the 1666 Fire of London, *London's Flames Reviv'd*.[115] William Bedloe was responsible for the publication of *A Narrative and Impartial Discovery of the Horrid Popish Plot: carried on for the Burning and Destroying of the Cities of London and Westminster* (1679), a work that cribbed from two earlier pamphlets, *Trap ad Crucem* (1670) and *History of the Fires* (1666).[116]

Because it was perceived, no doubt, as the foundation of English anti-Catholic mythology, a new edition of the Protestant martyrology by John Foxe was brought out in 1684 (which, like the previous 1641 edition, added material on the St. Bartholomew's Day Massacre and the Gunpowder Plot).[117] In 1680, in a paranoid political atmosphere in which invasion by the forces of the absolutistic Louis XIV could be envisioned, there appeared a reprint of Thomas Digges's Elizabethan tract, *Englands defense, a treatise concerning invasion, or, A brief discourse of what orders were best for repulsing of foreign forces if at any time they should invade us by sea in Kent or elsewhere: exhibited in writing to the Right Honourable Robert Dudley, Earl of Leicester, a little before the Spanish Invasion, in the year 1588*. A text about the conversion of a Capuchin friar to Protestantism supposedly originally written in 1603 was published as *Francis Broccard (Secretary to Pope Clement the Eighth) His Alarm to All Protestant Princes. With a Discovery of Popish Plots and Conspiracies. After his Conversion from Popery to the Protestant Religion. Translated out of the Latin Copy Printed in Holland* (1679). This work emphasizes the international context of all "popish plots," in effect, encouraging those who read it in 1679 to insert the current Popish Plot into a long history of Catholic perfidy. The work, interestingly, makes the Jesuits the archconspirators behind the parliamentary assault on the monarchy in the Civil Wars, the religious radicals allegedly serving only as their dupes. This is a case of anti-Catholic rhetoric and anti-Jesuitism being leveled at the political left.

In pope-burning processions[118] and in other Whig political propaganda (like earlier parliamentary propaganda during the Civil Wars), Queen Elizabeth and the Elizabethan era were nostalgically portrayed as truly Protestant:[119] hence it is not surprising that when a new Parliament was being elected in 1679, Queen Elizabeth's speech to her 1601 Parliament was republished (*The Last Speech and Thanks of Queen Elizabeth of Ever Blessed Memory, to the Last Parliament, after her Delivery from the Popish Plots, etc.*) and in 1683 there appeared Samuel Clarke's *History of the glorious life, reign, and death, of the illustrious Queen Elizabeth.*[120] Also, in the wake of the Popish Plot, a bilingual Latin-English broadside was issued commemorating Elizabeth as an English Deborah who rescued Protestants after the Marian persecutions: *Carmen in Serenissumae Reginae ELIZABETHAE Natalia, Classem Hispanicam ab ipsa devictam, & Conspirationem Papisticam Antiquam & Modernam. A Song upon the Birth-day of Queen ELIZABETH, the Spanish Armado, the Gun-Powder Treason, and the Late Popish Plot* (n.d.), a work celebrating "a new Deliverance" from Catholic plotters who would "drink" the "bloud of Protestants" and

> . . . slay both Young and Old, like savage beasts,
> To make the Streets run down with bloud, to fire
> The Houses; this was their vile hearts desire;
> But God in time this wickeness prevented.

The piece was published to coincide with one of the several pope-burning processions:

> Burn up the Cursed Pope, that *Man of Sin,*
> *Who doth upon the Seven Mountains dwell,*
>
> .   .   .   .
>
> Up *Protestants,* repay the Pope his due,

And *do to him as he hath done to you.*
In *Smithfield* Flames Saints were to Ashes turned,
In *Smithfield* Flames this day let him be burned.

The new fires of Smithfield are a Protestant revenge for the heretic burnings of
the mid-sixteenth century.

Supposedly Jesuit-sanctioned Elizabethan assassination plots were rehearsed in *The Jesuites Ghostly Wayes to Draw other Persons over to their Damnable
Principle, of the Meritoriousness of destroying Princes; Made clear in the two
barbarous Attempts of William Parry, and Edward Squire on our late Gracious
Sovereign Elizabeth Of Ever Blessed Memory* (1679). Thomas Morton's post–
Gunpowder Treason anti-Jesuit tract was republished in 1679, highlighting its
supposed relevance to the current Popish Plot: *An exact account of Romish doctrine: in the case of conspiracy and rebellion by pregnant observations collected
out of the express dogmatical principles of popish priests and Jesuites written and
printed immediately after the discovery of the Gunpowder Treason: and now upon
the discovery of the present Popish Plot against the life of His Sacred Majesty and
government reprinted and published by Ezerel Tonge.*[121] The Gunpowder Plot
engraving of 1612, withdrawn in its own time, was reissued in 1679.[122] John
Donne's *Ignatius His Conclave* was reprinted in 1680.[123] Thomas Scott's old
propaganda against the Spanish Match was recycled as *A narrative of the wicked
plots carried on by Seignior Gondamore for advancing the popish religion and Spanish faction: heartily recommended to all Protestants by Rich[ard] Dugdale, Gent*
(1679). James Wadsworth Jr.'s *English Spanish Pilgrim* reappeared in 1679 as
*The memoires of Mr. James Wadswort [sic], a Jesuit that recanted: discovering a
dreadful prospect of impiety, in the blasphemous doctrines (or Gospel) of the Jesuits, with their atheistical lives and conversations faithfully published to the world
out of the authors own original notes, with the particular places, persons, and cir-
cumstantial actions &c., of which he himself was both an eye and ear-witness
from time to time.* In 1679 a new edition appeared of Sir John Temple's history
of the Irish Rebellion, *The Irish Rebellion, or, An history of the beginnings and
first progress of the general rebellion raised within the kingdom of Ireland upon
the three & twentieth day of October, in the year 1641: together with the barbarous
cruelties and bloody massacres which ensued thereupon.*[124] During the time the
House of Commons was targeting the earl of Danby,[125] Charles II's chief minister, the work recounting the trial of an earlier impeachment victim, the earl

of Strafford, was reprinted (*An Impartial Account of the Arraignment, Trial and Condemnation of Thomas Late Earl of Strafford 1641* [1679]).[126]

Some anti-Catholic and anti-Jesuit works offered historical surveys of Catholic perfidy. For example, Henry Foulis's voluminous work, *The history of Romish treasons and usurpations* (1671), was reprinted in 1681.[127] In the general political context of the Popish Plot and Exclusion Crisis, it was inevitable to see points of comparison between the Parliament-Crown conflicts on the eve of the Civil War with the present moment: hence "Theophilus Rationalis" [Henry Duke] published in 1681 *Multum in parvo, aut vox veritatis: wherein the principles, practices, and transactions of the English nation, but more especially and in particular by their representatives assembled in Parliament anno Domini 1640, 1641: as also, 1681 are most faithfully and impartially examined, collected, and compared together for the present seasonable use, benefit and information to the publick.* As Alexandra Walsham has pointed out, many older broadside prints rehearsing the history of Protestant deliverances from Catholic menaces were reprinted during the Popish Plot era (and at the time of the Glorious Revolution).[128] Clearly there was a market for sensationalistic visual material portraying Catholic atrocities and cruelties.

In his study of Whig propaganda in the Exclusion Crisis, Tim Harris notes some of the popular anti-Catholic representations that resorted to the usual tropes and structure of English Protestant history. For example, he notes, "One pack of playing cards contained 'an History of all the Popish Plots that have been in England' from Elizabeth's time to 1678, and a similar history was offered in an illustrated almanac of 1681."[129] He points to some of the representations of Catholic atrocities that repeat the kinds of descriptions associated earlier with the Irish Rebellion:

> [T]he *Protestant Tutor,* was illustrated with prints showing children being eaten, people hung by their feet, or being burnt or boiled alive. . . . Richard Janeway recalled how catholics in Maryland were using Indians to murder protestants. . . . *A Scheme of Popish Cruelties* contained a number of prints illustrative of its title: jesuits, monks and friars ravishing and abusing women; popish villains beating the brains out of tender infants and putting their mothers to the sword; and bloody papists cutting the throats of protestants or burning "Martyrs for the True Religion."[130]

With the expiration of the Licensing Act in 1679, as was the case when censorship had ended in 1642, political and polemical texts could be published that in other times might not have seen the light of day.[131]

In the wake of the Popish Plot prosecutions and executions, there appeared a four-page quarto poem, *Faux's Ghost: or, Advice to Papists Novemb. 5. 1680*. Its author inserts the supposed current Catholic threat into the long history of Catholic assaults on Protestant England, using the diabolical Gunpowder Plot figure of Guy Fawkes to damn the contemporary plotters before focusing finally on the "popish midwife," Elizabeth Cellier, whom he associates with witchcraft.[132] The final plea in the poem is directed to the monarch and the Tories not to let popery into England. *The Protestant Tutor* (1679) has a section entitled "A prospect of Popery, or A Short View of the Cruelties, Treasons, and Massacres committed by the Papists since the beginning of the Reign of Q[u]een Mary," an account that moves from Marian persecutions to the Spanish Armada, the Gunpowder Treason, the "Massacre of Ireland, acted by the Papists upon the Protestants in that Kingdom, in the Year, 1642" (67), "The Massacre of Paris, acted by the French Papists upon the Protestants of that Kingdom, and the Cruelties of the Papists since in Piedmont, Lithuania and Poland, in the Year 1655 and 1656" (73), the 1666 Fire of London, and, finally, "the Horrid and Damnable Plot in the Year 1678. Contrived by the Papists for the Murdering of His Majesty, Destruction of the Protestant Religion, and Overthrowing of the Government by Law Established. With a Relation of the Murder of Sir Edmund-Bury Godfrey" (83)—each Catholic outrage illustrated with crudely executed woodcuts.

Many other pamphlets and broadsides kept the plot furor alive during this period, but by 1682 the Tory reaction had gained strength and effective counterpropaganda was being disseminated. The lead was taken by Roger L'Estrange, who not only debunked the plot in the periodical, *The Observator*,[133] but also later, during the brief reign of James II, published the most devastating refutation of Oates in his *Brief History of the Times* (1687–88). In his retrospective assessment L'Estrange diagnoses a social pathology that was hard to resist:

> Popery was so Dreadfull a Thing, and the Danger of the Kings Life, and of the Protestant Religion so Astonishing a Surprize, that People were almost bound in Duty, to be Inconsiderate, and Outrageous upon't; And

Loyalty it Self, would have look'd a little Cold, and Indifferent, if it had not been Intemperate. . . . [T]he Passions of the People already Dispos'd for Violence, and Tumult, there needed no more then Blowing the Cole of Otes's Narrative, to put All into a Flame. . . . The people were first Haryr'd out of their Senses, with Tales, and Jelousies, and Then made Judges of the Danger, and Consequently of the Remedy: Which upon the Main, and Briefly, came to no more than This. The Plot was Laid, all over the Three Kingdoms; France, Spain, and Portugal, Tax'd their Quotas to't; we were All to be Burnt in our Beds, and Rise with our Throats Cut; and no way in the world, but Exclusion [of James, Duke of York], and Union, to help us.[134]

The conditions would have been unfavorable, of course, during the height of the Popish Plot hysteria for such an argument to have been advanced.

Gathering arguments he had made in earlier English works, the Jesuit provincial John Warner published in Latin for an international audience his compendious history of the plot, which he calls "Presbyterian." He lays the main blame on a "Faction," led by the earl of Shaftesbury, that set out to diminish royal authority and win greater constitutional power for Parliament, especially the Commons:

Religion was only a pretext; they were really bent upon reducing the King's power and so increasing their own, because they were all sure that whatever the King lost would be their gain. The aim in which all the great ring-leaders of the Faction agreed was the reduction within the narrowest possible limits of the royal power. Many members of the Lower House, demented by Calvin's witchcraft and blinded by clouds off Lake Leman, were in favour of going even further and doing away with both the King and the royal title, so as to be able to introduce a democratic constitution like that of Geneva. (1: 212)[135]

From a Jesuit point of view sympathetic to strong if not absolutist monarchy, Warner articulates a vision of the Popish Plot ironically similar to that of later Whig historiography. To Warner, innocent Catholic priests and laymen who suffered and died as a result of a fiction constructed on the perjured testimony of Titus Oates, William Bedloe, Stephen Dugdale, and others and on the skimpy evidence of some indiscreet letters of Edward Coleman to the French king's confessor were sacrificial lambs, victims of those whose primary target was James, duke of York, the Catholic heir apparent to the throne. The Catholics who were executed were also victims of the more general constitutional struggle for power between king and Parliament.[136] And, it could be argued, they were also scapegoats for internecine Protestant conflicts between conformists and nonconformists. Because of the need to protect his brother and to counteract the perception that he was too favorable towards Catholics and too close to the powerful Louis XIV of France, on whom he depended for repeated subsidies, the king was not in a position to save the victims of the Popish Plot scare from condemnation and execution, or the general Catholic population from increased persecution. To stay in a relatively secure political position, he had to appear to be investigating the charges of conspiracy thoroughly, punishing those judged guilty, and controlling the exaggerated threat posed by the (numerically insignificant) English Catholic community.

The English Jesuits, given their place as the most hated antagonists of English Protestantism and their reputation for Machiavellian political mischief, were the safest target for the accusers, for Parliament, and for the government. In his tract Warner quotes a French observer's letter about the atmosphere in England at the height of the turmoil: "The name of 'Jesuit' is hated above all else — even by priests both secular and regular, and by the Catholic layfolk as well, because it is said that the Jesuits have caused this raging storm, which is likely to overthrow the whole Catholic religion" (1: 214). The Popish Plot was designed by Titus Oates as revenge against the Jesuits for rejecting his application to the order, but it also suited the popular mythology to see Jesuits as the masterminds of king-killing plans and threats against both English Protestantism and constitutional government.

Oates had been successfully prosecuted for perjury in 1685[137] and the Popish Plot had been generally discredited, but, despite the unmasking of the perjuries on which the treason trials of numerous Catholic victims were based, there was a reluctance on the part of popular opinion (and even the House of Commons) to reject the established historiographical model of popish plotting and providential Protestant deliverance. In the aftermath of the subsequent Glorious Revolution, a number of works were published or republished justifying the change of ruler by recalling the continuing Catholic danger that was averted. For example, a 1601 Appellant anti-Jesuit work by William Watson was reprinted as *A brief historical account of the behaviour of the Jesuites and their faction, for the first twenty five years of Q. Elizabeth's reign* (1689): this pamphlet warns about the dangers posed by Jesuits, but it is also an argument against the toleration of Catholics. In 1690, with James II and his trusted Jesuit advisor-confessor Edward Petre out of England,[138] Edward Gee published for the first time Robert Persons's *Memorial for the Reformation of England* (which had circulated only in manuscript) as *The Jesuit's memorial for the intended reformation of England under their first popish prince: published from the copy that was presented to the late King James II* (1690).[139] The previous year Gee had published *A catalogue of all the discourses published against popery* (1689), a list of 228 pamphlets published during James II's rule, almost all of them by Anglicans.[140] A collection of anti-Catholic satiric poetry, later published as *Poems on the Affairs of State* (1697), first appeared as *The Muses Farewel to Popery and Slavery* in 1689 and 1690. As John Kenyon points out, after the Glorious Revolution (and the partial rehabilitation of Titus Oates):

> the last of the Penal Laws, the Act of 1700 "for the further preventing the Growth of Popery," referred ominously to "such treasonable and execrable designs and conspiracies against his Majesty's person and government and the established religion as have lately, as well as frequently heretofore, been brought to light and happily defeated by the wonderful Providence of God"—a phrase which can be construed as applying primarily to the Assassination Plot of 1696, but which had other implications.[141]

Revision of the revisionist history of popish plotting was under way.

Intolerable Catholicism

One of the stress points in early modern English culture was the conflict between the growth of Protestant demands for liberty of conscience and the general opinion of the intolerability of Catholicism.[142] From Robert Southwell's late Elizabethan *Humble Supplication*[143] through pressure for either official or de facto toleration in the early and late Stuart periods[144] to the settlement of the issue in the Glorious Revolution,[145] toleration of Catholicism was impossible. John Milton's last pamphlet, "Of True Religion," unequivocally opposed toleration for Catholics and associated Catholicism not only with an intrusive for-

eign authority (of a pope who claimed temporal supremacy and the deposing power) but also with monarchical absolutism.[146] The demands for liberty of
conscience, which might point to the need for broad religious toleration, were
trumped by the demands for protection of "ancient liberties" of citizens—that
is, the wish for a strong Parliament and either a republic or a mixed monarchy
rather than for an absolute monarchy in which the king's prerogative powers
overrode the law proved stronger than the religious ideal. In this context Catholicism had to be portrayed as politically intolerable, and therefore religiously
intolerable, since church and state were inseparable (despite the existence of
Protestant dissenters and nonconformists, most of whom had to be accommodated). The closest the early modern English state came between 1558 and 1685
to official toleration of Catholics was, perhaps, in the chartering of the colony
of Maryland, where the only religious requirement of the inhabitants was belief in the Trinity (thus Socinians were excluded, along with Jews, Moslems, and
other non-Christians).[147]

Catholic apologists such as Robert Southwell and Robert Persons could
criticize Protestants for the inconsistency between their belief in religious freedom and their persecution of Catholics. Protestants countered with the charge
of hypocrisy: they claimed that Catholics, especially through the Spanish Inquisition and the persecution of Huguenots in Louis XIV's France, would not
tolerate Protestants and were, thus, asking for something they did not practice. They also pointed out that tolerating Catholics meant tolerating citizens
whose loyalty was suspect or flawed since it was divided politically between
England and a foreign power, the papacy, which claimed the right to excommunicate and depose monarchs, releasing Catholic citizens from their bonds
of political obedience if not also encouraging them to engage in active political
subversion. Thus developing English nationalism, growing opposition to royal
absolutism, and the desire for more representative government made Catholicism, which in the seventeenth century was associated with the kind of monarchical absolutism found in Louis XIV's France, religiously and politically intolerable. England and English identity were now Protestant. Although some
social and economic accommodations were made, there was still no ideological or legal space for English Catholics.[148]

Afterword

ANY STUDY OF EARLY MODERN RELIGIOUS CULTURE IS NECESSARILY A partial one. Therefore, this examination of Catholic and anti-Catholic discourses in early modern England can present only a selection of the issues and evidence relevant to the religious struggles of the age. My own interests and biases have, of course, determined some of the emphases evident in this study: for example, the attention given to Jesuits as a cultural presence and of individual Jesuits as religious and political agents in the early modern era. To some degree, this is the product of my surprise at the extraordinary visibility of the Jesuit order in the religious writing of the time (both as targets in anti-Catholic texts and as prolific writers of controversial as well as devotional prose). It is also the result of recent, historiographically responsible (rather than biased or apologetic) scholarship by John O'Malley, Thomas McCoog, and others dealing with the Jesuit order in its first century and a half of existence and particularly with the English Jesuit mission.[1]

Another emphasis in this study is Catholic martyrdoms and the brutality associated with them. This reflects the interests of an earlier era of archival scholarship by Catholic historians and antiquarians such as Henry Hungerford Pollen, Dom Bede Camm, John Morris, and Henry Foley, who were more interested in an apologetic "heroes of the faith" approach to English Catholic history than in a more nuanced account of religious conflict.[2] The documents they have gathered and preserved, however, especially caught my attention, and I am convinced these are an indispensable resource for scholars studying early modern Catholic culture. My emphasis on the physical aspects of martyrdom and its aftermath (including relic collection and transmission, the display of body parts, the care for all sorts of "remains" of the martyrs) is also the result of my wishing to stress the materialization of spiritual practices in Catholicism, a feature of

traditional Catholicism that was an essential part of the "old religion" but which
Protestant reformers criticized, associating it with idolatry, superstition, and
magical trickery. I find useful the term used by Michael O'Connell to describe
a distinctly Catholic perception of the interpenetration of the spiritual and physical in religious experience, "incarnational aesthetic."[3] Recent interest in the controversy about the Eucharist by Stephen Greenblatt and others reflects the importance of the religious and cultural issues involved.[4] Of course, earlier work
on Protestant iconoclasm by John Phillips and Margaret Aston is relevant to the
general question of the physicalization of the spiritual.[5] Except in passing, however, I have not dealt in this study with the Catholic aspects of architecture and
the visual arts, which relate to this issue.[6]

There are, of course, many important and rich topics that I have omitted
or glanced at briefly. For example, the whole question of religious tolerance is
only really dealt with briefly in the last chapter of this book. As W. K. Jordan's
four-volume study suggests,[7] it certainly deserves extensive treatment, attention
that would not only deal with those texts that approach the subject from theological and philosophical points of view but also set them in the context of the
social history of practical tolerance that, as Christopher Haigh and Anthony
Milton have observed, demonstrates the ways the values of local community
harmony and practical social functioning could often trump religious antago-
nisms and factionalism.[8]

I have paid little attention to another large sector of early modern English
Catholic culture, the continental Catholic exiles: a world of convents, seminaries, and schools training young people from English Catholic families, but
also one of politically estranged activists working for the restoration of English Catholicism.[9] I touch on some of the texts emanating from that sphere,
but other scholars have and will in the future pay more attention to this field
of inquiry.[10] I do not discuss most of the Catholic texts written in Latin, mainly
aimed at sympathetic continental Catholic readers, because I want to concentrate on English polemical debates, which were usually couched in the vernacular. An international controversy such as that associated with the Jacobean Oath
of Allegiance, was, of course, mostly conducted in Latin as the international
language of learning.

Another topic that certainly deserves more attention than I have given
to it is that of religious devotion. Here is an area of inquiry in which confessional lines were often blurred, as Protestants, for example, found value and
practical use in Catholic devotional texts. The classic example of this is Edmund

Bunny's appropriation of Robert Persons's *A Christian Directory* and his marketing it, with relatively few changes, as a Protestant work of devotion.[11] I have suggested in chapter 1 that Robert Southwell's religious poetry could also appeal to devout Protestants. Because I am more interested in the contrasting arguments, stances, and styles of Catholics and Protestants in the period, I largely put this whole area of inquiry to the side, except insofar as it relates to the experience of conversion.

Because I did not want to foreground conventional literary texts in my discussion or be diverted into extended treatment of particular canonical authors such as Spenser, Shakespeare, Milton, and Crashaw, and also because some of the recent books on these authors have dealt with the topic of religion,[12] I have severely limited the space given to such works in my individual chapters. Although we have a long way to go to understand and appreciate the importance of Catholic literature in the early modern period, I did not conceive of my study as primarily a "literary" one, in the narrow sense of the term, but rather as a broader cultural study of discourses. This said, I think it is time to rewrite the literary history of the period to give a more prominent place to Catholic texts, to continue discussing English Catholic writing, especially largely ignored authors such as William Alabaster, Thomas Lodge, and Sir John Beaumont, and to reexamine writings of authors who had a "Catholic period," particularly Ben Jonson.[13]

Finally, although I discuss Margaret Clitherow's case in chapter 2 and I allude to other recusant women there as well as in other sections of the study, I do not consistently highlight the topic of gender and religion—because the polemical battles that so interest me were all-male rhetorical contests, because the clerical focus of early modern Catholic history included women only as mainly adjutors and shelterers of priests, and also because I did not have anything important to add to the discussions of Elizabeth Cary or of gender and Catholicism beyond what perceptive feminist scholars such as Frances Dolan, Marie Rowlands, Heather Wolfe, and Margaret Ferguson have offered.[14] I am, of course, quite well aware of the centrality of women to the survival of English Catholicism and to the polemical uses of misogynistic language (on both sides of the religious divide).

It was hard to know which terminal date to select for this study: this is particularly a problem, because we are not dealing with questions of literary periodization or with change of reigns or with dynastic shifts but rather with deep cultural currents that flow beyond the sixteenth and seventeenth centuries into the modern era — many still detectable in the twenty-first century in both England and America. Because, however, processes of secularization have continued to change British and American culture since at least the late seventeenth century, religious language has diminished in usefulness and importance as a discourse in which all psychological, social, and political conflicts could be expressed. As I suggest in the last chapter of this study, the old anti-Catholic rhetoric that resurfaced at the time of Titus Oates's Popish Plot already came, for many, with an understood translation into more secular, political meaning. This is not to say that the social impact of religious bigotry steadily diminished over the past three hundred years — far from that, as Ian Paisley and his atrocious Web site testify — for, from time to time, fragile modern church-state separation is threatened (usually for cynical political gain) by individuals and groups who seek to appropriate religious and divine sanction for a particular political agenda. In the past three or four centuries a secular "public sphere"[15] has had space made for it in some modern societies, so that it became possible for citizens in some states to find public spaces free from rigid control by either the church or government authorities.

As my study makes clear, religious history is an integral part of cultural history, especially for an era in which people interpreted the world through religious understanding and used religious language to define most areas of individual experience and social intercourse. Since large political and social issues manifested themselves in situations of religious conflict and crisis as well as in the sectarian religious discourses, what might initially seem to us odd textual remains from the period — for example, particular polemical pamphlet wars — can be discovered to be culturally symptomatic and revelatory. Now that there has been a new "turn to religion" in literary and cultural studies as well as in historical scholarship, we are now more disposed, perhaps, than previously to hear voices from the past that speak about the world in religious language and codes. This book about Catholic and anti-Catholic discourses in early modern England is intended to join a conversation already taking place among literary scholars and historians. I hope to help open up a wide field of inquiry to new or further investigation by scholars interested in the texts and culture of early modern England but also to engage general readers interested in the development of modern out of early modern culture.

Notes

Preface

1. Alison Shell, *Catholicism, Controversy and the English Literary Imagination, 1558–1660* (Cambridge: Cambridge University Press, 1999), 16–17, remarks: "religious polemic thrives on distortion; its generic links with satire are a commonplace, but, more generally, it is perhaps nearer to imaginative writing than any other theological mode."

2. For this information, see David Armitage, "Literature and Empire," in *Origins of Empire, Oxford History of the British Empire,* vol. 1 (Oxford: Oxford University Press, 1998), 100; and John Stachniewski, *The Persecutory Imagination: English Puritanism and the Literature of Religious Despair* (Oxford: Clarendon Press, 1991), 17.

3. *The Book in Britain,* vol. 4, *1557–1695,* ed. John Barnard and D. F. McKenzie (Cambridge: Cambridge University Press, 2002), 29–93.

4. See, for example, John King, *English Reformation Literature: The Tudor Origins of the Protestant Tradition* (Princeton: Princeton University Press, 1982), *Tudor Royal Iconography: Literature and Art in an Age of Religious Crisis* (Princeton: Princeton University Press, 1989), *Spenser's Poetry and the Reformation Tradition* (Princeton: Princeton University Press, 1990), and *Milton and Religious Controversy* (Cambridge: Cambridge University Press, 2000); Deborah Shuger, *Habits of Thought in the English Renaissance: Religion, Politics, and the Dominant Culture* (Berkeley: University of California Press, 1990), and *Sacred Rhetoric: The Christian Grand Style in the English Renaissance* (Princeton: Princeton University Press, 1988); Linda Gregerson, *The Reformation of the Subject: Spenser, Milton and the English Protestant Epic* (Cambridge: Cambridge University Press, 1995); Huston Diehl, *Staging Reform, Reforming the Stage: Protestantism and Popular Theater in Early Modern England* (Ithaca: Cornell University Press, 1997); Donna Hamilton, *Shakespeare and the Politics of Protestant England* (Lexington: University Press of Kentucky, 1992); Peter McCullough, *Sermons at Court: Politics and Religion in Elizabethan and Jacobean Preaching* (Cambridge: Cambridge

University Press, 1998); and Kristen Poole, *Radical Religion from Shakespeare to Milton: Figures of Nonconformity in Early Modern England* (Cambridge: Cambridge University Press, 2000).

5. Stephen Greenblatt, *Renaissance Self-Fashioning: More to Shakespeare* (Chicago: University of Chicago Press, 1980).

6. On the methodological value of attending to fantasy materials, see Peter Lake, with Michael Questier, *The Antichrist's Lewd Hat: Protestants, Papists and Players in Post-Reformation England* (New Haven: Yale University Press, 2002), xviii–xxvi.

7. For an interesting set of reflections on the historiographical method of John Foxe in his *Actes and Monuments,* see Patrick Collinson, "Truth, Lies, and Fiction in Sixteenth-Century Protestant Historiography," in *The Historical Imagination in Early Modern Britain: History, Rhetoric, and Fiction, 1500–1800,* ed. Donald R. Kelley and David Harris Sacks (Cambridge: Cambridge University Press, 1997), 37–68.

8. Ethan Howard Shagan, "Constructing Discord: Ideology, Propaganda, and English Responses to the Irish Rebellion of 1641," *Journal of British Studies* 36 (January 1997): 4–34, argues that revisionist historians have not paid enough attention to the way popular beliefs, conditioned by political propaganda, had a large impact on events such as the English Civil Wars.

9. Brad Gregory, *Salvation at Stake: Christian Martyrdom in Early Modern Europe* (Cambridge, Mass.: Harvard University Press, 1999), 8–15.

10. I have in mind especially the voices of Catholics. Lake and Questier, *The Antichrist's Lewd Hat,* 323, point to the value of this technique: "Looking at events from the catholic perspective, putting Catholicism back in, provides the historian of early modern England with the ultimate counter factual, the most obvious and pertinent of control groups. This can be used to test and assess claims and analyses that are otherwise all too likely to be framed or at least stained by a sort of assumed manifest-destiny protestant triumphalism. . . . Used judiciously, such a hermeneutic manoeuvre can provide not so much a distorting as a refining mirror, in which things assumed to be normal or inevitable can appear fruitfully odd and contingent."

11. The religiously more open and ambiguous Shakespeare, on the other hand, does not fit into this dominant Protestant-nationalistic point of view. See my essay, "Shakespeare and Catholicism," in *Theatre and Religion: Lancastrian Shakespeare,* ed. Richard Dutton, Alison Gail Findlay, and Richard Wilson (Manchester: Manchester University Press, 2003), 218–41.

12. Frances Dolan, *Whores of Babylon: Catholicism, Gender and Seventeenth-Century Print Culture* (Ithaca: Cornell University Press, 1999); Shell, *Catholicism, Controversy and the English Literary Imagination;* Anne Dillon, *The Construction of Martyrdom in the English Catholic Community, 1535–1603* (Aldershot: Ashgate, 2002); Raymond D. Tumbleson, *Catholicism in the English Protestant Imagination: Nationalism, Religion and Literature, 1600–1745* (Cambridge: Cambridge University Press, 1998).

13. Shell, *Catholicism, Controversy and the English Literary Imagination,* 10.

14. "Shakespeare and Catholicism," in Dutton, Findlay, and Wilson, eds., *Theatre and Religion,* 218–41, and "John Donne's Conflicted Anti-Catholicism," *Journal of English and Germanic Philology* 101.2 (2002): 358–79.

1. Southwell's Remains: Catholics, Relics, and Print Culture in Early Modern England

1. L. Hicks, S.J., ed., *Letters and Memorials of Father Robert Persons, S.J.,* vol. 1, Catholic Record Society 39 (London: John Whitehead & Sons, 1942), 83 (cited hereafter as Persons, *Letters*). The Latin original of this passage is found on p. 73.

2. See Peter Lake, "Anti-Popery: The Structure of a Prejudice," in *Conflict in Early Stuart England: Studies in Religion and Politics, 1603–1642,* ed. Richard Cust and Ann Hughes (London: Longman, 1989), 72–106.

3. This occasioned the addition of "An Homilie Against Disobedience and Wilfull Rebellion" to the official Church of England *Book of Homilies,* along with "A Thanksgiving for the Suppression of the Last Rebellion," which concludes the volume.

4. See David Cressy, *Bonfires and Bells: National Memory and the Protestant Calendar in Elizabethan and Stuart England* (London: Weidenfeld and Nicolson, 1989); William Haller, *The Elect Nation: The Meaning and Relevance of Foxe's Book of Martyrs* (New York: Harper, 1963); and Christopher Hill, *Antichrist in Seventeenth-Century England* (London: Oxford University Press, 1971). I discuss the pattern of Catholic outrage and Protestant deliverance in chapter 5 of this study.

5. See Carol Z. Wiener, "The Beleaguered Isle: A Study of Elizabethan and Early Jacobean Anti-Catholicism," *Past and Present,* no. 51 (May 1971): 31–33. Thomas Clancy, S.J., "English Catholics and the Papal Deposing Power, 1570–1640, Part I," *Recusant History* 6.3 (October 1961): 114, points out that the earls' stated reasons for the rising were that "the old nobility had been replaced in the counsels of the Queen by new men and . . . that a new and heretical religion had been introduced." In his justification of the Armada, Cardinal Allen mentions the elevation by Elizabeth of unworthy, lower-rank men as one of the crimes justifying the 1570 papal bull of excommunication. See "A Declaration of the Sentence and deposition of Elizabeth, the usurper and pretensed Quene of Englande," in M. A. Thierney, *Dodd's Church History of England,* vol. 3 (Westmead, Farnborough, U.K., 1971), xliv–xlviii.

6. Paul L. Hughes and James F. Larkin, eds., *Tudor Royal Proclamations,* 3 vols. (New Haven: Yale University Press, 1964–69), 2: 490.

7. Bernard Basset, *The English Jesuits from Campion to Martindale* (New York: Herder and Herder, 1967), 109, writes: "Of the 182 men and women executed as Catholics under Queen Elizabeth, eleven at most could be classed as Jesuits. Of these only

Campion, Walpole and Southwell were Jesuit trained. All the others were seminary priests who, in the final crisis, had asked to be admitted to the Society. On Fr. William Holt's reckoning in 1596, six hundred priests had been sent into England in thirty-eight years. The Jesuits, after sixteen years in England, could claim, at most, twenty-five of these." For a recent account of the English Jesuit mission, see Thomas M. Mc-Coog, S.J., *The Society of Jesus in Ireland, Scotland, and England, 1541–1588: "Our Way of Proceeding?"* (Leiden: E. J. Brill, 1996).

8. Thomas Bell, *The Golden Balance of Tryall. Wherein the Reader shall plainly and briefly behold, as in a Glasse of Crystall; as well by what rule all controversies in Religion, are to be examined, as also who is, and of right ought to be the upright Judge in that behalf. Whereunto is also annexed a Counterblast against a masked Companion, terming himself E. O. but supposed to be Robert Parsons the trayterous Jesuite* (1603), M3ᵛ. See Victor Houliston, "The Fabrication of the Myth of Father Parsons," *Recusant History* 22.2 (October 1994): 141–51. Persons kept the polemical heat high on both the Protestant and the Catholic side over several decades of publication, beginning with his 1580 pamphlet defending recusancy, a work that elicited three immediate responses by Protestant antagonists. See Peter Milward, *Religious Controversies of the Elizabethan Age: A Survey of Printed Sources* (London: Scolar Press, 1977), 52.

9. Quoted in Basset, *The English Jesuits,* 455. Persons similarly composed a letter to the London magistrates defending himself and the Jesuit mission. In it, he too boldly (or arrogantly) challenged his Protestant adversaries to theological debate:

> I demand to be allowed to defend this faith. . . . *[Y]our ignorant Ministers have never dared to submit to the test of any disputation.* . . . I beg most earnestly that either here or elsewhere at your pleasure I may join battle in some kind of disputation with some of your ministers or prelates. I bar none of them, but in this cause I challenge the lot of them, knowing full well that when they have been stripped of a certain sort of parade and pretense, they can make no defense of their perversions of the truth. (English translation in Persons, *Letters,* 39)

For a discussion of the larger polemical context of Campion's and Persons's challenges, see McCoog, *The Society of Jesus,* 148; and "'Playing the Champion': The Role of Disputation in the Jesuit Mission," in *The Reckoned Expense: Edmund Campion and the Early English Jesuits: Essays in Celebration of the First Centenary of Campion Hall, Oxford (1896–1996),* ed. Thomas M. McCoog, S.J. (Woodbridge: Boydell & Brewer, 1996), 119–29; Thomas M. McCoog, S.J., "'The Flower of Oxford': The Role of Edmund Campion in Early Recusant Polemics," *Sixteenth-Century Journal* 24 (1993): 899–913.

10. McCoog, *The Society of Jesus,* 141–42, points out that even before Campion's and Persons's arrival in England "William Charke . . . translated from Latin Christian

Francken's *A conference or dialogue discovering the sect of Iesuits: most profitable for all Christendome rightly to know their religion* [London, 1580]. Franken, a Jesuit from 1568 until his apostacy from the Roman Catholic Church in 1579, bitterly attacked the Society and its founder, and contended that only those with a natural tendency towards hypocrisy 'either gotten by servile education, or apprehended by some blockishness of mind' could become good Jesuits. This controversial work set the tone for the popular presentation of the Society of Jesus."

11. On homosexuality as an Italian, papist, and Jesuit vice, see Alan Bray, *Homosexuality in Renaissance England* (London: Gay Men's Press, 1982), 14–16, 19–21, 29 (I am grateful for this reference to Garry Wills, *Witches and Jesuits: Shakespeare's* Macbeth [New York and Oxford: New York Public Library and Oxford University Press, 1995], 175).

12. Persons, *Letters,* 63n.

13. Ibid., 64.

14. Ibid., 84.

15. A. I. Doyle's review article of A. F. Alison and D. M. Rogers's bibliography, *The Contemporary Printed Literature of the English Counter-Reformation between 1558 and 1640. Volume I: Works in Languages Other than English,* in *Recusant History* 20.2 (October 1990): 146, notes that this "most frequently-printed work in their survey" appeared in "forty-five Latin editions between 1581 and 1632, two in Czech, one Dutch, four Flemish, nine German, one Hungarian and two Polish" (I am grateful for this reference to Alexandra Walsham, "'Domme Preachers': Post-Reformation English Catholicism and the Culture of Print," *Past and Present,* no. 169 [August 2000]: 100). It appeared in English in 1632 as *Campion Englished. Or a translation of the Ten Reasons in which E. Campian Insisted in his Challenge.* This work was also printed in 1687 during the reign of the Catholic James II in an English translation as *Reasons of a Challenge Sent to the Universities of England in Matters of Religion.*

16. See Milward, *Religious Controversies,* 57–58.

17. See McCoog, "'Playing the Champion,'" 135–36. Richard Simpson, *Edmund Campion: A Biography* (London: J. Hodges, 1867), 369, notes that Campion made converts during these debates, including Philip Howard, earl of Arundel. For a discussion of the four conferences, see Simpson, *Edmund Campion,* 363–78. Milward, *Religious Controversies,* 60, cites *A true report of the Disputation of rather private Conference had in the Tower of London, with Ed. Campion Jesuite, the last of August, 1581. Set downe by the Reverend learned men them selves that dealt therin. Whereunto is joyned also a true report of the other three dayes conferences had there with the same Jesuite. Which now are thought meete to be published by authoritie* (1583) and *The three last dayes conferences had in the Tower with Edmund Campion Jesuite, the 18: 23: and 27. of September, 1581. collected and faithfully set downe by M. John Feilde student in Divinitie. Now perused by the learned men*

themselves, and thought meete to be published (1583). For a recent edition and discussion of Campion's Tower debates, see James V. Holleran, ed., *A Jesuit Challenge: Edmund Campion's Debates at the Tower of London in 1581* (New York: Fordham University Press, 1999). Another conference with an imprisoned priest, John Hart, was published as propaganda by the Elizabethan authorities: *The summe of the Conference betweene John Rainolds and John Hart: Touching the Head and the Faith of the Church. . . . Penned by John Rainolds, according to the notes set downe in writing by them both: perused by John Hart, and (after things supplied, and altered, as he thought good) allowed for the faithfull report of that which past in conference betweene them. Whereunto is annexed a Treatise intituled, Six Conclusions Touching the Holy Scripture and the Church, written by John Rainolds. With a defence of such things as Thomas Stapleton and Gregorie Martin have carped at therein* (1588).

18. Persons, *Letters,* 119.

19. This work was printed by Richard Verstegan. Stephen Vallenger, who had a copy of it in his own hand and who may have written one or more of the poems appended to the narrative, was charged and convicted of libel as the supposed author of the work. See Sir Walter Mildmay's Star Chamber speech and the notes in Anthony G. Petti, ed., *Recusant Documents from the Ellesmere Manuscripts,* Catholic Record Society 60 (London: Catholic Record Society, 1968), 13–18. Petti, 17n., claims that the authorities knew Alfield was the real author of the work but nevertheless prosecuted and punished Vallenger, who lost his ears and was imprisoned until his death in 1591. See Henry Garnet, Letter to Claudio Aquaviva, 20 June 1595, Achivum Romanum Societatis Iesu (hereafter ARSI) Anglia.31, fols. 93–105, transcript and translation in Garnet letter file in English Jesuit Archive, London. Anne Dillon, *The Construction of Martyrdom in the English Catholic Community, 1535–1603* (Aldershot: Ashgate, 2002), 76–77, argues that the speed with which the Catholic side published an account of Campion's death was a reaction to the earlier experience of the publicity following the execution of Edward Hanse, which was dominated by government propaganda. See also her discussion of Alfield's text and its publication, pp. 78–80, 90.

20. Helen C. White, *Tudor Books of Saints and Martyrs* (Madison: University of Wisconsin Press, 1963), 212, notes that the story of Campion's capture had already been put in print by the man who betrayed him, George Eliot, *A Very True Report of the Apprehension and Taking of that Arche Papist Edmond Campion the Pope his Right Hand, with Three Other Jesuite Priests, and Divers other Laie People, Most Seditious Persons of Like sort* (1581). The rabidly anti-Jesuit Anthony Munday's *A Discoverie of Edmund Campion, and his Confederates, their Most Horrible and Traiterous Practises, against Her Majesties Most Royal Person, and the Realme* appeared shortly after the executions in January 1582 (White, *Tudor Books,* 215). Munday also published *A Breefe Aunser made unto two seditious Pamphlets . . . Contayning a Defence of Edmund Campion and his Com-*

plices, their most Horrible and Unnaturall Treasons, against her Majestie and the Realme (1582), a work that contains, at the end, answer-poems to the laudatory pieces published at the end of Alfield's *True Report.* Brad S. Gregory, *Salvation at Stake: Christian Martyrdom in Early Modern Europe* (Cambridge, Mass.: Harvard University Press, 1999), 19–20, points out the remarkable similarity of the accounts in Munday's *Discoverie* and Alfield's *True Report.*

21. Allen includes the same story in *A Briefe Historie of the Glorious Martyrdom of XII. Reverend Priests* (1582), distancing himself in his final remark from its content: "[He] after his beheading, him self dismembred, his hart, bowels, and intrailes burned, to the great admiration of some, being laid upon the blocke his belly downeward, lifted up his whole body then remayning from the ground: and this I adde upon report of others, not mine owne sight" (fivᵛ).

22. White, *Tudor Books,* 248, cites the story Southwell recounts of how a judge at Campion's sentencing found one of his gloves bloody when he pulled it off (in *An Epistle of Comfort* [Paris, n.d. (ca. 1587–88)], Bb3).

23. See the discussion of competing Protestant and Catholic treatment of wonders and miracles in Alexandra Walsham, *Providence in Early Modern England* (Oxford: Oxford University Press, 1999), 225–80.

24. Allen, *Briefe Historie,* cviiᵛ. Gregory, *Salvation at Stake,* 301, states: "The desire to collect, distribute, and venerate the martyrs' relics was driven by the widespread conviction that the holy sacrifice of their deaths had made them saints in heaven. Blotches of blood and bits of bone were quasi-sacramental, traces of the grace that had sustained the martyrs seconds before they passed to eternity. Of all objects on earth (aside from the consecrated host), these relics were the closest to heaven."

25. *The Elizabethan Jesuits: Historia Missionis Anglicanae Societatis Jesu (1660) of Henry More,* ed. and trans. Francis Edwards, S.J. (London: Phillimore, 1981), 137. Elizabeth Hanson, citing Simpson's biography of Campion, discusses the obtaining of Campion's finger as a relic in her essay, "Torture and Truth in Renaissance England," *Representations* 34 (spring 1991): 68.

26. Simpson, *Edmund Campion,* 466–67.

27. Ibid., 468.

28. See the discussion of the suppression of relics in the English Reformation in Eamon Duffy, *The Stripping of the Altars: Traditional Religion in England, 1400–1580* (New Haven: Yale University Press, 1992), 384–85, 390, 407–15, passim; and Robert Whiting, *The Blind Devotion of the People: Popular Religion and the English Reformation* (Cambridge: Cambridge University Press, 1989), 72–74. Duffy notes, "A major feast of England's most important saint, Thomas Becket, [was] the translation of his relics" (47). Gregory, *Salvation at Stake,* 264, suggests that the comparison of the Henrician martyrs, especially Bishop John Fisher, with Thomas à Becket, "influenced Henry's

1538 decision to obliterate the shrine to the slain Archbishop of Canterbury." For an insightful discussion of Thomas à Becket's shrine and of how "the metaphorics of the relic were transformed" in the sixteenth century, see Clark Hulse, "'Dead Man's Treasure': The Cult of Thomas More," in *The Production of Renaissance Culture,* ed. David Lee Miller, Sharon O'Dair, and Harold Weber (Ithaca: Cornell University Press, 1994), 190–225. The rediscovery in 1578 of the Roman catacombs with their rich treasure of relics of early Christian saints and martyrs created fresh interest in relics. Dillon, *Construction of Martyrdom,* 170–71, points out the relevance of the discovery to a general interest in Christian martyrdom. In his polemically charged *English Romayne Life,* Anthony Munday mocked the relics he saw in Rome (Anthony Munday, *The English Romayne Life 1582,* ed. G. B. Harrison [New York: Barnes & Noble, 1966], 40–57). In Protestant anti-Catholic discourse, of course, the notion of "popish relics" was broadened to include all the material remains of the old religion (vestments, rosaries, crucifixes, holy water, etc.): see, for example, Richard Overton, *New Lambeth fayre newly consecrated and presented by the Pope himselfe, cardinals, bishops, Jesuits &c: wherein all Romes reliques are set at sale . . .* (1642).

29. Hughes and Larkin, *Tudor Royal Proclamations,* 2: 118.

30. Ibid., 123. Early in the Elizabethan period one of John Calvin's works was published as *A very profitable treatise declarynge what great profit might come yf there were a regester made of all reliques,* trans. S. Wythers (1561). There is a discussion of relics in Andrew Willet's *Synopsis Papismi, That is, A General View of Papistrie,* 5th ed. (1634 [orig. pub. 1592]), 445–55.

31. For a discussion of relics and their uses in folk medicine, exorcisms, and other official and nonofficial religious practices, see Keith Thomas, *Religion and the Decline of Magic* (New York: Scribners, 1971), 26–31, 44–45, 53, passim; Whiting, *Blind Devotion of the People,* 56–59; and Dillon, *Construction of Martyrdom,* 98–99, 102, 171. The anti-Catholic and anti-Puritan Samuel Harsnett's *A Declaration of Egregious Popish Impostures* mocks the use of relics of Campion and his fellows in ritual exorcisms, especially of Campion's thumb (in F. W. Brownlow, ed., *Shakespeare, Harsnett, and the Devils of Denham* [Newark: University of Delaware Press; London and Toronto: Associated University Presses, 1993], 294–97). John Gee, *The Foot out of the Snare* (1624), sarcastically recounts some of the stories of cures attributed to Campion's relics: "One M. Anderton, a Lancashire Gentleman, was cured of the Stone, by the Reliques he had of F. Campian the blessed Saint: & being afterwards of another disease, laid out so for dead . . . that his thumbs were bound; by the help of the said Martyr, his flesh beeing laid upon his body, he was raised to life" (43 [misnumbered 53]). He exclaims: "What prodigies are these? What horrible impieties? Are they not forgeries? that shame not to affirme, that the bones of a Traytor can raise a dead man, as did Elias his bones? or that the flesh of Campian, could performe that which was so

much admired in our Saviour himselfe, when hee was amongst us in the flesh" (43–44). Dillon, *Construction of Martyrdom,* 98, notes that a piece of Campion's rib circulated on the Continent as a valued relic.

32. See Simpson, *Edmund Campion,* 322, 385, cited in Ruth Hughey, *The Arundel Harington Manuscript of Tudor Poetry,* 2 vols. (Columbus: Ohio State University Press, 1960), 2: 60. Hughey discusses the poem Walpole wrote about Campion (which William Byrd set to music) that was appended to Thomas Alfield's account of the execution.

33. Robert Persons, *Of the Life and Martyrdom of Father Edmund Campian,* ed. Br. H. Foley, *Letters and Notices* (December 1877) (n.p.: Manresa Press, 1877), 2. Robert Southwell wrote to the Jesuit general, Claudio Aquaviva, in 1585 from the English College at Rome, hoping to be sent on the English mission, "which promises the highest hope of martyrdom" (23 January 1585, ARSI. Rome, Fondo Gesuitico 651/648, in Thomas M. McCoog, S.J., "The Letters of Robert Southwell, S.J.," *Archivum Historicum Societatis Jesu* 63 [1994]: 103; translation separately provided in typescript by Thomas McCoog, to whom I am grateful). Gregory, *Salvation at Stake,* 279–80, calls attention to Southwell's expression of the desire for martyrdom in his *Epistle of Comfort,* which has a chapter praising martyrdom.

34. See J. T. Rhodes, "English Books of Martyrs and Saints of the Late Sixteenth and Early Seventeenth Centuries," *Recusant History* 22.1 (May 1994): 7–25; and John Knott, *Discourses of Martyrdom in English Literature, 1563–1694* (Cambridge: Cambridge University Press, 1993).

35. Quoted in Simpson, *Edmund Campion,* 463. See the description in William Weston's autobiography of the sympathetic popular response to an execution of some newly converted Catholics: *The Autobiography of an Elizabethan,* trans. Philip Caraman (London: Longmans, Green, 1955), 154–55.

36. Letter of 1586 quoted in Christopher Devlin, *The Life of Robert Southwell Poet and Martyr* (London: Longmans, Green, 1956), 139. Lord Burghley's secret memorandum, *An Antidote against Jesuitism* (Petyt MSS, ser. 538, vol. 43, fols. 304 ff.), printed in James Spedding, *The Letters and Life of Francis Bacon* (London: Longman, Green, Longman, and Roberts, 1861), 1: 47–56, discussed in Devlin, Appendix B, also makes the same point.

37. *Serious Considerations for repressing of the increase of Jesuites, priests, and Papists, without shedding Blood* (1641), 32.

38. Although on a popular level those who were executed for their religion were called "martyrs" and their remains venerated like those of saints, the Roman authorities were reluctant officially to canonize martyr-saints in this period (see Peter Burke, "How to Be a Counter-Reformation Saint," in *The Historical Anthropology of Early Modern Italy: Essays on Perception and Communication* [Cambridge: Cambridge University Press, 1987], 56).

39. See the discussion of this poem in Alison Shell, *Catholicism, Controversy and the English Literary Imagination, 1558–1660* (Cambridge: Cambridge University Press, 1999), 184–85.

40. For an anti-Catholic ballad treating the execution of Campion, Sherwin, and Bryant, see Hyder Rollins, ed., *Old English Ballads, 1553–1625* (Cambridge: Cambridge University Press, 1920), 64: "A Triumph for true Subjects, and a Terrour unto al Traitours: By example of the late death of Edmund Campion, Ralphe Sherwin, and Thomas Bryan, Jesuites and Siminarie priestes: who suffered at Tyburne, on Friday, the first Daye of December: Anno Domini 1581."

41. *Records of the English Province of the Society of Jesus,* ed. Henry Foley, S.J., 7 vols. (London: Burns and Oates, 1877–83), 4: 129–30, citing "Papers relating to the English Jesuits," BL MS Add. 21203, Plut. clii. F. The same account describes a red halo visible about Garnet's head. See also John Gerard's narrative of the Gunpowder Plot for an account of the miraculous occurrences associated with the death of Garnet, including the "miracle of the straw," the supposed appearance of a micro-miniature image of Garnet after his execution in a speck of his blood that had fallen on a wheat straw during his dismemberment: in *The Condition of Catholics under James I: Father Gerard's Narrative of the Gunpowder Plot,* ed. John Morris, S.J. (London: Longmans, Green, 1871), 296–307. See also Philip Caraman, *Henry Garnet 1555–1606 and the Gunpowder Plot* (New York: Farrar, Straus, 1964), 443–47, and the interesting discussion of the straw in Julian Yates, *Error, Misuse, Failure: Object Lessons from the English Renaissance* (Minneapolis: University of Minnesota Press, 2003), 37–45. The convert William Alabaster wrote a Latin poem on the straw: see *Unpublished Works by William Alabaster,* ed. Dana F. Sutton, Salzburg Studies in English Literature, Elizabethan and Renaissance Studies 126 (Salzburg: University of Salzburg, 1997), 10–11. The straw was debunked in Robert Pricket's poem, *The Jesuits Miracles, or new Popish Wonders. Containing the Straw, the Crowne, and the Wondrous Child, with the Confutation of them and their follies* (1607), which contains an engraving of the straw as a frontispiece. John Gee, *The Foot out of the Snare* (1624), 66, refers disparagingly to the effects of the straw and to the claim that "the very sight of Garnets straw hath made (at least) five hundred in our kingdom good Catholiques." He also mocks the use of Campion's relics for miracle cures. As late as the Restoration Popish Plot era, the straw was still part of religiopolitical discourse: in *A Panegyre upon Oates* (1679), ll. 51–57, the poet refers to the straw image as Catholic idolatry and delusion (*Poems on Affairs of State: Augustan Satirical Verse,* vol. 2: 1678–1681, ed. Elias F. Mengel Jr. [New Haven: Yale University Press, 1965], 129).

42. Raphael Holinshed, *The First and Second Volumes of the Chronicles of England, Scotlande, and Irelande* (1587), 1329 (I cite the Huntington Library copy, which contains pages [1328–31] excised from most other copies of the edition). See the discussion of the "castrations" of the 1587 Holinshed in Annabel Patterson, *Reading Holin-*

shed's *Chronicles* (Chicago: University of Chicago Press, 1994), 234–39, 253–63. In his 17 November 1580 letter to the rector of the English College at Rome, in which he alludes to the large political context of the Jesuits' arrival in England, Robert Persons not only mentions the Spanish invasion force sent to Ireland, the influence of the Catholic Lord d'Aubigny over James VI of Scotland, and Spain's conquest of Portugal but also the collapse of the French marriage negotiations: "suspicion as to the good faith of the French after the rejection of the marriage proposals" in conjunction with "the coming of the Jesuits to this island" (*Letters,* 57) troubled the authorities. In a letter of 14 June 1581 to Pope Gregory XIII, Persons explicitly connects the French party's leaving London with the fate of English Catholics: "To-day the French representatives left London: it is commonly thought that nothing was accomplished, for there is a great silence about the marriage. We are in daily expectation of a new and bitter storm of persecution" (ibid., 66). See McCoog, *The Society of Jesus,* 156.

43. For a discussion of the Catholic/Protestant propaganda struggle in the Elizabethan public sphere through various media — print, manuscript, and performance — and for the importance for the Jesuit mission of the context of the proposed French marriage (which they interpreted as an opportunity for Catholic advancement if not also toleration), see Peter Lake and Michael Questier, "Puritans, Papists and the 'Public Sphere' in Early Modern England," *Journal of Modern History* 72.3 (September 2000): 587–627. Lake and Questier argue that despite their claims for the religious, not political, purpose of their mission, Campion and Persons were in England to pose a political challenge to the English Protestant state and its structures of law and authority.

44. Holinshed, *Chronicles,* 1330.

45. Persons, *Letters,* 133.

46. For a discussion of Catholic martyrologies from the time of Campion's execution, see White, *Tudor Books,* 217–39; and Thomas H. Clancy, S.J., *Papist Pamphleteers: The Allen-Persons Party and the Political Thought of the Counter-Reformation in England, 1572–1615* (Chicago: Loyola University Press, 1964), 126–42. Michael E. Williams, "Campion and the English Continental Seminaries," in McCoog, ed., *The Reckoned Expense,* 285–99, discusses the use of Catholic martyrologies as instruments to raise funds to support English Continental seminaries.

47. This work was originally written and published in Latin, then translated and published in French (Milward, *Religious Controversies,* 65). Milward points out that the "literature of consolation" that grew out of this includes Southwell's *Epistle of Comfort.* For the centrality of consolation for Jesuits and its special meaning, see John W. O'Malley, *The First Jesuits* (Cambridge, Mass.: Harvard University Press, 1993), 19–20.

48. Dillon, *Construction of Martyrdom,* 274, notes that this work was a bestseller, printed in eight editions in Latin and French before 1609. See her discussion of it, pp. 243–76.

49. Verstegan, *A true reporte of the death & martyrdom of M. Campion,* 23; further page numbers cited in text. Dillon, *Construction of Martyrdom,* 138, discusses Verstegan's association of ecclesiastical despoliation with violence against the bodies of the Catholic martyrs.

50. As White notes, such Latin works about the English persecution were aimed at a Continental and educated, rather than an English and popular, audience (*Tudor Books,* 232). The Catholic book she suggests as "the nearest approach to Foxe's Book of Martyrs" is John Gibbons's *Concertatio Ecclesiae Catholicae in Anglia, adversus Calvinopapistas et Puritanos* (Trier, 1583; 2d [expanded] ed., 1588). Frescoes of the English martyrs' sufferings were painted on the walls of the English College, Rome, and reproduced in *Ecclesiae Anglicanae Trophaea* (Rome, 1589). See Dillon, *Construction of Martyrdom,* 175–231, for a discussion of these murals, especially in terms of their functioning as a counterforce to the depiction of Protestant martyrdom and English Church history by John Foxe and John Bale.

51. Dedication to *Jesuitismi,* quoted in Simpson, *Edmund Campion,* 462.

52. Robert M. Kingdon, ed., *The Execution of Justice in England by William Cecil and A True, Sincere, and Modest Defense of English Catholics by William Allen* (Ithaca and London: Cornell University Press for the Folger Shakespeare Library, 1965), 8–9.

53. This became, as Milward, *Religious Controversies,* 71, notes, "the most popular book on England in sixteenth-century Europe, going into fifteen editions—including translations into French, Spanish, Italian, and German—within ten years of its first appearance."

54. *Anti Sanderus. Duos continens Dialogos non ita pridem inter viros quosdam doctos Venetiis habitos.* See Milward, *Religious Controversies,* 72.

55. Hughes and Larkin, *Tudor Royal Proclamations,* 3: 86–93. See Nancy Pollard Brown, "Robert Southwell: The Mission of the Written Word," in *The Reckoned Expense,* ed. McCoog, 193–213. For a discussion of Catholic interiority and the topic of toleration dealt with in Southwell's *Humble Supplication* and his letter to Robert Cecil, as well as in Campion's "Brag," see Ronald J. Corthell, "'The Secrecy of Man': Recusant Discourse and the Elizabethan Subject," *ELR* 19 (autumn 1989): 272–90.

56. See Henry Garnet's "A brief discourse of the condemnation and execution of Mr. Robert Southwell, priest of the Society of Jesus," in Foley, *Records of the English Province of the Society of Jesus,* 1: 373.

57. Letter to Claudio Aquaviva of 7 March 1595 (ARSI. Rome. Angl. Hist. II.107; transcription of the Italian original and English translation in Jesuit Archives, London, kindly made available to me by Thomas McCoog, S.J., who is editing Garnet's letters for publication). In a letter to Robert Persons (9 April 1598), Garnet also mentions that he had had the copy of the Breviary Southwell used during his imprisonment and sent it to Alfonso Agazzari (Stonyhurst Coll. P.551, ARSI Angl.38. II, fol. 182).

58. See Basset, *English Jesuits,* 119.

59. Garnet to Aquaviva, 7 March 1595. I have changed McCoog's translation slightly, in one case to correct the reference to Montjoy from Montague ("Montago" in the Italian). In his letter describing Campion's execution, Robert Persons says Charles Howard stopped the executioner from cutting down Campion while he was still alive (*Letters and Memorials,* 1: 132).

60. Quoted in Devlin, *Life of Robert Southwell,* 324. Brown, "Robert Southwell: The Mission of the Written Word," 212, notes that the countess of Arundel "had a relic [of Southwell], one of the bones of his feet, and wore it constantly, exerting herself in every possible way to follow his edicts." The author of *A Yorkshire Recusant's Relation* (printed in John Morris, ed., *The Troubles of Our Catholic Forefathers,* vol. 3 [London: Burns and Oates, 1877]) refers to the authorities' desire to prevent Catholics from collecting relics at sites of execution: "[T]hey use singular diligence and wariness in martyring us, that no part of blood, or flesh, or garment, or anything belonging to the martyr be either unburnt or escape their hands. The sacred blood they conculcate and cast into the fire. The apparel the murderers take and disperse, the pins, points, buttons, and all, lest Catholics get them and use them for relics" (98–99).

61. *An Epistle of Comfort to the Reverend Priestes, & to the Honorable Worshipful, & Other of the Laye Sort Restrayned in Durance for the Catholicke Faythe* (1587), Aa7. In one of his letters, however, Southwell refuses to dignify the remains of a contemporary radical Protestant martyr:

> At Norwich in England, a certain leader of a new sect, until a short time ago a tanner . . . held that neither Christ nor the Holy Spirit was God; that Christ was not born of the Virgin Mary; that no one should swear for any reason whatever; that there should be no magistrates in a Christian republic; that all children ought not to be baptized; and other things of this sort which Anabaptists wisely believe. This man, after having been condemned to death by persons almost like himself, was shortly afterward burned—[while displaying] wonderful, as they say, obstinacy and the perverse appearance of piety. But shortly after, neither the fellow's bones nor his very ashes could be found so eagerly did the foes of pious relics try to get these faeces. (Robert Southwell to Claudio Aquaviva, 26 August 1587, ARSI. Fondo Gesuitico 651/648, in McCoog, "Letters of Robert Southwell," 106; translation separately provided by the editor)

In his satirical treatment of relics and pilgrimages, Erasmus treats all relics as excremental (see "A Pilgrimage for Religion's Sake," in *Ten Colloquies of Erasmus,* trans. Craig R. Thompson [New York: Liberal Arts Press, 1957], 56–91). What Southwell is doing in denying martyr status to a Protestant is but one example of the interconfessional competition in which it was normal to brand those of the opposite side who died for their beliefs as pseudomartyrs. Peter Lake, with Michael Questier, *The Antichrist's Lewd Hat: Protestants, Papists and Players in Post-Reformation England* (New Haven: Yale University Press, 2002), discuss this phenomenon at length, especially in chapter 8 (281–314). Lake and Questier note that Robert Persons's *Treatise of Three Conversions* (1603–4), "his attempt at a systematic reply to Foxe, contained contrasting tables of true catholic, as opposed to Foxe's false protestant, martyrs" (283). See the extensive discussion of the pseudomartyr debate in Dillon, *Construction of Martyrdom,* 18–71.

62. For a discussion of the relationship of writings to relics, see chapter 1, "Writing as Relic: The Mythologizing of Alphabetic Writing as Body Trace," in Laura Kendrick, *Animating the Letter: The Figurative Embodiment of Writing from Late Antiquity to the Renaissance* (Columbus: Ohio State University Press, 1999), 11–35.

63. See James H. McDonald, *The Poems and Prose Writings of Robert Southwell, S.J.: A Bibliographical Study* (Oxford: Roxburghe Club, 1937). The printing of this work may have been allowed by the authorities to foment further dissension in the Catholic ranks between the Jesuits and the anti-Jesuit Catholics during the "Appellant Controversy" prompted by the appointment of George Blackwell as "Archpriest" for England (White, *Tudor Books,* 257). Henry Garnet implies as much in a letter to Persons (5 May 1602) in which he indicates he tried to prevent the publication because it might "breed new troubles" and further anti-Jesuit hostility among the more accommodationist Catholics (Stonyhurst Coll. P.547). Victor Houliston, "The Lord Treasurer and the Jesuit: Robert Persons's Satirical *Responsio* to the 1591 Proclamation," *Sixteenth-Century Journal* 32.2 (2001): 385, suggests that the *Humble Supplication* was "brought out to contrast Southwell's moderate tone with Persons's alleged intransigence." Shell, who discusses the importance and influence of Southwell, notes that the sales of his published works "were . . . kick-started by martyrdom" (*Catholicism, Controversy and the English Literary Imagination,* 66).

64. When Philip Howard's *A Foure-Fould Meditation* was published in 1606 its author was identified as "R. S. the author of S. Peters Complaint."

65. Quoted in McDonald, *Poems and Prose Writings of Robert Southwell,* 95.

66. Ibid., 99.

67. See Hulse's discussion of how, in the case of Sir Thomas More, not only writings but also biographies and portraits of the saint became "substitute relics" ("'Dead Man's Treasure,'" 219). See also "The Book as Authorial Body," in Leah S. Marcus, *Unediting the Renaissance: Shakespeare, Marlowe, Milton* (London: Routledge, 1996), 192–98. For a discussion of how Catholics treated books as objects of reverence akin to images and rosary beads, see Patrick Collinson, Arnold Hunt, and Alexandra Walsham, "Religious Publishing in England," in *The Cambridge History of the Book in Britain,* vol. 4,

1557–1695, ed. John Barnard and D. F. McKenzie (Cambridge: Cambridge University Press, 2002), 59.

68. See Walter Ong, *Orality and Literacy: The Technologizing of the Word* (London: Routledge, 1982).

69. *Areopagitica,* in John Milton, *Complete Poems and Major Prose,* ed. Merritt Y. Hughes (New York: Odyssey Press, 1957), 720. Milton's opposition in his *Eikonoklastes* to the hagiographic *Eikon Basilike,* however, was related to his opposition to the use of print for idolatrous and superstitious purposes.

70. Collinson, Hunt, and Walsham, "Religious Publishing in England," 65.

71. "Typography and Meaning: The Case of William Congreve," in *The Book and the Book Trade in Eighteenth-Century Europe,* ed. Giles Barber and Bernhard Fabian (Hamburg: Ernst Hauswedell, 1981), 93–94. McKenzie illustrates the person-book connection in Shakespearean imagery from *Othello, Twelfth Night, Troilus and Cressida, Richard II, Coriolanus,* and *The Winter's Tale.*

72. See Samuel Daniel, *Poems and A Defence of Ryme,* ed. Arthur Colby Sprague (Chicago: University of Chicago Press, 1930), 9.

73. Nancy Pollard Brown notes that Southwell's letter followed Ralegh's own *Instructions to His Son* in this publication (Robert Southwell, *Two Letters and Short Rules of a Good Life,* ed. Nancy Pollard Brown and James H. McDoland [Charlottesville: University of Virginia Press for the Folger Shakespeare Library, 1973], xlviii–xlix). For an account of the surviving manuscript and print versions of Southwell's letter to his father, see Brown, "Robert Southwell: The Mission of the Written Word," 206–7. Other seventeenth-century works using the same metaphor in their titles include [Richard Brathwayte] *Remains after Death* (1618); *Reliquiae sacrae Carolinae: the workes of that great monarch and glorious martyr, King Charles the 1st* (1648); *The Remaines of the Right Honourable Francis Lord Verulam* (1648); *Reliquiae Wottonianae. Or a collection of lives, letters, poems, with characters of sundry personages: and other incomparable pieces of language and art. By the curious pencil of the ever memorable Sr Henry Wotton Kt* (1651); *J. Cleaveland Revived: poems, orations, epistles, and other of his genuine incomparable pieces never before publisht: with some other exquisite remains of the most eminent wits . . . that were his contemporaries* (1659); Simon Ford, *Londini quod reliquum, or, Londons remains* (1667, following the fire of 1666); Joseph Glanvill, *Some Discourses, Sermons, and Remains* (1681); *Golden remains of Sir George Freeman, Knight of the Honourable Order of the Bath: being choice discourses on select subjects* (1682); *The Works of Mr. John Oldham: together with his remains* (1686); *Some genuine remains of the late pious and learned John Lightfoot D.D.* (1700). In 1687 the son of the martyred lawyer Richard Langhorne published his father's tract on toleration, *Considerations touching the great question of the king's right in dispensing with the penal laws written on the occasion of His late Blessed Majesties granting free toleration and indulgence,* as his "Remains" (a2). By contrast, the

severed head of another Popish Plot martyr, the Franciscan John Wall, was sent to Douai as a relic for preservation (John Kenyon, *The Popish Plot* [1972; rpt. London: Phoenix Press, 2000], 250).

74. This acronym, the first three letters of "Jesus" in Greek, also stood for "Iesus Hominorum Salvator." Interestingly, the "Root and Branch" petition of 1640 portrayed the Laudian church's use of "the Jesuits' badge" on the cloth covering the pulpit as a sign of its popishness (*Constitutional Documents of the Puritan Revolution, 1625–1660,* ed. Samuel Rawson Gardiner, 3d ed. rev. [Oxford: Clarendon Press, 1951], 140).

75. McDonald, *Poems and Prose Writings of Robert Southwell,* 77. McDonald notices that the 1616 St. Omer's edition of *S. Peters Complaint and Saint Mary Magdalens Funerall Teares* has "the emblem of the Society of Jesus . . . the letters 'I H S,' surmounted by a cross rising from the cross-piece of the 'H'; below the letters, three nails; around the letters and the nails, a radiance of light" (91). He does not notice the similarity to the ornament at the top of the Cawood title page.

76. John R. Roberts and Lorraine Roberts, "'To Weave a New Webbe in their owne Loome': Robert Southwell and Counter-Reformation Poetics," in *Sacred and Profane: Secular and Devotional Interplay in Early Modern British Literature*, ed. Helen Wilcox, Richard Todd, and Alasdair MacDonald (Amsterdam: VU University Press, 1996), 74, suggest that Southwell chose the figure of St. Peter as one who had denied Christ as a way of reaching lapsed English Catholics who needed to be reclaimed for the faith.

77. McDonald remarks: "Apart from Saint Peters Complaint most of the poems he printed occur toward the end of the manuscripts" (*Poems and Prose Writings of Robert Southwell,* 77).

78. Folger Shakespeare Library, Harmsworth MS.

79. McDonald, *Poems and Prose Writings of Robert Southwell,* 82–83, suggests this as a likely date.

80. Ibid., 82, 85.

81. Ibid., 98. White notes that in *Moeoniae* "[i]n the case of the cycle on Mary and her Son, poems on 'The Death of Our Ladie' and 'The Assumption of Our Lady' found in manuscripts were not included" by the printer of the volume (*Tudor Books,* 270). See the discussion in Brown, "Robert Southwell: The Mission of the Written Word," 200, 204, 206–7, of the attempts to suppress the Catholic content and make the writings more acceptable to Protestant readers.

82. The Continental Catholic press issued the work as *A Christian Directorie* (1585) after Bunny's version had appeared. See the discussion of this work in Milward, *Religious Controversies,* 73–76. See also Victor Houliston, "Why Robert Persons Would Not Be Pacified: Edmund Bunny's Theft of the Book of Resolution," in McCoog, ed., *Reckoned Expense,* 159–77.

83. "Catholic Texts and Anti-Catholic Prejudice in the 17th-Century Book Trade," in *Censorship and the Control of Print in England and France, 1600–1900,* ed. Robin Myers and Michael Harris (Winchester: St. Paul's Bibliographies, 1992), 53.

84. See Hughey, *Arundel Harington Manuscript,* 1:106–11, 2: 57–66; and Edward Doughtie, ed., *Liber Lilliati: Elizabethan Verse and Song* (Bodleian MS Rawlinson Poetry 148) (Newark: University of Delaware Press; London and Toronto: Associated Universities Presses, 1985), 83. Harington's opinion was reported by his son, Sir John Harington of Kelston (Hughey, *Arundel Harington Manuscript,* 2: 63).

85. I note both this poem and the previous one in my book, *Manuscript, Print, and the English Renaissance Lyric* (Ithaca: Cornell University Press, 1995), 6.

86. This is cited in McDonald, *Poems and Prose Writings of Robert Southwell,* 134. Leah Marcus points out that the cult of the infant Jesus, which Southwell brought to England, represents a response to the Calvinist view of fallen nature and of the corrupt child (*Childhood and Cultural Despair: A Theme and Variations in Seventeenth-Century Literature* [Pittsburgh: University of Pittsburgh Press, 1978], 70–71).

87. Letter of 5 May 1601; cited in McDonald, *Poems and Prose Writings of Robert Southwell,* 134. White, *Tudor Books,* 270–74, notes the direct imitation of Southwell's poetry and of *Marie Magdalens Funeral Teares* by non-Catholic writers such as Nicholas Breton (in *Marie Magdalens Love* [London, 1595] and *Auspicante Jehova. Maries Exercise* [London, 1597]) and Gervase Markham (in *The Teares of the Beloved* [London, 1600]).

88. Walsham, "'Domme Preachers,'" 106–7, points out that there were several Catholic publications in the period that appeared in mainstream presses, including Southwell's *Saint Peters Complaint,* which had thirteen editions "in the public domain between 1595 and 1640, compared with just two clandestine impressions."

89. See the discussion of the terms "Counter-Reformation" and "Catholic Reformation" in John W. O'Malley, *Trent and All That: Renaming Catholicism in the Early Modern Era* (Cambridge, Mass.: Harvard University Press, 2000).

2. Alienating Catholics: Recusant Women, Jesuits, and Ideological Fantasies

1. *The Tudor Constitution: Documents and Commentary,* ed. and intro. G. R. Elton (Cambridge: Cambridge University Press, 1965), 363.

2. Ibid., 367.

3. Ibid., 366.

4. Ibid., 367.

5. As early as 1535 a royal proclamation commanded Anabaptists to leave the country under pain of death: *Tudor Royal Proclamations,* ed. Paul L. Hughes and James F. Larkin, C.S.V., 3 vols. (New Haven: Yale University Press, 1964–69), 1:

227–28. See also Queen Elizabeth's proclamation of 22 September 1560 ordering the deportation of Anabaptists (ibid., 2: 148–49). On the perception of Puritans in the 1590s as a subversive force at least at dangerous as Catholics, see John Guy, "The Elizabethan Establishment and the Ecclesiastical Polity," in *The Reign of Elizabeth I: Court and Culture in the Last Decade,* ed. John Guy (Cambridge: Cambridge University Press, 1995), 129.

6. See Alexandra Walsham, *Church Papists: Catholicism, Conformity and Confessional Polemic in Early Modern England* (Woodbridge, Suffolk: Royal Historical Society and Boydell Press, 1993).

7. See Hughes and Larkin, *Tudor Royal Proclamations,* 2: 488–91.

8. See Elton, *Tudor Constitution,* 410–32; and J. E. Neale, *Elizabeth I and Her Parliaments, 1559–1581* (London: Jonathan Cape, 1953), 116–21. There are, however, cases in which the husband was not forced to pay the fine exacted on the wife: in the Court of Common Pleas case of 1617 "The King and Richard Parker *against* Sir John Webb, and Katherin his Wife," it was observed that "the woman here being married hath no lands or goods, and therefore the King cannot have any thing, and the goods or lands of her husband cannot be taken for his wifes offence, she being convicted by indictment only, to which the husband is no party" (*The English Reports,* vol. 123, Common Pleas I [Edinburgh: William Green & Sons; London: Stevens & Sons, 1912], 1245), though it was recognized that "married women are the most dangerous recusants, because that they have the education of their children and the government of their servants" (1246).

9. The first Douai missionaries arrived in England in 1574, the first Jesuit missionaries in 1580.

10. Brad S. Gregory, *Salvation at Stake: Christian Martyrdom in Early Modern Europe* (Cambridge, Mass.: Harvard University Press, 1999), 275, points to an international context for this harsh statute: 1585 was the "year after the formation of the Catholic League in France and the startling assassination of William of Orange in the Netherlands." Writing in the aftermath of World War II, and silently analogizing Catholic missionaries and Nazi spies, Neale, *Elizabeth I and Her Parliaments, 1584–1601,* 37, wholeheartedly defended the extremity of this law:

> [I]t was a humane and reasonable attempt to resolve the dilemma of a state, exposed by ideological warfare to insidious and deadly peril. If a society has the right to defend its existence, the individual can hardly claim a conflicting right to remain within the community while acknowledging an external allegiance that threatens to destroy it. English Catholic priests were at liberty to retain their religion, provided they lived abroad. The sanction behind banishment was the penalty of treason. It proved—such is man's unconquerable mind—inadequate.

This may evoke our admiration, as the courage of the secret agent does in wartime; but we can hardly argue that the penalty was too severe. In the ideological state treasons multiply: they are no less treason because of that.

11. The most important loyalty oaths were the Elizabethan Oath of Supremacy and the early Stuart Oath of Allegiance.

12. *The Court of King James the First,* ed. John S. Brewer, 2 vols. (London: Richard Bentley, 1839), 1: 86–87. It is surprising that Goodman's account of the Gunpowder Plot is full of excuses for it: he sets it in the context of the long history of the persecution of Catholics and exculpates the convicted Jesuit, Henry Garnet, from any blame (72–115).

13. For an extensive treatment of Catholic women and of the gendering of Catholicism in the period, see Frances Dolan, *Whores of Babylon: Gender and Catholicism in Seventeenth-Century Print Culture* (Ithaca: Cornell University Press, 1999).

14. See, for example, Andrew Marvell's attack on Mary of Modena in his *An Account of the Growth of Popery, and Arbitrary Government in England* (1677), in *The Complete Prose Works of Andrew Marvell,* vol. 3, ed. Alexander Grosart (n.p.: Printed for private circulation, 1875), 296–97.

15. *Vox Regis* (1624), 13–14. For a discussion of Scott's work, especially his anti-Hispanicism, see William S. Maltby, *The Black Legend in England: The Development of Anti-Spanish Sentiment, 1558–1660* (Durham, N.C.: Duke University Press, 1971), 102–8.

16. *Paradise Lost,* 1.444–46, in John Milton, *Complete Poems and Major Prose,* ed. Merritt Y. Hughes (New York: Odyssey Press, 1957). For a discussion of Milton's portrayal of the recusant Catholic wife as a threat to the Protestant husband, see Cedric C. Brown, "Milton and the Idolatrous Consort," *Criticism* 35 (1993): 419–39.

17. See the Geneva Bible gloss on Revelation 17:4: "This woman is the Antichrist, that is the Pope with the whole bodie of his filthy creatures, as is expounded, ver. 18, whose beauty onely standeth in outwarde pompe & impudencie and craft like a strumpet."

18. See John N. King, *English Reformation Literature* (Princeton: Princeton University Press, 1982), 381–87; and Eamon Duffy, *The Stripping of the Altars: Traditional Religion in England c. 1400–c. 1580* (New Haven: Yale University Press, 1992), 155–206, 256–65. Dolan, *Whores of Babylon,* 102–18, discusses Protestant anti-Marianism. As an example of this phenomenon, see the fifth poem in William Prynne's *A Pleasant Purge for a Roman Catholike* (1642), 31–35, "On, and against, Popish Pictures of the Virgin Mary as a Queene, sitting on a Throne with a Triple Crown on her head, and holding Christ, painted like a sucking Infant in her Armes; and on the Reliques of her milke, which they keepe and shew."

19. See John N. King, *Spenser's Poetry and the Reformation Tradition* (Princeton: Princeton University Press, 1990), 91–97. Catholics could also deploy misogynistic language for their own purposes. Nicholas Sander, for example, in *De Origine ac Progressu Schismatis Anglicani* (Cologne, 1585), viciously attacked Ann Boleyn as a Lutheran seducer of King Henry VIII. He charged her with sexual promiscuity, alleging she was the mistress of Francis I of France, a lover of Sir Thomas Wyatt, an adulteress with Henry and, after their marriage, with other courtiers, and even the incestuous lover of her own brother. Sander connects Ann's supposedly low sexual morals with her Protestantism and claims that after her execution the pope had hopes that Henry might have been reconciled to the Catholic church once again: see Nicholas Sander, *The Rise and Growth of the Anglican Schism,* trans. David Lewis (1877; rpt. Rockford, Ill.: Tan Books and Publishers, 1988), 25–34, 101, 132–34. In Henry Stanford's manuscript poetic anthology, there is a misogynistic Catholic libel accusing Queen Elizabeth of having secretly borne three bastard daughters; see Steven May, ed., *Henry Stanford's Anthology: An Edition of Cambridge University Library Manuscript Dd.5.75* (New York: Garland, 1988), item 275.

20. David Norbrook, "Macbeth and the Politics of Historiography," in *The Politics of Discourse: The Literature and History of Seventeenth-Century England,* ed. Kevin Sharpe and Steven N. Zwicker (Berkeley: University of California Press, 1987), 82. In the context of the discussion of the succession question in the Parliament of 1563, Mary's non-Englishness was stressed: Sir Ralph Sadler referred to her as a "foreign prince" (quoted in Neale, *Elizabeth and Her Parliaments, 1559–1581,* 104).

21. "A Letter to Queen Elizabeth," in *Miscellaneous Prose of Sir Philip Sidney,* ed. Katherine Duncan-Jones and Jan Van Dorsten (Oxford: Clarendon Press, 1973), 48.

22. Samuel Butler, *Characters and Passages from Note-Books,* ed. A. R. Waller (Cambridge: Cambridge University Press, 1908), 62.

23. See Deborah Willis, *Malevolent Nurture: Witch-Hunting and Maternal Power in Early Modern England* (Ithaca: Cornell University Press, 1995), 118–22; and Garry Wills, *Witches and Jesuits: Shakespeare's* Macbeth (New York and Oxford: New York Public Library and Oxford University Press, 1995).

24. Anthony Weldon's *Secret History of James I,* which concentrates on the Robert Carr–Frances Howard affair and marriage and on the murder of Sir Thomas Overbury, has an ongoing anti-Catholic theme, sometimes inserted by way of the popular rumors that circulated at various stages of the scandal. The crypto-Catholic earl of Northampton and his niece are prime targets of this account, Carr himself portrayed as being seduced through the charms and witchcraft of the poisonous Catholic woman. For a discussion of Frances Howard's demonization as a (crypto-) Catholic woman, see David Lindley, *The Trials of Frances Howard: Fact and Fiction at the Court of King James* (London: Routledge, 1993), 49, 165. Later the duke of Buckingham's Catholic (convert) mother was rumored to have hastened the death of King James by poison.

25. She is associated with Catholic Mariolatry (1.2.72–86, 90) and portrayed as a sexually transgressive "Amazon" (1.2.104). Though warned that "women are shrewd tempters" (1.2.123), Charles, the French Dauphin, is charmed by her and practices a kind of idolatry of her (1.2.144–45): "Bright star of Venus, fallen down on earth, / How might I reverently worship thee enough?" (1.2.144–45). Joan is identified as a "witch" (1.5.21; 3.2.38), "damned sorceress" (3.2.38), "vile fiend and shameless courtezan" (3.2.45), and "railing Hecate" (3.2.64). When the duke of Burgundy betrays the English to join the French forces, he does so because he is "bewitch'd" (3.3.58) by her: Charles, the Dauphin, had urged her to "enchant him with [her] words" (3.3.40). The full treatment of Joan as a witch comes in the third scene of act 5, in which she calls on her magical powers and the evil spirits that have assisted her (5.3.2–12).

26. See, for example, Robert Southwell's letter dealing with Catholic women expelled, or in fear of being expelled, by their Protestant husbands (Thomas M. McCoog, S.J., ed., "The Letters of Robert Southwell, S.J.," *Archivum Historicum Societatis Iesu* 63 [1994]: 10). Walsham, *Church Papists,* 78–80, discusses the topic of recusant women with church papist husbands. She points out that a statute of 1606 made a wife's nonconformity "adequate grounds for depriving her husband of civil promotion and appointment" (80). The husband of Lady Blount, for example, refused to post bail for her after she was arrested (see Archives of the Archdiocese of Westminster MSS, 12:139 ff.) In the Parliament of 1593 members debated the problem of recusant wives of Protestant (or church papist) husbands (see Neale, *Elizabeth and Her Parliaments, 1584–1601,* 280–97). In one of his letters Robert Persons writes of church papist husbands' threatening to leave their wives (L. Hicks, S.J., ed., *Letters and Memorials of Father Robert Persons, S.J.,* vol. 1, Catholic Record Society 39 [London: John Whitehead & Sons, 1942], 1: 62). Dolan, *Whores of Babylon,* 17, points out that recusant wives were fined by the state at half-rate for nonattendance at religious services.

27. Henry Garnet addressed women in his "Treatise of Renunciation": "your husbands over your soul have no authority and over your bodies but limited power" (quoted in Marie Rowlands, "Recusant Women, 1560–1640," in *Women in English Society, 1500–1800,* ed. Mary Prior [London: Methuen, 1985], 165). Robert Persons refers to Catholic wives' being stronger than their husbands (*Letters,* 1: 62). Robert Southwell praised Catholic widows for their "virile hearts" (McCoog, "The Letters of Robert Southwell," 4). Since it was more dangerous for a man to be an active recusant, it is not surprising, for example, that the majority of people on the recusancy lists from the 1590s in Staffordshire are women (*Roman Catholicism in Elizabethan and Jacobean Staffordshire: Documents from the Bagot Papers,* ed. Anthony G. Petti [Staffordshire: Staffordshire Record Society, 1979], 47–49). For a discussion of the spiritual authority of Catholic wives, see Alison Shell, *Catholicism, Controversy and the English Literary Imagination, 1558–1660* (Cambridge: Cambridge University Press, 1999), 153–60.

28. Mary Claridge [Katharine Longley], *Margaret Clitherow (1556?–1586)* (New York: Fordham University Press, 1966), 139, points out that the only Catholic woman executed for her faith previously was Margaret Pole, countess of Salisbury, who was killed in 1541. See also the second edition of this biography, *Saint Margaret Clitherow* (Wheathampstead, Herts.: Anthony Clarke, 1986), which corrects some of the information of the first edition—particularly Clitherow's age at marriage (18, not 15) and the date of her execution, 25 March 1586. There is a recent discussion of Clitherow in Megan Matchinske, *Writing, Gender, and State in Early Modern England* (Cambridge: Cambridge University Press, 1998), 53–85. Matchinske's main interest is in the construction of female subjectivity and possibilities of empowerment within specific cultural constraints. The best discussion of Margaret Clitherow is found in Anne Dillon, *The Construction of Martyrdom in the English Catholic Community, 1535–1603* (Aldershot: Ashgate, 2002), 277–322. I completed this chapter before having access to Dillon's fine work, but I have attempted to incorporate her ideas and insights. Dillon is especially perceptive in relating the narrative of Clitherow's life and death to the conventions of saints' lives in the context of depicting her as "a type or example of the new Counter-Reformation sainthood" (281).

29. *An Abstract of the Life and Martirdome of Mistris Margaret Clitherow* (Mackline, 1619). This radical abridgment of John Mush's biography concentrates on her arrest, imprisonment, arraignment, and execution.

30. Claridge, *Margaret Clitherow*, 54, points out that before he went abroad for seminary training, Mush had been a servant of Dr. Thomas Vavasour and his wife, Dorothy (a friend of Margaret Clitherow), two strong Yorkshire Catholics. Dillon, *Construction of Martyrdom*, 280, argues that the life had dual authorship, that it was a fusion of two separate manuscript accounts, by William Hutton and John Mush, which were circulated separately before their conflation.

31. On the influence of Greek romance on hagiography in the sixteenth century, see Helen White, *Tudor Books of Saints and Martyrs* (Madison: University of Wisconsin Press, 1963), 279–90.

32. This point is also made by Dillon, *Construction of Martyrdom*, 278. She sees the target audience of this narrative as "primarily artisan" (281).

33. Dillon, *Construction of Martyrdom*, 290, states: "Margaret's spiritual regime forms a paradigm of recusant behaviour and belief and she functions as a model to demonstrate the new Tridentine practice, heavily influenced by Ignatian spirituality. These practices placed a premium on the Mass, frequent confession, twice weekly communion and the veneration of the Eucharist."

34. "A True Report of the Life and Martyrdom of Mrs. Margaret Clitherow," in *The Troubles of Our Catholic Forefathers Related by Themselves,* ed. John Morris (London: Burns and Oates, 1877), 3: 393–94. Citations of Mush's biography are by page numbers from this volume.

35. An earlier confessor had been William Hart, who was tried and executed in 1583 (Claridge, *Margaret Clitherow*, 60). Claridge states that he was "the priest who perhaps more than any other influenced Margaret Clitherow in both life and death" (94).

36. For a discussion of how Clitherow was attracted to the cult of martyrdom associated with Jesuit spirituality, see Claire Cross, "An Elizabethan Martyrologist and His Martyr: John Mush and Margaret Clitherow," in *Martyrs and Martyrologies: Papers Read at the 1992 Summer Meeting and the 1993 Winter Meeting of the Ecclesiastical History Society,* ed. Diana Wood (Oxford: Blackwell Publishers for the Ecclesiastical History Society, 1993), 271–81.

37. Claridge, *Margaret Clitherow,* 182, corrects Morris's use of the word *harlotry* here. Dillon, *Construction of Martyrdom,* 311, says, "Mush uses the sexual allegations made against Margaret for allegorical purposes. They represent persecution of the sanctity of family life and motherhood and the persecution of the Church as the Whore of Babylon."

38. In another account (published from manuscript by Morris as "Notes by a Prisoner in Ousebridge Kidcote") there is a description of the slanders of the Protestant ministers who tried to convert the martyr in her last days: "[W]hen they saw they could by no means prevail, they used slanderous speeches against her, and said she was reported to be of evil demeanour with priests, using more familiarity with them than with her husband" (309).

39. Claridge, *Margaret Clitherow,* 113.

40. Ibid., 141, quoting from manuscript a phrase censored from Morris's text.

41. Dillon, *Construction of Martyrdom,* 312, associates this element of the narrative with "the themes of sexual humiliation and sexual mutilation which are an identifying motif in the lives of women saints."

42. Dillon, *Construction of Martyrdom,* 266–67, notes the representation of Clitherow's execution in Richard Verstegan's *Theatrum Crudelitatum Haereticorum Nostri Temporis* (Antwerp, 1587).

43. Claridge, *Margaret Clitherow,* ix, notes that Mush's biography, which circulated in manuscript in Catholic circles, inspired Jane Wiseman, "when arraigned on the same charge as Margaret Clitherow[,] . . . to follow the same course," and it also inspired Mary Ward, who founded a religious order active in education and works of charity.

44. See Henry Garnet's 11 March 1601 letter about her (letter to the Jesuit General, Arch. S.J. Rom., Anglia 31, fols. 179–81—I am grateful to Thomas McCoog, S.J., who is editing Garnet's letters, for providing me with an English translation of this document).

45. See John Gerard, *The Autobiography of a Hunted Priest,* trans. Philip Caraman (New York: Pellegrini & Cudahy, 1952), 52–54. Henry Garnet's 15 July 1598 letter to the Jesuit General (Stonyhurst MS Anglia II, n. 40) describes Wiseman's exemplary behavior at her sentencing.

46. See Rowlands, "Recusant Women," 158; and Henry Foley, S.J., ed., *Records of the English Province of the Society of Jesus,* 7 vols. (London: Burns and Oates, 1877–83), 4: 84. Foley (4: 102) calls her Henry Garnet's "patroness." See Garnet's letter to Anne Vaux of 3 April 1606 (Foley, 4:102–5). She was the dedicatee of the translation of Ribadeneira's life of Ignatius, published in English in 1616.

47. *A True and Perfect Relation of the proceedings at the several Arraignments of the Late Most barbarous Traitors* (1606), Fff2ᵛ.

48. *The Life of the Most Honourable and Vertuous La. Magdalen Viscountesse Montague* (St. Omer, 1627), 26.

49. Ibid., 29.

50. See also A. C. Southern, ed., *An Elizabethan Recusant House, Comprising the Life of the Lady Magdalen, Viscountess Montague (1538–1608)* (London: Sands, 1954).

51. See Henriette Peters, *Mary Ward: A World in Contemplation,* trans. Helen Butterworth (Leominster, Herefordshire: Gracewing, 1994); and Lowell Gallagher, "Mary Ward's 'Jesuitresses' and the Construction of a Typological Community," in *Maids and Mistresses, Cousins and Queens: Women's Alliances in Early Modern England,* ed. Susan Frye and Karen Robertson (New York: Oxford University Press, 1999), 199–217.

52. For her biography and a discussion of her place in recusant literature, see Elizabeth Cary, Lady Falkland, *Life and Letters,* ed. Heather Wolfe, Renaissance Texts from Manuscript No. 4 (Cambridge: RTM Publications, 2001); and *The Tragedy of Mariam the Fair Queen of Jewry with the Lady Falkland: Her Life by One of her Daughters,* ed. Barry Weller and Margaret W. Ferguson (Berkeley: University of California Press, 1994).

53. For a good discussion of Henrietta Maria's court, see Caroline Hibbard, "The Role of a Queen Consort: The Household and Court of Henrietta Maria, 1625–1642," in *Princes, Patronage, and the Nobility: The Court at the Beginning of the Modern Age c. 1450–1650,* ed. Ronald G. Asch and Adolf M. Birke (London: German Historical Institute and Oxford University Press, 1991), 393–414.

54. "Puritan Jesuits" is a term used by Richard Montagu, whose hopes for a rapprochement between the English church and Rome led him to view Jesuits as an impediment (Anthony Milton, *Catholic and Reformed: The Roman and Protestant Churches in English Protestant Thought, 1600–1640* [Cambridge: Cambridge University Press, 1995], 353). His *Appello Caesarem. A Just Appeal from Two Unjust Informers* (1625) was ecumenical but anti-Jesuit. At King James I's accession the earl of Northumberland identified as a minority of the Catholic population "puritane papists that thirst after a spanish style," including Jesuits and their adherents (quoted in Mark Nicholls, *Investigating Gunpowder Plot* [Manchester: Manchester University Press, 1991], 114). See also the Jesuit-Puritan association made by the Civil War royalist poem, *Sampsons*

Foxes Agreed to fire a Kingdom: Or, The Jesuit, and the Puritan, met in a Round, to put a Kingdom out of Square (Oxford, 1644). Peter Lake, with Michael Questier, *The Antichrist's Lewd Hat: Protestants, Papists, and Players in Post-Reformation England* (New Haven: Yale University Press, 2002), 285, looks on hard-line recusant culture (promoted by the Jesuits) as a "puritan" wing of English Catholicism.

55. The Jesuits backed off a policy of active resistance in the last years of Queen Elizabeth's reign, though their reputation as activists persisted, reenergized by the government's successful association of the Jesuit superior, Henry Garnet, with the Gunpowder Plot. See Peter Holmes, *Resistance and Compromise: The Political Thought of the Elizabethan Catholics* (Cambridge: Cambridge University Press, 1982), 205–23. On anti-Jesuitism as a particularly strong form of anti-Catholicism, see Carol Weiner, "The Beleaguered Isle: A Study of Elizabethan and Early Jacobean Anti-Catholicism," *Past and Present*, no. 51 (May 1971): 27–62, esp. 36–39, 43–44; see also Arnold Pritchard, "The Myth of the Evil Jesuit," in *Catholic Loyalism in Elizabethan England* (Chapel Hill: University of North Carolina Press, 1979), 175–91. John W. O'Malley, S.J., "The Historiography of the Society of Jesus: Where Does It Stand Today?" in *The Jesuits: Cultures, Sciences, and the Arts, 1540–1773* (Toronto: University of Toronto Press, 1999), 29n.1, cites other scholarly sources that list European anti-Jesuit works and Jesuit responses.

56. See his *Dialogue betwixt a Secular Priest, and a Lay Gentleman . . .* (Rheims, 1601).

57. Hughes and Larkin, *Tudor Royal Proclamations*, 3: 251.

58. William Barlow, *An Answer to a Catholike English-man* (1609), B2. For a particularly virulent attack on Persons, see the anti-Jesuit Appellant Anthony Copley's *Another Letter of Mr. A. C. to his Dis-Jesuited Kinseman* (1602).

59. R. Doleman, pseud., *A Conference about the Next Succession to the Crowne of Ingland* ([Antwerp,] 1594). Persons may have coauthored this work. For a discussion of the hostile attitudes of English Protestants to Persons and to other Jesuits, see Victor Houliston, "The Fabrication of the Myth of Father Parsons," *Recusant History* 22.2 (October 1994): 141–51.

60. See Thomas H. Clancy, S.J., *Papist Pamphleteers: The Allen-Persons Party and the Political Thought of the Counter-Reformation in England, 1572–1615* (Chicago: Loyola University Press, 1964).

61. *A Sparing Discoverie of our English Jesuits* (n.p., 1601), a2.

62. Ibid., 7.

63. Thomas James, *The Jesuits Downefall* (Oxford, 1612), 3.

64. *Vox Populi. or Newes from Spayne* (1620), A4ᵛ.

65. "A Briefe discourse against succession knowen. Discoveringe a most assuered meane for your majesties safetye, and to cutt of all serchinge for eny other heir

or sucessour durying your Majesties Lyfe, and yet fully to content all such faithfull dutifull subjectes as desier the safetye of the Realme joyned with the securitie of your royal Person" (State Papers Domestic, Elizabeth 176/32, fols. 78–79).

66. *The Double PP. A Papist in Armes* (1606), B3^{r-v}.

67. See *Aphorismes. Or, Certaine Selected Points of the Doctrine of the Jesuits, with a treatise concerning their secret practises and Close studies* (1609), 15–16.

68. Ibid., 23. Thomas S. Nowak, "Propaganda and the Pulpit: Robert Cecil, William Barlow and the Essex and Gunpowder Plots," in *The Witness of Times: Manifestations of Ideology in Seventeenth-Century England,* ed. Katherine Z. Keller and Gerald J. Schiffhorst (Pittsburgh, Pa.: Duquesne University Press, 1993), 34–52, 264–67, points out in his discussion of William Barlow's sermons on the Essex Rebellion and the Gunpowder Plot that the Jesuits were propagandistically connected with both. In the case of the second conspiracy, however, the first Paul's Cross sermon "insists that the plot was not a Catholic conspiracy at all, but the work of a few lone fanatics" (48), but "the subsequent Gunpowder sermons [over the next five decades] made slight use of Fawkes, preferring to blame the whole affair on the Jesuits and . . . the Pope" (49). For a useful discussion of the Gunpowder Plot's reverberations in the literary texts of the time, see Wills's *Witches and Jesuits.* See chapter 5 below for a discussion of the Gunpowder Plot and its place in English national mythology.

69. See Maltby, *The Black Legend.*

70. For a discussion of the influence of French anti-Jesuit and anti-Spanish writing on England, see Lisa Ferraro Parmelee, *Good Newes from Fraunce: French Anti-League Propaganda in Late Elizabethan England* (Rochester: University of Rochester Press, 1996).

71. Jean Lacouture, *Jesuits: A Multibiography,* trans. Jeremy Leggatt (Washington, D.C.: Counterpoint, 1995), 352.

72. Thomas M. McCoog, S.J., *The Society of Jesus in Ireland, Scotland, and England, 1541–1588: "Our Way of Proceeding?"* (Leiden: E. J. Brill, 1996), 141–42, points out that before the first Jesuit missionaries arrived in England, William Charke, who later attacked them in print, published a translation of a Latin anti-Jesuit work, Christian Francken's *A Conference or Dialogue Discovering the Sect of Jesuites* (1580). In 1581 a translation of Pierre Bouquin's anti-Jesuit work, *A Defense of the Olde, and True Profession of Christianitie against the New, and Counterfeite Secte of Jesuites, or Fellowship of Jesus,* was published in England. O'Malley, "Historiography of the Society of Jesus," 7–8, also refers to two Latin anti-Jesuit works written by former Jesuits, Elias Hasenmüller's *Historia jesuitici ordinis* (1593) and Hieronymus Zahorowski's *Monita secreta* (Crakow, 1614); the latter had "twenty-two editions in seven languages by the end of the century" and was "reprinted and cited into the twentieth century" (8).

73. Quoted in Jenny Wormald, "Gunpowder, Treason, and Scots," *Journal of British Studies* 24 (April 1985): 147.

74. *Quo Vadis? A Just Censure of Travel as it is commonly undertaken by the Gentlemen of our Nation* (1617), 70.

75. See, for example, accounts of this fight published in English: *A Journal of all Proceedings Between the Jansenists, and the Jesuits* (1659), *A Journal of Monsr. De Saint Amour, doctor of Sorbonne: Containing a Full Account of all the Transactions both in France and Rome, concerning the five Famous Propositions Controverted between the Jansenists and the Molinists . . .* (1664), and *The Mystery of Jesuitism: Discovered in Certain Letters . . .* (1679), the last a translation of Blaise Pascal's *Lettres Provinciales*. Thomas H. Clancy, S.J., *A Literary History of the English Jesuits: A Century of Books, 1615–1714* (San Francisco: Catholic Scholars Press, 1996), 159, notes: "In no other country outside France did [Pascal's] polemic have greater success than in England. His works were promptly translated and enjoyed a wide circulation there. Four editions of *The Mystery of Jesuitism*, the preferred English title, were published before 1659. In reply *An Answer to the Provinciall Letters*, a translation by Martin Greene of a volume in French by Jacques Nouet and François Annat, was published in 1658."

76. The Spanish landed in Cornwall in 1595 and a new attack was turned back by bad weather. In 1597 another armada was foiled by bad weather. The threat persisted during the last years of Elizabeth's reign.

77. See *Leicester's Commonwealth: The Copy of a Letter Written by a Master of Art of Cambridge (1584) and Related Documents*, ed. D.C. Peck (Athens: Ohio University Press, 1985).

78. See Timothy H. Wadkins, "The Percy-'Fisher' Controversies and the Ecclesiastical Politics of Jacobean Anti-Catholicism, 1622–1625," *Church History* 57 (June 1988): 153–69. Percy's manuscript account of the second day's debate with King James has been published by Wadkins, "King James I meets John Percy, S.J. (25 May, 1622)," *Recusant History* 19.2 (October 1988): 146–54.

79. See Thomas McCoog, S.J., "The Establishment of the English Province of the Society of Jesus," *Recusant History* 17.2 (October 1984): 121–39.

80. For the former, see, for example, *The Jesuites Plot Discovered Intended against the Parliament and City of London very lately* (1641); for the latter, see the discussion in chapter 5, especially in relation to the execution of five Jesuits during the Titus Oates Popish Plot hysteria.

81. See Pritchard, "Myth of the Evil Jesuit," 107–19; McCoog, *The Society of Jesus in Ireland, Scotland, and England, 1541–1588*, 106–8; and Cardinal Gasquet, *A History of the Venerable English College, Rome* (London: Longmans, Green, 1920), 79–106.

82. See Pritchard, "Myth of the Evil Jesuit," 78–102; and P. Renold, ed., *The Wisbech Stirs, 1595–1598*, Catholic Record Society 51 (London: Catholic Record Society, 1958). One of the anti-Jesuit Appellants, Christopher Bagshaw, published *A True Relation of the Faction Begun at Wisbich, by Fa. Edmunds, alias Weston, a Jesuite,*

1595, and Continued since by Fa. Walley, alias Garnet . . . and Fa. Parsons in Rome, with there Adherents: Against us the Secular Priests their Brethren and Fellow Prisoners (1601).

83. See Thomas Graves Law, *The Archpriest Controversy: Documents Relating to the Dissension of the Roman Catholic Clergy, 1597–1602* (1896–98; rpt. New York: Johnson Reprint, 1965) and *A Historical Sketch of the Conflicts between Jesuits and Seculars in the Reign of Queen Elizabeth* (London: D. Nutt, 1889); and Holmes, *Resistance and Compromise,* 186–211. On the pamphlets connected with the controversy, see Gladys Jenkins, "The Archpriest Controversy and the Printers, 1601–1603," *The Library,* 5th ser., 2 (1948): 180–86.

84. See Philip Hughes, *Rome and the Counter-Reformation in England* (London: Burns & Oates, 1944), 306–11. Clancy, *A Literary History of the English Jesuits,* 166, points out, however, that English Jesuits, after 1615, switched from polemical assaults on the Oath to "saying simply that the Oath was forbidden."

85. See John Bossy, *The English Catholic Community, 1570–1850* (London: Darton, Longman & Todd, 1975), 49–59; Hughes, *Rome and the Counter-Reformation in England,* 212–46; and A. F. Alison, "Richard Smith, Richelieu and the French Marriage: The Political Context of Smith's Appointment as Bishop for England in 1624," *Recusant History* 7.4 (1964): 148–211. I am grateful for these references to Suzanne Gossett, who has edited a play dramatizing the Jesuit-secular battle over the appointment of the bishop, *Hierarchomachia or The Anti-Bishop* (Bucknell: Bucknell University Press; London and Toronto: Associated Universities Presses, 1982).

86. "Blacklo" was the pen name of Thomas White, a secular priest who looked for accommodation between the English church and Catholicism and who opposed Jesuit hard-line attitudes. On Blackloism as anti-Jesuitism, see Robert I. Bradley, S.J., "Blacklo and the Counter-Reformation: An Inquiry into the Strange Death of Catholic England," in *From the Renaissance to the Counter-Reformation: Essays in Honor of Garrett Mattingly,* ed. Charles H. Carter (New York: Random House, 1965), 348–70; and Shell, *Catholicism, Controversy,* 165–66. Blackloists wanted to strike a deal with the English government for toleration: this involved establishing an English chapter with a bishop and having the Jesuits expelled from England (see John Miller, *Popery and Politics in England, 1660–1688* [Cambridge: Cambridge University Press, 1973], 43). At the time of the Popish Plot, two secular priests, John Sergaunt and David Maurice, supposedly cooperated with the authorities in hunting Jesuits. See Bernard Basset, S.J., *The English Jesuits from Campion to Martindale* (New York: Herder and Herder, 1968), 248, citing Foley, *Records of the English Province,* 5: 81.

87. This work was used in a pamphlet issued after the publication of the speeches of the five Jesuits executed together in the later Popish Plot persecution: *Auto-katakritoi, or, the Jesuites condemned by their own Witness, Being an Account of the Jesuits*

Principles, In the matter of Equivocation, The Popes Power To Depose Princes, The King-
Killing Doctrine. Out of a Book Entituled An Account of the Jesuits Life and Doctrine. By
M.G. [a Jesuit] Printed in the Year 1661. And found in possession of one of the five Jesuits
Executed on the 20th of June last past. Together, with Some Animadversions on those pas-
sages, shewing, that by the Account there given of their Doctrine in the three points above-
mentioned, those Jesuits lately Executed, were, in probability, guilty of the Treasons for which
they suffered, and died Equivocating (1679).

88. Clancy, *A Literary History of the English Jesuits,* 159, points out that the context of this Restoration pamphlet was both a general English one and the recent attack on the Jesuits by Pascal and the Jansenists in France. Clancy notes: "Some years
later James Forbes, a Scots Jesuit, wrote in 1680 that he had presented Greene's book
to James, Duke of York, the future King James II. His Highness and the Duchess, his
wife, both found it excellent and wanted it reprinted" (160).

89. This loyalty test included six questions, one of which attempted to elicit
self-incriminating evidence of (potential) treason by posing the hypothetical case to
Catholics of a papally ordered invasion of England and asking whether the individual
Catholic's loyalty would be to the queen or the pope. There is a published version of
the actual questions put to Catholic prisoners in court in *A Particular Declaration or*
Testimony of the Undutiful and Traitorous Affection borne against her Majesty, by Edmond
Campion, Jesuit, and other condemned Priests (1582), cited in Sander, *Rise and Growth*
of the Anglican Schism, 320–21n.4.

90. See Perez Zagorin, "England and the Controversy over Mental Reservation," in *Ways of Lying: Dissimulation, Persecution, and Conformity in Early Modern Eu-*
rope (Cambridge, Mass.: Harvard University Press, 1990), 186–220; Steven Mullaney,
The Place of the Stage: License, Play and Power in Renaissance England (Chicago: University of Chicago Press, 1988), 116–34; and Janet E. Halley, "Equivocation and the Legal
Conflict over Religious Identity in Early Modern England," *Yale Journal of Law and the*
Humanities 3 (1991): 33–52. Southwell was the first English Jesuit to use equivocation
and the practice of mental reservation during his imprisonment, interrogations, and
trial. Garnet wrote his notorious treatise on equivocation, which circulated in manuscript, to defend Southwell's use of the practice. See Garnet's letter to Persons, 22 April
1598 (Stonyhurst Coll. P.552). A manuscript copy of the treatise, with Garnet's correc-
tions (in anticipation of its publication) and with the marginal notes of Sir Edward
Coke, who prosecuted Garnet after the Gunpowder Plot, is to be found in the Bodleian
Library, Oxford, among the Laudian manuscripts (No. 968 [E.45], 2821—noted by
Frank L. Huntley, "Macbeth and the Background of Jesuitical Equivocation," *PMLA*
79 [1964]: 391). See the discussion of Garnet's trial in chapter 5.

91. See M.G., *An Account of the Jesuites Life and Doctrine,* 113–14. Mariana
defended the latter in his notorious *De Rege et Regis Institutione* (Toledo, 1599): see

Sidney Anglo, "More Machiavellian than Machiavel," in *John Donne: Essays in Cele-bration,* ed. A. J. Smith (London: Methuen, 1972), 375. For a discussion of Jesuit atti-tudes towards tyrannicide, see Clancy, *Papist Pamphleteers,* 96–106. Anti-Jesuit propa-ganda and libels following the assassination of Henri IV were answered in a work translated by Anthony Hopkins for an English audience, *The Apologies of the Most Christian Kings of France and Navar, Henry IIII and Lewis XIII. As also of the most wor-thy Bishop of Paris, for the Fathers of the Society of Jesus* (St. Omer, 1611). In the Restora-tion era, the author of *Some General Observations upon Dr. Stillingfleets Book, and way of Wrighting. With A Vindication of St. Ignatius Loyola, and his followers the Jesuits. From the foul Aspersions he has lately cast upon them, in his discourse concerning the Idolatry, &c.* (1672) dealt with the charge that Jesuits defended the pope's power to depose princes and taught the lawfulness of king killing: regarding the former, he wrote that "they have [not] taught . . . nor writ one word of that subject, these fifty or sixty years" (39), since Jesuit General Aquaviva forbade doing so, and the latter was also forbidden by Aquaviva, who suppressed Mariana's writings on tyrannicide.

92. The Jesuits' association with the political assassinations of William of Or-ange in 1584 and the French king Henri III in 1589 are omitted.

93. J. C. H. Aveling, *The Handle and the Axe: The Catholic Recusants in England from Reformation to Emancipation* (London: Blond & Briggs, 1976), 77.

94. Bossy, *English Catholic Community,* 182–94, points out that the numbers of Catholics grew steadily in the first half of the seventeenth century.

95. See, for example, *Autokatakritoi,* 8: "As the Jesuits are the Popes Janizaries, so are the Benedictines his Spahi." Cf. *Pyrotechnica Loyolana, Ignatian Fire-works* (1667), which refers to "these Popish Janizaries the Jesuits" (89). In his *Satires upon the Jesuits,* John Oldham also makes this association (*Poems on Affairs of State: Augustan Satirical Verse, 1660–1714,* vol. 2: 1678–1681, ed. Elias F. Mengel Jr. [New Haven: Yale Univer-sity Press, 1965], 50 [Satire 2, l. 50]).

96. Thomas Scott, the Puritan polemicist who strongly opposed the Spanish Match, referred to Jesuits and those influenced by them as "the Hispaniolated, and Romanized, natures in England" (*Vox Dei. The Voyce of God* [1623] in *Vox Populi, Vox Dei. Vox Regis. Digitus Dei et al.,* [n.p., n.d.], 83).

97. See John W. O'Malley, S.J., *The First Jesuits* (Cambridge, Mass.: Harvard University Press, 1993), 147–49. On women and boys as dangerous occasions of scan-dal for Jesuits, see the set of instructions to Campion and Persons at the start of the En-glish Jesuit mission: "Familiar conversation with women, even the best of them, will be a thing to be shunned, as also with boys, thus preserving the decorum and gravity due to our state of life" (Persons, *Letters,* 320). McCoog, *The Society of Jesus,* 138n.32, says: "Missionaries were always advised to hear the confessions of women and young boys in open, visible spaces lest there be an occasion for gossip." He cites *Instructiones ad Provin-ciales et Superiores Societatis* (Antwerp, 1635), 62.

98. The sermon was printed as *A Counter-Plea to an Apostataes Pardon. A Sermon preached at Paules Crosse* (1618), cited in Millar MacClure, *The Paul's Cross Sermons, 1534–1642* (Toronto: University of Toronto Press, 1958), 240. It did not go unnoticed that Queen Anne had a Scottish Jesuit confessor, Robert Abercrombie. For this information and for a discussion of Anne of Denmark's Catholicism, see Albert J. Loomie, S.J., "King James I's Catholic Consort," *Huntington Library Quarterly* 34 (1970–71): 303–16. Queen Anne was not the only woman close to the throne about whom James had to worry. In 1602 King James expressed concern about the possibility that the Jesuits had converted Arabella Stuart, who was too close for comfort to the line of royal succession (*Letters of King James VI & I*, ed. G. P. V. Akrigg [Berkeley: University of California Press, 1984], 191). Robert Persons, in his unfinished life of Edmund Campion, retailed a story of the conversion of Protestant women of the Jacobean court by Jesuits (*Of the Life and Martyrdom of Father Edmund Campian*, ed. Br. H. Foley, *Letters and Notices* [December 1877] [n.p.: Manresa Press, 1877], pt. 2, p. 60). In Caroline England Protestant critics of the regime attacked "the French Queen and her Jesuites" (*Jesuites Plots and Counsels Plainly discovered To the most unlearned* [1642])—this despite the fact that Henrietta Maria had less to do with Jesuits than with the Capuchins who arrived at her court in 1630 and the Oratorian priest who was her confessor (Hibbard, "Role of a Queen Consort," 404). In the Restoration era King James II had a Jesuit confessor, John Warner, who was the Jesuit Provincial (see Bossy, *English Catholic Community*, 73).

99. [H. Compton,] *The Jesuites Intrigues* (London, 1669), 35–36.

100. *The Jesuits Character* (1642), A2ᵛ–3.

101. *The Letters of John Chamberlain*, ed. Norman Egbert McClure (1939; rpt. Westport, Conn.: Greenwood Press, 1979), 1: 392. I owe this reference to Donna Hamilton, who cites it in her book, *Shakespeare and the Politics of Protestant England* (New York: Harvester Wheatsheaf, 1992), 177.

102. See Elizabeth Heale, "Spenser's Malengine, Missionary Priests, and the Means of Justice," *Review of English Studies* n.s. 41 (1990): 171–84. Heale cites John Baxter's *A Toile for Two-Legged Foxes* (1600) as an anti-Jesuit work that uses some of the stock imagery found in Spenser's account.

103. See Philip Caraman, *Henry Garnet, 1555–1606, and the Gunpowder Plot* (New York: Farrar, Straus, 1964), 39, 129, 263.

104. Foley, *Records of the English Province*, 4: 110.

105. Caroline Hibbard, *Charles I and the Popish Plot* (Chapel Hill: University of North Carolina Press, 1983), 66; and Wadkins, "Percy-'Fisher' Controversies," 158.

106. Hibbard, *Charles I and the Popish Plot, 66.*

107. See Dolan, *Whores of Babylon*, 85–94, on the slanders circulated about priests and the women with whom they had contact.

108. James, *The Jesuits Downefall*, 41.

109. Copley, *Another Letter*, G1ᵛ.

110. *Anti-Coton, or A Refutation of Cottons Letter Dedicatorie: lately directed to the Queene Regent, for the Apologizing of the Jesuits Doctrine, touching the killing of Kings* (London, 1611), 66.

111. John Gee, *The Foot out of the Snare* (1624), 61–62. Gee then describes how the Jesuits repeated this performance in other venues to deceive the gullible.

112. See, for example, the story of the fraudulent exorcism staged by the Jesuits with the help of a French female con artist, in Lewis Owen's *Speculum Jesuiticum* (1629), 42–44. A Jesuit trickster-exorcist, Jean-Joseph Surin, also figures in the supposed diabolical possession of the nuns at Loudun, France: see Michel de Certeau, *The Possession at Loudun,* trans. Michael B. Smith (Chicago: University of Chicago Press, 2000).

113. *New Shreds of the Old Snare* (1624), 1–8. Subsequent citations appear in the text. Jesuit trickery in staged exorcisms is the special target of Samuel Harsnett's *A Declaration of Egregious Popish Impostures* (1603). See the edition and commentary of F. W. Brownlow in *Shakespeare, Harsnett, and the Devils of Denham* (Newark: University of Delaware Press; London and Toronto: Associated Universities Presses, 1993). The apostate former priest Richard Sheldon published in 1616, and dedicated to the militantly Protestant earl of Pembroke, his exposure of alleged Jesuit deceits in *A Survey of the Miracles of Rome, proving them to be Antichristian. Wherein are examined and refuted the six fundamental Reasons of John Flood Ignatian, published by him in defence of Popish Miracles.*

114. *The State-Mysteries of the Jesuites . . . Translated out of the French* [by Peter Gosshin] (1623).

115. Owen, *Speculum Jesuiticum,* 5. Subsequent citations from this pamphlet are given in the text.

116. *Pyrotechnica Loyolana,* 69.

117. This is appended to *Aphorismes.* Other versions were printed as *Discoverie of the most secret and subtile practises of the Jesuites* (1610) and "A Discoverie of the Secret Designes and Bloodie Projects of the Society of Jesuites of later yeares" (in *Two Spare Keyes to the Jesuites Cabinet* [1632], 39 ff.).

118. Another anti-Jesuit work, *A Bloody Tragedie, Or Romish Maske. Acted by Five Jesuites, and Sixteen Young Germaine Maides* (1607), tells the story of the capture, rape, murder, and mass burial of sixteen German maids by five Jesuits—an atrocity story at the extreme edge of anticlerical fiction. I am grateful for this reference to Joseph Kruppa, "John Donne and the Jesuits" (Ph.D. diss., Johns Hopkins University, 1965), 232n.83.

119. *Cabal,* 10. Subsequent citations are given in the text.

120. For a discussion of Donne's association of Jesuits with Machiavellianism, see Anglo, "More Machiavellian than Machiavel," 349–84. Lori Anne Ferrell, *Government*

by Polemic: James I, the King's Preachers, and the Rhetorics of Conformity, 1603–1625 (Stanford, Calif.: Stanford University Press, 1998), 89–109, discusses the ways the polemical battle over the Jacobean Oath of Allegiance made King James more receptive to anti-Jesuit rhetoric in the Gunpowder Plot anniversary sermons.

121. It was argued in the Star Chamber trials of presbyterians in 1591 that they and the Jesuits posed the same threat to the state: see Guy, "The Elizabethan Establishment," 129. For a discussion of Catholic resistance theory in its contemporary context of political thought, see Holmes, *Resistance and Compromise,* 147–60. The charge that Jesuits favored popular sovereignty extended to an even more radical charge by William Charke in *A Replie to a Censure* (1581), Ci, where Jesuits, like Anabaptists, are supposed not to believe in private property: Jesuits' unworldliness "savou[rs] not a litle of Anabaptistrie, in condemning the propertie or private possession of earthly blessings."

122. John Donne, *Ignatius His Conclave,* ed. T. S. Healy, S.J. (Oxford: Clarendon Press, 1969), 43. Subsequent citations appear in the text. Healy points out that the three reprintings of Donne's anti-Jesuit work came at politically significant times: "That of 1626 corresponds to the first year of a new reign when, under a young monarch and his Catholic queen, there was a suspicion of a sharp rise in Catholic activity. The second reprinting came when that suspicion had become a self-evident conclusion from the conduct of the Court and the arrival in London in 1634 of Gregorio Panzini as papal observer. The third and last reprinting of the century came in 1680 in the middle of the stirs provoked by Titus Oates" (xxvii).

123. In the seventeenth century, however, Jesuits came to be associated with the strong defense of royal absolutism, so that it is not surprising to encounter in a republican, pro-Parliament pamphlet of 1642 the assumption that they are "utterly against Parliaments, and all Government where Commons have any hand. . . . [T]hey laboured these 100. yeares as stories tell us, to bring people every where to slavery, and Kings to be absolute" (*Jesuites Plots and Counsels,* 2). By the mid-seventeenth century the Jesuits are habitually, but contradictorily, associated with democratic subversion of monarchy *and* with defense of royal absolutism. Clancy, *A Literary History of the English Jesuits,* 82, claims that the 1610 order by Jesuit General Aquaviva that "no Jesuit should treat either in print or by word of tyrannicide," and his subsequent order in 1614 that "any book written by a Jesuit which dealt with the power of the pope over princes [be] sent to Rome for approval before being printed . . . spelled the end of Jesuit speculation about the origin and nature of political authority." He says that "[t]he theme of Jesuit writers from 1615 on was loyalty to the Stuart kings" (82–83). He points out, however, that Persons's *Conference about the next succession* was a touchstone for antiroyalist sentiment and that it was reprinted at various times in the seventeenth century (155, 157). "Jesuit authors suddenly became respectable in the Interregnum. . . . Juan de Mariana was cited by Samuel Rutherford, a Scots Presbyterian, in his *Lex Rex* (1644).

In the month before King Charles was executed both John Canne in his *Golden Rule* and the author of *The Armies Vindication* cited Mariana. Both argued for the right of the people to kill a tyrant. During King Charles' trial Oliver Cromwell had discussed 'the nature of royal power according to the principles of Mariana and Buchanan' according to Gilbert Burnet" (157). "Later on during the Exclusion Crisis of 1679–81 the Whigs followed the Commonwealth men in their dependence on Jesuit sources. Despite the fact that numerous royalist preachers and pamphlets denounced the republicans in the 1640s and 1650s for depending on Jesuit sources, Suarez' *De Legibus* was published in London in 1679 and Doleman [Persons] was reprinted once more in 1681, this time unedited and uncut. Doleman has been called 'the chief storehouse of facts and arguments by nearly all opponents of royal claims for more than a century'" (157, citing G. H. McIlwain's introduction to *The Political Works of James I* [Cambridge: Cambridge University Press, 1918], li).

124. This is the mythic Pope Joan, a favorite target of Protestant anti-Catholic satire—for example, Alexander Cooke's *Pope Joane. A Dialogue betweene a Protestant and a Papist. Manifestly Proving, that a Woman Called Joane was Pope of Rome* ... (1610), a work issued in the context of the Oath of Allegiance controversy. See C. A. Patrides, "'A Palpable hieroglyphick': The Fable of Pope Joan," in *Premises and Motifs in Renaissance Thought and Literature* (Princeton: Princeton University Press, 1982), 152–81.

125. For a discussion of the political context of this play, see Thomas Middleton, *A Game at Chesse,* ed. R. C. Bald (Cambridge: Cambridge University Press, 1929), 1–18 passim; Margot Heinemann, *Puritanism and Theater: Thomas Middleton and Opposition Drama under the Early Stuarts* (Cambridge: Cambridge University Press, 1980), 151–71; Thomas Cogswell, "Thomas Middleton and the Court, 1624: A Game at Chess in Context," *Huntington Library Quarterly* 47 (1984): 273–88; Jerzy Limon, *Dangerous Matter: English Drama and Politics in 1623/24* (Cambridge: Cambridge University Press, 1986), 98–129; and Shell, *Catholicism, Controversy,* 36–55. See the discussion of the popular celebrations accompanying Charles's and Buckingham's return in David Cressy, *Bonfires and Bells: National Memory and the Protestant Calendar in Elizabethan and Stuart England* (London: Weidenfeld and Nicolson, 1989), 93–109.

126. For a discussion of the sexualization of the Jesuit threat in this play, see Limon, *Dangerous Matter,* 114–18.

127. Thomas Middleton, *A Game at Chesse,* ed. T. H. Howard-Hill (Manchester: Manchester University Press, 1993), 1.1.50–51. Subsequent citations are from this text. John Holles saw the play as arguing "that the Jesuits mark is to bring all the Christian world under Rome for the spirituality, and under Spayn for the Temporality"— quoted in A. R. Braunmuller, "'To the Globe I rowed': John Holles Sees *A Game at Chess,*" *English Literary Renaissance* 20 (1990): 342.

128. See 1.1.53–62, 109–15.

129. See, for example, 2.2.182; 4.2.53–57, 111–32.

130. The Black Knight's Pawn says the Black Bishop's Pawn wears an "epicene chasuble" (1.1.232). In *Ignatius His Conclave,* Donne associates sodomy with "Ecclesiastique Princes" (39, 41, 43) and retails the false tale of Pier Liugi, Pope Paul III's son, who was supposed to have sexually assaulted the bishop of Fano (see Healy's notes, 123). Healy notes that Barnabe Barnes in *The Devil's Charter* (1607) has Pope Alexander VI try to seduce a young man he later murders. Peter Lake remarks: "for many Protestants buggery became an archetypally popish sin, not only because of its proverbially monastic provenance but also because, since it involved the abuse of natural faculties and impulses for unnatural ends, it perfectly symbolized the wider idolatry at the heart of popish religion" ("Anti-Popery: The Structure of a Prejudice," in *Conflict in Early Stuart England: Studies in Religion and Politics, 1603–1642* [London: Longman, 1989], 75). Bruce Smith, *Homosexuality in Shakespeare's England,* (Chicago: University of Chicago Press, 1991), 43–44, claims that Henry VIII's antisodomy law was anti-Catholic. On the connection of priests and the accusation of sodomy, see Dolan, *Whores of Babylon,* 88–92.

131. This would appear to be a code for celibacy and, possibly, homosexuality.

132. Protestant polemicists habitually criticized the demands of Catholicism for obedience to the pope and to other ecclesiastical authorities. And Catholic texts, such as the life of Margaret Clitherow, idealized lay obedience to priestly authority.

133. See Hibbard's discussion of the Habernfeld Plot and anti-Jesuit paranoia: *Charles I and the Popish Plot,* 157–62.

134. Jesuits and missionary priests, in the biblical language of Revelation 9.3, were called "locusts" and "venomed wasps" (*Letters of James VI and I,* ed. Akrigg, 205) in Protestant discourse. In one of his sermons Lancelot Andrewes described Jesuits as monstrous locusts, "a kind of creatures who have a man's face, woman's hair but lion's teeth, and their tails the stings of scorpions" (*Ninety-Six Sermons* [Oxford: J. H. Parker, 1841–43], 5: 75, quoted in Alvin Kernan, *Shakespeare, the King's Playwright: Theater in the Stuart Court, 1603–1613* [New Haven: Yale University Press, 1995], 75). John Gee refers to Jesuits also as "the Locusts of the wildernesse, with their Scorpion-like tayles" (*The Foot out of the Snare,* 24). Alison Shell, "Catholic Texts and Anti-Catholic Prejudice in the 17th-Century Book Trade," in *Censorship and the Control of Print in England and France, 1600–1910,* ed. Robin Myers and Michael Harris (Winchester: St. Paul's Bibliographies, 1992), 43, points out "Jesuits were often compared to the locusts of the Apocalypse." See also Michael Questier, "'Like locusts over all the world': Conversion, Indoctrination and the Society of Jesus in Late Elizabethan and Jacobean England," in *The Reckoned Expense: Edmund Campion and the Early English Jesuits,* ed. Thomas M. McCoog, S.J. (Woodbridge, Suffolk: Boydell Press, 1996), 265–66.

135. Canto II, st. 9. I use the edition of this poem in *The English Spenserians: The Poetry of Giles Fletcher, George Wither, Michael Drayton, Phineas Fletcher, and Henry*

More, ed. William B. Hunter Jr. (Salt Lake City: University of Utah Press, 1977). Subsequent citations appear in the text.

136. In his polemical assault on the pending match between Queen Elizabeth and the Catholic duke of Alençon, John Stubbs had also used Solomon and Samson in a discussion of the evils of a mixed marriage (*John Stubbs's Gaping Gulf with Letters and Other Relevant Documents,* ed. Lloyd E. Berry [Charlottesville: University Press of Virginia for the Folger Shakespeare Library, 1968], 10).

137. See J. B. Broadbent, *Some Graver Subject* (London: Chatto & Windus, 1960), 96, 126, 131, 183; and David Quint, *Epic and Empire* (Princeton: Princeton University Press, 1993), 270–81 (both cited by Wills, *Witches and Jesuits,* 174). For a discussion of the influence of the Gunpowder Plot and of Gunpowder Plot commemorative sermons on Milton's poetry, see Stella Purce Revard, *The War in Heaven* (Ithaca, N.Y.: Cornell University Press, 1980), 87–107.

138. Milton, like most fellow Protestants, was strongly anti-Jesuit. He regarded Jesuits as king killers ("Observations upon the Articles of Peace with the Irish Rebels," in *Complete Prose Works of John Milton,* gen. ed. Don M. Wolfe, 8 vols. [New Haven: Yale University Press, 1953–82], 3: 316). He not only disparagingly referred to Marie de Medici as Henrietta Maria's "Jesuited mother" (*Eikonoklastes,* in *Complete Prose Works of John Milton,* 3: 421–42), but he also referred to his fear, during his trip to Italy, of Jesuits conspiring against him and to a warning that he should stay out of Rome (*Defensio Secunda,* in *Complete Prose Works of John Milton,* 4: 124). On Milton's anti-Catholicism and the ecclesiastical satire in *Paradise Lost,* see John N. King, *Milton and Religious Controversy: Satire and Polemic in* Paradise Lost (Cambridge: Cambridge University Press, 2000).

139. Catherine Canino, "The Discourse of Hell: *Paradise Lost* and the Irish Rebellion," *Milton Quarterly* 31.1 (March 1998): 20, remarks: "One might argue that all the devils in *Paradise Lost* are thinly disguised Jesuit casuists. . . . [Satan's] seduction of Eve is a masterpiece of casuistry. . . . Satan is, in spirit as well as practice, a Jesuit." Richard Carpenter, *The Jesuit, and the Monk: Or, The Serpent, and the Dragon: Or, Profession, and Practice. Being a Sermon Preached on the fifth of November, 1656* (1656), 6, likens the serpent who tempted Eve to Jesuits: "It was a Serpent that could move, turn, wind all manner of ways; and had . . . part of the motions, windings, turnings, returnings, and overturnings of the blessed Father Garnet, when he was religiously instructing his godly Ghostly Children in Confession, and . . . under the sacred Seal, to blow up the Parliament House." Toby Matthew, a Jesuit who was in the inner circle of the court of Henrietta Maria in the late Caroline period, was identified in anti-Catholic discourse as a dangerous influence on the queen. The pamphlet *The Confession of John Browne, A Jesuite in the Gate-house* (1641), identifies him as a member of her "Cabinet Counsell" along with Sir John Winter and Walter Montagu (A3) and also as one of the papal

nuncio's main advisors, along with Sir Kenelm Digby and Montagu (A3v). A story is told about Matthew's relationship with court ladies that portrays him as the seducing Jesuit working through powerful women to restore Catholicism in England:

> He visited one of the best ladies in the Land alone, and being found by her husband, and being asked why he durst be so bold, he was in feare to have bin precipitated out at a window. His manner was in the morning, sometimes two houres before day, to visit Ladies and Gentlewomen, enquiring of them, how they had slept that night. . . . I heard a French-man of good worth say, that he had seene a Breve from Rome with the Iniscript. TOBIAE MATHEW SACERDOTI, SOCIETATIS JESU. That is, to Toby Mathewes Priest of the order of JESUS: wherein (inter alia) was Confirma Amazonas illas quae strenue laborant in vita pro Christo. First confirm those Amazonian Court-Ladies, that is, those brave Catholicks, Catamountaines or the Popish-Faction, that labour lustily for the advancement of popery. (A3, A4)

Perhaps, if there is any contemporary model for Satan in *Paradise Lost* as a confidant of Eve, squatting toadlike beside her infusing a religious seduction dream into her ear, it is the Jesuit Matthew. For a discussion of Matthew as an important political agent, see chapter 4. The writer of *The Quacking Mountebank. Or the Jesuit turn'd Quaker . . .* (1655) refers to the Jesuits as religious seducers of women: "These English Crocodiles leave no polytick ways untried to work upon Weak Proselites, they prevaile most upon the femall Sex, as knowing the Woman was first seduced, and then seduced the man" (20). In the 17 December 1680 issue of his newsletter, *A Weekly Pacquet of Advice from Rome,* the Whig propagandist Henry Care summarized the myth of diabolical and Jesuit control: "Gallants manage Affairs of State; and the Ladies manage the Gallants; and the Jesuits manage the Ladies; and the Pope manages the Jesuits; and the Devil manages them all" (223).

140. See Brown, "Milton and the Idolatrous Consort," for the recurrence of this motif in Milton's work, culminating in *Samson Agonistes,* a poem in which Dalila, the foreign wife of a true believer, must be rejected by her godly spouse for her false religion.

3. Manuscript Transmission and the Catholic Martyrdom Account

1. See Clark Hulse, "Dead Man's Treasure: The Cult of Thomas More," in *The Production of English Renaissance Culture,* ed. David Lee Miller, Sharon O'Dair, and Harold Weber (Ithaca: Cornell University Press, 1994), 217. Brad S. Gregory, *Salvation at Stake: Christian Martyrdom in Early Modern Europe* (Cambridge, Mass.: Harvard

University Press, 1999), 270, says of Nicholas Harpsfield's account, "Eight extant manuscripts from the sixteenth and seventeenth centuries suggest a fairly wide, long-standing
circulation." Cresacre More's *The Life and Death of Sir Thomas Moore* (1630) circulated
in manuscript long before its publication. See Anne Dillon, *The Construction of Martyrdom in the English Catholic Community, 1535–1603* (Aldershot: Ashgate, 2002), 45, for
a discussion of how these manuscript lives were circulated in Marian England to support the regime's religiopolitical program. Although this chapter was completed before
I had access to Dillon's study, I have tried subsequently to incorporate her insights and
arguments.

2. This work was printed in 1584: see *Leicester's Commonwealth: The Copy of
a Letter Written by a Master of Art of Cambridge (1584) and Related Documents,* ed. D. C.
Peck (Athens: Ohio University Press, 1985). It subsequently circulated widely in manuscript: see H. R. Woudhuysen, *Sir Philip Sidney and the Circulation of Manuscripts,
1558–1640* (Oxford: Clarendon Press, 1996), 148. William Shelley, a layman, was sentenced to death for owning a copy of this work; see John Hungerford Pollen, ed., *Acts of
English Martyrs Hitherto Unpublished* (London: Burns and Oates, 1891), 307 (hereafter
cited in the text as Pollen, *Acts*).

3. See the discussion of this document in F. W. Brownlow, "John Shakespeare's
Recusancy: New Light on an Old Document," *Shakespeare Quarterly* 48 (summer 1989):
186–91; and Richard Wilson, "Shakespeare and the Jesuits," *Times Literary Supple-
ment,* 19 December 1997, 11–13. Persons and Campion brought printed copies of this
with them on the English mission in 1580, but there were also manuscript versions
produced, such as the one for Shakespeare's father.

4. See Woudhuysen, *Sir Philip Sidney,* 52–53, citing John Hungerford Pollen
and William MacMahon, eds., *The Ven. Philip Howard Earl of Arundel, 1557–1595,*
Catholic Record Society 21, English Martyrs vol. 2 (London: Catholic Record Society,
1919), 99, 142–43, 281, 338. This much-copied text circulated very widely in the Catholic community.

5. Dennis Flynn, *John Donne and the Ancient Catholic Nobility* (Bloomington: Indiana University Press, 1996), 218n.10, notes that this circulated in manuscript after 1596.

6. Woudhuysen, *Sir Philip Sidney,* 124, notes that eight manuscripts of this
work survive, that Holinshed used it for his *Chronicles* (1577), but that it was not printed
until 1631.

7. Southwell's poetry, despite its publication, continued to appear in manuscript collections in the seventeenth century. See, for example, Bod. MSS Eng. Poet.
b.5 and e.113 and BL MS. Harl. 6910. Robert Southwell's famous letter to his father
was reproduced in many copies and circulated widely. Other literary texts circulated in
manuscript include freshly copied versions of banned old mystery play cycles (Woudhuysen, *Sir Philip Sidney,* 145).

8. See Bod. MS Eng. Poet. e.122, fols. 31–36; BL MS Add. 15225, fols. 25–27ᵛ, for copies of this poem: Hyder Rollins, ed., *Old English Ballads, 1553–1625* (Cambridge: Cambridge University Press, 1920), 88–94, prints the British Library version.

9. BL MS Add. 15225, fols. 2ᵛ–3, in Rollins, *Old English Ballads,* 149–51 (I emend in two places).

10. Thomas Alfield, *A True Reporte of the Death & Martyrdome of M. Campion Jesuit and Preiste, & M. Sherwin, & M. Bryan Preistes . . .* (1582); and Anthony Munday, *A breefe Aunswer made unto two seditious Pamphlets. . . . Contayning a defence of Edmund Campion and his complices . . .* (1582). See the discussion of this work in chapter 1. In response to the execution of Everard Hanse, 31 July 1581, there was a libel published to counter the circulation of manuscript accounts of his death: *A true report, of the Araignment and execution of the late Popish traitor, Everard Haunce, executed at Tyborne, with reformation of the errors of a former untrue booke published concerning the same* (1581). See the text published in *Miscellanea,* Catholic Record Society (London: John Whitehead & Son, 1932)—noted in *Lives of the English Martyrs Declared Blessed by Pope Leo XIII. in 1886 and 1895,* written by the Fathers of the Oratory, of the Secular Clergy, and of the the Society of Jesus, completed and edited by Dom Bede Camm, O. S. B., 2 vols. (London: Burns and Oates, 1904–5), 1: 261.

11. For a rich comparative study of martyrdom in the early modern period, see Gregory, *Salvation at Stake,* esp. chap. 7, "The New Saints: Roman Catholics and Martyrdom," 250–314. Dillon, *Construction of Martyrdom,* particularly emphasizes the Continental audience of Catholic martyrdom accounts (especially the printed compilations), though, of course, she acknowledges their domestic functions in relation to the English Catholic community.

12. Reprinted from Grene's Collectanea M. part ii (fols. 206–9) in John Hungerford Pollen, ed., *Unpublished Documents Relating to the English Martyrs,* vol. 1: *1584–1603* (London: Catholic Record Society, 1908), 62. Hereafter cited in the text as Pollen, *Unpub. Doc.*

13. See, in particular, Garnet's letters of 1594 (in Pollen, *Unpub. Doc.,* 227–33) and March 1601–2 (ARSI. Rom. Anglia 31, 172–83), which contain reports of many martyrs.

14. See Anthony Petti, "Richard Verstegan and Catholic Martyrologies of the Later Elizabethan Period," *Recusant History* 5.1 (1959): 64–90. Dillon, *Construction of Martyrdom,* 78, discusses the functions of Catholic "postmasters" such as Verstegan. See her lengthy discussion in chapters 3–5 of Verstegan and his importance for Catholic pictorial depictions of martyrdom.

15. Dillon, *Construction of Martyrdom,* 82, discusses the primacy of the Continental context, in which these martyrdom stories served as a counterbalance to the Protestant martyrologies of John Foxe and Jean Crespin. England was the only country producing Catholic martyrs.

16. Pollen, *Unpub. Doc.*, 140–43, prints four letters written by Englishmen intended for Gibbons to use in revising his *Concertatio* for a second edition but intercepted by the English authorities. Alexandra Walsham, "'Domme Preachers': Post-Reformation English Catholicism and the Culture of Print," *Past and Present*, no. 168 (August 2000): 84, points out that Dr. Humphrey Ely was one of a number of correspondents who sent biographical material to Gibbons. See Gregory, *Salvation at Stake*, 287–97, for a discussion of the flow of communication and publication about the martyrs. He notes that "[b]etween 1580 and 1640, at least 203 editions of more than 50 different works either about the English Catholic martyrs or in which they occupy an important place were published throughout Europe, in English, Latin, French, Italian, Spanish, German, and Dutch" (289). See Dillon, *Construction of Martyrdom*, 78–81, for a discussion of the making of the Continental compendia of martyrdom accounts. She quotes Robert Persons's statement that he regularly received "books, dialogues, treatises, poems, satires, which have been composed and published, some in print, some in manuscript in praise of these martyrs and in blame of their adversaries" (79; citing L. Hicks, S.J., ed., *Letters and Memorials of Father Robert Persons, S.J.*, vol. 1, Catholic Record Society 39 [London: John Whitehead & Sons, 1942], 133).

17. Pollen, *Unpub. Doc.*, 393, connects many of the notes found in the Archives of the Archdiocese of Westminster (hereafter AAW) 4: 1–14, 117–32, etc., with the responses to this call. In the context of the Jesuit-secular conflicts over Smith's appointment and authority, Smith's information gathering was an attempt to compete with accounts of Jesuit martyrs by focusing on non-Jesuit clerical and lay martyrs. See Thomas H. Clancy, S.J., *A Literary History of the English Jesuits: A Century of Books, 1615–1714* (San Francisco: Catholic Scholars Press, 1996), 102.

18. This, as Pollen points out, *Unpub. Doc.* 144, was a translation of Allen's work, with Gibbons putting the lives in chronological order. Dillon, *Construction of Martyrdom*, 80–81, points out that Allen's book was translated into Italian and published in editions in 1583, 1584, and 1585.

19. Pollen, *Unpub. Doc.*, 1–3, mentions, in addition to these works, the following publications that contain accounts of martyrdoms or lists of martyrs: Nicholas Sander's *De origine et progressu Schismatis Anglicani Liber* (1585; 2d ed., 1586), *Relatione del presente stato d'Inghilterra* (Rome, 1590) (containing Dr. Richard Barrett's list of martyrs, also appearing in Tomaso Bozio's *De Signis Ecclesiae* [1591], Gregorio Nuñez Coronel's *De Vera Christi Ecclesia* [Rome, 1594], Juan Lopez Mancano's broadside sheet, *Breve Catalogo de los Martyres que han side de los Collegios y Seminarios Ingeses* [Valladolid, 1590], and Pedro de Ribandeneira's *Historia ecclesiastica del cisma de Inglaterra* [1593]), Persons's *Elizabethae Angliae Reginae saevissimum edictum . . . cum responsione* (Lyons, 1592), which has a catalog of laymen who died for the faith, and Fray Diego Yepes's *Historia particular de las persecucion de Inglaterra* (Madrid, 1599).

20. See Dillon, *Construction of Martyrdom,* 72–276, for the best discussion of the visual depiction of Catholic martyrdoms in printed books and paintings. She demonstrates the centrality of Richard Verstegan to this work: the visual imagery in his broadsheet, *Praesentis Ecclesiae Anglicanae typus* (Rheims, 1582), his blockbook, *Descriptiones quaedam illius inhumanae et multiplicies persecutiones, quam in Anglia propter fidem sustinent Catholicè Christiani* (Paris, 1583–84), and his landmark martyrology, *Theatrum Crudelitatum Haereticorum Nostri Temporis* (Antwerp, 1587), were a major influence on subsequent work. Dillon, *Construction of Martyrdom,* 146–47, emphasizes the connections of Verstegan and Persons with the French Catholic League and its militant Catholic program in relation to their depictions of martyrdom.

21. A manuscript version of this martyrdom account (by James Young) survives (Stonyhurst MS Anglia vi.117). There is an interesting four-page folio pamphlet containing the story of Gennings's life and martyrdom and of a devout Catholic woman's seizure of one of his thumbs as a relic after his death: *Strange and Miraculous News from St. Omers: Being an Account of the Wonderful Life and Death of a Popish Saint and Martyr, named Mr. Edmund Gennings, Priest, who was Executed for Treason some Years since: with a Relation of the Miracles at, and after his Death. Wherein may be observed, what Lying Wonders the Credulous Papists are made to believe, both against Sense and Reason* (n.p., n.d.). This has a short anti-Catholic introductory section and a short, mocking concluding paragraph, but the body of the pamphlet is a Catholic account. The work may therefore have been posing as anti-Catholic propaganda so as to put into circulation a Catholic martyrological text.

22. As Woudhuysen and others note, Catholic printed books and pamphlets from the Continent often returned to manuscript circulation when they were given to copyists in England for reproduction and sale. See Woudhuysen, *Sir Philip Sidney,* 82, citing Leona Rostenberg, *The Minority Press and the English Crown* (Nieuwkoop, Netherlands: B. De Graaf, 1971), 81.

23. Stonyhurst MS. M. fol.157, cited in Pollen, *Acts,* 2–8.

24. This letter is dated 16 March 1583[4].

25. D. Shanahan, "Petticoats on the Gallows," *Essex Recusant* 11 (1968): 107; the text of this martyrdom account is reproduced on pp. 108–10.

26. See J. G. O'Leary, "A Recusant Manuscript of Great Importance," *Essex Recusant* 10 (1968): 17–20.

27. Nancy Pollard Brown, "Paperchase: The Dissemination of Catholic Texts in Elizabethan England," *English Manuscript Studies,* vol. 1 (Oxford: Basil Blackwell, 1989), 120–43. Brown traces a paper supply, with its distinctive watermark, to Henry Garnet, who distributed it to be used both for some printed works and for manuscript copying. Garnet, she guesses, probably took possession of the papers of Robert Southwell after the latter's arrest and saw to it that a number of his works were copied and printed.

28. There are four extant manuscripts of the life. One sixteenth-century version was used by John Morris for his nineteenth-century edition in *Troubles of Our Catholic Forefathers,* vol. 3 (London: Burns and Oates, 1877), 360–440; another is a copy of selected chapters dealing with the arrest, trial, and execution (St. Mary's College, Oscott, in Peter Mowle's collection); another sixteenth-century version of the selected chapters is York Minster Library Add. MS 151; and a seventeenth-century version is Vatican Library Barberini Latini, Codex 3555 (information provided in Mary Claridge [Katherine Longley], *Saint Margaret Clitherow* [Wheathampstead, Herts.: Anthony Clarke, 1986]). See the discussion of Clitherow's martyrdom in chapter 2.

29. *An Abstracte of the Life and Martirdome of Mistres Margaret Clitherowe* (Mackline, 1619).

30. Cf. the eight-sheet quarto quire now in the Archives of the Archdiocese of Westminster containing "Of Mr Roger Cadwallader Pr. and martyr who suffered at Le[o]m[in]ster, 27. Aug. 1610" plus some other items (AAW 9: 211–26, the last two sheets of which are blank). There are two accounts of the 10 December martyrdoms of Roberts and Wilson in AAW 9: 343 ff. An account of the martyrdom of John Lathom is preserved in manuscript in a small quarto booklet formerly among the Douay MSS (AAW 11: 627 ff. [item #221]). Dillon, *Construction of Martyrdom,* 373, points out that when Richard Challoner was compiling material for his *Memoirs of Missionary Priests* (1741–42), he "drew on the original texts, letters, and manuscripts that were available at Douai"—that is, on many of the manuscripts that are now in the Archives of the Archdiocese of Westminster.

31. See Michael E. Williams, "Campion and the English Continental Seminaries," in *The Reckoned Expense: Edmund Campion and the Early English Jesuits,* ed. Thomas McCoog (Woodbridge: Boydell Press, 1996), 295–96. See also Dillon, *Construction of Martyrdom,* 83–84.

32. For an excellent discussion of the problematic and disputable meanings of these executions for contemporaries, see Peter Lake and Michael Questier, "Agency, Appropriation and Rhetoric under the Gallows: Puritans, Romanists and the State in Early Modern England," *Past and Present,* no. 153 (November 1996): 64–107. They highlight the Jesuits' activism and ideological zealotry (92–95). Although most of this chapter was written before I read this study, I have learned much from and am indebted to it. Lake and Questier's essay has become part of Peter Lake, with Michael Questier, *The Antichrist's Lewd Hat: Protestants, Papists and Players in Post-Reformation England* (New Haven: Yale University Press, 2002), 229–80. In chapter 8 of this same volume, "Discourses of Vice and Discourses of Virtue: 'Counter-Martyrology' and the Conduct of Intra-Catholic Dispute," 281–314, they emphasize the functions of martyrdom accounts and of countermartyrological discourse within a faction-ridden English Catholicism as part of intra-Catholic struggles. For example, in the context of the many

conflicts between the secular priests and the Jesuits, the writing of martyrdom accounts of secular priests could be seen as an argument that they were just as faithful Catholics as their zealous and hard-line competitors (300–301). In *Construction of Martyrdom*, in her discussion of "the pseudomartyr debate" (18–71 passim), Dillon examines the competing Catholic and Protestant martyrologies and accounts of English Church history. She identifies "the three intentions of any martyrology: political polemic, narrative history and religious manifesto" (255).

33. See Alexandra Walsham, *Church Papists: Catholicism, Conformity and Confessional Polemic in Early Modern England* (Woodbridge, Suffolk: Royal Historical Society and Boydell Press, 1993).

34. William Trimble, *The Catholic Laity in Elizabethan England, 1558–1603* (Cambridge, Mass.: The Belknap Press, 1964), 175, points out that, although the government distrusted time-serving church papists, "an occasional conformist was a lost Catholic, a fact increasingly true as Elizabeth's reign progressed."

35. Louise I. Guiney, *Recusant Poets* (New York: Sheed and Ward, 1939), 181.

36. Geoffrey F. Nuttall, "The English Martyrs, 1535–1680: A Statistical Review," *Journal of Ecclesiastical History* 22.3 (July 1971): 193–94.

37. See AAW 7: 339–42. This manuscript is the source for the (not always accurate) version in Pollen's *Acts* (238–48), which completes the story from Bishop Challoner's version.

38. A 1602 letter from a Jesuit correspondent to Robert Persons refers to the death of Duckett and to his having been used as an instrument by the (anti-Jesuit) Appellant party to print Southwell's work, which the (pro-Jesuit) "Archpriest" George Blackwell had not wished to be published at that time (Pollen, *Unpub. Doc.,* 390–91).

39. Lake and Questier, "Agency, Appropriation and Rhetoric under the Gallows," 81, also cite this example. Guiney, *Recusant Poets,* 174, prints from Peter Mowle's manuscripts a poem by Wells, "To Christ Crucified." See her discussion of Wells's life (171–73).

40. Dillon, *Construction of Martyrdom,* 61–62, discusses the European context of the martyrological competition. In the context of Catholics' and Protestants' claims that their religious antagonists were celebrating "pseudomartyrs," Dillon, 64–66, notes the refutation of Foxe found in Nicholas Harpsfield's *Dialogi sex* (Antwerp, 1566).

41. Lake, with Questier, *The Antichrist's Lewd Hat,* xvii–xviii.

42. Gregory, *Salvation at Stake,* 277.

43. Ibid., 280. For a discussion of the Protestant technique of turning the body into a text and other features of Protestant martyrdom accounts, see Catharine Randall Coats, *(Em)bodying the Word: Textual Resurrections in the Martyrological Narratives of Foxe, Crespin, de Bèze and d'Aubigné* (New York: Peter Lang, 1992). Coats argues, "Unlike Catholic hagiographical writing which may be characterized by a focus

on the image, and the spatial rendering and localization of that image, Calvinist martyrologies are above all typified by an insistence on the word—be it of the martyr,
of the author or of God" (2). For discussions of Protestant martyrdom, see also John
Knott, *Discourses of Martyrdom in English Literature, 1563–1694* (Cambridge: Cambridge University Press, 1993); and Huston Diehl, *Staging Reform: Reforming the Stage:
Protestantism and Popular Theater in Early Modern England* (Ithaca: Cornell University
Press, 1997), 185–94 passim.

44. *The Sermons of John Donne,* ed. George R. Potter and Evelyn Simpson, 10
vols. (Berkeley: University of California Press, 1953–62), 5: 382.

45. See also Thomas J. McCann, "Some Unpublished Accounts of the Martyrdom of Blessed Thomas Bullaker O. S. F. of Chichester in 1642," *Recusant History* 19.2
(October 1988): 171–82. McCann points to four surviving manuscript accounts of Bullaker's martyrdom and concludes that "the accounts of his martyrdom must have enjoyed a large readership" (173).

46. This is noted by Antonia Fraser, *Faith and Treason: The Story of the Gunpowder Plot* (New York: Nan A. Talese and Doubleday, 1996), 267.

47. See the discussion of Almond's execution in Lake and Questier, "Agency,
Appropriation and Rhetoric under the Gallows," 74.

48. See Richard Simpson, *Edmund Campion: A Biography* (London: John Hodges,
1896), 454–55. Pollen, *Unpub. Doc.,* 246–69, prints the later "confessions" of Walpole,
who was repeatedly threatened and tortured by the authorities before his death.

49. Garnet, letter to the Jesuit General, 11 March 1601 (ARSI Rom. Anglia 31,
172–83), translation in the English Jesuit Archives, London, kindly made available by
Thomas McCoog, S.J.

50. Nuttall, "The English Martyrs," 195.

51. Ibid., 195.

52. Lake and Questier, "Agency, Appropriation and Rhetoric under the Gallows," 70, point out that "[f]ourteen priests executed in 1588 in the closest the Elizabethan regime ever got to a 'terror' were sent off to 'sundry places neere London' to die."

53. *Life and Death of Mr Edmund Geninges, Priest,* 84.

54. Garry Wills, *Witches and Jesuits: Shakespeare's* Macbeth (New York and Oxford: New York Public Library and Oxford University Press, 1995), 101.

55. Thomas Laqueur, "Crowds, Carnival and the State in English Executions,
1604–1868," in *The First Modern Society,* ed. A. Beier, D. Cannadine, and J. Rosenheim
(Cambridge: Cambridge University Press, 1989), 322, notes that the "*hilaritas* of the
martyr . . . would have been . . . familiar to English audiences in Foxe's *Book of Martyrs.*" Knott, *Discourses of Martyrdom in English Literature,* 82, however, points out the
difference between Foxe's emphasis on the holy joy and cheerfulness of the Protestant
martyr and the jesting in which a Catholic martyr such as Thomas More engaged.

56. See the text printed in Henry Foley, ed., *Records of the English Province of the Society of Jesus*, vol. 1 (London: Burns and Oates, 1877), 373–75.

57. Dillon, *Construction of Martyrdom*, 88, points out that a regular feature of scaffold speeches of Catholic martyrs was a profession of political loyalty to monarch and country meant to signal that the death was for religion, not for treason.

58. *Life and Death of Mr Edmund Geninges, Priest*, 84–85.

59. Ibid., 85–86.

60. Cf. the examples discussed by Lake and Questier, "Agency, Appropriation and Rhetoric under the Gallows," 73–75.

61. See, for example, the exchange between William Cecil, Lord Burghley, and William Cardinal Allen, in their two works: *The Execution of Justice in England* (1584) and *A True, Sincere, and Modest Defense of English Catholics* (1584). I discuss this exchange in chapter 1.

62. Queen Henrietta Maria's visit to Tyburn in 1626 to pray at the site of the martyrdoms acknowledged this (see Alison Shell, *Catholicism, Controversy and the English Literary Imagination, 1558–1660* [Cambridge: Cambridge University Press, 1999], 153).

63. Pollen is citing "R. B." (Robert Barnes?), the author of *Two Obstinate and Notorious Traitors, Slade and Body, their Execution and Confession* (1583?), a work that seems to use a veneer of hostility to disguise its sympathy for the martyrs. Cf. the account of their martyrdoms in AAW 2: 341 ff. See also Shell, *Catholicism, Controversy and the English Literary Imagination*, 112.

64. Gregory, *Salvation at Stake*, 280, states: "Sometimes priests viewed martyrdom with eucharistic overtones. Edmund Campion, for example, referred to martyrs as 'holy hosts and oblations' pleasing to God." On the eucharistic signals in martyrdom accounts, see Dillon, *Construction of Martyrdom*, 107–8. She connects the Tridentine emphasis on the Mass as sacrifice with the visual imagery associating the martyr with Christ in broadsheets and other illustrated Catholic texts (136–37).

65. Lake and Questier, "Agency, Appropriation and Rhetoric under the Gallows," 69, 73.

66. Dillon, *Construction of Martyrdom*, 49, notes, however, that the Protestant faithful treated George Wyatt's remains as relics. She points out also that Miles Huggarde in *The displaying of the protestantes with a description of divers their abuses* (1556) had mocked Foxe's depiction of Protestants "swarming over the embers of the fires after the burnings [of the Marian victims] to collect the relics of their brethren" (52). This unusual activity displayed behavior associated with the "old religion" and took place despite the consistent Protestant attacks on Catholic superstitious practices connected to saints' relics.

67. See Gregory, *Salvation at Stake*, 307–10, for a discussion of this phenomenon. Dillon, *Construction of Martyrdom*, 66–67, discusses Thomas Stapleton's pointing out

the irony that John Foxe used the idea of the miraculous in some of his Protestant martyrdom stories, given the Protestant criticism of Catholic miracle mongering. She also discusses the deliberate exclusion of references to miracles from some verbal and pictorial depictions of Catholic martyrdom so as to suggest the difference between converting pagans (a process in which miracles were more appropriate) and maintaining the fidelity of Catholics to a papally centered church or reconciling those who had fallen away from it (97–98, 207–11). She acknowledges, however, the Jesuits' wish to accommodate community beliefs by retaining the miraculous in some narratives. She notes (86–87) Stapleton's defense of miracles in the preface to his translation of Venerable Bede's *The Historie of the Church of Englande* (1565). Patrick Collinson, "Truth, Lies, and Fiction in Sixteenth-Century Protestant Historiography," in *The Historical Imagination in Early Modern Britain: History, Rhetoric, and Fiction, 1500–1800*, ed. Donald R. Kelley and David Harris Sacks (Cambridge: Cambridge University Press, 1997), 55–57, points out that Foxe's conception of the miraculous differed from the Catholic one in not conceiving of the miraculous as an exception from the ordinary workings of nature. See the discussion of rivalrous Protestant and Catholic accounts of wonders and miracles in Alexandra Walsham, *Providence in Early Modern England* (Oxford: Oxford University Press, 1999), 225–80.

68. More, *Life and Death of Sir Thomas More*, 357–58.

69. Ibid., 359.

70. In his long-winded speech at Garnet's Gunpowder Treason trial, the earl of Northampton punned on Bull's name in relation to papal bulls (*A True and Perfect Relation of the proceedings at the several Arraignments of the Late Most barbarous Traitors* [1606], ZZ3^v).

71. Cited in Camm, *Lives,* 1: 260–61.

72. In one of his letters to Cardinal Allen, William Barret reported three striking examples of divine punishment having been visited on the persecutors of Catholics: see *Letters of William Allen and Richard Barret, 1572–1598*, ed. P. Renold (London: Catholic Record Society, 1967), 96–97.

73. A description of authorities' vigilance about Catholic relic hunters at executions can be found in *A Yorkshire Recusant's Relation* (in Morris, *Troubles,* 3: 98–99):

> [S]pies are set abroad to mark the countenances and behaviour of the bystanders, and to note it any be there which by word, gesture, or any other way seem favourable to us, lament our unjust deaths, or show any sign of charitable compassion towards us in our agony, or endeavour to get of our blood or other relics, for all such they apprehend as traitors and enemies to the Queen. Moreover, they use singular diligence and wariness in martyring us, that no part of blood, or flesh, or garment, or anything belonging to the martyr be either unburnt or

escape their hands. The sacred blood they conculcate and cast into the fire. The apparel the murderers take and disperse, the pins, points, buttons, and all, lest Catholics get them and use them for relics. They boil also the quarters in some filthy mixture, and the heads they bedaub with some black matter, to cause them to seem more loathsome and grizzly.

74. *Life and Death of Mr Edmund Geninges, Priest,* 96. Gregory, *Salvation at Stake,* 298, notes the woman's name was Lucy Ridley.

75. *Life and Death of Mr Edmund Geninges, Priest,* 93.

76. Ibid., 94. Lake and Questier, "Agency, Appropriation and Rhetoric under the Gallows," 101, note: "[I]n early modern England the hands of the hanged were thought to possess curative powers. In the events surrounding Gennings's death, élite religion, a Counter-Reformation sensibility obsessed with martyrs' relics, popular beliefs about the body of the hanged man, and garbled versions of humoral medical theory were all clustered together around the rites of state violence in a fascinating, overlapping pattern of meaning and gesture."

77. See Garnet's 11 March 1601 letter to Claudio Aquaviva, ARSI. Anglia 31, fols. 172–83.

78. Gregory, *Salvation at Stake,* 269, notes that the martyrologist Maurice Chauncy sent to Rome, in addition to the executed Carthusian John Houghton's prison writings, "part of the bloodstained shirt in which [he] had been slain." See Gregory's discussion, 298–300, of the mania for relic collection and the international circulation of relics.

79. John Kenyon, *The Popish Plot* (1972; rpt. London: Phoenix Press, 2000), 250, notes that the severed head of the Franciscan John Wall, who was executed in 1679 at the height of the Popish Plot hysteria, was sent to Douay, where the Poor Clares kept it, returning it to England at the beginning of the French Revolution, from which it was returned again to France in 1815.

80. See Peter Burke, "How to Be a Counter-Reformation Saint," in *The Historical Anthropology of Early Modern Italy* (Cambridge: Cambridge University Press, 1987), 48–62, 243.

81. Francis W. Steer, "St. Philip Howard, Arundel and the Howard Connexion in Sussex," in *Studies in Sussex Church History,* ed. M. J. Kitch (Falmer, East Sussex: Leopard's Head Press and the University of Sussex, 1981), 209–22, and *Archdiocese of Westminster. Cause of the Canonization of Blessed Martyrs John Houghton, Robert Lawrence, Augustine Webster, Richard Reynolds, John Stone, Cuthbert Mayne, John Paine, Edmund Campion, Alexander Briant, Ralph Sherwin, and Luke Kirby Put to Death in England in Defence of the Catholic Faith (1535–1582). Official Presentation of Documents on Martyrdom and Cult,* Sacred Congregation of Rites, Historical Section, 148 (Vatican:

Vatican Polyglot Press, 1968). The latter document refers to "353 Servants of God, martyred between 1535 and 1681" (ix). Cf. Stephen and Elizabeth Usherwood, *We Die for the Old Religion: The Story of the 85 Martyrs of England & Wales Beatified 22 November 1987* (London: Sheed & Ward, 1987).

82. This manuscript (Stonyhurst MS Collectanea P.76–148) was published only in the late nineteenth century: Robert Persons, *Of the Life and Martyrdom of Father Edmund Campian,* ed. Br. H. Foley, *Letters and Notices* (December 1877) (n.p.: Manresa Press, 1877), 1–68, 219–42, 308–39.

83. In his letter to the Privy Council ("Campion's Brag"), Campion wrote: "And touching our Society be it known to you that we have made a league—all the Jesuits of the world, whose succession and multitude must overreach all the practices of England—cheerfully to carry the cross you shall lay upon us and never to despair your recovery, while we have a man left to enjoy your Tyburn, or to be racked with your torments or consumed with your prisons" (text printed in Bernard Basset, *The English Jesuits: From Campion to Martindale* [New York: Herder and Herder, 1968], 456).

84. See John Bossy, "The Heart of Robert Persons," in McCoog, ed., *The Reckoned Expense,* 146–47: "Acquaviva insisted that there was an obligation on Jesuits in England to be careful, which Campion had not been. . . . Persons . . . abandoned the 'Life' for an account of the persecution of Catholics in England, and did not return to it for thirteen years. Then he produced a torso which was a good deal more conventional than what Acquaviva seems to have had in mind, and stopped before Campion's arrest. In practice Persons surely made it his business to din into departing missioners the message that they were being sent to do a job not, if they could help it, to get martyred." Gregory, *Salvation at Stake,* 486n.174, thinks, however, that Bossy "seems to overestimate the extent to which Acquaviva sought to restrain the missionaries' desire for martyrdom."

85. Not only did the king consider himself an international peacemaker, but he expressed also an aversion to the severer forms of punishment for religious dissent. "Our nature bene ever so enclined to clemencie, especially we have ever bene so loath to shed blood in any case that might have any relation to conscience," he remarked in a 1610 royal proclamation (*Stuart Royal Proclamations,* vol. 1: *Royal Proclamations of King James I, 1603–1625,* ed. James F. Larkin, C.S.V., and Paul L. Hughes [Oxford: Clarendon Press, 1973], 246).

86. Michael G. Finlayson, *Historians, Puritanism, and the English Revolution: The Religious Factor in English Politics before and after the Interregnum* (Toronto: University of Toronto Press, 1983), 98, observes: "[B]y 1628 Catholics were clearly living under conditions of much less tension than at any time since the 1570s. No Catholic, priest or layman, had been executed under the provisions of the anti-recusant legislation since 1618." By 1640 "the *de facto* toleration of Catholics constituted a major problem" (ibid., 105) for the king and Parliament.

87. Clancy, *Literary History of the English Jesuits,* 127, points out, however, with reference to the Jesuits: "The period between the outbreak of Civil War and the death of Charles II was a difficult period for the Jesuits. From 1615 through 1640 only one English Jesuit, Edward Arrowsmith, had been executed for religion. In the next forty-four years twelve were put to death and eleven more died in prison. The Jesuits had to endure two grievous times of trial. The first was during the Civil War. The second and more serious was during the Oates plot." Hugh Aveling, *The Handle and the Axe: The Catholic Recusants in England from Reformation to Emancipation* (London: Blond and Briggs, 1976), 215, notes that during the Popish Plot era, 100 missionary priests were arrested, 17 of whom were executed and 23 of whom died in jail or as a result of imprisonment. Of the 90 Jesuits in England, 40 were arrested, 9 were executed, and 19 died in prison.

88. E. E. Reynolds, *John Southworth, Priest and Martyr* (London: Burns & Oates, 1962), 68, notes: "He was attended to the place of execution by two hundred coaches, and great many people on horseback, who all admired his constancy." For the political context of Southworth's prosecution and execution, see Ian Y. Thackray, "Zion Undermined: The Protestant Belief in a Popish Plot during the English Interregnum," *History Workshop: A Journal of Socialist and Feminist Historians* 18 (autumn 1984): 28–42. John Coffey, *Persecution and Toleration in Protestant England, 1558–1689* (Harlow: Longman, 2000), 157, says, "Cromwell protested against the execution, and when Southworth's body had been quartered, he paid a surgeon to sew the pieces together, so that it could be returned to Douai for a Catholic burial."

89. Reynolds, *John Southworth,* 71.

90. Ibid., 72–73.

4. Performing Conversion

1. The first of the missionary priests to be martyred in the Elizabethan period, Cuthbert Mayne, was a convert.

2. This was a stronger loyalty oath than that tendered under the Elizabethan regime because it specifically included a rejection of papal claims of temporal authority. See 3 Jac. I, c.4: "An Act for the better discovering and repressing of Popish recusants, 1606," in *The Stuart Constitution, 1603–1688: Documents and Commentary,* 2d ed., ed. and intro. J. P. Kenyon (Cambridge: Cambridge University Press, 1986), 170–71.

3. For a historically comprehensive study of the phenomenon of conversion in the period from 1580 to 1625, see Michael Questier, *Conversion, Politics and Religion in England, 1580–1625* (Cambridge: Cambridge University Press, 1996). This work deals extensively with the different Protestant and Catholic understandings of conversion and of the change of religion, relating conversion accounts to the larger field

of polemical and devotional discourse. See also Questier's articles, "John Gee, Archbishop Abbot, and the Use of Converts from Rome in Jacobean Anti-Catholicism," *Recusant History* 21.3 (May 1993): 347–60; and "Crypto-Catholicism, Anti-Calvinism and Conversion at the Jacobean Court: The Enigma of Benjamin Carier," *Journal of Ecclesiastical History* 47.1 (January 1996): 45–64. See also the outline of the "Convertite Controversies" in Peter Milward, *Religious Controversies of the Jacobean Age* (Lincoln: University of Nebraska Press, 1978), 165–71; and the discussion of conversion tracts in James Shapiro, *Shakespeare and the Jews* (New York: Columbia University Press, 1996), 139–41.

4. See chapter 4, "Jonson's Duplicity: The Catholic Years," in Ian Donaldson, *Jonson's Magic Houses: Essays in Interpretation* (Oxford: Clarendon Press, 1997), 47–65.

5. David Howarth, *Lord Arundel and His Circle* (New Haven: Yale University Press, 1985), 3.

6. See his and William Tedder's sermons published together as *The Recantations as They Were Severallie Pronounced by Wylliam Tedder and Anthony Tyrrell* (1588). For the account of Tyrrell's final reconciliation to Catholicism, edited by Robert Persons, see "The True and Wonderful Story of the Lamentable Fall of Anthony Tyrrell, Priest, from the Catholic Faith, Written by his own Hand, before which is Prefixed a Preface Showing the Causes of Publishing the Same unto the World," in *The Troubles of Our Catholic Forefathers Related by Themselves,* 2d ser., ed. John Morris (London: Burns and Oates, 1875), 310–510.

7. See Milward, *Religious Controversies,* 170. For a discussion of these and other apostate priests, see Patrick McGrath, "Apostate and Naughty Priests in England under Elizabeth I," in *Opening the Scrolls: Essays in Catholic History in Honour of Godfrey Anstruther,* ed. Dominic Aidan Bellenger (Bath: Downside Abbey, 1987), 50–83. For short biographical accounts of Tyrrell and Tedder, see Godfrey Anstruther, *The Seminary Priests: A Dictionary of the Secular Clergy of England and Wales, 1558–1850,* vol. 1: *I Elizabethan 1558–1603* (Durham: Ushaw College; Ware: St Edmund's College, [1968]), 347–48, 361–63. Robin Clifton, "The Popular Fear of Catholics during the English Revolution," *Past and Present,* no. 52 (August 1971): 37, regards the narratives and sermons of former Catholics as an important subgenre of writing in the period. In addition to Sheldon's work, he cites John Gee's *The Foot out of the Snare* (1624); James Wadsworth Jr.'s *The English Spanish Pilgrim* (1629) (discussed below); H. Yaxlee's *Morbus et Antidotus* (1630); and T. Abernathie's *The Abjuration of Poperie* (Edinburgh, 1638).

8. Questier, *Conversion,* 47, notes: "Archbishop Bancroft made use of various renegades including Bell, Ralph Ithell, John Scudamore and Christopher Perkins. . . . [They] were also used as persuaders. Thomas Clarke preached in London while Thomas Bell was sent back to the North to proselytise there, and he took part in disputations against the Jesuit Henry Walpole in York" (159).

9. M. C. Questier, "Loyalty, Religion and State Power in Early Modern England: English Romanism and the Jacobean Oath of Allegiance," *Historical Journal* 40.2 (1997): 311–29, argues that this oath was cunningly framed to create widespread divisions in the Catholic lay and clerical communities and, thus, seriously to weaken English Catholicism.

10. John P. Feil, "Sir Tobie Matthew and His Collection of Letters" (Ph.D. diss., University of Chicago, 1962), 43–44. This is the best account of Matthew's life and works.

11. *The Sermons of John Donne,* 10 vols., ed. George R. Potter and Evelyn Simpson (Berkeley: University of California Press, 1953–62), 10: 161. In the same passage, however, Donne also cites the example of a mercenary convert who became a Catholic to receive an ecclesiastical pension.

12. The translator of this latter work from Latin to English was Edward Coffin, S.J. For a discussion of de Dominis, see Thomas Middleton, *A Game at Chesse,* ed. R. C. Bald (Cambridge: Cambridge University Press, 1929), 7–10. I cite the text in Thomas Middleton, *A Game at Chess,* ed. T. H. Howard-Hill (Manchester: Manchester University Press, 1993), 122. For a sympathetic account of de Dominis and his sharing with King James a vision of a reunited Christianity, see W. B. Patterson, *King James VI and I and the Reunion of Christendom* (Cambridge: Cambridge University Press, 1997), 220–59.

13. Note in A. H. Mathew, ed., *The True Historical Relation of the Conversion of Sir Tobie Matthew* (London: Burns and Oates, 1904), xvi.

14. *The Romish Priest Turn'd Protestant: With the Reasons of his Conversion. Wherein The True Church is Exposed to the View of Christians, and Derived out of the Holy Scriptures, Sound Reason, and the Ancient Fathers, Humbly presented to both Houses of Parliament. By James Salgado, a Spaniard, formerly a Priest of the Order of the Dominicans* (1679).

15. Ibid., 31, 28.

16. In *The Riverside Shakespeare,* 2d ed., ed. G. Blackmore Evans et al. (Boston: Houghton Mifflin, 1997).

17. See *The Coppy of a Letter Sent from France by Mr. Walter Montagu to his Father the Lord Privie Seale, with his answere thereunto. Also a second answere to the same Letter by the Lord Faulkland* (1641). Two refutations of the arguments set forth by Montagu follow the text of his notorious letter. See also Feil, "Sir Tobie Matthew," 236–67.

18. On Caroline court conversions, see Gordon Albion, *Charles I and the Court of Rome: A Study in Seventeenth-Century Diplomacy* (London: Burns, Oates and Washbourne, 1935), chap. 8. See also Caroline Hibbard, *Charles I and the Popish Plot* (Chapel Hill: University of North Carolina Press, 1983), 38–71.

19. Ibid., 236.

20. Patricia Crawford, *Women and Religion in England, 1500–1720* (London: Routledge, 1993), 84.

21. Thomas H. Clancy, S.J., *A Literary History of the English Jesuits: A Century of Books, 1615–1714* (San Francisco: Catholic Scholars Press, 1996), 53, 75n.10.

22. Ibid., 71.

23. Questier, *Conversion,* observes: "Conversion is as much a declaration of freedom from institutions as a pledge of allegiance to them" (75).

24. Technically, after the 1598 Edict of Nantes France tolerated Protestantism, but religious persecution of Protestants did not cease.

25. Dorothy Shirley was the daughter of the earl of Essex and Frances Walsingham (Sir Philip Sidney's widow). Anthony Milton, *Catholic and Reformed: The Roman and Protestant Churches in English Protestant Thought, 1600–1640* (Cambridge: Cambridge University Press, 1995), 85, notes that Cary's conversion to Rome was an embarrassment to Laudians. Ann Hyde, the first wife of James II, was denounced by her father, the earl of Clarendon, for her conversion.

26. Dana F. Sutton, ed., *Unpublished Works by William Alabaster (1568–1640)* (Salzburg: University of Salzburg, 1977), xix, suggests this person was Hugh Holland, "a lifelong friend who had been with him both at Westminster and at Trinity [College, Cambridge]." I cite Sutton's edition of Alabaster's conversion narrative (99–178) by page number in the text.

27. See *The Elisaeis of William Alabaster,* ed. and trans. Michael O'Connell, *Studies in Philology,* Texts and Studies, 76.5 (1979); and Michael O'Connell, "William Alabaster," in *Dictionary of Literary Biography,* vol. 132, ed. David A. Richardson (Detroit, Mich.: Gale Research, 1993), 3–12. See also the short autobiographical account Alabaster wrote on his entry to the English College in Rome, in *Records of the English Province of the Society of Jesus,* ed. Henry Foley, vol. 1 (London: Burns and Oates, 1877), 66–69.

28. James P. Crowley, "'He took his religion by trust': The Matter of Ben Jonson's Conversion," *Renaissance and Reformation* 23.1 (1998): 58, points out that Wright, who also converted Ben Jonson, was notable as a Catholic clergyman who resisted the hard-line politics of Cardinal Allen and Robert Persons, S.J., and tried to "find a middle way between London and Rome in the battle for tolerance." Alabaster apparently encountered Wright before he was imprisoned but while he was under house arrest with the dean of Westminster, after he "surrendered himself publicly to Essex's secretary, Anthony Bacon, in what was a first attempt at gaining tolerance—if not support—of loyalist Catholics in the English legal system" (59). See Wright's letter to Robert Cecil, 20 January 1598, in which he writes: "The conversion of Mr Alabaster I doubt not shalbe able in justice to prevale against me, being urged by the Dean of Westminster to dispute with him in particular" (Public Record Office, State Papers, Domestic, Elizabeth [PRO SPDE] 12/266/23). On Wright's loyalism and his connection with

the earl of Essex's possible cryptopopery, see Alison Shell, *Catholicism, Controversy and the English Literary Imagination, 1558–1660* (Cambridge: Cambridge University Press, 1999), 127–33.

29. See the discussion of Alabaster in Shell, *Catholicism, Controversy and the English Literary Imagination,* 88–92. Shell highlights the influence on Alabaster of Robert Southwell.

30. William Rainolds, *A Refutation of Sundry Reprehensions, Cavils, and False Sleights, by which M. Whitaker Laboureth to Deface the Late English Translation, and Catholike Annotations of the New Testament* (Paris, 1583). J. C. H Aveling, *The Handle and the Axe: The Catholic Recusants in England from the Reformation to Emancipation* (London: Bland and Briggs, 1976), 230, points out that John Dryden's conversion to Catholicism was related to his reading of the biblical criticism of Richard Simon, a French Oratorian priest.

31. *The Confessions of St. Augustine,* trans. E. B. Pusey (New York: Dutton; London: Dent, 1951), 177.

32. Ibid., 187–88.

33. See Southwell's letter to his cousin printed before the 1595 edition of *Saint Peter's Complaynt* defending religious poetry and criticizing contemporary amorous verse (in James H. McDonald and Nancy Pollard Brown, eds., *The Poems of Robert Southwell, S.J.* [Oxford: Clarendon Press, 1967], 1).

34. *The Complete Works of Thomas Lodge,* vol. 3 (New York: Russell & Russell, 1963), 13. Shell, *Catholicism, Controversy and the English Literary Imagination,* 77, remarks: "Lodge supplies a case-study of one whose public conversion to Catholicism resulted in a complete change of subject-matter"; his "conversion seems to have been secret and prolonged; but on a public level, it culminated in 1596 with his publication of the religious meditation *Prosopopeia,* and a renunciation of his previous writing."

35. See, for example, the series of seventeen religious sonnets Constable composed after his conversion in 1589 (preserved in BL MS Harleian 7553), printed in *The Poems of Henry Constable,* ed. Joan Grundy (Liverpool: Liverpool University Press, 1960), 183–92. See Grundy's account of Constable's life and conversion, 15–50, and the account given in George Wickes, "Henry Constable, Poet and Courtier (1562–1613)," *Biographical Studies 1534–1829* 2.4 (1954): 272–300. See the discussion of Constable's poetry in Shell, *Catholicism, Controversy and the English Literary Imagination,* 107–8, 122–26.

36. *The Sonnets of William Alabaster,* ed. G. M. Story and Helen Gardner (Oxford: Oxford University Press, 1959), 3 (Sonnet 5, l. 10). Subsequent citations, by sonnet and line number, are given in the text.

37. O'Connell, "William Alabaster," 9, sees in Alabaster's poetry "a blending of Counter-Reformation traditions of affective meditation with a stamp of Protestant

inwardness," and he argues that "Alabaster is clearly aware of a difference in style in the devotion of contemporary Catholics and Protestants."

38. See Story and Gardner, *Sonnets of William Alabaster,* xiii.

39. See Shell, *Catholicism, Controversy and the English Literary Imagination,* 88–94, on the relationship of the contemporary literature of tears to Alabaster's poetry and prose.

40. On the importance of required "conferences" for high-profile Catholic converts, see Questier, *Conversion,* 151.

41. See James V. Holleran, *A Jesuit Challenge: Edmund Campion's Debates at the Tower of London in 1581* (New York: Fordham University Press, 1999), for the Catholic accounts. For the Protestant versions, see John Field's *A True Report of the Disputation or Rather Private Conference Had in the Tower of London, with Ed. Campion Jesuite, the Last of August, 1581* (1583) and *The Three Last Dayes Conferences Had in the Tower with Edmund Campion Jesuite, the 18: 23: and 27. Of September, 1581* (1583).

42. This work was answered in print by John Racster, *William Alablasters Seven Motuies* [sic] *Removed* (1598), and Roger Fenton, *An Answere to W. Alabaster his Motives* (1599).

43. Alabaster is contemptuous of Ithell for "play[ing] the Apostata" (136).

44. See John Gerard's account of Alabaster's staying with him (from *The Autobiography of a Hunted Priest, by John Gerard,* trans. Philip Caraman [New York: Pellegrini & Cudahy, 1952], 140):

> I gave shelter here to a gentleman who had been the Earl of Essex's chaplain in the expedition against Spain which captured Cadiz.
>
> He was a learned man and spoke several languages. In order to become a Catholic he had declined many offers of high preferment in his Church. Already he had had a taste of prison, and when he was offered the chance of escaping, I told him he could stay at my house.
>
> I looked after him there for two or three months. During this time I gave him the Spiritual Exercises, and he made up his mind to enter the Society. He was a man who had been nurtured, so to speak, in Calvin's bosom. He had spent his life in the army, and he was used to having his own way over other people.

45. Robert Caro observes the convergence of meditation and rhetoric in Alabaster and Wright: writing of the poetry, Caro claims that "Alabaster's concern, like Wright's in his lengthy meditative discourse, is to find accord between mind and will on the one hand, and his affections on the other, as he prayerfully strives for a heartfelt union of all his powers in the love of God" ("William Alabaster: Rhetor, Meditator, Devotional Poet—II," *Recusant History* 19.2 [1988]: 165).

46. In *A Search Made into Matters of Religion* (1609), Francis Walsingham reports that during his third meeting with the archbishop of Canterbury, the archbishop was very angry (having been questioned by King James on how he had handled Walsingham's case) and threatened him: "[M]y L. proceeded in his wrathfull speaches, and after many fierce & angry words, he added: I will even send thee to Bridewell: thou art worthy to be set on the Pillory, and to have thine eares cut of for a libelling knave as thou art. . . . I will handle thee as thou art, before I have done with thee" (46).

47. See the account of Alabaster's return to England, his imprisonments, his travel to the Continent, his conflict with Persons, and his return to the English church in Story and Gardner, *Sonnets of William Alabaster,* xvii–xx.

48. O'Connell, "William Alabaster," 10.

49. Ibid., 10–11. Cf. Questier, *Conversion,* 189. Questier also notes that "Alabaster's long-running doctrinal conflicts with both Churches generally failed to coincide with his professions of institutional allegiance to one side or the other" (55).

50. O'Connell, "William Alabaster," 11, lists *De Bestia Apocalyptica* (1621), *Ecce Sponsus Venit* (1633), *Spiraculum Tubarum Sive Fons Spiritualium Expositionum ex Aequivocis Pentaglotti Significationibus* (1633), and *Schindleri Lexicon Pentaglotton, in Epitomen Redactum a G.A.* (1635) ("an abridgement of a Hebrew lexicon").

51. Walsingham explains his background: he was raised "by the care of the Right Honorable, [his] very good Patron *Syr Francis Walsingham,* Counsellour & Secretary to the late Queene, under the Fatherlike tuition and sicret government of *M. Humfrey Walsingham,* [his] neere Kinsman" (*A Search made into matters of Religion* [1609], **2r–v). In a letter accompanying a gift of his book to Humphrey Walsingham (Sir Francis Walsingham's nephew), the convert expresses his indebtedness to his kinsman and to the deceased Sir Francis, at the same time that he hopes he and other relatives may be persuaded to become Catholic (in Stonyhurst MS Anglia vii, cited in Henry Foley, ed., *Records of the English Province of the Society of Jesus,* vol. 2 [2d, 3d, and 4th ser.] [n.p.: Manresa Press, 1875], 379–80). Although the convert's mother was Catholic, as were some of his siblings, his familial and educational background was strongly Protestant. Subsequent citations from *A Search* are noted in the text by page number.

52. Preface to *Pseudo-Martyr,* ed. Anthony Raspa (Montreal: McGill-Queen's University Press, 1993), 13.

53. Similarly, in *A Lost Sheep Returned Home: Or, The Motives of the Conversion to the Catholic Faith, of Thomas Vane, Doctor of Divinity, and lately Chaplain to His Majesty the King of England, &c.* (1648), the conversion is only the pretext for a general polemical argument for the claim that the Roman Catholic Church is the only true Christian church.

54. He refers to Perkins's *The Reformed Catholicke* and "Minister Willet his booke; intituled *A Retection &c.*" (476) and John Foxe's *Actes and Monuments* as all playing that trick.

55. Questier, *Conversion,* 85, claims that Walsingham's spiritual counselor here is a Jesuit.

56. Whereas Augustine, in Books 7 and 8 of the *Confessions,* dramatizes the transformative power of reading Scripture, particularly the writings of St. Paul, Walsingham and some other Catholic converts concentrate on the extratextual as well as extrarational character of the experience of grace and the turning of the will towards God.

57. Questier, *Conversion,* 59.

58. Trans. Henry Beveridge (Grand Rapids, Mich.: Eerdmans, 1989), 253–56.

59. Questier, "Crypto-Catholicism, Anti-Calvinism and Conversion," 61, points to the importance of Ignatian spiritual exercises to Benjamin Carier's conversion. He argues that the Jesuits "presented him with a model for evangelical conversion" and that he yearned for and accepted "the evangelical counsels of perfection [poverty, chastity, and obedience] as represented to him by the Society of Jesus" (62).

60. For a discussion of these debates in their larger polemical context, see Timothy H. Wadkins, "The Percy-'Fisher' Controversies and the Ecclesiastical Politics of Jacobean Anti-Catholicism, 1622–1625," *Church History* 57 (1988): 153–69; Milward, *Religious Controversies,* 216–27; and Clancy, *Literary History of the English Jesuits,* 56–60. A Caroline work, *The Converted Jew or Certain Dialogues between Michaeas a Learned Jew, and others, Touching Diverse Points of Religion Controverted betweene Catholicks and Protestants. Written by M. John Clare a Catholic Priest of the Society of Jesus* (1630), presents, in a "Poetical fiction of Dialogues" (a3v) (the first, for example, with Cardinal Bellarmine, Michaeas "a learned Jewish Rabine," and "Doctour Whitakers of Cambridge" [a1v]), the theological differences of Protestantism and Catholicism in order to position Caroline Catholics alongside conservative Protestants as loyal subjects and radical Protestants as theologically and politically dangerous.

61. Feil, "Sir Tobie Matthew," 148, says that "by 1619 . . . he was undoubtedly bound to the Jesuits." An anti-Catholic pamphlet of 1641, *The Confession of John Browne a Jesuite in the Gate-house,* alludes to a supposed papal breve addressed to *Tobiae Mathew Sacerdoti, Societatis Jesu* (A4), indicating that some contemporaries saw Matthew as a Jesuit.

62. For a discussion of Matthew's relation with Donne, see Robert Parker Sorlien, "Apostacy Reversed: Donne and Tobie Matthew," *John Donne Journal* 13 (1994): 101–12.

63. William Crashaw, Richard's father, was an aggressively Protestant controversialist who was particularly outraged by the Jesuits and by the feminine aspects of Catholic practice, especially devotion to the Blessed Virgin. See, especially, *The Jesuites*

Gospel (1610)—answered by the Jesuit John Floyd's *Overthrow of the protestants pulpit babels* (1612). Henry Constable's conversion supposedly "killed his father from sorrow, and lost both his reputation and the advancement which the Lord Treasurer would have procured him" (John Bossy, "A Propos of Henry Constable," *Recusant History* 6 [1962]: 231). In his conversion account (cum political treatise), Benjamin Carier remarks: "You shall scarce heare of a Puritane father, but his sonne proves either a Catholike or an Atheist" (*A Treatise Written by Mr. Doctour Carier* [Brussels, 1614], 30).

64. BL MS Harl. 6987/108, cited in Feil, "Sir Tobie Matthew," 186.

65. Feil, "Sir Tobie Matthew," 192, observes: "behind a façade of foppishness and foolery which put people off their guard, a shrewd and tenacious mind, tempered by vanity, was at work for the Catholic cause as it was understood by the Society of Jesus."

66. Ibid., 27, 76, 79, 148.

67. On the topic of Matthew's homoerotic bond with his longtime companion, George Gage, with whom he lived for many years and named as his heir, see Feil, "Sir Tobie Matthew," 74. Feil also describes how Matthew used the homoerotic inclinations of William Cecil, Lord Roos (a great nephew of Lord Burghley) to try to convert him to Catholicism. They traveled together in a group of young Englishmen, with Matthew, as the (older) leader, taking steps to provide Roos with "attractive Catholic servants" (70), finally with one young Spaniard (Diego) who came between Roos and the woman he married (118). In May 1611 Roos acted out his religious alienation by urinating as he approached the Protestant town of Sluys. Shortly after, he "'displayed his privy member' five or six times before mixed groups, and then, exhilarated by the reaction he was provoking, displayed himself again while waiting for a ferry to carry the party to the local church. To cap the performance, he laid his member on Matthew's shoulder" (72). Feil cites BL MS Harl. 7002/199–200.

68. Feil, "Sir Tobie Matthew," 243.

69. Clancy, *A Literary History of the English Jesuits,* 127, points out that the high point of Jesuit numbers working in England was 193 in 1640, as it was for the total number of missionary priests, 750. What followed, during the Civil Wars and Interregnum, was a considerable drop in these figures.

70. For a discussion of "priest-virtuosi," see Edward Chaney, *The Grand Tour and the Great Rebellion: Richard Lassels and the "Voyage of Italy" in the Seventeenth Century* (Geneva: Slatkine, 1985); cited in Shell, *Catholicism, Controversy and the English Literary Imagination,* 179n.7.

71. Feil, "Sir Tobie Matthew," 19, explains Matthew went to Naples out of religious curiosity after hearing the report of the annual liquefaction of St. Januarius's blood.

72. This Catholic translation of Augustine was attacked by Protestants. See, for example, William Crompton's *Saint Austin's Religion* (1625) and Matthew Sutcliffe's *The Unmasking of the Masse-Monger* (1626).

73. *The Life of Lady Lucy Knatchbull,* ed. Dom David Knowles (London: Sheed and Ward, 1931).

74. For the identification of this work as Matthew's, see A. F. Allison, "Sir Toby Matthew the Author of *Charity Mistaken," Recusant History* 5.3 (October 1959): 128–30. This book, which argues that Protestants are outside the church and cannot be saved, was the one that William Chillingworth answered in his landmark work, *The Religion of Protestants* (1638). Chillingworth himself had converted to Catholicism and then returned to the (Laudian) English church.

75. Feil, "Sir Tobie Matthew," 137–38, also lists as books Matthew prepared for the press during his second exile (1619–22) *The Widdowes Mite* (St. Omer, 1619) and *Of the Love of our Only Lord and Saviour* (1622) and, in addition to the translation of Augustine's *Confessions,* translations of Vincenzo Puccini's *The Life of the Holy and Venerable Mother Suor Maria Maddalena de Patsi* (St. Omer, 1619), Juan de Avila's *The Audio Filia, or a Rich Cabinet full of Spirituall Jewells* (St. Omer, 1620), and Guiseppe Biondo's *A Relation of the Death, of the most Illustrious Lord, Signor Troilo Savelli, a Baron of Rome* (St. Omer, 1620).

76. See Feil, "Sir Tobie Matthew," 231–32, and the discussions of the Toby Matthew poems from Huntington Library MS HM 198 in Anthony G. Petti, "Unknown Sonnets by Sir Toby Matthew," *Recusant History* 9.2 (1967): 123–58. The sonnets in this collection by Matthew open with a dedicatory poem addressed to his "soveraigne friend" (fol. 88), probably George Gage.

77. Questier, *Conversion,* 80, notes he was a former pupil of William Perkins at Emmanuel College, Cambridge, and was a friend of William Bedell and Joseph Hall. See also John Walter Stoye, *English Travellers Abroad, 1604–1667: Their Influence in English Society and Politics* (London: Jonathan Cape, 1952), 338–39.

78. St. Omer, 1615. A facsimile edition of this appears in volume 150 of *English Recusant Literature,* ed. D. M. Rogers (Menston, Yorkshire: Scolar Press, 1973). Signature and page numbers are cited in the text.

79. Questier underplays the implicit polemical content of this text, saying it "excludes almost all references to confessional division" (*Conversion,* 80).

80. See, for example, pp. 39–40, for his emphasis on the importance of Marian devotion.

81. On the importance of this subgenre, see Nancy Armstrong and Leonard Tennenhouse, *The Imaginary Puritan: Literature, Intellectual Labor, and the Origins of Personal Life* (Berkeley: University of California Press, 1992), 199–216 passim.

82. In general terms many Protestant, especially Puritan, conversion narratives psychologically portray the individual's coming to grace as a deliverance from the captivity of sin. See Patricia Caldwell, *The Puritan Conversion Narrative: The Beginnings of American Expression* (Cambridge: Cambridge University Press, 1983), 8 passim. Because

I am concerned with the phenomenon of change of religion, I do not discuss this other notion of conversion.

83. For a modern annotated edition of this work that places it in its religio-political context, see *John Gee's Foot out of the Snare (1624)*, ed. Theodorus Hendrikus Bernardus Maria Harmsen (Nijmegen: Cicero Press, 1992).

84. See Juan de Nicholas y Sacharles, *The Reformed Spanyard* (1621), which retails a story of the Spanish convert who dramatizes an attack in London, after his defection, by a papist who leaves him for dead (E1r–E2r).

85. In this other work he describes at length Philip II's monastery-palace, the Escorial, recounts the persecution of Englishmen who fell into the hands of the Spanish Inquisition, and criticizes the Order of the Immaculate Conception of Our Lady as a military order designed to undertake political subversion.

86. *DNB*, 20: 425–26. See also Martin J. Havran, *The Catholics in Caroline England* (Stanford, Calif.: Stanford University Press, 1962), 125–26, for an account of Wadsworth's sorry career after he came to England.

87. Foley, *Records of the English Province of the Society of Jesus*, 1: 551: "I have known this gentleman beyond the seas at St. Omer's, a student, and after that in Spaine, amongst the Jesuits, where the custome is that all students take an oath to receive Orders in so many months. And in Madrid I was present when he was brought by the archest Jesuit of them all, Sir Toby Matthews, to pronounce an oration in the name of all the Jesuits, before his Majesty, then Prynce of Wales. He spoke somewhat in the beginning of the month of May; then he shewed how gratefull the Prynce's arrival was unto them, and that all hoped he would not degenerate from the religion and worth of his ancestors. And last of all he went to kisse the Prynce's hand, but the Prynce refused to give him his hand, thinking it was a disgrace to let any Jesuite touch his hand."

88. Donne, *Sermons*, 10: 145.

89. *Texeda Retextus: or the Spanish Monke His Bill of Divorce against the Church of Rome* (1623), 32.

90. See the discussion of the trope by Diana Treviño Benet, "The Escape from Rome: Milton's *Second Defense* and a Renaissance Genre," in *Milton in Italy: Contexts, Images, Contradictions*, ed. Mario A. Di Cesare (Binghamton, N.Y.: Medieval & Renaissance Texts and Studies, 1991), 29–49. However, a Catholic convert such as Humphrey Leech could also use the escape-from-Babylon trope. See Questier, *Conversion*, 81.

91. Sig. B1ᵛ. Musgrave was a Carthusian monk before he became a Protestant.

92. Sig. D2.

93. *The Recantations*, 11.

94. *The Foot out of the Snare (1624)*, Aa1.

95. *A Triumph of Truth* (1609), 108. For a discussion of Leech's path to Catholicism by way of anti-Calvinism, see Nicholas Tyacke, *Anti-Calvinists: The Rise of English*

Arminianism, c. 1590–1640 (Oxford: Clarendon Press, 1987), 62–64. See also Questier, *Conversion,* 53–54, 89–93.

96. *A Treatise Written by Mr. Doctour Carier,* 19, 44. Carier addresses King James: "[I] doe know that your Majestie by your birth, hath so great an Interest in the Saincts of heaven, as you shal never cease to have untill you cease to be the sonne of such a mother, as wold rejoice more then all the Rest for your conversion. And therefore I assure my self that she with all the rest doe pray that your Majestie before you die may be militant in the communion of that church wherin they are triumphant" (20). Carier's *Treatise,* however, is less an account of his conversion than an argument for King James to turn away from radical Protestants towards the Catholic church in order to pursue his goal of Christian unity and peace.

97. Compare this with Francis Walsingham's discussion of the unflattering motives of apostates from Catholicism:

> I have heard some of that Religion to make sundry observations of such as have fallen from them, which they tearme Apostates, who fell, as they say, from them principally upon these motyves of good fellowship, good cheare, loose life and women: and they give for examples, *Bell, Shaw, Tyrrell, Atkinson, Tydder, Mayre, Sacheverall, Bayly, Ithell, Skidmore, Rouse,* and such like, who yet (say they) notwithstanding never lightly changed their judgements in Religion, but only their affections for injoying their appetites for some tyme: but yet afterward, that being satisfied, they had many motions to returne, if they might do it with their safety, as they say hath bene made manifest but such as have in deed returned, as namely *Shaw,* and *Tyrrell,* who after many yeares lyving with wyves, left them, and went over the sea to do penance, which they performed with great austerity against themselves for their former loosenesse, the one dying in *Naples,* the other in *Flanders,* and confessing publikely, that whilst they preached most earnestly in defence of Protestant Religion, they never believed it to be true, but only desire therby to injoy their sensualityes. And the like they protested to know of sundry of their fellowes before mentioned, though they have not yet receyved (say they) so great grace, as the other did, to breake from all at once, and to put their better desyres in execution. (*A Search,* 358–59)

For a contemporary work on apostasy, see John Floyd's *Synopsis Apostosiae,* translated into English by Henry Hawkins as *A Survey of Apostacy* (1617).

98. See Feil, "Sir Tobie Matthew," 216. Feil cites the *Earl of Strafford's Letters and Dispatches,* ed. W. Knowles (London, 1739), 1: 390; and *Historical Manuscripts Commission* 12 R App. IX, p. 127, "Notebook and Journal of Sir Richard Hutton."

99. For the report of Elizabeth I's alleged deathbed reconciliation to Catholicism, see Shell, *Catholicism, Controversy and the English Literary Imagination,* 141, 268n.1.

nothon of a deathbed conversion

For a discussion of the rumor of the deathbed conversions of Bishop John King and other prominent political figures, see Alan Davidson, "The Conversion of Bishop King: A Question of Evidence," *Recusant History* 9.5 (April 1968): 242–54. Henry King delivered a Paul's Cross sermon on 25 November 1621 to deny the rumor of his father's deathbed conversion (*A Sermon Preached at Pauls Crosse . . . Whereunto is annexed the Examination . . . of Thomas Preston* [1621], cited in Millar MacLure, *The Paul's Cross Sermons, 1534–1642* [Toronto: University of Toronto Press, 1958], 243). Late in life when he was ill, Bishop Godfrey Goodman was converted to Catholicism by the Franciscan Christopher Davenport, a former chaplain of Henrietta Maria (see the article on Goodman in the online *Catholic Encyclopedia* www.newadvent.org/cathen/06646a.htm). Perhaps the most famous deathbed conversion was that of Charles II, who had promised in the secret Treaty of Dover (1670) to become a Catholic and reestablish Catholicism in England. John Miller, *Popery and Politics in England, 1660–1688* (Cambridge: Cambridge University Press, 1973), 22, notes that this was handled by "John Huddlestone, the Benedictine who had helped save the king's life after the battle of Worcester." See the polemically charged papers allegedly found in Charles's writing desk after his death that acknowledge the truth of the Roman Catholic religion, in John Warner, S.J., *The History of English Persecution of Catholics and the Presbyterian Plot,* ed. T. A. Birrell, trans. John Bligh, S.J., 2 vols. (London: Catholic Record Society, 1953), 2: 512–14. Miller, *Popery and Politics,* 208, points out that James II, who wanted to exploit every opportunity to convert English Protestants to Catholicism, "published two documents found among Charles's papers which purported to give the late king's reasons for his conversion" (Miller cites *State Tracts,* 2 vols. [1689–92], 2: 273–74).

5. Plots, Atrocities, and Deliverances: The Anti-Catholic Construction of Protestant English History

1. English Protestants, especially the radical reformers, expressed feelings of solidarity with European Protestant states, territories, and communities (especially during the Dutch revolt against the Spanish in the late sixteenth century and during the Thirty Years' War), but the English national interests usually trumped religious sympathies, especially during the reign of King James I. For a discussion of British xenophobia in relation to religious identity, see David Loades, "The Origins of English Protestant Nationalism,"in *Religion and National Identity,* ed. Stuart Mews (Oxford: Basil Blackwell for the Ecclesiastical History Society, 1982), 297–307.

2. Alexandra Walsham, *Providence in Early Modern England* (Oxford: Oxford University Press, 1999), examines the ways "providentialism played a pivotal role in forging a collective Protestant consciousness, a sense of confessional identity which fused anti-Catholicism and patriotic feeling and which united the elite with their social

inferiors" (5). Although both Catholics and Protestants used a language of providentialism, she claims that "Protestant polemicists . . . made the repeated interventions of the Almighty in English history the centrepiece of an enduring and chauvinistic national myth" (225). For a discussion of a series of nationalistic (anti-Catholic) popular celebrations, see David Cressy, *Bonfires and Bells: National Memory and the Protestant Calendar in Elizabethan and Stuart England* (London: Weidenfeld and Nicolson, 1989).

3. See Cressy, *Bonfires and Bells,* 110–29, for a discussion of its commemoration.

4. Jonathan Scott, *England's Troubles: Seventeenth-Century English Political Instability in European Context* (Cambridge: Cambridge University Press, 2000), 29–30, has recently reminded us that English Protestant fears of Catholicism were set in a pan-European context:

> What one notices first about the seventeenth-century English fear of popery are its range and power: it spanned the century; it crossed all social boundaries; as a solvent of political loyalties it had no rivals. What one should notice next is that it is inexplicable in a purely national context. Within England in the seventeenth century catholics made up a tiny and declining proportion of the population: Protestantism was secure, and was becoming more so. It was in Europe that the opposite was the case. Between 1590 and 1690 the geographical reach of Protestantism shrank from one-half to one-fifth of the land area of the continent. The seventeenth century in Europe was the century of the victories of the counter-reformation, spearheaded by Spain in the first half of the century and France in the second. It was the century in which Protestantism had to fight for its survival. This was the context of the fear of popery in England, which found itself thrust into the front line against the European counter-reformation advance.

While the fear of domestic Catholic subversion was overblown, the threat of foreign Catholic assaults was real.

5. For recent discussions of the Gunpowder Plot, see Mark Nicholls, *Investigating Gunpowder Plot* (Manchester: Manchester University Press, 1991); and Antonia Fraser, *Faith and Treason: The Story of the Gunpowder Plot* (New York: Doubleday, 1996). See Fraser, 254–60, for a discussion of Garnet's trial.

6. *A true and perfect relation of the whole proceedings against the late most barbarous traitors, Garnet a Iesuite, and his confederats: contayning sundry speeches deliuered by the Lords Commissioners at their arraignments, for the better satisfaction of those that were hearers, as occasion was offered; the Earle of Northamptons speech hauing bene enlarged vpon those grounds which are set downe. And lastly all that passed at Garnets execution* (1606). This work was printed by Robert Barker, the king's printer. A second edition came out the same year.

7. John Chamberlain refers to the hidden audience at Garnet's arraignment: "The King was there privately and held yt out all day, besides many courtiers and Ladies, as the Lady Arbella, the Ladies of Suffolke, Walsingham, Sir James Hayes Lady *cum multis aliis*" (*The Letters of John Chamberlain,* ed. Norman Egbert McClure [1939; rpt. Westport, Conn.: Greenwood Press, 1979], 1: 220).

8. Linda Levy Peck, *Northampton: Patronage and Policy at the Court of James I* (London: George Allen & Unwin, 1982), 111–12.

9. Lori Anne Ferrell, *Government by Polemic: James I, the King's Preachers, and the Rhetorics of Conformity, 1603–1625* (Stanford, Calif.: Stanford University Press, 1998), 92, refers to "the almost paranoiac concern by many in James's government, especially the Earl of Salisbury, about the possibility that papists would prevaricate under examination. . . . While the doctrine of equivocation had a real existence . . . it had an exaggerated cultural presence as the foundation of a Protestant monitory myth."

10. Coke reiterates the English government's retroactive association of Pius V's 1570 bull, *Regnans in Excelsis,* with the 1569 Northern Rebellion (P2^{r-v}), which set the pattern of papal authorization of Catholic subversion, rebellion, assassination attempts, and treason.

11. Nicholls, *Investigating Gunpowder Plot,* 73, notes that Garnet admitted in posttrial interrogation that the Tesimond conference was not a real confession.

12. Supposedly King James, who was in hiding listening to Garnet's trial, found the frequent interruptions of Garnet unfair. See Philip Caraman, *Henry Garnet, 1555–1606, and the Gunpowder Plot* (New York: Farrar, Straus, 1964), 418.

13. For a fuller account of Garnet's speeches of self-defense, see the rival narrative of the Gunpowder Plot by John Gerard: *The Condition of Catholics under James I: Father Gerard's Narrative of the Gunpowder Plot,* 2d ed., ed. John Morris (London: Longmans, Green, 1872), 243–62. For another Catholic account of the plot, see that of Oswald Tesimond: *The Gunpowder Plot: The Narrative of Oswald Tesimond alias Greenway,* ed. and trans. Francis Edwards, S.J. (London: Folio Society, 1973).

14. See Nicholls, *Investigating Gunpowder Plot,* 67–68, on Sir Edmund Baynham's mission to Rome.

15. See, for example, his not very original play on the metaphor of the "two Bulls" about the succession issued by the pope at the end of Elizabeth's reign (Z4^{v}–Aa1).

16. Peck, *Northhampton,* 113, calls Cotton "the seventeenth-century version of a technocrat; his role [was] to organise royal commissions, to compile data — in this case historical precedents — for use in backing government decisions."

17. Ibid., 112.

18. For a discussion of the harsh antirecusancy legislation (3 Jac. I, cap. iv) passed by Parliament in the wake of the plot, see Wallace Notestein, *The House of Commons, 1604–1610,* (New Haven: Yale University Press, 1971), 141–61.

19. Garry Wills, *Witches and Jesuits: Shakespeare's* Macbeth (New York: Oxford University Press, 1995), 174n.48. On Milton's response to Gunpowder Plot commemoration, see Stella P. Revard, "Milton's Gunpowder Poems and Satan's Conspiracy," *Milton Studies* 4 (1972): 63–77.

20. On commemorative sermons associated with this event, see Thomas S. Nowak, "'Remember, remember, the fifth of November': Anglocentrism and anti-Catholicism in the English Gunpowder Sermons, 1605–1651" (Ph.D. diss., State University of New York at Stony Brook, 1992), and "Propaganda and Pulpit: Robert Cecil, William Barlow and the Essex and Gunpowder Plots," in *The Witness of Times: Manifestations of Ideology in Seventeenth-Century England,* ed. Katherine Z. Keller and Gerald J. Schiffhorst (Pittsburgh, Pa.: Duquesne University Press, 1993), 34–52, 264–67. Bishop Launcelot Andrewes preached ten anniversary sermons on the plot. In the immediate aftermath of the plot, however, as Ferrell, *Government by Polemic,* 75–89, argues, James wished to avoid wholesale anti-Catholic propaganda and to use the occasion of the anniversary sermon for attacks on what he perceived as the more dangerous political threat, Puritanism.

21. David Cressy, "The Fifth of November Remembered," in *Myths of the English,* ed. Roy Porter (Cambridge: Cambridge University Press, 1992), 68. Cressy notes: "Some features of Gunpowder commemoration were neglected or suppressed in the revolutionary 1650s. There was awkwardness and uncertainty as to whether the republican regime should commemorate a Stuart dynastic deliverance" (74). With the Restoration, "[f]ormal observance of the Gunpowder Plot was fully reinstated.... But in Charles II's reign the anniversary took on alternative and oppositional meanings" (75). There were attempts to scale back the celebrations during the brief reign of the Catholic James II, but "after 1688[,] the anniversary of the landing of William of Orange—significantly but fortuitously on 5 November—focused attention on the double deliverance of liberty and religion" (76), and they resumed. See also Cressy's discussion of the memorialization of the Gunpowder Plot in *Bonfires and Bells,* 141–55.

22. Cressy, "The Fifth of November Remembered," 71, 73.

23. A second edition followed in 1625, then a third, revised (and illustrated) edition in 1627, and a fourth, and final, edition in 1630.

24. Walsham, *Providence in Early Modern England,* 255, notes the muting of the anti-Catholic vehemence in the Gunpowder Plot commemorative sermons in the period in which James was cultivating warmer relations with Spain (1618–23)—until, of course, the failure of the Spanish Match. After the brief revival of anti-Spanish feeling, the polemical anti-Catholic heat was turned down again in the Caroline period of Laudianism and the Catholic Queen Henrietta Maria.

25. Walsham, *Providence in Early Modern England,* 249, points out that Vicars's work was refused a license for a second edition in 1637 by Archbishop Laud's chaplain,

Samuel Baker, but that it was finally republished in 1641. For a discussion of this and other early poems on the plot, see Richard F. Hardin, "The Early Poetry of the Gunpowder Plot: Myth in the Making," *English Literary Renaissance* 22.1 (winter 1992): 62–79. Hardin cites Edward Hawes's *Trayterous Percyes and Catesbyes Prosopopoeia* (1606), Michael Wallace's *In Serenissimi Regis Jacobi . . . Liberationem* (1606), John Ross's *Apostrophe and Praesens Tempus* (1607), William Gager's *Pyramis* (1608), and, of course, Milton's "In Quintem Novembris" as works dealing with the plot and its protagonists. For a listing of Gunpowder Plot poems, mostly from the mid-seventeenth century, see Gerald MacLean, *Time's Witness: Historical Representation in English Poetry, 1603–1660* (Madison: University of Wisconsin Press, 1990), 299n.46.

26. *The Divine Weeks and Works of Guillaume de Saluste, Sieur du Bartas,* 2 vols., trans. Joshua Sylvester, ed. Susan Snyder (Oxford: Clarendon Press, 1979), 1: 52. See II.iii.4.1251–55, 1219–95, of DuBartas's poem.

27. On this alleged plot, see Caroline Hibbard, *Charles I and the Popish Plot* (Chapel Hill: University of North Carolina Press, 1983), 157–62.

28. See Robin Clifton, "The Popular Fear of Catholics during the English Revolution," *Past and Present,* no. 52 (August 1971): 23–55, for a discussion of this in relation to the longer history of anti-Catholic prejudices.

29. Hibbard, *Charles I,* 95–156; and Dolan, *Whores of Babylon: Catholicism, Gender, and Seventeenth-Century Print Culture* (Ithaca: Cornell University Press, 1999), 95–156. Of the many pamphlets from the time, see especially William Prynne, *Romes Master-peece* (1643).

30. Hugh Trevor-Roper, *Catholics, Anglicans and Puritans: Seventeenth-Century Essays* (Chicago: University of Chicago Press, 1988), 113.

31. Ibid., 103.

32. See the chapter "The Origins of the Irish Rebellion November 1640–December 1641," in Conrad Russell, *The Fall of the British Monarchies, 1637–1642* (Oxford: Clarendon Press, 1991), 373–99. See also Raymond Gillespie, "The End of an Era: Ulster and the Outbreak of the 1641 Rising," in *Natives and Newcomers: Essays on the Making of Irish Colonial Society, 1634–1641,* ed. Ciaran Brady and Raymond Gillespie (Dublin: Irish Academic Press, 1986), 191–213.

33. See the discussion of the various motives behind the propagandistic pamphlets in M. Perceval-Maxwell, "The Reaction in Britain to the Rebellion," in *The Outbreak of the Irish Rebellion of 1641* (Montreal and Kingston: McGill-Queen's University Press, 1994), 269–84. Keith Lindley, "The Impact of the 1641 Rebellion upon England and Wales, 1641–4," *Irish Historical Studies* 18 (September 1972): 166, notes that "[t]he accusation that the king and his chief advisers had favoured, if not encouraged, the Irish Rebellion was an important part of a propaganda campaign launched by the parliamentarians to identify the royalist party with popery, tyranny, and barbarity, and

to present themselves as the upholders of the protestant religion, the rights of parliament, and the fundamental liberties of the kingdom." As David Loewenstein, *Representing Revolution in Milton and His Contemporaries: Religion, Politics, and Polemics in Radical Puritanism* (Cambridge: Cambridge University Press, 2001), 192, points out, John Milton, for example, in *Eikonoklastes* (*Complete Prose Works of John Milton,* gen. ed. Don M. Wolfe, 8 vols. [New Haven: Yale University Press, 1953–82], 3: 470–85), argues for a politically devious involvement of Charles in the Irish Rebellion. See Loewenstein, 191–201, for a discussion of Milton's treatment of this topic. See also Catherine Canino, "The Discourse of Hell: *Paradise Lost* and the Irish Rebellion," *Milton Quarterly* 32.1 (March 1998): 15–23.

34. Temple was a member of the Irish Privy Council.

35. Ethan Howard Shagan, "Constructing Discord: Ideology, Propaganda, and English Responses to the Irish Rebellion of 1641," *Journal of British Studies* 36 (January 1997): 4–34, points out that there were two kinds of pamphlets published during the time of the Irish Rebellion—a radical Protestant and antimonarchical sort that drew on the anti-Catholic rhetoric of atrocity descending from John Foxe's *Book of Martyrs* and a royalist form of propaganda that characterized the rebellion in terms of its threat to (monarchical) order. The first kind of propaganda, however, dominated the media and had the greater public impact, building on popular anti-Catholic (and anti-Irish) prejudices. For a discussion of the English depiction of the Irish as northern barbarians in a tradition of such discourse descended from classical times, see Deborah Shuger, "Irishmen, Aristocrats, and Other White Barbarians," *Renaissance Quarterly* 50.2 (summer 1997): 494–525.

36. *A Perfect Relation of the Beginning and Continuation of the Irish Rebellion, From May last, to this present 12th of January, 1641[2]* (1641[2]), 7.

37. The pagination of this section is in error: the order of the page numbers in this edition is 96–97, 102–3, 100–101, 98–99, 104–5. This list of atrocities was obviously imitated by and assimilated to other lists from such sources as Foxe's *Book of Martyrs* in the propagandistic Popish Plot–era work, *The Protestant Tutor* (1679), which has a section entitled "A short Account of the Varieties of Popish Tortures practiced by those Bloody Idolaters upon poor Protestants" (131–35), a list of twenty-five sorts of atrocities.

38. See Milton's "Observations upon the Articles of Peace," in *Complete Prose Works,* 3: 308.

39. This reprises the story of Perotine Massey from Foxe's *Actes and Monuments.* For a discussion of this episode, see Steven Mullaney, "Reforming Resistance: Class, Gender, and Legitimacy," in *Print, Manuscript, and Performance: The Changing Relations of the Media in Early Modern England,* ed. Arthur F. Marotti and Michael D. Bristol (Columbus: Ohio State University Press, 2000), 235–51.

40. This text is unpaginated.

41. Henry Care, *A Weekly Pacquet of Advice from Rome: or, The History of Popery . . . Perform'd by a Single Sheet, Coming out every Friday, but with a continual Connexion. To each being added, The Popish Courant: or, Some occasional Joco-serious Reflections on Romish Fopperies* (1679), 23. This Whig propagandist, in his newsletter of 17 October 1679, has a Catholic speaker refer to a "good Lady . . . whose pious hands frequently made Candles of the Hereticks Fat, and then had them Consecrated to the Honour of the Blessed Virgin" (119). Care's newsletter (1679–83) contains, serially, a history of the papacy and discussions of what are presented as false Catholic practices and doctrines, followed in each issue by comic "news." For a discussion of Care, see Richard L. Greaves, *Secrets of the Kingdom: British Radicals from the Popish Plot to the Revolution of 1688–1689* (Stanford, Calif.: Stanford University Press, 1992), 15–16; and Lois G. Schwoener, *The Ingenious Mr. Henry Case, Restoration Publicist* (Baltimore: Johns Hopkins University Press, 2001), esp. 44–75. Raymond Tumbleson, *Catholicism in the English Protestant Imagination: Nationalism, Religion, and Literature, 1660–1745* (Cambridge: Cambridge University Press, 1998), 88–89, cites some of the atrocity stories summarized in George Fox's *The Arraignment of Popery* (1667).

42. See Perceval-Maxwell, "The Reaction in Britain," 261–84; and Lindley, "The Impact of the 1641 Rebellion," 143–76. For later uses of the Irish Rebellion in English-dominated Ireland both before and after the Glorious Revolution, see T. C. Barnard, "The Uses of 23 October 1641 and Irish Protestant Celebrations," *English Historical Review* 106 (October 1991): 889–920.

43. *The First Sermon, Preached to the Honourable House of Commons now assembled in Parliament at their Publique Fast. Novemb. 17. 1640.* By Cornelius Burges Doctor of Divinitie. Published by Order of that House. London, 1641, in *The English Revolution I, Fast Sermons to Parliament, Volume 1, 1640–1641,* Reproductions in facsimile with notes by Robin Jeffs (London: Cornmarket Press, 1970). Page numbers are cited in the text. Perceval-Maxwell, "The Reaction in Britain," 263–64, points out that "Charles initiated the Fast Sermons, which . . . were intended to generate support for action in Ireland, although they later became a form of parliamentary propaganda." See Hugh Trevor-Roper, "The Fast Sermons of the Long Parliament," in *Religion, the Reformation and Social Change* (London: Macmillan, 1967), 294–344; and John F. Wilson, *Pulpit in Parliament: Puritanism during the English Civil Wars, 1640–1648* (Princeton: Princeton University Press, 1969). Trevor-Roper points out that the Fast Sermons "were preached before Parliament on the last Wednesday of every month from 1642 to 1649" (294) but that earlier Fast Sermons were preached at times of crisis or on other important occasions (such as the opening of Parliament): "[W]ell-timed sermons would not only declare the general party line, but also, on particular occasions, prepare the way for dramatic episodes. They would foretell the death first of Strafford,

then of Laud; declare the civil war; initiate the iconoclastic programme; and, finally, they would announce the most dramatic, most revolutionary gesture of all: the execution of the king himself" (296). For Cornelius Burges, see *DNB*, 3: 301–3.

44. One short pamphlet connects the English outrage with the Irish Rebellion by way of reporting an alleged plot to blow up the main Protestant church in Dublin: *A Gunpowder-Plot in Ireland. For the blowing up of the chiefest Church in Dublin, when the Lords and others were at Sermon, on Sunday, October 31, 1641. Which Conspiracie was plotted to bee done by the Papists and Priests in Dublin. With a further Discovery of their bloody intentiion for the Massacring of the English Protestants in Ireland* (1641).

45. *Another Sermon Preached to the Honorable House of Commons. . . November the fifth, 1641.* By Cornelius Burges, D. D. London, 1641, in *The English Revolution I*, 333–401.

46. For this document, see *The Constitutional Documents of the Puritan Revolution 1625–1660*, ed. Samuel Rawson Gardiner, 3d rev. ed. (Oxford: Clarendon Press, 1951), 202–32. It blamed all the evils in England on "those malignant parties, whose proceedings evidently appear to be mainly for the advantage and increase of Popery, is [*sic*] composed, set up, and acted by the subtile practice of the Jesuits and other engineers and factors for Rome" (203).

47. Perceval-Maxwell, "The Reaction in Britain," 286, notes the shift in government policy "towards Catholicism in Ireland from tacit toleration to annihilation." He says: "Pym and his followers believed that Catholicism was about to try to destroy Protestantism in England, but in resisting this supposed threat, he created a similar, if reversed, fear in Ireland. The Irish, in turn, in countering what they believed to be Puritan intentions, appeared to confirm every suspicion the militant Protestants in England possessed" (290).

48. Stephen Marshall, *A Sermon Preached before the Honourable House of Commons . . . At their publike Fast, November 17. 1640* (1641), in *The English Revolution I*, 97–152. Marshall was a client of John Pym, but in this sermon he pressed a primarily religious agenda for Parliament—the anti-Laudian emphasis on the need for measures to protect a preaching ministry.

49. *Meroz Cursed, or, A Sermon Preached To the Honourable House of Commons, At their late Solemn Fast, Febr. 23.1641[2]* (1641[2]). Trevor-Roper identifies Marshall as "the most important of the preachers [of the Fast Sermons] . . . . In the Long Parliament he would emerge as the inseparable political and spiritual ally of Pym, the interpreter of Pym's policy after Pym's death. At every stage of the revolution we can see him. . . . From beginning to end Marshall was the clerical tribune of the Parliament" ("Fast Sermons," 297–98). This sermon was published in 1641/2, 1642, and 1645. Trevor-Roper points out that this day was the first on which "Parliament, City and country would celebrate the fast on the same day" (306).

50. Trevor-Roper, "Fast Sermons," 307. Glenn Burgess, "Was the English Civil War a War of Religion?" *Huntington Library Quarterly,* 61.21 (1998): 173–201, argues against the importance of the religious basis of the Civil Wars, and he does not view the Fast Sermons as attempts to justify a holy war: "The sermons worked on an altogether different plane, as encouragements to a certain kind of introspection. God may have approved of what men were doing, but it was not his approval that legitimated it. The godly should, no doubt, fight with the belief that God was on their side, but he was on their side *because* their fight was *already* a justifiable one" (191). He refuses to read Marshall's "Meroz Cursed" as a "literal call to arms" (192).

51. Trevor-Roper, "Fast Sermons," 308, notes that the words inciting to brutal violence found in this sermon "would become the commonplaces of many a later preacher."

52. Lindley, "The Impact of the 1641 Rebellion," 156. The pamphlet is *An alarum to warre: proclaimed by our soveraigne and his parliament, to subjugate the papists and vindicate the protestants of Ireland* (1642). Lindley, says that "the whole series of rumoured catholic plots and popery scares from November 1641 up to the outbreak of the English civil war must be interpreted in the light of the impact of the Irish rebellion upon England and Wales, for it was that rebellion that gave even the wildest rumours credibility" (159). Cf. the report in *A Perfect Diurnall of the Passages in Parliament* (21–28 February 1641[2]) of a Catholic plot in Lancashire to use "ten Barrels of powder . . . to make Balls of wildfire, wherewith to set on fire divers chief Towns in this Kingdome . . . that when those Towns should be set on fire, all the Papists in England would rise" (in *Making the News: An Anthology of Newsbooks of Revolutionary England, 1641–1660,* ed. Joad Raymond [New York: St. Martin's Press, 1993], 45–46).

53. *The Writings and Speeches of Oliver Cromwell,* ed. Wilbur Cortez Abbott, vol. 2 (*The Commonwealth, 1649–1653*) (1937–47; rpt. New York: Russell & Russell, 1939), 205.

54. For a discussion of Milton's pamphlet, see Thomas N. Corns, "Milton's *Observations upon the Articles of Peace:* Ireland under English Eyes," in *Politics, Poetics, and Hermeneutics in Milton's Prose,* ed. David Loewenstein and James Grantham Turner (Cambridge: Cambridge University Press, 1990), 123–34.

55. Milton's Sonnet XVIII is printed in *Milton's Sonnets,* ed. E. A. J. Honigmann (London: Macmillan; New York: St. Martin's Press, 1966). Honigmann, 164–65, quotes some of the atrocity stories from contemporary newsletters that reached England. They closely resemble the brutality ascribed to the Irish rebels, and, in fact, some of the soldiers serving the duke of Savoy were Irish. For the importance of the persecution of the Waldenses before and after the Piedmont massacre, see, for example, Samuel Clarke, *A General Martyrologie, Containing a Collection of all the greatest Persecutions which have befallen the Church of Christ From the Creation to our present Times, Both in*

England and all other Nations. Whereunto are added two and twenty Lives of English Modern Divines, Famous in their Generations for Learning and Piety, and most of them great Sufferers in the Cause of Christ. As also the Life of the Heroical Admiral of France, slain in the Parisian Massacre, and of Joane Queen of Navar, poisoned a little before, 2d ed. (1660), chap. 41–45. In chapter 40 Clarke presents an account of atrocity stories connected to the Irish Rebellion, illustrating these and the other episodes of Protestant martyrdom with crude and shocking woodcuts.

56. *Poems on Affairs of State: Augustan Satirical Verse, 1660–1714* [hereafter *POAS*], vol. 2: 1678–1681, ed. Elias F. Mengel Jr. (New Haven: Yale University Press, 1965), 94 (l. 350). Caryll's 1679 publication, at the height of the Popish Plot turmoil, attacks Titus Oates, William Bedloe, and Sir William Scroggs. *The New Plot of the Papists to Transform Traitors into Martyrs* (1679), which is actually a Catholic pamphlet questioning the reality of the Popish Plot, questions Oates's motives and the truth of his narrative of the plot: "is there not some reason, a little to hesitate, and to doubt at least, whether Mr. Oats (overpowerd by the two prevailing Motives, first of revenge against the jesuites, for not receiving and entertaining him any longer; and next of procuring a subsistance; which he then wanted) may not have invented that voluminous History of his Plott (which to all people knowing in the world hath the perfect air of a Romance)" (11). The writer compares the contemporary "plot" with the Gunpowder Plot, whose participants fled and for which there was physical evidence, and finds it insubstantial. Also, by invoking Nero's blaming Christians for the burning of Rome, he suggests that Catholics were scapegoated for some disasters (such as the 1666 Fire of London). On the other hand, the newswriter Henry Care associates romance and untruth with Roman Catholicism: "We have now learn'd why people are wont to call lying Fables, Romances; no doubt, at first, from the Legends and Lives of our Roman Saints, which exceed for extravagant Conceits the whimsies of the Talmud, and the Dotages of the Alchoran: nay Ovid's Metamorphosis, or Lucian's true History, contain not Stories more silly and incredible" (*Weekly Pacquet of Advice from Rome,* 23 May 1679, 199).

57. Harold Love, "The Look of News: Popish Plot Narratives, 1678–1680," in *The Cambridge History of the Book in Britain,* vol. 4, *1557–1695,* ed. John Barnard and D. F. McKenzie (Cambridge: Cambridge University Press, 2002), 654. Love calls Titus Oates "one of the great pioneers . . . of literary realism." Sharon Achinstein, *Milton and the Revolutionary Reader* (Princeton: Princeton University Press, 1994), 7, says political pamphleteers of the era of the English Revolution were engaged in "fiction-making."

58. Jonathan Scott, "England's Troubles: Exhuming the Popish Plot," in *The Politics of Religion in Restoration England,* ed. Tim Harris, Paul Seaward, and Mark Goldie (Oxford: Basil Blackwell, 1990), 118–19.

59. Ll. 114–15 in *POAS,* 461.

60. Concentrating on the Exclusion Crisis and on court and opposition politics, Mark Knights, *Politics and Opinion in Crisis, 1678–81* (Cambridge: Cambridge University Press, 1994), 142, says that "whilst religious sympathies helped fire the clamour for the subject's legal rights, which were necessary for the security of Protestantism, a significant part of the constitutional debate took place on a purely secular level about the rights and powers of Parliament and the King. Religion was part of a citizen's liberty and property, which was why those words became such important slogans." Looking at the larger, international cultural picture, Michel de Certeau, *The Writing of History,* trans. Tom Conley (New York: Columbia University Press, 1988), sees the gradual change from religious to secular culture in terms of the Protestant-Catholic oppositions. De Certeau, 193–94n.27, claims, for example, that around 1660, in both England and France, doctrinal conflict changed to social and political conflict. Of course, religious conflict facilitated the relativizing of religious belief and the objectification of it as an object of knowledge rather than as an epistemology, so, ironically, it precipitated the conditions for the marginalization of religion in civil society. See C. John Sommerville, *The Secularization of Early Modern England: From Religious Culture to Religious Faith* (New York: Oxford University Press, 1992).

61. Oates's narrative was published in 1679 when a new (more oppositionist) Parliament was in place. For a discussion of the political activities and propaganda of radical Whigs from the Popish Plot and Exclusion Crisis to the Glorious Revolution and its aftermath, see Melinda S. Zook, *Radical Whigs and Conspiratorial Politics in Late Stuart England* (University Park: Pennsylvania State University Press, 1999). Cf. Greaves, *Secrets of the Kingdom.*

62. See Introduction to Ole Peter Grell, Jonathan I. Israel, and Nicholas Tyacke, eds., *From Persecution to Toleration: The Glorious Revolution and Religion in England* (Oxford: Clarendon Press, 1991), 11–16; and John Bossy, "English Catholics after 1688," 369–87, in the same volume. Bossy points out that 1689 Toleration Act, despite its exclusion of Catholics, actually benefited Catholics in many ways and that King William's wish to treat Catholic subjects leniently counteracted the force of more hostile parliamentary acts.

63. Thomas M. McCoog, S.J., "Richard Langhorne and the Popish Plot," *Recusant History* 19.4 (1989): 507, says: "Charles sacrificed Jesuits on the altar of political expediency." McCoog notes that nine Jesuits were executed during the Popish Plot crisis, twelve more died in prison, and three more of injuries or infirmity, totaling twenty-four Jesuit victims. These figures differ from those given by J. C. H. Aveling, *The Handle and the Axe: The Catholic Recusants in England from Reformation to Emancipation* (London: Blond and Briggs, 1976), 215: "Of their ninety missioners . . . forty were arrested, nine were executed and eighteen died of imprisonment." Aveling calculates: "Of the 600–700 missioners [Jesuit and non-Jesuit], about one hundred were

arrested. Of these seventeen were executed. . . . Another twenty-three died in gaol or
later, as a result of imprisonment."

64. *The Complete Prose Works of Andrew Marvell,* vol. 3, ed. Alexander Grosart
(n.p.: Printed for private circulation, 1875), 247–424. The work was reprinted in 1678,
after Marvell's death, and answered by Roger L'Estrange's *The Parallel or An Account of
the Growth of Knavery* (1678). L'Estrange attempted to expose the fictions of propaganda, referring, for example, to events in the 1640s when he exclaimed: "what were all
their Stories of Popish Plots, Intercepted Letters, Dark Conspiracies, but only Artifices
to gull the Credulous and Silly Vulgar" (10). In his *History of the Plot* (1679), A2, he remarked: "We are come to govern our selves by Dreams, and Imaginations; We make
every Coffee-house Tale an Article of our Faith, and from incredible Fables we raise
Invincible Arguments." For a broader discussion of both Marvell's and Milton's use of
anti-Catholic discourse, see Cedric C. Brown, "'This Islands watchful Centinel': Anti-
Catholicism and Proto-Whiggery in Milton and Marvell," in *The Cambridge Companion to English Literature: 1650–1740,* ed. Steven N. Zwicker (Cambridge: Cambridge
University Press, 1998), 165–84. Brown, 167, notes that Marvell's *Account* was brought
out in a French translation in 1680, and "a Whig continuation" in 1680, reprinted in
1688 also to justify the Glorious Revolution, then excerpted for its description of Catholicism in a short 1689 pamphlet, *Mr. Andrew Marvell's Character of Popery.*

65. For a discussion of the *Growth of Popery* in the context of the country party's
political propaganda in the mid-1670s, see Warren Chernaik, *The Poet's Time: Politics
and Religion in the Work of Andrew Marvell* (Cambridge: Cambridge University Press,
1983), 90–100. Chernaik says, "[I]t is likely that *The Growth of Popery* was written in direct consultation with Shaftesbury and other Country Party leaders" (96).

66. Scott, *England's Troubles,* 8, 24, argues that there were "three crises of popery and arbitrary Government," 1618–49, 1678–83, and 1688–89. For a discussion of
Marvell's *Growth* in relation to foreign affairs, see Knights, *Politics and Opinion in Crisis,* 17–25.

67. Tumbleson, *Catholicism in the English Protestant Imagination,* 48, sees Marvell's prime interest as secular politics, not religion.

68. Conal Condren, "Andrew Marvell as Polemicist: His *Account of the Growth
of Popery, and Arbitrary Government,*" in *The Political Identity of Andrew Marvell,* ed.
Conal Condren and A. D. Cousins (Aldershot: Scolar Press, 1990), 170–71. For a discussion of Marvell's ("loyalist") politics in this tract, see John M. Wallace, *Destiny His
Choice: The Loyalism of Andrew Marvell* (Cambridge: Cambridge University Press,
1968), 207–31. Wallace claims Marvell is not antimonarchical in this work in the way
some of the political radicals of the time were. He argues that in addition to criticizing royal policies, he blamed "a Parliament that in large part had corrupted itself without outside help" (213).

69. He makes the exception of the four peers whose exercise of parliamentary free speech landed them in the Tower: the duke of Buckingham, the earl of Shaftesbury, the earl of Salisbury, and Lord Wharton.

70. Chernaik, *The Poet's Time,* 90, points out that many who, like Marvell, supported toleration did not approve of the Declaration because they saw it as an absolutistic expansion of the royal prerogative and a cooptation of Parliament's law-making powers.

71. The same year James married Mary of Modena he refused to comply with the Test Act, thus signaling his Catholicism.

72. Condren, "Andrew Marvell as Polemicist," argues that Marvell's main concern was the welfare of "the Protestant cause" (172): "Marvell's cause in 1678 is close to being the Good Old Cause which, if it was not overtly republican, was focused on Christian liberty, the continuation of the European Reformation and the extirpation of Catholicism" (173).

73. Here Marvell replicates John Milton's view of Catholicism. For a discussion of Milton's anti-Catholicism, see John N. King, *Milton and Religious Controversy: Satire and Polemic in* Paradise Lost (Cambridge: Cambridge University Press, 2000); and Tumbleson, *Catholicism in the English Protestant Imagination,* 41–68.

74. Marvell refers to the fears of royal military action, specifically that the army camped outside London at Black Heath— commanded by "Monsieur Schomberg, a French Protestant," and "Colonel Fitzgerald, an Irish Papist, major general," who might, respectively, be working for "advancing the French governement" and "promoting the Irish religion" (293)— might pose a real threat to the staunchly Protestant city.

75. Chernaik, *The Poet's Time,* 98.

76. John Miller, "Public Opinion in Charles II's England," *History* 80 (October 1995): 369, states: "Th[e] sense that England was threatened by the might of international Catholicism persisted under Charles II, with Louis XIV now seen in the role (once occupied by the Habsburgs) of aspirant to universal monarchy."

77. Aveling, *The Handle and the Axe,* points out, "In 1678 *some* conspiring certainly was afoot within the Catholic community" (207). "Edward Coleman, a Catholic convert layman employed in the Duke of York's household, had for years been writing to Louis XIV's Jesuit confessor about a 'grand design' of a Catholic takeover of the Establishment, presumably when his master became king. A number of leading activist Papist peers had lately been meeting more frequently and traveling backwards and forwards to France. They were associated with numbers of unemployed Catholic English and Irish army officers. In Catholic activist circles in the provinces by 1678 there were signs of almost apocalyptic expectation of the Catholic religion coming in again" (208). Although Oates's plot "had a slender basis in fact" (210) then, it reflected some real if low-scale activity on the part of some Catholics. Coleman's

correspondence with the French was published in *A Collection of Letters and other Writings Relating to the Horrid Popish Plott: Printed from the Originals in the Hands of George Treby Esq.; Chairman of the Committee of Secrecy of the Honourable House of Commons. Published by Order of that House* (1681). Earlier, as Knights, *Politics and Opinion in Crisis,* 180, notes, two of the letters were published in *Mr Coleman's two letters to Monsieur L'Chaise . . . together with the D[uke] of Y[ork's] letter to the said Monsieur L'Chaise* (1678).

78. I cite the facsimile of Oates's *Narrative* found in *Diaries of the Popish Plot,* comp. and introd. Douglas C. Greene (Delmar, N.Y.: Scholars' Facsimiles & Reprints, 1977). See pp. 166–67 for references to the Jesuit plotting and Milton. Subsequent references appear in the text, using the pagination of this volume. See the summary of Oates's pamphlet in John Kenyon, *The Popish Plot* (1972; rpt. London: Phoenix Press, 2000), 63–67, 73–76.

79. Steven C. A. Pincus, *Protestantism and Patriotism: Ideologies and the Making of English Foreign Policy, 1650–1668* (Cambridge: Cambridge University Press, 1996), 443, has argued that the first Restoration Dutch War was fought to counter republicanism and religious fanaticism and to restore power to the prince of Orange.

80. *Scribal Publication in Seventeenth-Century England* (Oxford: Clarendon Press, 1993), 172.

81. Viscount Stafford was imprisoned with these four and was the only peer executed during the Popish Plot era, condemned by a majority vote in the House of Lords.

82. In the first of his "Satires against the Jesuits" (1680) John Oldham portrays the ghost of Henry Garnet delivering a bloodthirsty speech to stir the Jesuit popish plotters to ruthless action. Oldham portrays Jesuits as king killers and atheists (*POAS* 2: 25) and blames them for the fire of London (2: 30).

83. See Scott, "England's Troubles: Exhuming the Popish Plot," in Harris, Seaward, and Goldie, *The Politics of Religion in Restoration England,* 119–22.

84. Aveling, *The Handle and the Axe,* 216, observes that with the arrests and executions of Jesuits, "[t]he backbone of the Society of Jesus in England was broken swiftly in 1678–9. . . . Probably two-thirds of the Jesuit missions ceased to operate because the missioners were arrested, or fled overseas, or the patrons were removed."

85. Miller, "Public Opinion," 363.

86. Scott, "England's Troubles: Exhuming the Popish Plot," 120.

87. John Warner, *A Vindication of the Inglish Catholiks from the pretended conspiracy against the life and Government of his Sacred Majesty. Discovering the chiefe Falsities & Contradictions contained in the Narrative of Titus Oates* (Antwerp, 1680), 18, noted: "Provincial Congregations all over the Society are held every three yeares by the respective Provincials. And the yeare 1678 was of course assigned for them. So the Con-

gregation was nothing peculiar to *England,* for the same time like Congregations were held all over *Europe* in each Province of the Jesuits."

88. Kenyon, *Popish Plot,* 37, notes that James II was received into the Catholic church in 1669 by a Jesuit, Emmanuel Lobb.

89. Scott, *England's Troubles,* 186, cites *The Tryals of William Ireland, Thomas Pickering, and John Grove* (1678), 11.

90. Scott, *England's Troubles,* 14, cites William Bedloe, *A Narrative and Impartial Discovery of the Horrid Popish Plot* (1679).

91. Scott, *England's Troubles,* 186.

92. Ironically he later became the target of popular anger for his hand in the acquittal of Sir George Wakeman, the queen's physician, of the charge of planning the poisoning of Charles II.

93. Kenyon, *Popish Plot,* 199; also see pp. 131–46, 180–88, 193–201, for a discussion of Scroggs's behavior and temperament. For his conduct during the trial of the five Jesuits, see pp. 180–85. J. P. Kenyon, "The Acquittal of Sir George Wakeman: 18 July 1679," *Historical Journal* 14.2 (1971): 707, calls Scroggs's behavior at Wakeman's trial "a nice blend of anti-Catholic prejudice, social deference and a desire to see justice done in difficult circumstances." For some of the poetic attacks on Scroggs after the Wakeman verdict, see *POAS* 2: 280–91.

94. Quoted in Kenyon, "Acquittal of Sir George Wakeman," 705.

95. The full title is *An Answer to Blundell the Jesuites Letter; That was taken about him at Lambeth, on Munday the 23rd of this Instant June. Directed to the Jesuits at Cambra in Flanders: Wherein he gives them an Account of several Notorious Untruths, concerning the Proceedings in Court, against the Five Jesuits lately Executed: with several other Preposterous Relations. The which being duly weighed, it was thought fit to Exhibit this Responsary to confute his errers, and for Vindication of the wholesome Laws, and Impartial Judicature of this our English Nation, &c.* (1679).

96. Tim Harris, *London Crowds in the Reign of Charles II: Propaganda and Politics from the Restoration until the Exclusion Crisis* (Cambridge: Cambridge University Press, 1987), 96, notes: "With the breakdown of the Licensing Act in June 1679 there appeared a flood of lengthy and elaborate tracts in which the whigs sought to defend their policy by outlining the legal and historical precedents for exclusion. But they also sought to win mass support for their cause through propaganda which was aimed at the popular market: broadsides, newspapers, prints, ballads, plays, sermons, and public spectacles."

97. Blundell's letter might have been printed at the initiative of either English Catholics or the court party.

98. From a Tory vantage point, Roger L'Estrange's *The History of the Plot* (1679) portrays the series of trials of the alleged "plotters" as a miscarriage of justice. He pays

special attention to the proceedings against the five Jesuits, in a narrative in which they emerge as eloquent, credible, and long-suffering while Oates and his fellow perjurers are portrayed as disreputable.

99. There was only time to try the first before the commission by which the court sat expired. Later, the trial of Wakeman took placed in changed circumstances: Scroggs by that time expressed hostility to Oates's testimony and the jury was more sympathetic to the accused so that he was found not guilty.

100. Although Blundell does not mention it, Langhorne provided such information, which did great damage to the Jesuit mission but did not save his life. There is some dispute about whether Langhorne had the permission of the Jesuit provincial to make these damaging revelations—which might, perhaps, have been gleaned from the papers seized from the arrest of the five Jesuits.

101. *An Answer to Blundell the Jesuites Letter* (1679). In the absence of prepublication censorship between 1679 and 1685, charges of libel were brought against booksellers or publishers to curtail printing of radical political pamphlets.

102. Kenyon, *Popish Plot*, 207.

103. See Thomas H. Clancy, *A Literary History of the English Jesuits: A Century of Books, 1615–1714* (San Francisco: Catholic Scholars Press, 1996), 164–65, for a discussion of the dissemination of the scaffold speeches of the five Jesuits in Protestant texts.

104. *Animadversions on the last Speeches of the Jesuits* and *Impartial Considerations on the Speeches of the five Jesuits* (1679).

105. See also the translation and republication of an anti-Jesuit work originally addressed to Henri IV of France: *The King-Killing Doctrine of the Jesuites: Delivered in a Plain and Sincere Discourse to the French King, Concerning the Reestablishment of the Jesuites in his Dominions. Written in French by a Learned Roman Catholick, and now Translated into English, and humbly recommended to the Consideration of both Houses of Parliament* (1679). I discuss this work in chapter 2.

106. A contemporary pamphlet, *A Letter from a Jesuite: Or, The Mysterie of Equivocation* (1679), makes equivocation the quintessential Jesuit mark: "[T]heir very looks and garbs, as well as their words, are Equivocations, Wolves in sheeps clothing, and Ghostly fathers that have by vows abandon'd the world, ruffling in Courts, Exchanges, every where, in huffing habits of Hectoring Gallants. Their discourses capable of as many Constructions as an Almanack makers prognostications, not are their writings less full of crafty obscurity and hidden meanings" (2–3).

107. Scott, "England's Troubles: Exhuming the Popish Plot," 108–9.

108. Anne Dillon, *The Construction of Martyrdom in the English Catholic Community, 1535–1603* (Aldershot: Ashgate, 2002), 7, identifies Punket, who was executed in July 1581, as "the last English Catholic martyr."

109. There was a flood of anti-Catholic pamphlets published when James, duke of York, married Mary of Modena in 1673. See Clancy, *A Literary History of the En-*

glish Jesuits, 162. On the phenomenon of "recycling" of earlier political and religious propaganda in an earlier period, see Joseph Marshall, "Recycling and Originality in the Pamphlet Wars: Republishing Jacobean Texts in the 1640s," *Transactions of the Cambridge Bibliographical Society* 12.1 (2000): 55–85. Marshall estimates that between 10 and 15 percent of the Thomason Tracts could accurately be called "recycled." Knights, 189–91, points out that royalists or Tories as well as Whigs republished earlier pamphlets during the Popish Plot and Exclusion Crisis era.

110. See also *The True Narrative of the Popish Plot against King Charles I* (1680). In his *Brief History of the Times,* pt. 2, 58, L'Estrange alludes to the reprinting of Prynne's work and claims that the Habernfeld Plot story was the model for Israel Tonge's Popish Plot one, which Titus Oates then articulated for a broader audience.

111. *The arraignment, tryal and condemnation of Robert Earl of Essex and Henry Earl of Southampton, at Westminster the 19th of February, 1600 and in the 43 year of the reign of Queen Elizabeth for rebelliously conspiring and endeavouring the subversion of the government, by confederacy with Tyr-Owen, that popish traytor and his complices . . . were the 5th of March . . . arraigned, condemned, and executed* (1679).

112. *The Gunpowder-Treason: with a Discourse of the Manner of its Discovery; and A Perfect Relation of the Proceedings against those horrid Conspirators; Wherein is Contained their Examinations, Tryals, and Condemnations: Likewise King James's Speech to Both Houses of Parliament, On that Occasion . . .* (1679). Roger Widdrington's account of Garnet's trial, originally printed in Latin in 1616, was also republished: *The tryal and execution of Father Henry Garnet, superior provincial of the Jesuits in England for the powder-treason* (1679). See also Thomas Morton, *An Exact Account of Romish Doctrine: in the Case of Conspiracy and Rebellion* (1679), and John Williams, *A vindication of the history of the gunpowder-treason: and of the proceedings and matters relating thereunto, from the exceptions which have been made against it, and more especially of late years by the author of the Catholick apologie, and others: to which is added, A parallel betwixt that and the present popish plot* (1681). Cressy, *Bonfires and Bells,* 176, notes the 1680 republication of John Wilson's 1626 work, *Song or story for the lasting remembrance of divers famous works which God hath done in our time,* and three editions between 1671 and 1679 of Samuel Clarke's 1657 work, *Englands Remembrancer, containing a true and full narrative of those two never to be forgotten deliverances: the one from the Spanish Invasion in eighty eight: the other from the hellish Powder Plot, November 5. 1605.*

113. In a work first published in 1667 (after the Fire of London), William Lloyd says that if "Cecil did draw in those wretches into this Treason" "What [*sic*] i[t] ever the less Treason because He drew them into it?" (*The Late Apology In behalf of the Papists, Reprinted and Answered In behalf of the Royalists. The Fourth Edition Corrected* [1675], 31). Lloyd asserts that the threat of Catholic fanaticism persisted in the Restoration era: "who can deny that some Papists in this Age retain the Principles of them that were Consenting to [the Gunpowder Plot]" (35).

114. Other anti-Jesuit works are, for example, *The Jesuite Countermin'd, Or, An Account of a New Plot Carrying on by the Jesuites: Manifested by their present Endeavours (under all Shapes) to raise Commotions in the Land, by Aspersing His Sacred Majesties Counsels and Actions* (1679) and *A Truth known to very Few: viz. That the Jesuites Are down-right Atheists: Proved such, and condemned for it By Two Sentences of the Famous Faculty of Sorbonne* (1680).

115. The radical Protestant lord mayor of London, Sir Patience Ward, was responsible for putting the anti-Catholic inscription on the monument to the 1666 Fire. John Warner, S.J., *The History of English Persecution of Catholics and the Presbyterian Plot,* ed. T. A. Birrell, trans. John Bligh, S.J., 2 vols., Catholic Record Society Publications 47, 48 (London: John Whitehead & Son, 1953–55), 2: 492, records its text. In 1667 a pamphlet was published from a report to the House of Commons blaming the Jesuits for the Fire of London: *A true and faithful account of the several informations exhibited to the honourable committee appointed by the Parliament to inquire into the late dreadful burning of the city of London: together with other informations touching the insolency of popish priests and Jesuites.* A pamphlet issued soon after the fire rang an incredible number of metaphoric variations on the association of Jesuits and fire to blame the Jesuits for such disasters: *Pyrotechnica Loyolana, Ignatian Fire-works. Or, The Fiery Jesuits Temper and Behaviour. Being an Historical Compendium of the Rise, Increase, Doctrines, and Deeds of the Jesuits. Exposed to Publick view for the sake of London. By a Catholick-Christian* (1667). The writer sees Jesuit agency in the St. Bartholomew's Day Massacre (14), the assassinations or attempted assassinations of Henri III and Henri IV of France and Queen Elizabeth and King James of England, a plot to set London on fire at the end of Elizabeth's reign and the Gunpowder Plot in the early part of King James's, the "war betwixt England and Scotland 1639" (118), the warfare against Protestants in Bohemia, France, the Palatinate, the Netherlands, Germany, and elsewhere during the Thirty Years' War, the Irish Rebellion of 1641 (begun "[o]n the 23. Of Octob. 1641, being IGNATIUS DAY" [120]), the "cutting off King Charles I. On the 30. Jan. 1648[9]" (121), and, finally, the Fire of London (1666). Strangely, this work connects the Jesuits with the Army Independents of the Interregnum (121). For a recent discussion of the association of Catholics with the Fire of London, see Frances Dolan, "Ashes and 'the Archive': The London Fire of 1666, Partisanship, and Proof," *Journal of Medieval and Early Modern Studies* 31.2 (spring 2001): 379–408. Dolan notes that *London's Flames Reviv'd* was "reprinted whenever the political climate warranted or required another denunciation of papists: not just in 1667, just following the fire, but in 1679, at the time of the Popish Plot, and in 1689, when the Revolution was being justified in part through anti-Catholicism" (394).

116. Especially after the Fire of London, Catholics were repeatedly imagined to have set or to be ready to set fires or, as in the Gunpowder Plot, to set explosives to attack the English Protestant community.

117. See John Miller, *Popery and Politics in England, 1660–1688* (Cambridge: Cambridge University Press, 1973), 75.

118. Some of these events were publicized in print soon after their staging. See, for example, *The Solemn Mock Procession of the Pope, Cardinalls, Jesuits, Fryers, etc . . . November the 17, 1679* (1679), *The Solemn Mock Procession of the Pope, Cardinals, Jesuits, Fryers, Nuns, etc . . . November the 17th 1680* (1680), *The Solemn Mock Procession: Or, The Trial and Execution of the Pope and His Minister, on the 17 of Nov. at Temple Bar* (1680), and *The Procession; Or, The Burning of the Pope in Effigy* (1681). There is a description of a pope-burning procession from a Catholic point of view in Warner, *History*, 1: 186. Harris, *London Crowds*, 92–93, notes that the Whig Green Ribbon Club was responsible for the pope-burning processions starting in 1673. See also O. W. Furley, "The Pope-Burning Processions of the Late Seventeenth Century," *History* 44 (1959): 16–23; Sheila Williams, "The Pope-Burning Processions of 1679, 1680 and 1681," *Journal of the Warburg and Courtauld Institutes* 21 (1958): 104–18; and Cressy, *Bonfires and Bells*, 179–82. Cressy points out that the custom of burning the pope in effigy began in the Caroline period (*Bonfires and Bells*, 147).

119. For a discussion of the uses of Elizabethanism during the Popish Plot and Exclusion Crisis, see John Watkins, *Representing Elizabeth in Stuart England: Literature, History, Sovereignty* (Cambridge: Cambridge University Press, 2002), 127–35.

120. In 1680 a play was published with the title *The Coronation of Queen Elizabeth, with the restauration of the Protestant religion, or, The downfal of the Pope: being a most excellent play, as it was acted both at Bartholomew and Southwark fairs, this present year, 1680, with great applause and approved of and highly commended by all the Protestant nobility, gentry and commonalty of England, who came to be spectators of the same.*

121. The addle-brained zealot Israel Tonge was Oates's initial collaborator in the Popish Plot fabrication. Kenyon, *Popish Plot*, 278, points out that he took financial advantage of the plot hysteria by bringing out several other books in 1679: *Jesuitical Aphorisms, or a Summary Account of the Doctrines of the Jesuits; The New Design of the Papists Detected; Popish Mercy and Justice;* and *The Northern Star: the British Monarchy, or the Northern the Fourth Universal Monarchy.*

122. Fraser, *Faith and Treason*, 281.

123. John Donne, *Ignatius His Conclave,* ed. T. S. Healy, S. J. (Oxford: Clarendon Press, 1969), 84.

124. William Borlase's *History of the Execrable Irish Rebellion of 1641* was reprinted in 1680. Scott, *England's Troubles*, 199, notes the revival of fears of an Irish Rebellion during the 1680 Parliament.

125. Danby initially tried to use the Popish Plot to his and the Crown's advantage, pressing to have Edward Coleman, the duke of York's secretary, arrested and his papers (containing embarrassing correspondence with France) searched. See K. H. D. Haley, *The First Earl of Shaftesbury* (Oxford: Clarendon Press, 1968), 456.

126. See Scott, *England's Troubles*, 187.

127. He had earlier published an anti-Jesuit and anti-Presbyterian diatribe, *The history of the wicked plots and conspiracies of our pretended saints* (1662).

128. Walsham, *Providence in Early Modern England*, 265.

129. Harris, *London Crowds*, 110. For a discussion of playing cards and the anti-Catholic model for writing English history, see J. R. S. Whiting, *A Handful of History* (Dursley, Gloucestershire: Alan Sutton, 1978), 36–63.

130. Harris, *London Crowds*, 110.

131. Love observes: "[T]wice in the century the press became an agency of power in its own right. . . . The first of these periods was 1641–46 and the second 1677–82, the fiction in each case being a variant on the old theme of anti-Popery" (*Scribal Publication in Seventeenth-Century England*, 171).

132. For a discussion of Cellier in relation to the gendering of Catholicism, see Dolan, *Whores of Babylon*, 157–210.

133. Kenyon, *Popish Plot*, 280.

134. L'Estrange, *A Brief History of the Times*, pt. 1, 113–14. Relating the Popish Plot to the Gunpowder Plot, the Irish Rebellion, and the Great Fire of 1666, John Bunyan wrote: "then we began to fear cutting of throats, of being burned alive in our beds, and of seeing our Children dashed in pieces before our Faces" (*Israel's Hope Encouraged*, cited in *The Miscellaneous Works of John Bunyan*, ed. Roger Sharrock, vol. 4, ed. T. L. Underwood [Oxford: Clarendon Press, 1989], xviii).

135. Warner, *History*, 1: 212. Subsequent citations of this work appear in the text. Warner, who became Jesuit provincial in 1679 after the execution of his predecessor Thomas Whitebread, became King James II's confessor in 1687 (Miller, *Popery and Politics*, 235). He wrote pamphlets during the Popish Plot crisis: Birrell, in Warner, *History*, 1: ix, identifies him, along with L'Estrange, as the main anti-Plot propagandist in print. He published the following: *Concerning the Congregation of Jesuits held in London April 24, 1678, which Mr. Oates calls a Consult* (1679); *Harangues Des Cinq Pères de la Compagnie de Jesus, Executés à Londres le 20/30 Juin 1679* (n.p., n.d.); *Anti-Fimbria or An Answer to the Animadversions uppon the Last Speeches of the Five Jesuits Executed at Tyburne June 20/30 1679* (n.p., 1679), a work aimed at his polemical adversary, Thomas Barlow, bishop of London; *A Defence of the Innocency of the Lives, Practice and Doctrine of the English Priests, Jesuits, and Papists. relating to the Crimes of Murther and Treason unjustly charged on them by E. C. in his Narrative . . .* (n.p., 1680); and *A Vindication of the Inglish Catholiks from the pretended conspiracy against the life and Government of his Sacred Majesty. Discovering the chiefe Falsities & Contradictions contained in the Narrative of Titus Oates* (Antwerp, 1680) (cited above), the last reappearing with additions in second (1680) and third (1681) editions. During the reign of James II, he composed and circulated in manuscript his Latin history of the plot.

136. L'Estrange says of the Popish Plot that "the Shot was Manifestly Pointed at his Royal Highness [James], and through Him at the King, his Brother; and thorough his Late Majesty, at Monarchy it self" (*A Brief History of the Times*, pt. 1, 32).

137. See the discussion in Kenyon, *Popish Plot*, 282–94.

138. James had made Petre a member of his Privy Council in 1687.

139. Arnold Pritchard, *Catholic Loyalism in Elizabethan England* (Chapel Hill: University of North Carolina Press, 1979), 27–28, says that this work, probably completed around 1596, was intended by Gee "to blacken Parsons's character and to point out the horrible fate that England had recently escaped by the Glorious Revolution." John Bossy, *The English Catholic Community, 1570–1850* (London: Darton, Longman & Todd, 1975), 75, suggests that John Warner brought Persons's manuscript tract with him from France because he was sympathetic to its blueprint for Catholic restoration. In the work, however, Persons recommends only a temporary toleration of religious diversity during the period that a restored Catholic state worked to make all citizens conform to Catholicism.

140. See Miller, *Poetry and Politics*, 252.

141. Kenyon, *Popish Plot*, 300–301.

142. See Brad Gregory, *Salvation at Stake: Christian Martyrdom in Early Modern Europe* (Cambridge, Mass.: Harvard University Press, 1999), for a discussion of the inconceivability of toleration in a period of conflicting confessional commitments.

143. William Allen's *A True Sincere and Modest Defence of English Catholics* (1584) had, in its conclusion, made a plea for toleration. The libelous *Leicester's Commonwealth* also argued for toleration. At the start of the reign of James I, "The Catholics' Supplication unto the King's Majesty, for toleration of Catholic Religion in England" was submitted to him: see M. A. Tierney, *Dodd's Church History of England*, vol. 4 (1841; rpt. Westmead: Gregg International Publishers, 1971), lxxii–lxxiv.

144. Traditionally King James's promise of toleration of Catholics and his failure to follow through once he assumed the English throne has been linked to the Catholic fanatical response of the Gunpowder Plot. See James's 1603 letter to the earl of Northumberland, in *Letters of King James VI & I*, ed. G. P. V. Akrigg (Berkeley: University of California Press, 1984), 206–7, in which he promises: "As for the Catholics, I will neither persecute any that will be quiet and give but an outward obedience to the law, neither will I spare to advance any of them that will by good service worthily deserve it" (207). See also his 1603 letter to Sir Robert Cecil, 204–5, where he expresses a relatively moderate attitude towards the persecution of Catholics, favoring deportation rather than killing. In the second half of his reign, when James pursued a Spanish match for Charles, there was a sort of de facto toleration of Catholics but no legal mitigation of their plight. Charles I and Charles II may have softened the legal prosecution of recusants and priests, but they could not change the basic antirecusancy laws.

Charles II's attempt at toleration by royal edict in the Declaration of Indulgence (1672) politically backfired and James II's Declaration of Indulgence similarly failed. In 1687 an old pro-toleration treatise by the executed Richard Langhorne was issued to support Charles's action at a point James was about to do something similar: *Considerations Touching the Great Question of the King's Right in Dispensing with the Penal Laws. Written on the Occasion of His Late Blessed Majesties granting Free Toleration and Indulgence.*

145. The landmark Act of Toleration of 1689 gave broad freedom to Protestant nonconformists, but it did not really extend toleration to Catholics.

146. See Nathaniel H. Henry, "Milton's Last Pamphlet: Theocracy and Intolerance," in *A Tribute to George Coffin Taylor,* ed. Arnold Williams (Chapel Hill: University of North Carolina Press, 1952), 197–210; Tumbleson, *Catholicism in the English Protestant Imagination,* 56–63. For a long tract using an anti-Catholic version of modern Catholic history to argue against the toleration of Catholicism, see William Denton, *The Burnt Child dreads the Fire: or an Examination of the Merits of the Papists, Relating to England, most from their own Pens. In Justification of the late Act of Parliament for preventing the dangers which may happen from Popish Recusants. And further shewing, That whatsoever their Merits have been, no thanks to their Religion, and therefore ought not to be gratified in their Religion, by Toleration thereof* (1675).

147. See John D. Krugler, "Lord Baltimore, Roman Catholics, and Toleration: Religious Policy in Maryland during the Early Catholic Years, 1634–1649," *Catholic Historical Review* 65.1 (1979): 49–75. For a general treatment of the topic, see Harvey Kamen's article on toleration in the *Encyclopedia of the Renaissance,* ed. Paul F. Grendler, 6 vols. (New York: Charles Scribner's Sons, 1999), 6: 147–48. See also the discussion of religious toleration in Nigel Smith, *Literature and Revolution in England, 1640–1660* (New Haven: Yale University Press, 1994), 121–23; and John Coffey, *Persecution and Toleration in Protestant England, 1558–1689* (Harlow: Longman, 2000).

148. For a discussion of continuing anti-Catholicism in the eighteenth century, see Colin Haydon, *Anti-Catholicism in Eighteenth-Century England, c. 1714–80* (Manchester: Manchester University Press, 1993). The Catholic Relief Act of 1778, which ultimately led to the Gordon Riots, did away with the worst of the old Penal Laws, but Catholics were not "emancipated" until 1829, and there is a continuity of both popular and elite anti-Catholicism all the way to the present day. However, John Bossy, "English Catholics after 1688," points out that in the period of Whig control from the Glorious Revolution to 1760, Catholics functioned with a much milder degree of persecution and if they kept a low profile were able to worship and function socially in much better circumstances than they could earlier. After the lapsing of the Licensing Act in 1695, for example, it was possible to publish Catholic books in England.

Afterword

1. See, for example, John W. O'Malley, S.J., *The First Jesuits* (Cambridge, Mass.: Harvard University Press, 1993); Thomas M. McCoog, S.J., *The Society of Jesus in Ireland, Scotland, and England, 1541–1588: "Our Way of Proceeding?"* (Leiden: E. J. Brill, 1996); and *The Jesuits: Cultures, Sciences, and the Arts, 1540–1773,* ed. John W. O'Malley, S.J., Gauvin Alexander Bailey, Steven J. Harris, and T. Frank Kennedy, S.J. (Toronto: University of Toronto Press, 1999). In the last volume, see especially O'Malley's chapter, "The Historiography of the Society of Jesus: Where Does It Stand Today?" (3–37).

2. See, for example, John Hungerford Pollen, S.J., ed., *Unpublished Documents Relating to the English Martyrs,* vol. 1: *1584–1603,* Catholic Record Society 5 (Leeds: J. Whitehead & Sons for the Catholic Record Society, 1908); Dom Bede Camm, (comp. and ed., *Lives of the English Martyrs declared blessed by Pope Leo XIII, in 1886 and 1895. Written by fathers of the oratory, of the secular clergy and of the Society of Jesus,* 2 vols. (London: Burns & Oates, 1904–5), and *Forgotten Shrines: An Account of Some Old Catholic Halls and Families in England and of Relics and Memorials of the English Martyrs* (London: MacDonald & Evans; St. Louis: Herder, 1910); John Morris, ed., *The Troubles of Our Catholic Forefathers,* 3 vols. (London: Burns and Oates, 1872–77); Henry Foley, S.J., *Records of the English Province of the Society of Jesus,* 7 vols. (London: Burns and Oates, 1877–80).

3. Michael O'Connell, "The Idolatrous Eye: Iconoclasm, Antitheatricalism, and the Image of the Elizabethan Theater," *English Literary History* 52 (1985): 279–310.

4. See chapters 3 and 5 of Catherine Gallagher and Stephen Greenblatt's *Practicing New Historicism* (Chicago: University of Chicago Press, 2000) and the critique by David Aers, "New Historicism and the Eucharist," *Journal of Medieval and Early Modern Studies* 33.2 (spring 2003): 241–59.

5. See John Phillips, *The Reformation of Images: Destruction of Art in England, 1535–1660* (Berkeley: University of California Press, 1973); and Margaret Aston, *England's Iconoclasts* (Oxford: Clarendon Press, 1988).

6. For a recent discussion of "priest holes" found in English houses, see Julian Yates, *Error, Misuse, Failure: Object Lessons from the English Renaissance* (Minneapolis: University of Minnesota Press, 2003), 139–207.

7. W. K. Jordan, *The Development of Religious Toleration in England: From the Beginning of the English Reformation to the Death of Queen Elizabeth* (London: George Allen & Unwin, 1932); *The Development of Religious Toleration in England: From the Accession of James I to the Convention of the Long Parliament (1603–1640)* (London: George Allen & Unwin, 1936); *The Development of Religious Toleration in England:*

From the Convention of the Long Parliament to the Restoration, 1640–1660 (London: George Allen & Unwin, 1938); *The Development of Religious Toleration in England: Attainment of the Theory and Accommodations in Thought and Institutions (1640–1660)* (Cambridge, Mass.: Harvard University Press, 1940).

8. See, for example, Christopher Haigh, "The Church of England, the Catholics and the People," in *The Reign of Elizabeth,* ed. Christopher Haigh (Basingstoke: Macmillan, 1984), 195–219; and Anthony Milton, "A Qualified Intolerance: The Limits and Ambiguities of Early Stuart Anti-Catholicism," in *Catholicism and Anti-Catholicism in Early Modern English Texts,* ed. Arthur F. Marotti (Basingstoke: Macmillan; New York: St. Martin's Press, 1999), 85–115.

9. See, for example, Albert J. Loomie, *The Spanish Elizabethans: The English Exiles at the Court of Philip II* (New York: Fordham University Press, 1963).

10. In a forthcoming volume I have coedited with Ronald Corthell, Frances Dolan, and Christopher Highley, *Early Modern English Catholic Culture,* there are several essays dealing with the culture of continental English Catholics.

11. I discuss this example in chapter 1.

12. See, for example, John King, *Spenser's Poetry and the Reformation Tradition* (Princeton: Princeton University Press, 1990), and *Milton and Religious Controversy* (Cambridge: Cambridge University Press, 2000); Anthony Raspa, *The Emotive Image: Jesuit Poetics in the English Renaissance* (Fort Worth: Texas Christian University Press, 1983); and the two volumes from the conference on the Lancastrian Shakespeare: *Region, Religion and Patronage: Lancastrian Shakespeare,* ed. Richard Dutton, Alison Gail Findlay, and Richard Wilson (Manchester: Manchester University Press, 2003); and *Theatre and Religion: Lancastrian Shakespeare,* ed. Richard Dutton, Alison Gail Findlay, and Richard Wilson (Manchester: Manchester University Press, 2003).

13. Roger Sell, who has edited *The Shorter Poems of Sir John Beaumont* (Abo, Finland: Abo Akademi, 1974), is working on an edition of all of Beaumont's works. Nigel Smith and Peter Lake have undertaken a study of Ben Jonson's *Sejanus* in relation to Jonson's Catholicism and contemporary religious conflict. The latter has included a long study of Jonson's *The Alchemist* and *Bartholomew Fair* in *The Antichrist's Lewd Hat: Protestants, Papists, and Players in Post-Reformation England* (New Haven: Yale University Press, 2002), 579–620.

14. See Frances Dolan, *Whores of Babylon: Catholicism, Gender and Seventeenth-Century Print Culture* (Ithaca: Cornell University Press, 1999); Marie B. Rowlands, "Recusant Women: 1560–1640," in *Women in English Society, 1500–1800,* ed. Mary Prior (London: Methuen, 1985), 149–80; Elizabeth Cary, Lady Falkland, *Life and Letters,* ed. Heather Wolfe, Renaissance Texts from Manuscript no. 4 (Cambridge: RTM Publications, 2001); Elizabeth Cary, Lady Falkland, *The Tragedy of Mariam The Fair Queen of Jewry with The Lady Falkland Her Life by one of her Daughters,* ed. Barry Weller and Margaret Ferguson (Berkeley: University of California Press, 1994).

15. Habermas's starting date for the formation of this "public sphere" has been pushed back earlier in more recent scholarship. See, for example, Alexandra Halasz's *The Marketplace of Print: Pamphlets and the Public Sphere in Early Modern England* (Cambridge: Cambridge University Press, 1997) and the forthcoming issue of the journal *Criticism,* which collects papers from two Modern Language Association convention sessions, "The Public Sphere in Early Modern England."

Index

Page numbers in italics refer to illustrations.

ARTHUR F. MAROTTI

is professor of English at Wayne State University.